Nicholas Patrick Wiseman

Twelve lectures on the connexion between science and revealed religion

Delivered in Rome

Nicholas Patrick Wiseman

Twelve lectures on the connexion between science and revealed religion
Delivered in Rome

ISBN/EAN: 9783742843593

Manufactured in Europe, USA, Canada, Australia, Japa

Cover: Foto ©Lupo / pixelio.de

Manufactured and distributed by brebook publishing software (www.brebook.com)

Nicholas Patrick Wiseman

Twelve lectures on the connexion between science and revealed religion

TWELVE LECTURES

ON THE

CONNEXION BETWEEN SCIENCE

AND

REVEALED RELIGION.

DELIVERED IN ROME
BY THE LATE
CARDINAL WISEMAN.

NEW EDITION.

علم از بهر دین پرورد نست

"Science should be dedicated to the service of religion."—GULISTAN, viii.

DUBLIN:
JAMES DUFFY, 15, WELLINGTON-QUAY;
AND
22, PATERNOSTER-ROW, LONDON.
1866.

PREFACE.

In the following Lectures, the reader will hardly fail to observe a certain want of harmony between the different parts; and I know not how I can better apologize for it, than by briefly stating the manner and occasion of their composition. They were first drawn up for private instruction, and read by me in the English College at Rome, over which I had the happiness of presiding; being intended for an introductory course to the study of theology. At the request of several friends, I was induced to deliver them to a public audience; and, during the Lent of 1835, they were read to a large and select attendance, in the apartments of His Eminence Cardinal Weld.

It will be easily understood how many modifications were requisite for the second delivery; particularly as I pledged myself in my prospectus to simplify my subjects, so far as to make them intelligible to persons who had no previous acquaintance with them. Accordingly many topics were but lightly touched, which, in the original draught, had been more fully developed, while others were extended to a length unnecessary for an academical audience possessed of preliminary scientific knowledge. In fact, the greater part of the Lectures were written over again for the occasion.

Among my audience I counted men, whose reputation, in their respective departments of literature and science, might have made me shrink from my complicated task; yet I found them assiduous in their attendance, and encouraging in their judgment. They joined in a wish, repeatedly expressed by most of my hearers, that these Lectures should be communicated to the public: and I came over to England, chiefly to carry this desire into execution. But then a further change appeared necessary to prepare them for the press.

In the first place, many of the parts which had been suppressed in the second delivery, have been restored; while several elementary details, which were then introduced, have not been withdrawn. I wished to make the work interesting to different classes of readers; and hoped that the intermixture of some few topics, more exclusively addressed to the learned, would not detract from the interest which the general plan might possess for the ordinary reader. Still, a certain incongruity must thence result; as some passages will appear addressed to a different audience from the greater part of the course.

The second cause of change is, perhaps, more satisfactory. My long residence abroad had debarred me from the consultation of several modern works, treating on the subject of these Lectures, so that in regard to English books, I might say with the poet—

"Quod si scriptorum non magna est copia apud me,
Hoc fit quod Romæ vivimus, illa domus."*

Now, the perusal of these caused occasional modifications in the opinions which I had previously adopted. But, even when a work has appeared since the delivery of the Lectures, I have thought it advisable to introduce the mention of it into the text, rather than omit it, to avoid an anachronism. On the whole, I am sensible that I have had neither leisure nor opportunity to improve them, as might be expected; and that many more works might have been perused or consulted by me to great advantage.

* "Catullus ad Manlium," 33.

The form, therefore, in which my humble lucubrations appear before the public, is that of a third modification; and if the observation be true, that second thoughts are *not* the best, but third thoughts, which correct the second, and bring them back in part to the more vivid and natural impressions exhibited in the first,[*] I may appear to present this little narrative of what I have done, rather in the form of a recommendation than of an apology.

But, from my heart, I can say, that no reader's eye, however keen, will be more sensible than mine is, to the imperfections of my work. The subjects of which it treats are varied, and have rather formed a relaxation from severer pursuits, than objects of professed research. That its numerous faults will be observed, and, perhaps, severely criticised, I must naturally expect. Still, I shall always feel that the cause which I plead may well throw some of its protection over its least worthy advocates, and conciliate the benevolence of all that revere and love it. To succeed in its behalf, would, indeed, be glorious; but the attempt—the labour of which, in this case, has not been small—cannot surely be divested of all merit; and I shall

[*] "Guesses at Truth."

gladly hail the augury of the indulgent reader, if, at the conclusion of this my proem, he addresses me in the words of the poet:

Μέγας ἀγών· μεγάλα δ' ἐπινοεῖς ἑλεῖν.
Μακάριος γε μὴν κυρήσας ἔσει·
ΠΟΝΟΣ Δ ΕΥΚΛΕΗΣ.
EURIPID. *Rhes.* Act i. v. 195.*

---

* Great is the cause, and great thine aim;
Thrice happy, if success shall claim
Its due reward: yet honour'd still
May be the labour and the will.

CONTENTS.

	PAGE
LECTURE I. On the Comparative Study of Languages,	1
LECTURE II. The same subject continued,	46
LECTURE III. On the Natural History of the Human Race,	98
LECTURE IV. The same subject continued,	144
LECTURE V. On the Natural Sciences,	178
LECTURE VI. The same subject continued,	222
LECTURE VII. On Early History,	255
LECTURE VIII. The same subject continued,	292
LECTURE IX. On Archæology,	328
LECTURE X. On Oriental Literature,	361
LECTURE XI. The same subject continued,	408
LECTURE XII. Conclusion,	442

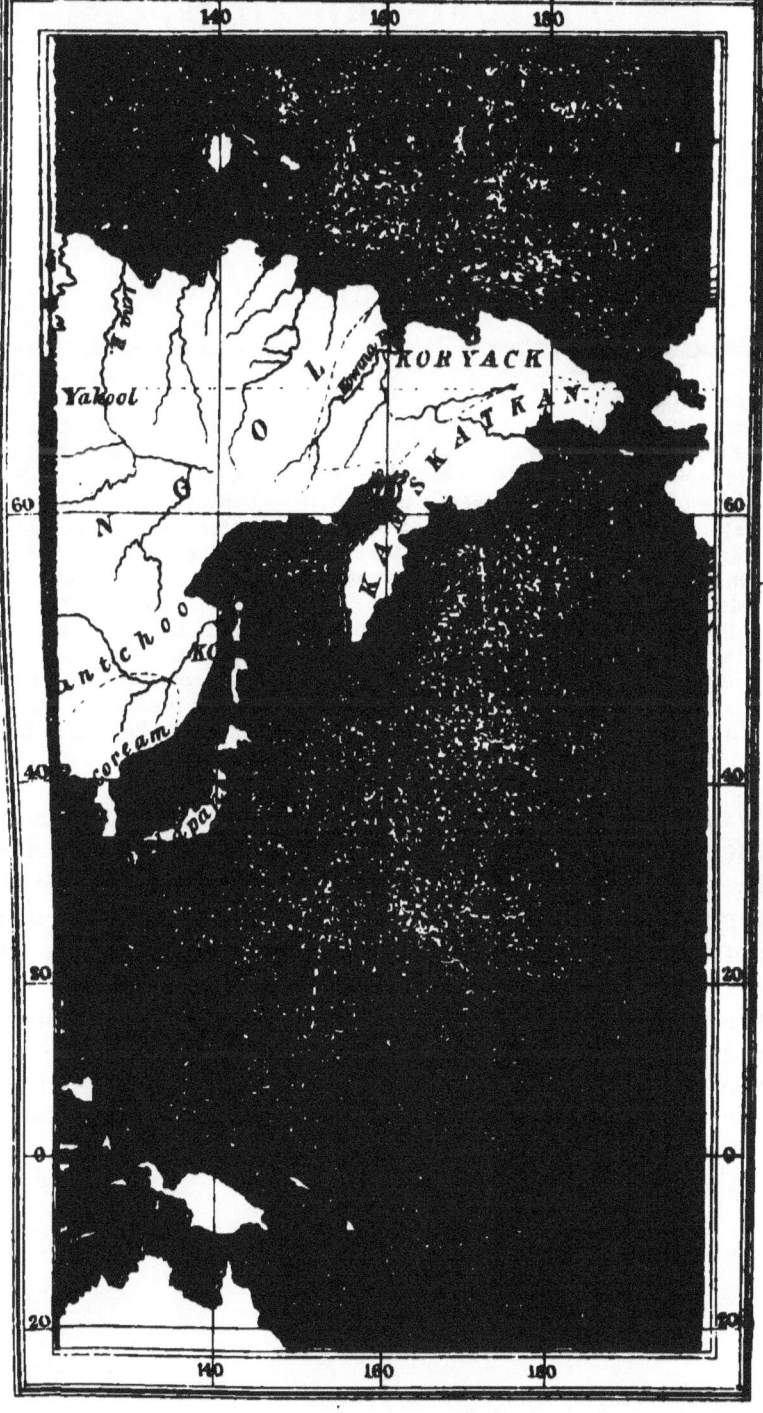

LECTURE THE FIRST;

ON THE

COMPARATIVE STUDY OF LANGUAGES.

PART I.

GENERAL INTRODUCTION.—Relation of these Lectures to the Christian Evidences.—Method to be therein followed.—Results to be anticipated.

ETHNOGRAPHY, or comparative study of languages.—HISTORY—*First* period: Search after the primary language; defects in the object and methods.—*Second* period: Collection of materials; lists of words, and series of Our Fathers.—*Third* period: Attempts at arrangement and classification; Leibnitz, Hervas, Catherine II., and Pallas, Adelung and Vater.—Dangerous appearance of the study at this period, from the apparent multiplication of independent languages.—RESULTS—*First:* Formation of families, or large groups of languages in close affinity, by words and grammatical forms.—Exemplification in the Indo-European, Semitic, and Malayan families.—*Second:* Progressive reduction of supposed independent languages into connection with the great families; Ossete, Armenian, Celtic.—Review of Sir W. Betham's System; Dr. Prichard; Recapitulation; Concluding Remarks.

WERE it given unto us to contemplate God's works in the visible and in the moral world, not as we now see them, in shreds and little fragments, but as woven together into the great web of universal harmony; could our minds take in each part thereof, with its general and particular connections, relations, and appliances,—there can be no doubt but religion, as established by Him, would appear to enter, and fit so completely and so necessarily into the general plan, as that all would be unravelled and destroyed, if by any means

LECTURE THE FIRST;

ON THE

COMPARATIVE STUDY OF LANGUAGES.

PART I.

GENERAL INTRODUCTION.—Relation of these Lectures to the Christian Evidences.—Method to be therein followed.—Results to be anticipated.

ETHNOGRAPHY, or comparative study of languages.—HISTORY—*First* period: Search after the primary language; defects in the object and methods.—*Second* period: Collection of materials; lists of words, and series of Our Fathers.—*Third* period: Attempts at arrangement and classification; Leibnitz, Hervas, Catherine II., and Pallas, Adelung and Vater.—Dangerous appearance of the study at this period, from the apparent multiplication of independent languages.—RESULTS—*First:* Formation of families, or large groups of languages in close affinity, by words and grammatical forms.—Exemplification in the Indo-European, Semitic, and Malayan families.—*Second:* Progressive reduction of supposed independent languages into connection with the great families; Ossete, Armenian, Celtic.—Review of Sir W. Betham's System; Dr. Prichard; Recapitulation; Concluding Remarks.

WERE it given unto us to contemplate God's works in the visible and in the moral world, not as we now see them, in shreds and little fragments, but as woven together into the great web of universal harmony; could our minds take in each part thereof, with its general and particular connections, relations, and appliances,—there can be no doubt but religion, as established by Him, would appear to enter, and fit so completely and so necessarily into the general plan, as that all would be unravelled and destroyed, if by any means it should be withdrawn. And such a view of its interweaving with the whole economy and fabric of nature, would doubtless be the highest order of evidence which could be given us of its truth. But this is the great difference between nature's and man's operation, that she fashioneth and moulds all the parts of her works at once, while he can apply himself only to the elaboration of one single part at a time;* and hence it comes, that in all our researches, the successive and partial attention which we are obliged to give to separate evidences or proofs; doth greatly weaken their collective force. For, as the illustrious Bacon hath well remarked, " the harmony of the sciences, that is, when each part supports the other, is, and ought to be, the true and brief way of confutation and suppression of all the smaller sorts of objections; but, on the other hand, if you draw out every axiom, like the sticks of a fagot, one by one, you may easily quarrel with them, and bend and break them at your pleasure."†

To the difficulties thus thrown in our way by the limitation of our faculties, prejudices of venerable standing have added much. For ages it has been considered, by many, useless and almost profane, to attempt any marriage between theology and the other sciences. Some men in their writings, and many in their discourse, go so far as to suppose that they may enjoy a dualism of opinions, holding one set which they believe as Christians, and another whereof they are convinced as philosophers. Such a one will say, that he believes the Scriptures, and all that they contain; but will yet uphold some system of chronology or history which can nowise be reconciled therewith. One does not see how it is possible to make accordance

---

* " For as when a carver cuts and graves an image, he shapes only that part whereupon he works, and not the rest; but contrariwise, when Nature makes a flower or living creature, she engenders and brings forth rudiments of all the parts at once."—Bacon, " De Augm. Scient." l. vii. p. 360, *Trans. Oxf.* 1640.

† Bacon, " De Augm. Scient." l. vii. p. 330.

between the Mosaic creation and Cuvier's discoveries; another thinks the history of the dispersion incompatible with the number of dissimilar languages now existing; a third considers it extremely difficult to explain the origin of all mankind from one common parentage. So far, therefore, from considering religion or its science, theology, as entitled to sisterhood with the other sciences, it is supposed to move on a distinct plane, and preserve a perpetual parallelism with them, which prevents them all from clashing, as it deprives them of mutual support. Hence, too, it is no wonder that theology should be always considered a study purely professional, and devoid of general interest; and that it should be deemed impossible to invest its researches with those varied charms that attract us to other scientific inquiries.*

Reflections such as these have led me to the attempt whereupon I enter to-day; the attempt, that is, to bring theology somehow into the circle of the other sciences, by showing how beautifully it is illustrated, supported, and adorned by them all; to prove how justly the philosopher should bow to her decisions, with the assurance that his researches will only confirm them; to demonstrate the convergence of truths revealed with truths discovered; and, however imperfectly, to present you with some such picture as Homer hath described upon his hero's shield; of things and movements heavenly, that appertain unto a higher sphere, hemmed round and embellished by the representations of earthlier and homelier pursuits.

My purpose, therefore, in the course of lectures to which I have invited you, is to show the correspondence between the progress of science and the development of the Christian evidences; and, before proceeding

---

* For a view of the unsatisfactory method by which the French eclectic school attempts at once to separate and reconcile science and revelation, see Damiron, "Essai sur l'Histoire de la Philosophie en France:" *Bruxelles*, 1829, pp. 471-474; or Carové, "Der Saint Simonismus und die neuere Philosophie:" *Leip.* 1831, p. 42.

further, I must be allowed to explain the terms and limits of my inquiries. By the simple statement of my theme, it will be seen that I do not intend to enter upon the well-occupied field of natural theology, or to apply the progress of science to the increasing proof thereby gained, of a wise all-ruling Providence. It is of revealed religion alone that I mean to treat—of the evidences which Christianity has received in its numberless connections with the order of nature or the course of human events. And, when I use the word evidences, I must be understood in a very wide and general signification. I consider that whatever tends to prove the truth of any narrative in the sacred volume, especially if that narrative, to merely human eyes, appears improbable, or irreconcilable with other facts, tends also essentially to increase the sum of evidence which Christianity possesses, resting, as it essentially does, upon the authenticity of that book. Any discovery, for instance, that a trifling date, till lately inexplicable, is quite correct, besides the satisfaction it gives upon an individual point, has a far greater moral weight in the assurance it affords of security in other matters. And hence a long research, which will lead to a discovery of apparently mean importance, must be measured according to this general influence, rather than by its immediate results.

But while, as has been observed, it is the interest of those who search after truth to generalize their proofs as much as possible, and take their stand upon the broadest ground, those who attack it will ever find their greatest advantage in particular objections, and piecemeal destruction. And such, on their part, has been the policy pursued. Each science has been individually ransacked, and many partial results of each separately urged, as sufficient to overthrow the defences of Christianity. These repeated attempts must form an additional motive for inquiry into the real results of modern science. It is true that the Christian revelation rests upon general arguments, not easily shaken by particular objections. It is true that its evidence, external and internal, consists of numerous and various considerations, dove-tailed and riveted so strongly together, that a partial attack upon one point is borne by the rest; so that we incur greater difficulties by supposing the whole system of Christianity false in consequence of a particular objection, than we do by confessing our inability to answer, and adhering nevertheless to the cause which it impugns.

But although the less-instructed Christian may thus preserve his conviction undisturbed by difficulties whereunto he sees not the immediate answer, there is another method of proceeding more satisfactory, more interesting, and, to those who have the power, almost of obligation; that is, boldly and patiently to examine the objections, and solve them individually; and for this purpose to neglect no means within their reach, of procuring the necessary information. Of our ultimate and complete success, we cannot allow ourselves to entertain a doubt.

Causa jubet melior superos sperare secundos.

If we are firmly convinced that God is as much the author of our religion, as he is of nature, we must be also thoroughly assured, that the comparison of His works, in both these orders, must necessarily give a uniform result. An essential part of my task will therefore be, to show how the very sciences, whence objections have been drawn against religion, have themselves, in their progress, entirely removed them; and hence my method of treating each science, with one or two exceptions, will necessarily be historical. I shall thus avoid an important difficulty—that of supposing all my hearers furnished with an accurate knowledge of so many different pursuits. Instead of this, I flatter myself, that while I show the signal services rendered to religion by the progress of each science, I shall present a short and simple introduction to its history and principles.

We shall see how the early stage of each furnished objections to religion, to the joy of the infidel and the dismay of the believer; how many discouraged these studies as dangerous; and then how, in their advance, they first removed the difficulties drawn from their imperfect state, and then even replaced them by solid arguments in favour of religion. And hence we shall feel warranted in concluding, that it is essentially the interest of religion to encourage the pursuit of science and literature in their various departments.

In the arrangement of my subjects, while I pay attention to a certain natural order of connection, I shall also be anxious to give them an increasing interest; and I almost fear I have been guilty of an error in tactics, by placing in my front the science whereupon I now enter, as it can hardly possess the general interest of most that will follow it, though I trust it will fully justify all I have advanced in these preliminary remarks. I mean *Ethnography*, or the classification of nations from the comparative study of languages—a science born, I may say, almost within our memory.

This science has also been properly called by the French *Linguistique*, or the study of language; and is also known by the name of comparative philology. These names will sufficiently declare the objects and methods of the study; and I will not premise any other definition, as I trust you will gradually, as my subject unfolds, become acquainted with its entire range.

I enter upon it with the full consciousness of the difficulties which surround it; it is a science which as yet has found no historian, and hardly possesses any elementary works; and I have had to collect from many writers the materials for the sketch which I shall endeavour to present to you; it is, indeed, by the simple history of this science, that we shall see the Mosaic account of the dispersion of mankind most pleasingly confirmed.

I need hardly recall to your memories this remnant of early history. That mankind descended from one family—spoke but one language; that, in consequence of their being united in a design which accorded not with the views of Providence, the Almighty confounded their speech, and introduced among them a variety of tongues, which produced a general dispersion; such, in brief, are the outlines of this venerable history, recorded in the eleventh chapter of Genesis.

Commentators upon this passage have generally considered that this confusion consisted, not so much in the abolition of the common tongue, as in the introduction of such a variety of modifications in it as would suffice to effect the dispersion of the human race. In fact, it was only on this hypothesis that the long and useless search after the original language could have been conducted.

But the whole of this narrative is of course treated by the adversaries of revelation as a fable, or a *mythus*.* We may allow philosophers, indeed, to discuss such abstract questions as whether speech could have been the gradual invention of the human species, or must have been the free gift of God, as Dr. Johnson, Anton, and Bonald maintain;† or neither a pure gift nor an invention, but, according to the later theory of the lamented Humboldt, a necessary and spontaneous result of man's organization.‡ We might even allow them the innocent amusement of

---

* "The Book of Genesis veiled, in a significant expressive *mythus*, a problem which no philosophy has satisfactorily solved."—Gensenius, "Geschichte der hebräischen Sprache und Schrift :" *Leip.* 1815, p. 13. (See Geddes's Preface to his Translation of the Pentateuch, 1792, p. xi.)

† Boswell's "Life," first ed. vol. ii. p. 447. R. G. Anton, "Ueber Sprache, in Rücksicht auf Geschichte der Menschen :" *Görlitz*, 1799, p. 31. Beattie's "Theory of Language :" *London*, 1788, p. 95. This position is the basis of Bonald's system, and is warmly attacked by Damiron, *ubi sup.* p. 224; Cousin, Preface to Maine de Biran's "Nouvelles Considérations :" *Paris*, 1834, p. xv.; and many others.

‡ "Speech, according to my fullest conviction, must really be considered as inherent in man; since, as the work of his intellect in its simple knowledge, it is absolutely inexplicable. This hypothesis is facilitated by supposing thousands and thousands of years; language could not have been invented without its type pre-existing in man."

discussing whether such an invention would have begun by substantives, as Dr. Smith is of opinion,* or by interjections, as the President de Brosses and Herder conjecture.† So long as an imaginary theatre is supposed for the actors in such a discovery, so long as we speak with the President, of children abandoned to the tuition of nature, or with Soave, of two insulated savages, the field is open, and the disquisition without danger.

But other writers have transferred their speculations upon this subject to the dominion of history; Maupertuis, for instance, supposes the human race to have been originally without speech, till its different divisions gradually invented separate dialects.‡ Rousseau and Volney represent man as the " mutum et turpe pecus " of the ancients, " thrown," according to the words of the latter, " as it were by chance, on a confused and savage land, an orphan abandoned by the unknown hand that had produced him,"§ and left to discover the first elements of social life, much on the principle, and by the process described in the Epicurean poet:—

> " Ergo si varii sensus animalia cogunt,
> Muta tamen quum sint, varias emittere voces;
> Quanto mortaleis magis æquum est tum potuisse
> Dissimileis alia, atque alia res voce notare."‖

This view of the origin of language is not unfre-

After several highly interesting remarks, he proceeds to observe, that still language must not be considered as a gift bestowed ready-formed to man (etwas fertig gegebenes), but as something coming from himself.—"Ueber das vergleichende Sprachstudium, in Beziehung auf die verschiedenen Epochen der Sprachentwickelung." In the Acts of the Royal Academy of Sciences of Berlin; historical and philosophical class, 1820-21: *Berlin*, 1822, p. 247.

* "Theory of Moral Sentiments:" *Edinb.* 1813, vol. ii. p. 364.
† De Brosses, "Traité de la Formation Méchanique des Langues" (anonym.): *Paris*, 1765, tom. ii. p. 220. Herder, "Nouveaux Mémoires de l'Académie Roy. des Sciences:" *Berlin*, 1783, p. 382.
‡ "Dissertation sur les différens moyens dont les hommes se sont servis pour exprimer leurs idées."—Hist. de l'Académie Roy.: *Berlin*, 1756, p. 335.
§ "Ruines:" *Paris*, 1820, p. 37. "Causes de l'Inégalité entre les Hommes, Œuvres complètes;" *Paris*, 1826, p. 40.
‖ Lucret. l. v. 1086.

quently repeated at the present day. Charles Nodier published a series of articles, entitled *Notions élémentaires de Linguistique*, in the *Temps* paper for September and October, 1833, wherein he maintains that languages were the handiwork of human powers acting by themselves. Even writers who were never suspected of having entertained opinions at variance with the inspired narrative, appear sometimes to indulge in the same imagination.*

The Marquis de Fortia d'Urban goes farther, and denies at once the history of the dispersion as given by Moses, and indeed the inspiration of the historical narratives of Scripture.†

The inquiry, when thus considered, seems to involve the authenticity of the Mosaic documents touching the early history of man. It then becomes our duty to investigate the very study which gave birth or strength to such objections: and we shall soon perceive that the nearer it has advanced towards perfection, the more it has confirmed the veracity of the Jewish historian.

The history of the comparative study of languages, presents the same features in the moral sciences, which chemistry does among physical pursuits. While the latter was engaged in a fruitless chase of the philosopher's stone, or a remedy for every disease, the linguists were occupied in the equally fruitless search after the primary language. In the course of both inquiries, many important and unexpected discoveries were doubtless made; but it was not till a principle of analytical investigation was introduced in both, that the real nature of their objects was ascertained, and results obtained, far more valuable than had first caused and encouraged so much toilsome application.

The desire of verifying the Mosaic history, or the ambition of knowing the language first communicated by divine inspiration, was the motive or impulse of the

* For instance, Dr. Murray, in his "History of European Languages:" *Edinb.* 1823, vol. i. p. 28.
† "Essai sur l'Origine de l'Écriture :" *Paris*, 1832, p. 10.

old linguists' chimerical research. For, it was argued, if it can only be shown that there exists some language which contains, as it were, the germ of all the rest, and forms a centre whence all others visibly diverge, then the confusion of Babel receives a striking confirmation; for that language must have been once the common speech of mankind.

But here such a host of rivals entered the lists, and their conflicting pretensions were advanced with such assurance, or such plausibility, as rendered a satisfactory decision perfectly beyond hope.

The Celtic language found a zealous patron in the learned Pezron;[*] the claims of the Chinese were warmly advocated by Webb, and several other writers.[†] Even in our own times—for the race of such visionaries is not yet extinct—Don Pedro de Astarloa,[‡] Don Thomas de Sorreguieta,[§] and the Abbé d'Iharce-Bidassouet-d'Aroztegui,[||] have taken the field as champions of the Biscayan, with equal success as, in former times, the very erudite and unwieldy Goropius Becanus brought up his native Low Dutch as the language of the terrestrial paradise.[¶]

Notwithstanding these ambitious pretensions, the Semitic languages, as they are called, that is, the languages of Western Asia, seemed to be the favoured claimants; but, alas! even here there was rivalry among the sisters. The Abyssinians boasted their language to be the mother stock, from which even Hebrew had

---

[*] "Antiquité de la Nation et de la Langue des Celtes:" *Paris*, 1704.

[†] "Essay on the Probability that the Language of China is the primitive Language:" *London*, 1669. "The Antiquity of China; or, an Historical Essay endeavouring a Probability that the Language of China is the primitive Language:" *Ibid*. 1678.

[‡] "Apologia de la Lengua Bascongada, o Ensayo criticofilosofico de su perfeccion y antiguedad sobre todas las que se conocen:" *Madrid*, 1803.

[§] "Semana Hispana-Bascongada la unica de la Europa, y la mas antigua del orbe:" *Ibid*. 1804.

[||] See his prospectus published in the French journals, 1824. His work has, I believe, since appeared.

[¶] "Origines Antuerpianæ:" *Antw*. 1569, pp. 534, *seq*.

sprung;* a host of Syriac authors traced the lineal descent of their speech, through Heber, from Noah and Adam :† but Hebrew was the pretender that collected the most numerous suffrages in its favour. From the Antiquities of Josephus, and the Targums, or Chaldee paraphrases of Onkelos and of Jerusalem,‡ down to Anton in 1800,§ Christians and Jews considered its pretensions as almost definitively decided; and names of the highest rank in literature—Lipsius, Scaliger, Bochart, and Vossius—have trusted the truth of many of their theories to the certainty of this opinion.

The learned and judicious Molitor, however, who has brought an immense store of Rabbinical literature to bear upon the demonstration of the Catholic religion which he has embraced, acknowledges that "The Jewish tradition which makes Hebrew the language of the first patriarchs, and even of Adam, is, in its literal sense, inadmissible;" though he adds very judiciously, that it is sufficient to acknowledge the inspiration of the Bible, for us to be obliged to confess that the language in which it is written is a faithful, though earthly, image of the speech of paradise; even as fallen man preserves some traces of his original greatness.‖

Such was the object towards which the comparative study of languages in general first directed its attention; and two essential faults may be observed in the manner of conducting it, both of which arose from the limited views of its cultivators.

* See the Advertisement to the Ed. Princ. of the New Testament: *Rome*, 1548.
† See their authority, given in Assemani's "Bibliotheca Orientalis," tom. iii. part i. p. 314. Ibn Kaledoon, Massoudi, Haider Razi, and other Arabic authors, maintain the same opinion. (See Quatremère's learned Essay, in the "Nouveau Journal Asiatique," March, 1835.)
‡ Josephus, "Archæolog." lib. i. c. i. tom. i. p. 6, ed. *Haverc.* Targumin on Gen. xi. 1.
§ "De Lingua Primæva:" *Wittemb.* 1800.
‖ "Philosophie der Geschichte, oder über die Tradition." Not having, at this moment, the original at hand, I must refer to the French abridgment, "Philosophie de la Tradition," par X. Quris, p. 211: *Paris*, 1834.

The first was, that hardly any affinity seems to have been admitted between languages, save that of filiation. Parallel descent from a common parent was hardly ever imagined: the moment two languages bore a resemblance, it was concluded that one must be the offspring of the other.* This mode of reasoning is most visible among the writers upon the Semitic dialects; but there are curious instances of it also in others.

Thus an affinity between the Persian and German languages had been early perceived by Lipsius and Salmasius:† but no solution could be devised of this phenomenon, except that one must have borrowed from the other. " Hodierna (lingua Persica)," says the learned David Wilkins, "ex *multis Europæ et Orientis vocibus composita est*, Latinis sc. Germanicis, Græcis."‡ Walton had before expressed the same opinion as quite certain: " Ut gens Persica ipsa Græcorum, Italorum, Arabum, Tartarorumque colluvies est, ita lingua quoque ejus ex horum linguis est conflata!"§

This principle led the acute and learned Reland into a different, but still more curious error upon the same subject. He had collected the Indian words preserved in ancient authors, and found that many of them could be illustrated from the Persian. Yet this did not lead him to suspect an affinity between the Indian and the

---

* The following passage, from an author with those opinions on most points I do not coincide, may explain this position. "Il ne faut pas se représenter les peuples et les langues en lignes perpendiculaires... Il n'y a entre elles ni droit d'aînesse, ni primogéniture. Cette question qu'on entend faire, la langue A est-elle plus ancienne que la langue B, est puérile, et tout aussi dénuée de sens que le sont ordinairement les controverses scholastiques touchant les langues mères."—Principes de l'Etude comparative des Langues, par le Baron de Mérian, p. 12: *Paris*, 1828.

† Lipsius, "Epist. ad Belgas." *Antw.* 1602-4. Salmasius, "de Lingua Hellanist." p. 378. Scaliger is often quoted as having observed this resemblance (*vide* Wilkins, *inf. cit.*); but in his 228th letter to Pontanus, he says:—"Nihil tam dissimile alii rei quam Teutonismus linguæ Persicæ."

‡ Preface to Chamberlayne's "Oratio Dominica," p. 7: *Amstel.* 1715.

§ Prolegom. xvi. § 2.

Persian languages. But as he knew no grounds on which to resort to the usual expedient of supposing that one had given birth to the other, he was unable, upon any principle then known, to solve this problem; and therefore concluded that the words so collected were not Indian, but Persian, and that the ancients had been mistaken in giving them as Indian.* Even in more modern times, the Abate Denina could devise no explanation of the affinity between Teutonic and Greek,† other than supposing the ancient Germans to have been a colony from Asia Minor: so that truly we might exclaim with the poet:

"Hic quoque sunt igitur Graiæ, quis crederet, urbes,
Inter inhumanæ nomina barbariæ;
Huc quoque Mileto missi venere coloni,
Inque Getis Graias constituere domos."‡

The second error in the method of this study, was that it was conducted almost entirely by etymology, and not by comparison. As the authors whom I have mentioned wish to prove the derivation of other languages from the one whose cause they espoused, they were necessarily driven to this expedient. Similarity of words or forms could have only established an affinity between the languages in which it occurred, and therefore it was preferable to find in the favourite language a supposed original word which contained in itself the germ, as it were, or meaning of the term examined, rather than trace the affinities through sister languages, or even condescend to derive it from obvious elements in its own native language. Thus, if I remember right, Jennings, somewhere in his Jewish

---

* "De Veteri Lingua Indica Dissertat. Miscellan." tom. i. p. 209. *Traject. ad Rhen.* 1713. (See Professor Tychsen's correction of them, Append. iv. to Heeren's "Researches," vol. ii. p. 376: *Oxford*, 1833.)
† "Sur les Causes de la Différence des Langues."—Nouveaux Mémoires de l'Académie Royale, 1783, p. 542: *Berlin*, 1785.
‡ Ovid, "Trist." lib. iii. El. ix.

Antiquities, derives the Greek ἄσυλον, *asylum*, from the Hebrew אשל, *eshel*, an *oak* or *grove*, in spite of the simple etymology given it by the ancients, *a priv.* and συλαω, forming together the signification of *inviolable*. With equal propriety might we derive the English verb to *cut off*, from the Syriac verb ܩܛܦ *cataf*, which signifies the same thing. These extraordinary etymologies swarm, even to this day, in popular writers advocating the pretended rights of the Hebrew language. Nor did other authors neglect this method. Becanus, for instance, explains from Dutch every name found in the early history of Genesis; and, discovering in his own language a possible analysis of them, concludes triumphantly that those names were given in that tongue. Who can for an instant doubt that Adam and Eve spoke Low Dutch, when he learns that the name of the first man clearly resolves itself into *Hat* (hate) and *dam*, because he was as a dam opposed to the serpent's hatred; and that of his consort into *E* (oath) and *vat*, she being the receptacle of the oath, or promise of a Redeemer?[*]

But to return. The defects I have pointed out in the early history of our science, were the natural consequence of the objects it pursued. It was necessary to enlarge at once the view, as well as the field of the philologer, before any good results could be expected. It was necessary to begin upon a new method, and without the mischievous spirit of system; and the collection of facts was the necessary basis to such improvements. "Ici, comme ailleurs," says Abel-Rémusat, "on a commencé par bâtir des systêmes, au lieu de se borner à l'observation de faits."[†]

Had the moderns been obliged to begin their studies at this first point, many years must have elapsed before they could have reached maturity; for the collection of materials would have occupied a considerable time.

---

[*] *Ubi sup.* p. 539.
[†] "Recherches sur les Langues Tartares :" *Paris*, 1820, p. xviii.

Fortunately, however, the older writers had done something in this way, though with no very definite purpose. Travellers, among other curiosities, had brought lists of words from countries which they had visited; missionaries, with more exalted views, learned the languages of nations whom they converted, and wrote elementary books for their instruction. These two sources produced the collections necessary for prosecuting the comparative study of languages.

The first traveller who thought of enriching his narrative with lists of foreign words, was the amusing and credulous Pigafetta, who accompanied Magelhaens, in the first voyage round the globe. At the conclusion of his journal, he presents us with three very meagre vocabularies; the first whereof is of the Brazilian language; the second, collected from his Patagonian giant, who makes so conspicuous a figure in his book, is of the Tehuel; the third is from Tidore, one of the Moluccas.* His example was followed by later navigators; almost every traveller who explored new lands, or gleaned fuller information upon those already known, collected specimens of this nature, though often injudiciously—almost always inaccurately.† Many of these collections were deposited in libraries, and used at subsequent periods by learned men. The judicious Reland, whose labours in this department of literature have been very much overlooked, published from manuscripts of this sort, preserved in the Leyden library, vocabularies of the Malayalim, Cingalese, Malabaric, Japanese, and Javanese. He also took particular pains to collect from travellers, specimens of American languages.‡ In like manner, the collections of Messerschmidt, made during

---

* Primo volumine, 3a editione, delle "Navigationi et Viaggi raccolti già da M. Gio. Bat. Ramusio:" *Ven.* 1563, p. 370. The words relating to religion in the vocabulary of Tidore, are Arabic.

† See Balbi's "Introduction à l'Atlas Ethnographique du Globe:" *Paris,* 1826, pp. 27, *seqq.* and p. c. of the Disc. Prélim.

‡ "De Linguis Insularum quarundam Orientalium Dissert. Miscell." pars 3 : *Traject.* 1708, p. 57. He adds short lists of words used in

his seven years' residence in Siberia, and deposited in the Imperial Library at St. Petersburg, were of signal service to Klaproth, in compiling his *Asia Polyglotta*.*
Books of devotion were naturally the first printed by missionaries, for the use of those nations whom they converted to Christianity, and these were sure to contain the Lord's Prayer. This was, therefore, the example most easy to be procured of a variety of languages, so as to have a uniform specimen for their comparison. Smaller collections of it had been made by Schildberger, Postel, and Bibliander; but the naturalist Gesner first conceived the idea of uniting it as a sample to a catalogue of known languages; and he published, in 1555, his *Mithridates*, better known in the extended, but less accurate, edition of Waser.† The merit of this little work is, that it formed a nucleus to later acquisitions; and though we must smile to see it standing beside its bulky namesake by Adelung and Vater, it is pleasing to trace this noble monument of human industry to the little dictionary of Gesner. Here the languages are arranged in alphabetical order, one-half thereof being erroneously entitled or described; and when I tell you that the language of the gods has a place there, because Homer has indulged in such a fiction, you will easily judge what critical merit it possesses. This, and the subsequent collections by Müller, Ludeke, Stark, and others, were completely eclipsed and superseded by the more extensive series of Wilkins and Chamberlayne,

---

Soloman's Island, Cocas, N. Guinea, Moses Island, Moo, and Madagascar, and concludes (p. 137), that Malay is the basis of them all. This we shall see has been substantially verified. "De Linguis Americanis." *Ibid.*

* *Paris*, 1823, p. viii.

† "Mithridates Gesneri," Gasper Waserus recensuit et libello commentario illustravit. *Tigur.* 1610. Between these two editions it was published in Rome, without any acknowledgment, as an "Appendix to F. Angelo Rocca's Bibliotheca Vaticana Illustrata;" *Rome*, 1591, pp. 291-376. The author pretends to have collected the materials himself (pp. 310-364), yet has transcribed the whole of Gesner's work, with its typographical mistakes, and has only made a few trifling additions.

published at Amsterdam, after the beginning of the last century.*

This date brings us to a period when the science, however imperfect its principles may have remained for a long time after, took at least a most extended field into cultivation, and varied the character of its observations and experiments, so as to prepare the way for more important discoveries. It is perhaps its critical moment both for ethnography and for religion.

The name of Leibnitz is the connecting link between the sciences at the period we have now reached. Had we to define in one word the pursuits of this great man, we could only do so by saying they were *philosophy*. But this would be an injustice to his fame; for many claim and obtain an equal credit, by casting some additional light upon some individual branch of science. The genius of Leibnitz was like the prism of his great rival; this one ray, on passing through it, was refracted into a thousand variegated hues, all clear, all brilliant, and connected in almost imperceptible gradations, not of shadow, but of light. In his writings, we follow the changeful beam, playing through the whole range of science; traced to his mind, we discover all its varieties diverging from one single principle—a bright and vivid current of philosophic thought. In him, mathematics and moral philosophy, history and philology, for the first time found a common seat; and persons even deeply versed in any one of these studies, bowed to the authority of the man who possessed sufficient genius to embrace them all, and make them contribute to their mutual advantage.

From such a man we might expect essential improvements in any science, where this combination of varied acquirements was singularly necessary. Such was Ethnography, and to Leibnitz, therefore, does it owe those principles which first allowed it to claim a place

* "Oratio Dominica in diversis omnium fere Gentium Linguis versa," editore J. Chamberlaynio: *Ams.* 1715. It is followed by "Letters" from Dr. Nicholson, Leibnitz, and Wotton.

among the sciences. Though, from some passages in his works, he is supposed to have patronized the rights of Hebrew to be the primary language, in his letter to Tenzel he clearly rejects those claims.* Be this as it may, so far as the mere comparison of words can go, he must be admitted to have proposed the first sound principles; nay, there is hardly an analogy announced by the followers of that comparative system in modern times, which he has not somewhere anticipated; several of his hopes have been fulfilled—many of his conjectures verified.

Instead of confining the study of languages to the useless object pursued by the earlier philologers, he saw and pointed out its usefulness for the advancement of history, for tracing the migrations of early nations, and penetrating even beyond the mist of their earliest and most unauthentic records.† This enlargement of view necessarily produced a variation of method. However he might occasionally indulge in trifling etymologies for a pastime, Leibnitz well saw that to extend the sphere of usefulness which he wished to give this science, a comparison must be instituted between idioms most separated in geographical position. He complains that travellers were not sufficiently diligent in collecting specimens of languages,‡ and his sagacity led him to suggest that they

---

* "G. Leibnitii Opera Omnia," edit. Dut. tom. vi. part ii. p. 232. A similar opinion is expressed in a letter to him from Hermann von der Hardt, p. 235.

† " Je trouve que rien ne sert davantage à juger des connexions des peuples que les langues. Par exemple, la langue des Abyssins nous fait connaître qu'ils sont une colonie d'Arabes."—Lettre au P. Verjus : *Ibid.* p. 227. " Quum nihil majorem ad antiquas populorum origines indagandas lucem præbeat quam collatio linguarum," &c.— Desiderata circa Linguas Populorum : *Ibid.* p. 228. Lacroze ("Commerc. Epistol." tom. iii. p. 79 : *Leips.* 1742) and Reland (*ubi sup.* p. 78) take the same view of this study.

‡ " C'est un grand défaut que ceux qui font des descriptions des pays, et qui donnent des relations des voyages, oublient d'ajouter des essais des langues des peuples, car cela servirait pour en faire connaître les origines."—Monumenta varia inedita, ex Musæo J. Feller, tom. xi. p. 595 : *Jena*, 1717.

should be formed upon a uniform list, containing the most elementary and simple objects.* He exhorted his friends to collect words into comparative tables, to investigate the Georgian, and to confront the Armenian with the Coptic, and the Albanese with German and Latin.† His attention to these pursuits, and the peculiar sagacity of his mind, led him to conjectures which have been curiously verified by modern research. For instance, he suspected there might be an affinity in words between the Biscayan and the Coptic, the languages of Spain and Egypt,‡ a conjecture which you will see has been put to the test of mathematical calculus by the late Dr. Young.

I remarked just now, that this was the critical moment of the study, in regard to religion, as well as to Ethnography; and the reason is plain. The old tie which had hitherto held all languages in a supposed affinity,—their assumed derivation from Hebrew,—was now broken or loosened, and no other substituted for it. The materials of the study, whence the modern science had to issue in fair proportions, were now in a state of fusion, without form or connection. In the search for new materials, each day seemed to discover a new language, independent of all previously known, and consequently to increase the difficulty of reconciling appearances with the narrative of Moses.§

It was not now sufficient to find a few words bearing some resemblance in three or four languages, and hence conclude the common origin of all. As an instance of this older practice, I will quote the word *sack*, as one of the favourite breathing-points of the old

---

* "Desiderata." (*ubi sup.*)   † Tom. v. p. 494.
‡ "S'il y avait beaucoup de mots Basques dans le Cophthe, cela confirmerait une conjecture que j'ai touché, que l'ancien Espagnol et Aquitanique pouvait être venu d'Afrique. Vous m'obligerez, en marquant un nombre de ces mots Cophtho-Basques."—*Ibid.* p. 503; also tom. ii. p. 219.
§ It was generally supposed that the number of primary languages could only be about seventy. (See Hervas, "Origine, Meccanismo, ed Armonia degl' Idiomi," p. 172 : *Cesena*, 1785.)

etymologists. Goropius Becanus, whom I must once more quote as representative of the ancient school, accounts for this word being found in so many languages upon the ingenious ground, that no one at Babel would have forgot his wallet, whatever else he might leave behind. This valuable psychological surmise he confirms from his own observation. Our learned doctor was once on a time called in to attend a German in a brain fever, who had stabbed himself during a paroxysm of his complaint; but though suffering dreadful pain, the patient would not allow him, or any of his brethren, to approach him. "The wretched man," says he, "did not remember that we were physicians, ready to put his disorder to flight." Yet, in spite of this manifest exhibition of madness and delirium, there was one object which he never forgot, and about which his reason seemed perfectly unclouded—a bag of dollars, which he kept under his pillow. "No wonder, therefore," exclaims our philosopher, cunningly transferring his argument from the contents to the container, and from the object to its name,—"no wonder, that at Babel none should forget the term for so interesting an article."[*] Yet the numerous examples collected of this word, will be hardly found to go out of two only families of languages,— the Semitic and the Indo-European. In like manner, Count de Gebelin, who made the last stand upon the old system, often draws the most sweeping conclusions of universal affinity, after comparing, among themselves, words from the different Semitic or Teutonic dialects.[†]

This method of reasoning was now, however, to be exploded, and in the mean time no general principle was to be substituted in its place. Only an analytical method would be admitted, whereby the grammatical

---

[*] *Ubi sup.* p. 578.
[†] "Monde Primitif," vol. iii. p. 30, *seq.*: *Paris*, 1775-81, in the illustration of his "Premier Principe: Les langues ne sont que des dialectes d'une seule." Also pp. 290, *seqq.*

elements of language were to be minutely decomposed and compared, as well as their words, and no affinity admitted between two languages which would not stand a very rigid test. It would therefore appear, that the farther the search proceeded, the more dangerously it would trespass upon the forbidden ground of inspired history.

An uneasiness on this head is clearly discernible in the works of an author, who, towards the close of last century, went far beyond all his forerunners, in laborious research, and in amassing materials for this interesting science. This was the indefatigable and learned Jesuit, Don Lorenzo Hervas y Pandura, who, in a series of works, mostly forming part of his *Idea dell' Universo*, laid before the public vast additions to the stores already described. He had, indeed, the advantage of belonging to a religious society, possessing within its own circle men who had travelled and preached in every district of the globe. Not only did he thus receive personal information on languages little known, but he was able to procure many grammars, vocabularies, and writings, which had scarcely been seen in Europe. With these materials at command, he published year after year, at Cesena,* his numerous quartos upon languages, which were translated and republished by his friends in Spain.†

The great merit of Hervas is his indefatigable zeal

---

* The following are his principal works : "Catalogo delle Lingue conosciute, e Notizia della loro Affinità e Diversità," 1784. "Origine, Formazione, Meccanismo, ed Armonia degl' Idiomi," 1785. "Aritmetica delle Nazioni, e Divisione del Tempo fra l'Orientali," 1785. This is one of the most interesting and valuable among Hervas's works, and there is a supplement to it at the end of the 20th volume of his works. "Vocabolario Poliglotto con Prolegomeni sopra più di 150 Lingue," 1787. "Saggio Prattico delle Lingue," 1787. This contains the Lord's Prayer in more than 300 languages and dialects, with grammatical analyses and notes.

† See "Voyage en Espagne," par C. A. Fischer : *Paris*, 1801, tom. ii. p. 52. The Spanish edition of Hervas is much the more complete. The "Catalogo de las Lenguas de las Naciones conocidas :" *Madrid*, 1800-5, is in six large 8vo. volumes.

and diligence in collecting; there is hardly an attempt at systematic arrangement in his works, but rather a degree of confusion and want of judgment are perceptible in his remarks. Mistakes must indeed be naturally expected in one who wandered over so wide a field, and who had generally to make his own path; yet so assiduous was he in collecting materials, that in spite of the caution wherewith his results must be adopted, the ethnographer is even at this day obliged to explore his pages for information which farther researches have not been able to procure or enlarge. At every step, however, he seems to fear that the study he is pursuing may be turned to the prejudice of revelation. He evidently labours under a great anxiety to prove the contrary; he opens some of his works, and concludes others, with long and elaborate dissertations on this subject.* But his manner of treating it is long and abstract, and his conclusions do not seem to follow easily from the facts which he quotes in evidence. So unsatisfactory, indeed, are the comparisons of words from different languages which he makes on these occasions, that the existence of one letter in common is sufficient with him to form an identity in an entire word.†

Whilst the south of Europe was thus promoting the interests of this science by means of this modest and learned clergyman, in the north it was more brilliantly encouraged by the personal application and patronage of an empress. Among the many literary merits of Catherine II., that of having planned, conducted, and afterwards directed a large comparative work on language, though nowhere mentioned by her English biographer, is far from being the least.‡ Ample justice

* "Saggio Prattico: Origine, Formazione," ec. pp. 156, *seqq.*
† See examples in his "Origine," ec. pp. 27, 29, 118, 128, 134; and "Vocab. Polig." pp. 33, *seqq.*
‡ See Tooke's "Life of Catherine II." 5th edition. Neither in the 13th nor in the 17th chapter is there any mention of the Tzarina's or Pallas's researches on this point, though their literary performances are there enumerated.

has, however, been done to her claims by Frederick Adelung, in a small treatise on this subject. We there learn, upon the authority of her letter to Dr. Zimmerman, that she drew out a list of one hundred Russian words, and had them translated into as many languages as possible. She soon discovered unexpected affinities, and with her own hand began to draw up comparative tables. The doctor's book on "Solitude" superseded this dry task; and accordingly, sending for the naturalist Pallas, she commissioned him to complete her undertaking, and prepare it for publication.* This commission was nowise suited to his taste or previous pursuits; it was imposed upon him against his will, and consequently came forth very imperfect.† Under the title of *Linguarum totius Orbis Vocabularia Comparativa, Augustissimæ cura collecta*, the two first volumes appeared at St. Petersburg, in 1787 and 1789. These contain only the European and Asiatic languages; the third was never published, but in a second edition by Jankiewitsch (1790-91), the African dialects were added.

Europe, thus occupied at its two extremities, received considerable succour from the farthest East. In the year 1784, the Asiatic Society was instituted at Calcutta; through the encouragement whereof the languages of eastern and southern Asia began to be cultivated, and *Grammars* and *Dictionaries* were published of languages and dialects till then almost unknown. The term *Oriental languages*, hitherto confined

---

* "Catherine der grossen Verdienste um die vergleichende Sprachkunde :" *St. Petersb.* 1815. This was not the first attempt made in Russia to promote this study. Bacmeister, in 1773, published there a prospectus of a similar work.

† We have Pallas's own acknowledgment on this point. "Pallas vergleichendes Wörterbuch de europäischen und asiatischen Sprachen, welches er, wie er selbst kurtz vor seinem Tode sagte, *invita Minerva*, und nur auf dringendes Verlangen der Kaiserin Katherine II., nach den von ihr gesammelten und bestellten Hülfsmitteln, eiligst zum Druck befördete, enthält zwar shätzbare Materialien, die aber ohne alle Kritik zusammengestellt sind."—Klaproth, "Asia Polyglotta :" *Paris*, 1823, p. vii.

to the Semitic dialects, now received a far more extensive meaning; Chinese, before considered an almost unconquerable language, began to be studied, till later it was stripped of its difficulties by the sagacity and diligence of the French orientalists; and Sanskrit, peculiarly the province of our countrymen, was cultivated by them with great success, and from them passed into the hands of continental scholars.

But in justice I am bound to say that Rome has the merit of having first seriously attended to the study of Indian literature. John Werdin, better known under the name of Father Paulinus a Sancto Bartholomæo, published, under the auspices of Propaganda, a series of works upon Sanskrit grammar, and upon the history, mythology, and religion of the Hindoos. He was, even during his life, severely handled by Anquetil du Perron and other French critics, but strenuously defended by his countrymen the Adelungs.* Abel-Rémusat has later still done justice to his reputation, and remarks that his misfortune has been, to have his unaided labours eclipsed by the combined exertions of the English society of Calcutta.† It is, farther, just to remark, that so far from any alarm being felt among learned members of the Church in Italy at the new and then highly mysterious class of literature thus opening before them, they hailed it as the prospect of fresh and important accessions to the proofs of early tradition. This feeling is expressed with peculiar earnestness in a letter from F. Angelo Cortenoris, long a missionary in Ava, to the munificent Cardinal Borgia.‡

I shall now mention only one work more, and so pass from this chronological part of my subject, to lay before you some of its results. I ought perhaps to have already mentioned, that from the time of Cham-

---

* "Mithridates," vol. i. p. 134, and vol. iv. p. 56.
† In the "Biographie Universelle," vol. xlii. p. 342, ed. *Ven.* 1828, printed also in his "Nouveaux Mélanges Asiatiques," tom. ii. *Paris*, 1829, p. 305.
‡ On the perusal of F. Paulinus's "Amarasinha," dated Udine, June 9, 1799.—Borgia Papers, in the Museum of Propaganda, C.

berlayne, there had been continually a series of publications containing collections of the Lord's Prayer; the most important of which was the one given by Hervas. Something new was perhaps given in each, but then each copied the errors of its predecessors. The plan was essentially defective, as intended to show the character of different languages; because a translation of a prayer so peculiar in its form must be more or less constrained in many languages, nor could ever form such a fair specimen as an original composition by a native would present. Then these collections were generally arranged in alphabetical order, and were unaccompanied with any philological or ethnographical illustrations. In fact, instead of improving, the system rather became worse, till, in the hands of Fry, Marcel, and Bodoni, these publications degenerated into a mere piece of typographical luxury, and became only specimens of their skill in making and printing foreign alphabets. One work, however, containing such a collection, forms a most honourable exception, and must be reckoned, in spite of its imperfections, among the most valuable and splendid ethnographic works. I allude to the *Mithridates*, begun by John Christopher Adelung, in 1806. He died before publishing the second volume, which appeared in 1809, under the care of Dr. J. Severinus Vater. Its materials were chiefly drawn from Adelung's papers, and extended to the European languages the researches confined in the first volume to Asia; the third volume, upon the African and American languages, was entirely contributed by Vater, and came out in parts, from the year 1812 to 1816. In 1817, this valuable compilation was completed by a supplementary volume, containing much additional matter, by Vater and the younger Adelung, besides a most interesting essay on the Cantaber, or Biscayan, by Baron W. von Humboldt.[*]

[*] Dr. Vater died March 28, 1826, at the age of fifty-five. Though he resided at Königsberg and Halle, the "Mithridates" was all published at Berlin.

In this work, the alphabetical classification is abandoned, and the languages are distributed into groups, or larger divisions, with a minute description and history of each. Lists of works useful for acquiring or examining them are likewise given, together with specimens, consisting principally of the Lord's Prayer. Adelung's views on the origin of languages seem to be that mankind may have invented them in different countries.* Noah's ark, or the tower of Babel, no way enters into his consideration, for he has no favourite hypothesis to maintain:† and it would appear that the Paradise whence the human race issued was, in his opinion, the seat of the present generation; thus excluding all interruption, by any great catastrophe, of the earliest history of man.‡ With such opinions we have nothing to do at present; they are not given by Adelung as resulting from his valuable researches.

Hitherto we have been occupied with the historical part of our subject, and this has now brought us fairly into our own times. You have therefore a right to expect that, according to my engagement, I lay before you the present state of this science, and show the confirmation which its latest developments have afforded to the scriptural history of man's dispersion.

You have seen, then, how, at the close of the last century, the numberless languages gradually discovered seemed to render the probabilities of mankind having originally possessed a common tongue, much smaller than before; while the dissolution of certain admitted connections and analogies among those previously known, seemed to deny all proof from comparative philology of their having separated from a common stock. Every new discovery only served to increase

---

* Erst. th. Einleitung. Fragmente, u. s. w. p. xi.
† " Ich habe keine Lieblingsmeinung, keine Hypothese zum Grunde zu legen. Ich leite nicht alle Sprachen von Einer her. Noah's Arche ist mir eine verschlossene Burg, und Babylon's Schutt bleibt vor mir völlig in seiner Ruhe."—*Ibid.* Vorrede, p. xi.
‡ *Ibid.* Einleit. p. 6, comparing pp. 14, 17.

this perplexity: and our science must at that time have presented to a religious observer the appearance of a study daily receding from sound doctrine, and giving encouragement to rash speculations and dangerous conjecture. But even at that period, a ray of light was penetrating into the chaos of materials thrown together by collectors; and the first great step towards a new organization was even then taken, by the division of those materials into distinct homogeneous masses, into continents, as it were, and oceans; the stable and circumscribed, and the movable and varying elements, whereof this science is now composed.

The affinities which formerly had been but vaguely seen between languages separated in their origin by history and geography, began now to appear definite and certain. It was now found that new and most important connections existed among languages, so as to combine in large provinces or groups, the idioms of nations whom no other research would have shown to be mutually related. It was found that the Teutonic dialects received considerable light from the language of Persia; that Latin had remarkable points of contact with Russian and the other Slavonian idioms; and that the theory of the Greek verbs in $\mu\iota$ could not well be understood without recourse to their parallels in Sanskrit or Indian grammar. In short, it was clearly demonstrated that one speech, essentially so called, pervaded a considerable portion of Europe and Asia, and stretching across in a broad sweep from Ceylon to Iceland, united, in a bond of union, nations professing the most irreconcilable religions, possessing the most dissimilar institutions, and bearing but a slight resemblance in physiognomy and colour. The language, or rather, family of languages, I have thus lightly sketched, has received the name of Indo-Germanic, or Indo-European. As this group is necessarily to us the most interesting, and has received most cultivation, I will describe it more at length; confining myself to a few passing observations upon other families. But in tracing the history of this one, you will be fully enabled to see how every new investigation tends still farther to correct the dangerous tendencies of the earlier periods of our science.

The great members of this family are the Sanskrit, or ancient and sacred language of India; the Persian, ancient and modern, formerly considered a Tartar dialect;* Teutonic, with its various dialects, Slavonian, Greek, and Latin, accompanied by its numerous derivatives. To these, as we shall later see, must be now added the Celtic dialects; the enumeration I have made being intended to embrace only the languages early admitted into this species of confederation. By casting your eyes over the ethnographic map which I present you, you will at once see the territory thus occupied; that is, the whole of Europe, excepting only the small tracts held by the Biscayan, and by the Finnish family, which includes Hungarian; thence it extends over a great part of southern Asia, here and there interrupted by insulated groups. It were tedious indeed to enumerate the writers who have proved the affinity between the languages I have named,† or between two or more members thereof: it will be sufficient for our purpose if I explain rather the methods they have pursued and the results they have obtained.

The first and most obvious mode of proceeding, and the one which first led to these interesting conclusions, was that of which I have often spoken: the comparison of words in these different languages. Many works have presented comparative tables to a very great extent: that of Colonel Vans Kennedy comprises nine hundred

---

* Pauw, for instance, mentions the affinity between German and Persian, "qui est un dialecte du Tartare."—*Recherches Philos. sur les Américains,* vol. ii. p. 303: *Berlin,* 1770. "La lingua Persiana moderna è un dialetto corrotto della Tartaro-Mongola."—Hervas, Catalogo, p. 124.

† See a copious list of the authors who have written in favour of these affinities, in Dr. Dorn, "Ueber die Verwandschaft des persischen, germanischen, und griechischlateinischen Sprachstammes," pp. 9!-120: *Hamb.* 1827; and of those who have opposed them, pp. 120-135.

words common to Sanskrit and other languages.* The words found thus to resemble one another in different idioms, are by no means such as could have been communicated by subsequent intercourse, but express the first and simplest elements of language, primary ideas, such as must have existed from the beginning, and scarcely ever change their denominations. Not to cite the numerals, which would require many accompanying observations; while I pronounce the following words, *pader, mader, sunu, dokhter, brader, mand, vidhava*, or *juvan*, you might easily suppose that I was repeating words from some European language; yet every one of these terms is Sanskrit or Persian. Again, to choose another class of simple words, in such words as *asthi* (Gr. ὀστοῦν), a bone; *denta*, a tooth; *eyumen*, the eye, in Zend; *brouwa* (Ger. *braue*), eyebrow; *nasa*, the nose; *lib*, a lip; *karu* (Gr. χείρ), a hand; *genu*, the knee; *ped*, the foot; *hrti*, the heart; *jecur*, the liver; *stara*, a star; *gela*, cold; *aghni*, (Lat. *ignis*), fire; *dhara*, (terra), the earth; *arrivi*, a river; *nau* (Gr. ναῦς), a ship; *ghau*, a cow; *sarpam*, a serpent; you might easily fancy that you heard dialects of languages much nearer home; and yet they all belong to the Asiatic languages I have already mentioned. So far indeed may this comparison be carried, that fanciful etymologists like Von Hammer, will derive such pure English words as *bedroom* from the Persian.*

But this verbal coincidence would have proved by no means satisfactory to a large body of philologers, had it not in due course been followed by a still more important conformity in the grammatical structure of these languages. Bopp, in 1816, was the first to examine this subject with any degree of accuracy; and by a minute and sagacious analysis of the Sanskrit verb, compared with the conjugational system of the

* "Researches into the Origin and Affinity of the principal Languages of Asia and Europe:" *London*, 1828, at the end of the work.
† See his comparative tables in almost every number of the "Wiener Jahrbücher," for several years past.

other members of this family, left no farther doubt of their intimate and primitive affinity;* since which time he has pushed his researches much farther, and commenced the publication of a more extensive work.†

By the analysis of the Sanskrit pronouns, the elements of those existing in all the other languages are cleared of their anomalies; the verb-substantive, which in Latin is composed of fragments referable to two distinct roots, here finds both existing in regular form; the Greek conjugations, with all their complicated machinery of middle voice, augments, and reduplications, are here found and illustrated in a variety of ways, which a few years ago would have appeared chimerical. Even our own language may sometimes receive light from the study of distant members of our family. Where, for instance, are we to seek the root of our comparative *better?* Certainly not in its positive *good,* nor in the Teutonic dialects, in which the same anomaly exists. But in the Persian we have precisely the same comparative بهتر *behter,* with exactly the same signification, regularly formed from its positive به *beh,* good; just as we have in the same language بدتر *badter,* worse, from بد *bad.*

Having brought these two languages into contact, I cannot forbear expressing some surprise at several observations upon the subject contained in the valuable work by Colonel Kennedy, to which I have already referred. He says, for instance, that "the slightest examination of Persian grammar must show it radically different from that of German. In neither words, therefore, nor in grammatical structure, do the German and Persian languages possess any affinity."‡ I cannot conceive how any one who has perused Bopp's

---

* "Franz Bopp, über das Conjugazionssystem der Sanskritsprache, in Vergleichung mit jenem der griech. latein. persisch. und germanischen Sprache:" *Frankfort,* 1816.
† "Vergleichende Grammatik des Sanskrit, Zend, Griechischen, Lateinischen, Littauischen, Gothisch. und Deutschen:" *Berlin,* 1833.
‡ Page 157.

work, and still less how any one who has read a hundred pages in the two languages, could deny the marked affinity between their respective grammars. I must at the same time observe, that to institute a fair comparison between them, we must not merely take the German as at present existing, but examine its older forms, as given and proved in Grimm's splendid grammar. We shall there discover, for instance, forms of the verb-substantive bearing the closest relation to the Persian conjugation. But of one part of his assertion the learned author, sixty pages later, affords sufficient confutation, when he tells us that " it must be farther remarked, that the only languages in which Sanskrit words exist, are the Greek, Latin, Persian, and Gothic, and the vernacular dialects of India."* Surely this acknowledged affinity of the two languages to a third, whereby they are, as it were, admitted into the family whereof it is the head, as in strict relationship with it, must imply a mutual connection between them. In another place, too, he seems to deny all affinity between the Sanskrit and Persian grammars;† and in the passage I have quoted, as well as elsewhere, he clearly excludes the Slavonian from this family, though its rights to enter it are now universally acknowledged. Throughout the course of his interesting work, it is certainly painful to see the author so unwilling to do justice to his predecessors' merits; and the severe censure which he has bestowed upon others, has been naturally enough the measure of consideration shown him in domestic, but still more in foreign reviews.

You see at once, and I shall have to return again to this subject, how the formation of this vast family greatly diminishes the number of independent original languages; and other great genera, if I may so call them, have been equally well defined. Of the Semitic languages I need not speak; for the intimate relationship between the dialects which form them, the Hebrew, Syro-Chaldaic, Arabic, and Gheez or Abyssinian, has

---

* Page 206, also p. 9. † Page 187.

long been acknowledged, and applied to another science so important as to deserve later a particular discourse.* But the Malay, as it has been generally called, presents a similar result in modern ethnography to that of our former investigation. According to both Marsden and Crawfurd, this language or family should be rather called the Polynesian, as the Malay, properly so called, is only one dialect of it, and may be called the *lingua franca* of the Indian Archipelago. In all the languages composing this group, there is a great tendency to the monosyllabic form, and to the rejection of all inflection; thus approximating to the neighbouring group of Transgangetic languages, with which, indeed, Dr. Leyden seems to unite them. "The vernacular Indo-Chinese languages on the continent," he writes, "seem to be in their original structure either purely monosyllabic, like the spoken languages of China, or they incline so much to this class, that it may be strongly suspected that the few original polysyllables they contain, have either been immediately derived from the Pali, or formed of coalescing monosyllables. These languages are all prodigiously varied by accentuation, like the spoken language of China."† Now, among these languages he reckons the Bugis, Javanese, Malayu, Tagala, Batta, and others, which are allied not only in words, but in grammatical construction.‡ Crawfurd, confining his observations within rather narrower limits, comes to the same conclusion. Javanese he considers as presenting most elements of the language which forms the basis of all in this class; and it is peculiarly deficient in grammatical forms,§ which may be said no less of the Malayan dialect.‖ Indeed, he too has recognized so strong a resemblance,

---

* See the Lecture on "Sacred Oriental Studies."
† "On the Language and Literature of the Indo-Chinese Nations." —Asiat. Res. vol. x. p. 162.
‡ Page 200.
§ "History of the Indian Archipelago:" *Edin.* 1820, vol. ii. pp. 5, seqq. 72, 78, 92, &c.
‖ Page 41.

not only of words but of structure, in the languages
spoken all through the Indian Archipelago, as to warrant
their being classed in one family.* Marsden is still
more explicit, and extends the limits of the group a
good deal farther. "Besides the Malayan," says he,
"there are a variety of languages spoken in Sumatra,
which, however, have not only a manifest affinity among
themselves, but also to that general language which is
found to prevail in, and be indigenous to, all the islands
of the Eastern Sea, from Madagascar to the remotest
of Captain Cook's discoveries; comprehending a wider
extent than the Roman or any other tongue has yet
boasted. Indisputable examples of this connection and
similarity I have exhibited in a paper which the Society
of Antiquaries have done me the honour to publish in
their *Archæologia*, vol. vii. In different places it has
been more or less mixed and corrupted, but between
the most dissimilar branches an evident sameness of
many radical words is apparent, and in some, very
distant from each other in point of situation—as, for
instance, the Philippines and Madagascar—the deviation
of the words is scarcely more than is observed in the
dialects of neighbouring provinces in the same kingdom.† Thus, again, we have an immense family
stretching over a vast portion of the globe, and comprising many languages which a few years ago were
considered independent; and though I have in my map
preserved the two perfectly distinct, it would almost
appear as if some affinity might be allowed between the
Transgangetic and Malayan groups.

This first great step of modern ethnographic science,
you will, I am sure, acknowledge to be of great interest
and importance, when viewed in reference to the early
history of man. Instead of being perplexed with a
multiplicity of languages, we have now reduced them
to certain very large groups, each comprising a great
variety of languages formerly thought to be unconnected, and thus representing, as it were, only one

* Page 78. † "History of Sumatra :" *London*, 1811, p. 200.

human family, originally possessing a single idiom. Now every succeeding step has clearly added to this advantage, and diminished still farther any apparent hostility between the number of languages and the history of the dispersion. For I have now to show you how farther research has deprived new idioms of their supposed independence, and brought them into classes already discovered, or, at least, into connection with distant languages. For example, the march of the Indo-European family was supposed by Malte Brun, in 1812, to be completely arrested in the region of the Caucasus by the languages there spoken, as the Georgian and Armenian; which, to use his own words, " formed there a family or group apart."* But Klaproth, by his journey to the Caucasus, has made it necessary to modify this assertion to a great extent. For he has proved, or at least rendered it highly probable, that the language of one great tribe, the Ossetes or Alans, belongs to the great family I have mentioned.† Again, Armenian, which Frederick Schlegel had formerly considered a species of intermediate language, rather hanging on the skirts of the same group than incorporated therewith,‡ has been by Klaproth, upon grammatical as well as lexical examination, proved fairly to belong to it.§ The Afghan or Pushtoo has shared the same fate.‖

But the greatest accession which this family has received by means of a diligent and judicious study of the analogies of languages, is undoubtedly that of the entire Celtic family, which, with its numerous dialects, must now be content to form only a province of the Indo-European. Balbi, in his Ethnographic Atlas, which I will describe to you later, has placed the

* " Précis de la Géographie Universelle," tome ii. p. 580.
† " L'analyse de la Langue des Ossètes fera voir qu'elle appartient à la souche Médo-Persane."—Voyage au Mont Caucase, et en Géorgie: *Paris*, 1823, vol. ii. p. 448 ; see pp. 470, *seqq.*
‡ " Ueber die Sprache und Weisheit der Indier :" *Heidelb*. 1808, p. 77.
§ " Asia Polyglotta," p. 99. ‖ *Ibid.* p. 57.

Biscayan and Celtic languages in one tableau: not of course, because he considers them as having anything in common, but because they were apparently out of the pale of those idioms by which they are surrounded. Colonel Kennedy boldly asserts, " that the Celtic has no connection with the languages of the East, either in words or phrases, or the construction of sentences."* But a still later writer has discussed the question with all the forms of the exploded school, and endeavoured to examine the origin of the Celtic nations, by processes which on the continent are almost forgotten. I allude to the work entitled " The Gael and the Cymbri."† To deny it the praise of ingenuity and curious research, would assuredly be unjust; but the two great ethnographical points therein treated, the radical difference between the Welsh and Irish languages, and the Phenician or Semitic origin of the latter, are certainly managed with all that unsatisfactory display of etymology which has been long since rejected from this study. If we wish to establish the Irish language as a Phenician dialect, the process is very simple. We know from the most undoubted sources that the Phenician and the Hebrew were two sister dialects: compare, therefore, the grammatical structure of this language and Irish, and the result will solve the problem. Now, instead of this simple method, see how our author proceeds. The names of places on the Spanish and other coasts, were given by the Phenicians; now these names can all be explained in Irish. Therefore the Irish and Phenician languages are identical. A few years ago, an eminent geographer published an essay in a French journal,‡ wherein he, by a similar process, derived many African names of places from Hebrew, so as to establish their Phenician origin. Klaproth, in a letter under the Danish name of Kierulf, confuted these etymologies by proposing two new ones for each name, the one from

---

* *Ubi sup.* p. 85. † By Sir W. Betham : *Dublin*, 1834.
‡ " Nouvelles Annales des Voyages," Feb. 1824.

Turkish, the other from Russian.* This may suffice to show how unsatisfactory such processes are. For the author never takes the pains to prove that the character of the places corresponds to the Irish interpretation of their names. To examine his etymologies in detail would be indeed tedious; but I cannot refrain from taking a few examples at random. Some names which we know to be Phenician, and which correspond in that language to the exact character of the places they represent, must go to Irish to receive new ones, which will do as well for any other. Thus Tyre, in Phenician, צור, *Tzur*, a rock, a meaning to which allusion is frequently made in Scripture, is derived, according to him, from *Tir*, a land or city; when we might just as well derive it from the Chaldaic טיר *Tir, a palace*. Palmyra and Tadmor, which are exact translations of one another, meaning the city of palms, must be derived from Irish words; the one meaning the *palace of pleasure*,† the other the *great house;* and Cadiz, or *Gadir*, as it was originally called, must no longer signify, as the word does graphically in Phenician, *the island* or *peninsula;* but after the Irish word *cadaz*, which only resembles the modern corruption of the name, must signify *glory*.‡ Again, taking a set of names, not of places but of people, ending by a common adjective termination in *tani;* these are cut in two, and the termination is made to be the Irish word *tana*, country. I might just as well go to the Malayan for their interpretation; for there also *tanah* means a country, as Tanah Papuah, the country of the Papuas.§ But just let us take one example: *Lacetani* means, according to our author, *the country of milk*. Why not, therefore, from *lac*, milk, by a regular formation, derive *lacetum*, like *spinetum*, or *rosetum*, a

---

* In an appendix to his "Beleuchtung und Widerlegung der Forschungen, u. s. w. des Herrn J. J. Schmidt:" *Paris*, 1824.
† The word *palas* is manifestly identical with palace, *palatium*, the Palatine hill, then the residence of the Cæsars, and so a *palace*. How did the Phenicians possess it?
‡ Pp. 100, 104.
§ See "Trans. of R. A. S." vol. iii. p. 1, 1831.

place abounding in milk; and so again, in regular order *Lacetani*, the inhabitants of such a country. Surely, if we are to make such etymologies, is not this more regular than the Irish one, *lait* milk, *o* of, *tana* country?* But suffice it to say, that Latin, Biscayan, and even Spanish words, suffer strange changes into Irish to work out this untenable hypothesis.† Then, as to the grammatical analysis proposed in this work, to prove that Welsh and Irish have nought in common, I must say that, in spite of its obscurities, it produced on my mind exactly a contrary impression, and seemed to me to prove, before I had seen the valuable work to which I shall just now refer, that both belonged to the same family, and that the Indo-European.

I may have appeared to you more full and severe in my remarks upon this work than my subject required; but I will own that, more than once, I have been exposed to the mortification of hearing our English ethnographers blamed, as falling far below the advanced position of foreign philologers; and assuredly, when, after perusing the learned, judicious, and satisfactory inquiries of Baron Humboldt, from the Biscayan, into the very names so disfigured in this book, and admiring the sound philosophical and philological principles which guide him at every step,‡ we take up a work published since his, and going over the same ground, upon a system of fanciful etymologies derided to scorn by continental linguists, it is hard to forbear feeling a lively regret that we should be subject to the

---

* Page 104.

† For instance, we are told that *Llanes* comes from *lean*, a swampy plain, while *llano* in Spanish is the strict representation of *planus*, and means precisely the same. Puenta Rio de la (Rio de la Puenta), from *puinte*, a point (again of Indo-Germanic origin), and not from the Spanish *puente*, a bridge. Cantabri means *heads high above!* &c. (pp. 107, 109, 111).

‡ In his interesting "Prüfung der Untersuchung über die Urbewohner Hispaniens:" *Berlin*, 1821. Compare Sir W. Betham's derivation of Asturias from *as*, a torrent, and *sir*, a country (p. 106), with the learned German's disquisition on that name as found in Spain and Italy, p. 114.

D

reproaches of our neighbours, and that what they have already done should be apparently overlooked amongst us. When we are obliged to put forward as our greatest ethnographer, one who, like Dr. Murray, blends the rarest erudition with the most ridiculous theories,—who, with a profound knowledge of many languages, maintains that all those of Europe have their origin from nine absurd monosyllables, expressive of different sorts of strokes:* when a philosopher held greatly in respect by his school, so late as 1827, speaks of the affinity between Greek and Sanskrit as something new and strange: refers to "a German publication of Francis Bopp," and an "Essay on the Language and Philosophy of the Indians, by the celebrated Mr. F. Schlegel," as works yet unknown to us except through the quotations of a review; mentions Gebelin, De Brosses, and Leibnitz, as the best authorities upon these studies; and occupies many pages in attempting to prove that Sanskrit is a *jargon* made up from Greek and Latin, and illustrates his position from *kitchen-Latin* and *macaronic verses:*† when a learned linguist professes to prove the conformity of the European with Oriental languages, and for that purpose confuses together primary and derivative, ancient and modern Semitic and Indo-European words, giving such terms from the Arabic as *astrolabe* and *melancholy*, which it, as well as we, received from the Greeks:‡ when, in short, in the very last year, we have a divine, I believe of some celebrity, bringing this very study to bear upon the Mosaic history, by completely overlooking all its

---

* These are:—1. *ag, wag, hwag.* 2. *bag* or *bwag.* 3. *dwag.* 4. *cwag.* 5. *lag.* 6. *mag.* 7. *nag.* 8. *rag.* 9. *swag.* "History," &c., *ut sup.* p. 31. "By the help of these nine words and their compounds, all the European languages have been formed !" (p. 39).

† These observations will all be found in Dugald Stewart's "Elements of the Philosophy of the Human Mind," vol. iii. *London*, 1827, pp. 100-137.

‡ See "A Specimen of the Conformity of the European Languages, particularly the English, with the Oriental Languages," by Stephen Weston, B.D. *London*, 1802.

modern results, and considering the Teutonic, Greek, and Semitic as forming the three principal ethnographic reigns; telling us that " the construction of the three great families of language, the Oriental, the Western, and the Northern, is actually so distinct that a new wonder arises from the perfect adequacy of each to perform all the purposes of human communication;[*] when we see so many others amongst us, whom it would be long to enumerate, pertinaciously clinging to the old dreams of Hebrew etymologies,

"Trattando l'ombre come cosa salda ;"

we cannot but feel that the reproach made against us is but too well grounded, that we have neglected to keep pace with the progress of this science upon the continent; and be keenly mortified when we meet, instead of amendment, another repetition of what has heretofore justified the charge.

But from this unpleasant and unwilling censure, which I trust will not be often called for in the course of our meetings, I am agreeably recalled by a work to which I am happy to say I can give unqualified praise:—

—— χαίρω δὲ πρόσφορον
'Εν μὲν ἔργῳ κόμπον ἱείς;[†]

and which leads us back to the matter whence we have so long digressed. For you may perhaps have almost forgotten, that we were discussing the propriety of uniting the Celtic dialects to the Indo-European family. This question may be now considered as fairly set at rest, by the valuable and interesting work of Dr. Prichard, *On the Eastern Origin of the Celtic Nations*.[‡]

[*] "Divine Providence; or, the Three Cycles of Revelation," by the Rev. G. Croly, LL.D. *London*, 1834, c. xxii. p. 301. Nothing can be more incorrect than the description which follows this passage of the characteristics of each family so formed.
[†] Pindar, Nem. viii. 82. [‡] Oxford, 1831.

In an earlier publication, to which I shall, on a future occasion, have to refer very frequently, he had entered into a partial analysis of the Welsh numerals and verbs, and concluded that the admission of this language into the family so often named, " would have been allowed if it had undergone a similar investigation to the others, from persons competent to form an opinion on its analogies."* But in the present work he has put the affinity of the Celtic with the Indo-European languages above all doubt. First, he has examined the lexical resemblances, and shown that the primary and most simple words are the same in both, as well as the numerals and elementary verbal roots.† Then follows a minute analysis of the verb, directed to show its analogies with other languages; and they are such as manifest no casual coincidence, but an internal structure radically the same. The verb-substantive, which is minutely analyzed, presents more striking analogies to the Persian verb than perhaps any other language of the family.‡ But Celtic is not thus become a mere member of this confederacy, but has brought it most important aid; for from it alone can be satisfactorily explained some of the conjugational endings in the other languages. For instance, the third person plural of the Latin, Persian, Greek, and Sanskrit, ends in *nt, nd, ντι, ντο,* and *nti* or *nt.* Now, supposing, with most grammarians, that the inflexions arose from the pronouns of the respective persons, it is only in Celtic that we find a pronoun that can explain this termination. For there, too, the same person ends in *nt,* and thus corresponds exactly, as do the others, with its pronoun *hwynt,* or *ynt.*§

* " Researches into the Physical History of Man :" *London,* 1826, vol. ii. p. 168 ; comp. p. 622.
† Pp. 36–88. It may, however, be worth while observing, that Jäkel has shown all the words given by the ancients as Celtic, to be German. "Der germanische Ursprung der lateinischen Sprache :" *Bresl.* 1830, p. 11. Does this arise merely from family affinity, or from confusion in the ancients, who took little pains to study what they deemed barbarous languages?
‡ See pp. 171, *seqq.* § Pp. 130–138.

This circumstance certainly gives Welsh an important place among the languages composing this great family. It must not, however, thereby receive any undue advantage over the others, or be considered as approaching nearer to the original stock. For this is yet an important problem to be solved, to ascertain, that is, the order of filiation, if it exist, or the rights of primogeniture, among its members. Sanskrit, instead of the made-up jargon it was supposed to be by Stewart, is considered by most ethnographers the oldest and purest form; Latin resembles it in many respects more than Greek, and yet Jäkel has lately endeavoured to prove that it is derived through Teutonic. He has, indeed, brought many examples of Latin words which want their signification unless we recur to German; as *fenestra*, which through the cognate word *fenster* is explained from *finster*, dark, having originally signified, according to him, the shutters or lattice; and of others which have no roots except there; such as *præsagire* and *sagus*, which find in German the verb *sagen*, whence *wahrsagen*, for sufficient root.* Such speculations must not, however, be indulged in too much; for a root once common to both languages may have been lost in one, and preserved in another, though both are independent in descent. Thus we are every moment obliged to recur to the Arabic for roots now wanting in Hebrew; yet no one would thence conclude the Arabic origin of the Hebrew tongue. Minute grammatical analysis will alone put us in possession of correct conclusions upon this subject.

While the Indo-European family is thus gradually more rounded as well as increased in its territorial limits, and the number of its members daily increases, other languages, the connections whereof were not formerly known, have been found allied to others separated by considerable tracts of country, so nearly as to form with them a common family. I will content

---

* *Ubi sup.* p. 13.

myself with one instance in Europe. Towards the close of the last century, Sainovic, followed by Gyarmathi, proved that Hungarian, which lies like an island surrounded by Indo-European languages, belongs essentially to the Finnish or Uralian family,* which stretches downwards, as it were, through the Esthonian and Livonian, to join it.† In Africa, too, the dialects whereof have been comparatively but little studied, every new research displays connections between tribes extended over vast tracts, and often separated by intermediate nations; in the north between the languages spoken by the Berbers and Tuariks, from the Canaries to the Oasis of Siwa; in central Africa, between the dialects of the Felatahs and Foulas, who occupy nearly the whole interior; in the south, among the tribes across the whole continent, from Caffraria and Mozambique to the Atlantic Ocean.‡

But it is time that we should pause; first looking back upon what we have hitherto gained, thence to take augury for those more interesting results which will occupy our next meeting. We have seen, then, the learned world slumbering, contented with the hypothesis that the few languages known might be all resolved into one, and that one probably the Hebrew. Aroused by new discoveries, which defied this easy vindication of the Mosaic history, they saw the necessity of a totally new science, which should dedicate its attention to the classification of languages. At first it seemed as though the infant science was impatient of control, and its earliest progress seemed directly at variance with the soundest truths. Gradually, however, masses which seemed floating in uncertainty, came together, and like the garden islands of the Mexican Lake, combined into

---

* "Sainovii Demonstratio Idioma Ungarorum et Lapponum idem esse:" *Copenhag.* 1770. "Gyarmathi, Affinitas Linguæ Hungaricæ cum Linguis Fennicæ originis, grammatice demonstrata:" *Götting.* 1799.
† See the "Ethnographic Map," prefixed to this volume.
‡ See Prichard, *ubi sup.* p. 7.

compact and extensive territories, capable and worthy of the finest cultivation. The languages, in other words, grouped themselves into various large and well-connected families, and thus greatly reduced the number of primary idioms from which others have sprung. And after this, we have seen how every succeeding research, so far from weakening this simplifying result, has, on the contrary, still farther strengthened it, by ever bringing new tongues, thought before to be independent, into the limits of established families, or uniting into new ones such as promised little or no affinity. Such are the two first results of this science, and I will reserve for another day its farther advance.

But before closing this lecture, I may not withhold a few reflections suggested to me by looking back on the sort of inquiry I have therein followed. For, when I consider how many different men have laboured almost unwittingly to produce the results I have laid before you—one, for no sensible purpose, hunting out the analogies of this speech; another, that knew not wherefore, noting the dialects of barbarous tribes; a third, comparing together, for pastime, the words of diverse countries;—when I see them thus, all like emmets bearing their small particular loads, or removing some little obstruction, and crossing and recrossing one the other, as though in total confusion, and to the utter derangement of each other's projects; and yet, when I discover that from all this there results a plan of exceeding regularity, order, and beauty; it doth seem to me as though I read therein signs of a higher instinct, and of a directing influence over the thoughtless counsels of men, which can bring them unto great and useful purposes. And such, methinks, is to be found in the history of all sound learning. For, as a day appearing now and then of brighter and warmer sunshine, doth foreshow that the full burst of summer's glory is about to break upon the earth, so do certain privileged minds, by some mysterious communication, ever foresee, as it were, or rather feel sometime beforehand, and announce the approach of some great and new system of truth; as did Bacon, of Philosophy; and Leibnitz, of our science; and Plato, of a holier manifestation. Then arise, and come in from all sides, we know not how, workmen and patient labourers, like those who cast down faggots under a foundation, or raise stones thereon; whom no one takes for the architects or builders of the house, for they know and comprehend nought of its plans or objects; and yet every stone which they place fitteth aright, and adds to the usefulness and beauty of its parts. And so, after this fashion, by the work of many conjoined, though not combined in any plan, a science is builded up in fair proportions, and seemeth to stand well and in its proper place among the others already raised; and so at length cometh to be a joint, as it were, in the general fitness of things, and a maxim in the universal truth, and a tone or accord in the harmony of nature.

Now I cannot persuade myself that there is not an overseeing eye in this ordering of things dissimilar to one great end, when I see that this great end is the confirmation of God's holy word; but rather of this seeming human industry I would say with the divine poet :

> "Lo Motor primo a lui si volge lieto,
> Sovra tant' arte di natura, e spira
> Spirito nuovo di virtù repleto
> Che ciò che truova attivo quivi, tira
> In sua sustanzia e fassi un' alma sola
> Che vive e sente, e sè in sè regira."*
>   DANTE, *Purgat*. xxv.

Not that He partaketh in the errors and follies of such as labour in these pursuits, but as He useth the evils of

> *——————— "Then turns
> The Primal Mover with a smile of joy
> On such great work of nature; and imbreathes
> New spirit replete with virtue, that what here
> Active it finds, to its own substance draws;
> And forms an individual soul that lives,
> And feels, and bends reflective on itself."
>   CARY'S *Translation*.

this world for the most holy purposes, and unfolds often therefrom the most magnificent passages of His blessed providence, so may He here overrule and guide even the ill-intended labours of many, and so dispose thereof, as that a new and beautiful light may come forth upon His truths, when such is most truly needed.

Thus would I consider the rise and development of any new science, as entering essentially into the established order of God's moral government; just as the appearance, from time to time, of new stars in the firmament, according to what astronomers tell us, must be a pre-ordained event in the annals of creation. And if you agree with me in these reflections, you will also, methinks, feel as I do, that in tracing the history of any pursuit, we are not so much indulging a fond curiosity, or following the progress of man's ingenuity, as watching the beautiful courses whereby God hath gradually removed the veil from before some hidden knowledge, first lifting up one corner thereof, then another, till the whole is rolled away: and you will with me delight in studying the purposes and applications thereby intended, both towards our humble instruction and His increasing glory.

LECTURE THE SECOND;

ON THE

COMPARATIVE STUDY OF LANGUAGES.

PART II.

SUMMARY OF RESULTS exposed in the preceding Lecture.—*Continuation.*—*Third:* Relationship between the different families.—Present state of the study; its two principal Schools, founded on the comparison of words, and of grammatical forms.—Remarks directed towards reconciling them.—Errors regarding the supposed power of development in languages; opinion of Humboldt.—Power of external circumstances to alter the grammatical structure of a language. Proposed rule for the comparison of words. Dr. Young's application of the calculus of probabilities to the discovery of the common origin of two languages, by a comparison of words.—Lepsius on the affinities between Hebrew and Sanskrit.—His farther and inedited researches into the connection between Hebrew and ancient Egyptian.—Proposed comparison of Semitic and Indo-European grammatical forms (referred to a note).—Conclusions of modern Ethnographers.—*First:* That all language was originally one; Alex. von. Humboldt, Academy of St. Petersburg, Merian, Klaproth, Fred. Schlegel.—*Secondly:* That the separation was by a violent and sudden cause; Herder, Turner, Abel-Rémusat, Niebuhr, Balbi.

AMERICAN LANGUAGES.—Difficulties arising from their multiplicity.—Attempts of Vater, Smith-Barton, and Malte-Brun, to trace them to Asiatic languages.—Unity of family proved by similarity of grammar; subdivision into groups.—Their number accounted for by the experience of the science; confirmation of their Asiatic origin from other coincidences.—General remarks on the providential connection of the different states of religion with different families of languages.

ALBEIT, in my last Discourse, after leading you through a compendious history of philological ethnography in ages past, I brought you into our own times, and endeavoured to make you acquainted with the labours of many who yet live; nevertheless, I may be said to have there only given you the proem, as it were, or introduction to the modern study, and to the principles whereon it is conducted. For, such was the abundance of matter furnished by my theme, that, after all convenient abridgment used, I saw myself compelled either to abuse your patience by too long a discourse, or divide my subject, to the disparagement of its better understanding. And so, choosing this part, which threw the difficulties upon myself rather than upon those who so courteously attend me—

> "Contro il piacer mio per piacerli,
> Trassi dell' acqua non sazia la spugna."

In requital for this, I must request you to summon back to your recollection the chiefest points whereof we seemed to have gained sufficient evidence; and these are, that the comparative study of languages has brought into certain relationship many which heretofore had seemed divided in sunder, forming thereof great groups or families, so that nations and tribes, covering vast tracts of territory, are, in this study, accounted as only one people; and that its subsequent researches tend in every instance to diminish the number of independent languages, to widen the pale of these larger provinces, and to bring the number of original stocks much nearer to what might be supposed to have arisen on a sudden, among the few inhabitants of the earlier world.

The next important point to be ascertained is, whether any relationship can be discovered between languages of different families, so as to deduce that they have once been in closer connection than at present; in other words, that they descend from a common stock. Now, the inquiries which have been carried on to ascertain this delicate and important point, are so intimately connected with the present state of the study, and the schools into which it is divided, that it becomes absolutely necessary for us to interrupt our course, and examine this actual condition of philological ethnography; if, indeed, we are to call 'an interruption what essentially enters into the design of our original plan. As one of the schools sets but little value upon the methods pursued by the other, and consequently upon the results thence gained, it would be unjust to receive them as undisputed; and I should be deceiving you were I to lay before you these results as the uncontested discoveries of the science, or without explaining how far they may be considered satisfactory. Two things I will premise; first, that so far as we have proceeded, all agree; so that the results I have laid before you may be considered as quite placed out of doubt; secondly, that you will find we have suffered nothing, or rather have gained, by the severer principles which one school has adopted.

The principal ethnographers of modern times may be divided into two classes; one whereof seeks the affinity of languages in their words, the other in their grammar; their methods may be respectively called *lexical* and *grammatical* comparison. The chief supporters of the first method are principally to be found in France, England, and Russia; such as Klaproth, Balbi, Abel-Rémusat, Whiter, Vans Kennedy, Gaulianoff, the younger Adelung, and Merian. In Germany, Von Hammer, and perhaps Frederick Schlegel, might be considered as of the same school. The principle followed by these writers may be perhaps summed up in the observation made somewhere by Klaproth, that " words are the stuff or matter of language, and grammar its fashioning or form." And in a work by the late Baron Merian, which Klaproth edited, we have all the principles whereon he and his school conduct the study clearly and systematically laid down, with all the results they have thence deduced.[*] The other class is confined, in a great measure, to Germany, and

---

[*] " Principes de l'Etude comparative des Langues:" *Paris*, 1828.

reckons W. A. von Schlegel and the lamented Baron W. von Humboldt among its most distinguished chiefs. No one has been more explicit or more energetic in denouncing the principles of the other school than the first of these two writers. "Viri docti," says he, "in eo præcipuè peccare mihi videntur, quod ad similitudinem nonnullarum dictionum qualemcumque animum advertant, diversitatem rationis grammaticæ et universæ indolis plane non curant. In origine ignota linguarum exploranda, ante omnia, respici debet ratio grammatica. Hæc enim à majoribus ad posteros propagatur; separari autem à lingua cui ingenita est nequit, aut seorsum populis ita tradi ut verba linguæ vernaculæ retineant, formulus loquendi peregrinas recipiant."* Here you see that we have two most important assertions; that grammar is an essential inborn element of a language; and that a new grammar cannot be separately imposed upon a people; but that if they accept the forms, they must adopt also the matter of a language.

Having thus stated the opinions, or rather the principles of these two schools, I will proceed to lay before you such reflections and conclusions as I have been led to in the prosecution of this study; hoping, that as they are presented with all becoming diffidence, they may be still somewhat useful towards narrowing the difference between the schools I have described.

First, then, I will say, that authors are often mistaken when they attempt to analyze a language, with a view of ascertaining its primitive form. Nothing is more common than to find, in very judicious writers, the idea that there is in languages a tendency to develop and improve themselves; like Horne Tooke or his adversary, they lead us back to periods where every auxiliary verb had its real meaning,† and when every

---

* "Indische Bibliothek," 1 Band, 3 Heft. : *Bonn*, 1822, pp. 285, 287. In the first number (1820) he expresses himself in still stronger terms.

† See, for instance, Fearn's "Anti-Tooke," vol. i. *London*, 1824, p. 244.

conjunction was an imperative. Murray, in like manner, speaks of the stage of languages when compounds and pronouns were first invented;* and indeed pretends, as I have mentioned at our last meeting, to trace all languages to a few absurd and jingling monosyllables. I will give an example which will fully explain my meaning. If we analyze the Semitic languages, especially the Hebrew, we can easily resolve all their conjugational system into mere additions of pronouns, made to the simple elementary form of the verb; and you may discover in their words, the traces of monosyllabic, instead of dissyllabic roots, which they now present. We should thus have a simple language composed of the shortest words, totally devoid of inflexion, and determining the value of its elements by position in a sentence; in other words, a language, in structure, closely resembling the Chinese. This, certainly, considered in reference to the actual state of the family, would be a more simple, or a primary state, from which the present might be thought to have arisen by the gradual development of many ages; and, in fact, learned men have not been wanting who so thought.† Now, from this opinion, which I confess I once held, I must totally dissent: for hitherto the experience of several thousand years does not afford us a single example of spontaneous development in any speech. At whatever period we meet a language, we find it complete as to its essential and characteristic qualities; it may receive a finer polish, a greater copiousness, a more varied construction; but its specific distinctives, its vital principle, its soul, if I may so call it, appears fully formed, and can change no more. If

---

* "History," &c. vol. i. p. 41.
† The reasoning whereon this theory rests is so obvious to all that are acquainted with these languages, that it is only a wonder that more authors have not pursued it. (See Adelung's "Mithridates," tom. i. p. 301; Klaproth, "Observations sur les Racines des Langues Sémitiques," at the end of "Merian's Principes," p. 209.) To these I might add the authority of professed Hebrew scholars; as Michaelis, Gesenius, Oberleitner, &c.

an alteration does take place, it is only by the springing up of a new language, phœnix-like, from the ashes of another; and even where this succession has happened, as in that of Italian to Latin, and of English to Anglo-Saxon, there is a veil of secrecy thrown over the change; the language seems to spin a web of mystery round itself, and enter into the chrysalis state; and we see it no more till it emerges, sometimes more, sometimes less, beautiful, but always fully fashioned, and no farther mutable. And even there we shall see that the former condition held already within itself the parts and organs ready moulded, which were one day to give shape and life to the succeeding state.*

The two languages which I have just mentioned, as to their essential features, or rather their personality and principle of identity, are as perfect in the oldest as in the latest writers. Of Dante, or the Guidos, I need not speak; but our Chaucer, too, assuredly found in his native tongue as fully-stringed and as sweetly-attuned an instrument whereon to sing his lay, as Wordsworth himself could desire. So it is with the Hebrew: in the writings of Moses, and in the earlier fragments incorporated into Genesis, the essential structure of the language is complete, and apparently incapable, in spite of its manifest imperfection, of any farther improvement. The ancient Egyptian, as written in hieroglyphics upon the oldest monuments, and in the Coptic of the liturgy, after an interval of three thousand years, you will see established by Lepsius to be identical. The same will be observed upon comparing the oldest with the latest Greek or Latin writers. The case of the last is particularly striking, if we consider the opportunity of improvement afforded it by coming

* Thus a very slight study of the decline of Latin will show us the words now pure Italian becoming common; as *pensare*, to think, in the writings of St. Gregory; or the preposition *de* for the genitive. Such forms were all doubtless common long before among the vulgar. In rude sepulchral inscriptions, we have the SS for the X, as BISSIT for VIXIT; nay, I remember one instance where this verb is written as in Italian (excepting the change of V into B), BISSE.

in contact with the former. But though the conquest of Greece brought into rude Latium sculpture and painting, poesy and history, art and science; though it rounded the forms of its periods, and gave new suppleness and energy to its language, yet did it not add a tense or declension to its grammar, a particle to its lexicon, or a letter to its alphabet.

For in sooth we may lay it down as a principle, that no nation, from a sense of defect in its present language, will, under ordinary circumstances, borrow from another, or produce any new germs within itself. How comes it else, that Chinese, so devoid of grammatical construction, that it seems the very copy of the forms of thought expressed in signs by the deaf and dumb,* has never contrived to frame what we consider indispensable to the understanding of speech? Why have the Semitic languages, after thousands of years' neighbourhood with languages of other families, never generated a present tense, or compound and conditional tenses and moods, the want whereof so much perplexes their discourse and writing; or invented some new conjunctions to relieve the copulative *vau* from the burthen of expressing all possible relation between the parts of a discourse? Nay, how comes it that, after ages of contact with more perfect alphabets, and fully owning the immense difficulties of one without vowels, those who speak them have never succeeded in introducing them here, but resort, to this day, to the clumsy expedient of troublesome points? And the one which

---

* The deaf and dumb cannot be brought to use the grammatical gestures invented for them by the Abbé Sicard, but content themselves with the simple signs of ideas, leaving the structure undetermined by any but the natural order of connection.—(See Degerando, "De l'Éducation des Sourds-muets:" *Paris*, 1827, tom. i. pp. 580, 588.) The following is the literal translation into words of the Our Father, as expressed by them in signs :—1. *Our*, 2. *Father*, 3. *heaven*, 4. *in* (sign of insertion), 5. *wish* (sign of drawing or attracting), 6. *your* (you), 7. *name*, 8. *respect;* 9. *wish*, 10. *your*, 11. (over) *souls*, 12. *kingdom*, 13. (that is) *providence*, 14. *arrive;* 15. *wish*, 16. *your*, 17. *will*, 18. *do*, 19. *heaven*, 20. *earth*, 21. *equality* (in like manner as) (p. 589).

has attempted a change, the Abyssinian, has only produced a more unnatural and complicated syllabic alphabet, full of trouble, and liable to innumerable mistakes. Were there such a thing as natural development in languages, surely so many ages must have produced it in these instances. But so far from this being the case, the earlier stages of a language are often the most perfect; and the late researches I have so often referred to, made by Grimm into the primitive forms of German grammar, are far from establishing the tendency of a language to improve; for many valuable forms have been therein lost.

To speak, therefore, of the secondary stages of a language, or to suppose it must have required centuries for it to arrive at any given point of grammatical development, is perfectly against experience. Languages grow not up from a seed or a sprout; they are, by some mysterious process of nature, cast in a living mould, whence they come out in all their fair proportions; and that mould is the mind of man, variously modified by the circumstances of his outward relations. Here again I cannot but regret our inability to comprehend in one glance the bearings and connections of different sciences; for, if it appears that ages must have been required to bring languages to the state wherein we first find them, other researches would show us that these ages never existed; and we should thus be driven to discover some shaping power, some ever-ruling influence, which could do at once what nature would take centuries to effect; and the book of Genesis hath alone solved this problem.

Although I may have already appeared to you diffuse upon this subject, I must not leave it without giving what I consider the strongest confirmation of my opinions—the judgment of the truly lamented William von Humboldt. This profound linguist, perhaps beyond any other, brought a spirit of analytical inquiry in contact with a vast store of practical ethnographic knowledge, and used the study of languages in a way that few have done besides, as a means to arrive at a better acquaintance with the forms of thought, and with the processes of mental improvement. And if to valiant knights it has been a praise that they loved to die with their harness buckled on, and if it has been a glory to some orators that their eloquence burnt with a brighter flame just before it was quenched for ever; assuredly his is a fairer commendation, to have given the best proof of the calm power of thought over the infirmities of our nature, and shown, almost in death, the concentrating hold which genius may keep upon the elements of a long and meditative life. For long ago he had announced to his friends his intention of drawing up, as his last legacy, a very compendious treatise upon the philosophy of language; and so, within these few months, the last of his life, reduced by illness to such a state of miserable weakness, as that he could now no longer hold in his hand either pen or book; bending over his table as one bowed down by years, he seemed to gather inward those varied energies which in earlier days had qualified him alike for a philosopher or a statesman; and dictated a profound work upon that most difficult subject, which, when published, will give to the world a noble instance, not of the ruling passion, but of the governing intellect, strong in death.

When, upon the advice of Abel-Rémusat, he had made himself acquainted in a short period with the Chinese language, he lost no time in requiting him by a most interesting letter upon grammatical forms. Not having met with this work till long after I had written down the reflections I have just made, I have been highly gratified by finding in it precisely the same views, though far more philosophically expressed. "Je ne regarde pas les formes grammaticales," he says, "comme les fruits des progrès qu'une nation fait dans l'analyse de la pensée, mais plutôt comme un résultat de la manière dont une nation considère et traite sa langue."* He observes, that in the Maya and Betoi, two American languages, there are two forms of the verb; one that marks time, the other simply the relation between the attribute and the subject. This appears highly philosophical, yet he well observes, " ces rapprochemens peuvent, ce me semble, servir à prouver que, lorsqu'on trouve de pareilles particularités dans les langues, il ne faut pas les attribuer à un esprit éminemment philosophique dans leurs inventeurs."† I will take the liberty of reading one more extract, as admirably expressing what I have wished to inculcate. " Je suis pénétré de la conviction qu'il ne faut pas méconnaître cette force vraiment divine que recèlent les facultés humaines, ce génie créateur des nations, surtout dans l'état primitif, où toutes les idées, et même les facultés de l'âme, empruntent une force plus vive de la nouveauté des impressions, où l'homme peut pressentir des combinaisons auxquelles il ne serait jamais arrivé par la marche lente et progressive de l'expérience. Ce génie créateur peut franchir les limites qui semblent prescrites au reste des mortels, et s'il est impossible de retracer sa marche, sa présence vivifiante n'en est pas moins manifeste. Plutôt que de renoncer, dans l'explication de l'origine des langues, à l'influence de cette cause puissante et première et de leur assigner à toutes une marche uniforme et mécanique, qui les traînerait pas à pas depuis le commencement le plus grossier jusqu'à leur perfectionnement, j'embrasserais l'opinion de ceux qui rapportent l'origine des langues à une révélation immédiate de la divinité. Ils reconnaissent aux moins l'étincelle divine qui luit à travers tous les idiomes, même les plus imparfaits, et les moins cultivés."‡ Thus, therefore, does this distinguished ethnographer agree, that languages do not reach their

---

* "Lettre à M. Abel-Rémusat, sur la Nature des Formes Grammaticales," &c., par M. Guill. de Humboldt : *Paris*, 1827, p. 13.
† Page 15.
‡ Page 55, compare p. 51. See also the quotation in Lect. i. p. 10, note.

peculiar development, as it is erroneously called, by slow degrees, but receive it from some unknown energy of the human mind; unless, like the first speech, we suppose them to have been communicated from above.

Having thus denied the power of languages to produce of themselves, and, under ordinary circumstances, even to alter their grammatical structure; and considering this not merely as the outward form of a language, but as its most essential element, we may well inquire how far Schlegel is correct, in assuming that under no circumstance can such a modification or change take place; and I will take the liberty of saying, that some instances seem to warrant us in maintaining, that under the pressure of peculiar influences, a language may undergo such alterations as that its words shall belong to one class, and its grammar to another. It is true that in that case, a new language will be formed, different from either of its parents, but still it will depart from the one which preceded it, by the adoption of new grammatical forms. Thus, Schlegel himself allows that Anglo-Saxon lost its grammar by the Norman conquest.* And may we not say that Italian has sprung out of the Latin, more by the adoption of a new grammatical system, than by any change in words? For if you will compare any works in the two languages, you will hardly perceive any difference in the verbs and nouns: but you find articles borrowed from the pronouns, a total loss of case, and consequently of all declension; and the verbs conjugated almost entirely by auxiliaries in the active voice, and totally deprived of a passive, properly so called. These, in fact, are the alterations which entitle it to be considered a new language. It is true, that in this case the language has not gone out of its own family for the types of its variations; for these peculiarities are all to be found in other languages of the Indo-Euro-

* "De Studio Etym." *ubi sup.* p. 284.

pean class, as German and Persian; but it is no less true, that the change is very great, and allies the new language to another subdivision, which forms one extreme, while the Latin is almost the other, of the family.

The ancient Pehlwi or Pahlavi has been supposed by some linguists to present a similar example: for Sir W. Jones observed that the words are Semitic, but the grammar Indo-European;* and hence Balbi has placed it in his *Tableau* of the Semitic languages. The fact is partly admitted, but the consequences denied, by Dr. Dorn, who supposes the Semitic words to have crept into the language by intercourse with the surrounding Aramean nations.† Another curious example of a similar phenomenon may be taken from the Kawi, a language of the Indian Archipelago; of which Mr. Crawfurd thus writes: " Were I to offer an opinion respecting the history of the Kawi, I should say that it is Sanskrit deprived of its inflections, and having in their room the prepositions and auxiliary verbs of the vernacular dialects of Java. We may readily suppose the native Brahmans of that island, separated from the country of their ancestors, through carelessness or ignorance, endeavouring to get rid of the difficult and complex inflexions of the Sanskrit, for the same reasons that the barbarians altered the Greek and Latin languages to the formation of the modern Romaic or Italian."‡

Perhaps, too, another instance may be found in the Tartar languages,—in which a profound scholar finds traces of similar departure from the original type of

* " Asiatic Researches," vol. ii. ed. *Calcutta*, p. 52.
† " Ueber die Verwandschaft," &c. p. 44.
‡ " On the Existence of the Hindu Religion in the Island of Bali."—Asiat. Res. vol. xiii. *Calcutta*, 1820, p. 161. In another work Mr. Crawfurd expresses his opinion in a rather modified form: " The opinion I am inclined to form of this singular language is, that it is no foreign tongue introduced into the island, but the written language of the priesthood."—History of the Indian Archipelago: *Edinb*. 1820, vol. ii. p. 18.

their grammatical construction. " Depuis l'extrémité de l'Asie," says Abel-Rémusat, " on ignore entièrement l'art de conjuguer les verbes; ou du moins les participes et les gérondifs jouent le principal rôle dans les idiomes Tongous et Mongols: où la distinction la personnes est inconnue. Les Turcs orientaux en offrent les premiers quelques traces; mais le peu d'usage qu'ils en font semble attester la pré-existence d'un système plus simple. Enfin ceux des Turcs qui touchaient autrefois la race Gothique dans les contrées qui séparent l'Irtich et le Jäik, que l'ont repoussée ensuite, et bientôt poursuivie jusqu'en Europe, ont de plus que les Turcs quelque chose qui leur est commun avec les nations Gothiques; la conjugaison par le moyen des verbes auxiliaires; et malgré cette addition, qui semble étrangère à leur langue, celle-ci conserve quelque chose du mécanisme géné des idiomes sans conjugaison."* Finally, another example may be drawn from the Amharic; and I will state it in the words of an able writer in a new periodical, deserving of every encouragement:—" So much has been stated merely to show that the question needs to be considered thoroughly, whether languages may not borrow each other's pronouns and inflexions, while the whole material remains incongruous. . . . Indeed, the Amharic language, which at first was supposed a dialect of the Gheez (Abyssinian), and then to be Shemitic, is now alleged by the most recent inquirers to be of African pedigree, and only to have imitated Shemitic inflexions."†

These are instances of languages clearly going even out of their own families to find grammatical forms and structure. Languages of the greatest distance display sometimes the most extraordinary coincidence of grammar, yet are not therefore supposed to stand in any affinity. For instance, the Biscayan presents many

---

* "Recherches sur les Langues Tartares :" *Paris*, 1820, tom. i. p. 306.
† "On Comparative Philology," in the *West of England Journal*, No. 3, July, 1835, p. 94.

curious analogies with several American languages,—such as the want of precisely the same letters, the tendency to combine the same consonants, and a similar complication of the conjugational system, formed by the insertion of syllables expressing different modifications of the simple verb; and, in the latter point, it resembles also the dialects of South-west Africa.* Yet Humboldt, at the very moment he denies that similar words are sufficient to establish a common origin for different languages, and mentions the points of resemblance I have just stated, is far from concluding that any affinity is to be admitted between these different idioms; but, on the contrary, says:—" Grammatical peculiarities of this sort have always appeared to me demonstrations rather of degrees in civilization, than of affinity between languages."†

But, to come to some conclusion upon this matter: it appears to me, that while, on the one hand, the comparers of words have carried their conclusions a great deal too far, the learned Von Schlegel has also been borne away by his indignation against their excesses, when he tells us that the common use of *a privativum* proves more for the affinity of Greek and Sanskrit than some hundreds of words.‡ Humboldt, no less a supporter of the superior deference due to grammatical resemblance, in a brief but able exposition of his views upon our study, allows proper weight to verbal affinities.§

I should therefore propose a rule for examining verbal affinities, and concluding therefrom, relationship between languages, which may prevent the arbitrary methods followed by the lexical, and come nearer the severer wishes of the other school. This is, not to take

---

* See " Balbi's Tableau des Langues de l'Afrique."
† " Prüfung der Untersuchung über die Urbewohner Hispaniens," p. 175 ; cf. p. 109.
‡ *Ubi sup.*
§ "An Essay on the best means of ascertaining the affinities of Oriental Languages," by Baron W. Humboldt. In the "Transactions of the Royal Asiatic Society," vol. ii. 1830, pp. 214, 215.

words belonging to one or two languages in different families, and, from their resemblance, which may be accidental or communicated, draw inferences referable to the entire families to which they respectively belong; but to compare together words of simple import and primary necessity, *which run through the entire families*, and consequently are, if I may so express myself, aboriginal therein. For instance, the numeral *six* is in Sanskrit षष् *shash*, in Persian شش *shesh*, in Latin *sex*, in German *sechs*. This is consequently a word strictly belonging to the entire family; yet it belongs as much to the entire Semitic family; for in Hebrew, its purest type, we have no less שש *shesh*, and in the other dialects this is modified according to the laws that always regulate the change of letters. Again, *seven* is in Sanskrit सप्तन् *saptan*, in old German *sibun*; comparing these with the Semitic languages, we have שבע *shevang*, in Hebrew, and شبعت *sheba't* in Arabic. *One* likewise is in Sanskrit एक *aika*, in Persian یک *yak*, in Hebrew אחד *echad*, and so in the other dialects. The word κέρας, if found only in Greek, might be supposed a derivative from the Hebrew or Phenician קרן *keren;* but this opinion seems excluded by finding it pervade members of the family which could not have so borrowed it; as the Latin *cornu*, and the German *horn*. Nor can even the Latin be derived from the Greek, for the insertion of the *n*, which brings it nearer to the Semitic, can hardly be accidental; particularly as it is found in the German, which cannot be suspected of communication either with Hebrew or Greek. Yet the word thus found in so many members of this family, is as universal in the Semitic, where the Syriac is ܩܪܢܐ *karno*, and the Arabic قرن *keren*. In the same manner, there seems no reason for doubting the pure Sanskrit origin of the word *ama*, mother; and yet it is essentially

Semitic; אם *em* in Hebrew, and اُمّ *omma* in Arabic, which have the same meaning; as well as *ama* in Biscayan, now used in Spanish for a nurse. These examples are sufficient to illustrate my rule. They present cases wherein words pervade all or most of the members of two families; so that we may consider them primary or essential to both. And only in such cases as these would I easily admit a comparison of words, as sufficient to demonstrate affinity between languages. When, therefore, a lexicon, such as Parkhurst's, derives an English word from a Hebrew root, I at once reject it as ungrounded: when a Greek one is derived from it, I admit it as possible, because it may have been communicated by intercourse with the Phenicians, but it proves nothing as to derivation. If, as in the foregoing examples, two or more of these languages have the same primary word, and this again recurs in several of the Semitic languages, I admit it as of weight towards framing the mysterious connection of all languages at some primeval period.

This leads us to another important inquiry—what number of words found to resemble one another in different languages, will warrant our concluding these to be of common origin. This point has been made, by the late Dr. Young, the subject of a curious mathematical calculation, which has not, to my knowledge, found its way into any ethnographic work; probably from its occurring in an essay upon subjects nowise connected with this study. After giving his various formulas, he thus concludes: "It appears, therefore, that nothing whatever could be inferred with respect to the relation of two languages from the coincidence of the sense of any single word in both of them; and that the odds would be three to one against the agreement of two words; but if three words appear to be identical, it would be then more than ten to one that they must be derived in both cases from some parent language, or introduced in some other manner; six words would give more than 1,700 chances to one, and eight, near 100,000; so that, in these cases, the evidence would be little short of absolute certainty. In the Biscayan, for example, or the ancient language of Spain, we find in the vocabulary accompanying the elegant essay of Baron W. von Humboldt, the words *beria*, new; *ora*, a dog; *guchi*, little; *oguia*, bread; *otzoa*, a wolf (whence the Spanish *onza*); and *zazpi* (or as Lacroze writes it, *shashpi*), seven. Now, in the ancient Egyptian, new is *beri;* a dog, *whor;* little, *kudchi;* bread, *oik;* a wolf, *ounsh;* and seven, *shashf;* and if we consider these words as sufficiently identical to admit of our calculating upon them, the chances will be more than a thousand to one, that at some very remote period, an Egyptian colony established itself in Spain; for none of the languages of the neighbouring nations retain any traces of having been the medium through which these words have been conveyed."*

This conclusion is undoubtedly too definite and bold; for these resemblances, if real, may be sufficiently explained by the supposition that both languages had the same original point of departure, and have both preserved in themselves some fragments of a common primary language. Still, to those who pursue this system of comparison, the general results of this mathematical calculation must be exceedingly interesting; inasmuch as it seems to prove, that a very limited number of words, if really alike and of such a character as could not have been communicated by later intercourse, are sufficient to establish an affinity between two languages.

Coming, therefore, at last to the consequences of this long disquisition, which was necessary for understanding the respective value of the results I am going to lay before you; I need hardly inform you that the followers of the lexical system, or of verbal comparison, more readily find analogies between languages at

---

* "Remarks on the Reduction of Experiments on the Pendulum."
—Philosophical Trans. vol. cix. for 1819, p. 70.

a great distance one from the other, and possessing no historical connection. Thus, the Biscayan, which we have seen by Dr. Young compared with the Egyptian, has been in like manner confronted by Klaproth with the Semitic languages, and a number of words really or apparently similar brought together from the two.* In like manner, he addressed a letter to the late M. Champollion, in which he pointed out curious verbal coincidences between the Coptic and very distant languages, particularly such as have their seat between the Oby and the Wolga.† But of his assiduous labour in this department, I shall have to speak again.

The two families which afford the greatest facilities for examining the connection between languages of totally different characters, are doubtless those you have so often heard mentioned—the Indo-European and Semitic; for we are better acquainted with their various members than with those of any other family. Hence it is that most attempts have been made to bring these into contact; but too often, from neglecting the rule I have proposed, of ascertaining the originality of the words so compared, in both the families, by seeing if they pervade all or many of their branches, the result is not always satisfactory. For instance, Dr. Prichard, in a comparative list which he has given,‡ does not appear to me sufficiently to have attended either to the primary character of the words, or to their being common to the entire family. Thus, he compares the Hebrew word יין—*yain* with the Latin *vinum,* and we might add the Greek οἶνον; and the comparison is probably correct. But, as it is more than probable that the cultivation of the grape, and the manufacture of wine, proceeded from east to west, and belonged in earliest times to Semitic nations, so may we likewise suppose that the

---

* "Mémoires relatifs à l'Asie:" *Paris,* 1824, tom. i. v. 214.
† Republished, *ibid.* p. 205.
‡ At the end of his "Eastern Origin of the Celtic Nations," p. 192.

name accompanied it; and thus it is a borrowed word. Again, he compares the Latin *lingua*—tongue, with the Hebrew בלע—*loang*, to swallow. Not to say that the connection of these two ideas is not a probable one in etymology, the word *lingua* is peculiar to Latin in the Indo-European family. But it becomes a family word, if we observe what Marius Victorinus says—" that the ancients said *dingua* for *lingua*."* The word, thus restored to its primitive form, enters into affinity with the German *zunge*, and loses all resemblance to the Semitic verb.

I have already given a few instances of what I consider more satisfactory verbal comparisons between the two families, when I laid down the rule for such inquiries; but I would farther suggest, that there are points in the grammatical characters of the two families, which will admit of a minuter comparison than has been hitherto attempted. I should find it difficult to explain my sentiments upon this head, without going into a minute and complicated comparative analysis, hardly intelligible without some acquaintance with the languages, and not interesting to a great portion of my audience. I will therefore only say, that I am convinced a closer grammatical affinity will be found between the families than we are at first inclined to suspect; and it is with pleasure that I mention a work which seems likely to open a field to new researches, and point out new elements of affinity between these and other families. I allude to Dr. Lepsius's " Palæography, as a means of Inquiry into Languages, exemplified in the Sanskrit," published last year, and full of the most curious and original researches. By means of this new element, he has established several very ingenious and striking resemblances between Sanskrit and Hebrew, so as to leave no doubt, according to his

* "Novensiles sive per *l* sive per *d* scribendum; communionem enim habuerunt literæ hæ apud antiquos, ut dinguam et linguam, et dacrimis et lacrimis."—Marii Victorini Grammatici et Rhetoris de Orthographia. Ap. Pet. Sanctand. *Lugd.* 1584, p. 32. Comp. p. 14.

own expression, of the existence of a common, though undeveloped germ, in both.*

Encouraged by his success in this instance, he was advised to apply himself to the study of Coptic, with a view to discover, if possible, its relations with other languages; seeing that hitherto it has been considered an isolated and independent tongue. By the generosity which characterizes the German governments, whenever the interests of literature are concerned, he has been enabled to pursue his researches; and they have been crowned with complete success. Through the kindness of the distinguished and learned individual, at whose suggestion he undertook them, I am enabled to lay before you their interesting results, down to a very late period. The first letter, whereof I have translated the following extracts, is dated Paris, Jan. 20, of the present year (1835), and is addressed to the Chev. Bunsen.

" My Egyptian and Coptic studies are going on well. They have brought me to results, by which I have been myself most agreeably surprised; and whose more universal interest for the history of languages becomes every day more striking. What alarmed me a little at first was the complete linguistic solitude in which the Coptic language appeared to be placed, and the little prospect I had of ever being able to use it as a help in my researches into Egyptian antiquities. At the same time I must confess, that the historical demonstrations of Quatremère, on the origin of the Egyptian language (which, indeed, are wholly independent of the language itself), had left in my mind many doubts unsolved as to the identity of the Egyptian and Coptic tongues. I have now discovered, in the essence of the language

* " Paläographie als Mittel für die Sprachforschung, zunächst am Sanskrit nachgewiesen :" *Berlin*, 1834, p. 23. A remarkable coincidence between the two, is the way in which ר *Resch*, is evidently considered as a vowel, in the rules regarding the Hebrew points, precisely as in Sanskrit the letter *R*. Not having any longer Lepsius's work at hand, I do not remember whether he dwells upon this resemblance.

itself, not only that there is no appearance whatever of any grammatical change, and that it possesses, perhaps, in a higher degree, the principle of stability so peculiar to the Semitic dialects, but also that it has preserved in its formation traces of a higher antiquity than any Indo-Germanic or Semitic language wherewith I am acquainted, which traces will therefore be most unexpectedly important even for these two families. At the same time, the Coptic cannot be termed either Semitic or Indo-Germanic; it has its own peculiar formation, though, at the same time, its fundamental relationship with these two families is not to be mistaken. Its degree of cultivation is about the same as that of the Semitic languages, and therefore the relationship is here more manifest. The progress pointed out by you from syllabic to alphabetic language, is also a most important element for the Coptic.

"The roots of the pronouns are a part of speech which seems to have worked the earliest in the formation of language, and to have influenced it in a very considerable degree. On these roots, and their comparisons with the Semitic and Indo-Germanic pronominal formations, I lay great stress. Let us, for example, compare for a moment the affixes of the personal pronoun in Coptic and Hebrew, in order to see the relationship between the formation of both.

	my sea	*our sea*	*thy sea*, m.	*thy sea*, f.
HEB.	jam-mi	jam-nu	jam-ka	jam-k (i)
COPT.	jom-i	jom-n	jom-k	jom-ti
	your sea	*his sea*	*her sea*	*their sea*
HEB.	jam-kem (ken)	jam-(o)-hu	jam-hâ (-t)	jam-m-u
COPT.	jom-ten	jom-f	jom-s	jom-u*

"I am at present occupied with the task of laying before the public a specimen of a Coptic grammar, so as to account for the new direction given to my studies.

---

* I will take the liberty of adding a few remarks. 1st. The resemblance in the first person singular is complete, because the reduplication of the ם—*m*, in the example chosen, is accidental, in consequence of its being supposed to be derived from the obsolete word

LECTURE THE SECOND.

I will, however, premise a comparative part, which will be founded principally upon the pronominal roots, and will secure to the Coptic language the ground on which it has arisen, and point out its place among the other better-known languages. The new and particular part of its formation, that part which gives to every language its proper individuality, will thus be linked in a more convenient manner, both for the writer and for the reader, with the older part, whereby it is connected with other dialects. Some important parts of my Coptic grammar are in substance finished already, and it is not after all so difficult a task to shed a little light upon that which before was in such utter darkness.

"I have been induced to pay particular attention to the names of the numerals, which I found bore a remarkable likeness to the figures which signify their respective numbers. What has struck me still more is, that the Indo-Germanic and Semitic numerals agree exactly, even in details, with the Egyptian system; that, further, the Sanskrit ciphers are essentially Egyptian; and that all this is found much more clearly, and in a greater degree of nearness to its natural origin, in the Egyptian. The numeral figures decidedly appear to me to have gone from Egypt to India, thence they were transported by the Arabs, who even now call them Indian, even as we now term them Arabic, because we received them from the Arabs. The remarkable agreement of the numerals in the Coptic, Semitic, and Indo-Germanic, and the demonstrable derivation of them, principally in Egyptian, from the three pronominal roots, and, from their cipher-like

ימם—*yamam*; so that the suffix is simply *i*, as in Coptic. 2ndly. The difference in the second person feminine singular is more apparent than real; inasmuch as the Hebrew in the second persons departs from the suffix suggested by analogy, *ta*, *ti* or *t*, *tem*, *ten*, and assumes a *c* instead of the *t*. The Coptic throws light upon this circumstance, by preserving here the regular suffixes, while in the masculine it accompanies the Hebrew in its change. 3rdly. This remark, it is evident, comprises the second person plural.

connection with one another, will lead me to bestow a more extensive discussion upon this important subject.

"Finally, one of the principal points which have occupied me, is the undeniable connection between the Semitic alphabet and the Demotic, and, consequently, the hieroglyphic alphabets of the Egyptians. What obstructs in great measure all research into the pronunciation of the Coptic, is the Greek character, which was adopted in the second or third century; when many of the nicer distinctions, which no doubt existed in the original domestic palæography, were necessarily abandoned. At the same time, the pronunciation of the Coptic tongue, which at first, owing to its extraordinary accumulation of vowels and other peculiarities, appeared to me quite chaotic, is become quite clear to me; especially since I have made more minute researches into the accents, which in the grammars are considered as quite unessential, and are generally, in published works, given very incorrectly. But I have now by me some manuscripts from the library, which have furnished me with a completely new light upon the subject."

The second extract which I will lay before you, is from a letter dated the 14th of last month (February).

"..... I have thought it would perhaps be better if I drew up and sent to the Academy my essay on the names and signs of the numerals, to which, as well as to their interesting relations, I believe I have unquestionably discovered the key in the Egyptian ciphers, and in the Coptic names of the numerals. It will be ready, at latest, in a week; and the results appear to me perfectly clear and satisfactory, inasmuch as they solve the riddle so often, but so remotely, attempted, respecting the meaning of these ancient numeral roots, and that not only as regards the Coptic, but also for the Semitic and Indo-Germanic languages; and they will place this whole cycle of dialects in a very remarkable harmony with one another, which, in my mind, may be of great importance for all the higher departments of comparative linguistic."

The conclusions to be drawn from these interesting documents, must be obvious to every mind. We have it ascertained, that the ancient Egyptian, now fully identified with the Coptic, is no longer to be considered an insulated language, void of connection with those around it, but presents very extraordinary points of contact with the two great families so often mentioned, not, indeed, sufficiently distinct to make it enter into either class, but yet sufficiently definite, and rooted in the essential constitution of the language, to prevent their being considered accidental, or a later engrafting thereupon. The effect of this intermediary character, according to Lepsius's expression, is to group together in a very remarkable harmony this cycle of languages; so that, instead of any longer considering the Indo-European and Semitic as completely insulated families, or being compelled to find a few verbal coincidences between them, we may now consider them as linked together, both by points of actual contact, and by the interposition of the Coptic, in a mysterious affinity grounded on the essential structure, and most necessary forms, of the three.

Now let us consider the further inquiries to which these researches must lead a thinking mind; how, for example, can such intermediary languages have arisen? Is it from both these great groups having been originally one, so that, as they separated, like masses cleft asunder by some natural convulsion, smaller fragments splintered away between and from both, partaking of the peculiar grain and qualities of both, so as to mark their points of former union? Or are the whole to be considered as equally derivatives of a common stock, modified into such varieties by circumstances now unknown, and dependent upon laws now, probably, abolished? Take any hypothesis, or rather, anticipate any result you please, likely to result from these discoveries and their further extension, and you come necessarily to a union and community of the great groups or families, partly by themselves, partly, like the polygonar structures of the ancients, through the medium of smaller connecting fragments, which nature or Providence has allowed to remain between them.

And this is further worthy of notice, that the severer school, the one which seemed to require a demonstration of affinity too rigid to be ever practical out of the limits of one family, has, in fact, discovered that affinity between the families themselves, and left no cavil tenable against this important fact. For, this must close all that can be expected from this study, as far as principles are concerned; all that remains now is to desire their further application, and to have the same process extended to other groups, apparently separated from the rest.

And here let us look back for a moment at the connection between our study and the sacred records. From the simple historical outline which I have laid before you, it appears that its first rise seemed fitter to inspire alarm than confidence, insomuch as it broke in sunder the great bond anciently supposed to hold them all together; then for a time it went on, still further severing and dismembering; consequently, to all appearance, ever widening the breach between itself and sacred history. In its further progress, it began to discover new affinities where least expected; till, by degrees, many languages began to be grouped and classified in large families acknowledged to have a common origin. Then, new inquiries gradually diminished the number of independent languages, and extended, in consequence, the dominion of the larger masses. At length, when this field seemed almost exhausted, a new class of researches has succeeded, so far as it has been tried, in proving the extraordinary affinities between these families,—affinities existing in the very character and essence of each language, so that none of them could have ever existed without those elements wherein the resemblances consist. Now, as this excludes all idea of one having borrowed them from the other; as they could not have arisen in each by independent processes; and as the radical difference among the languages forbids their being considered dialects or offshoots from one another, we are driven to the conclusion, that, on the one hand, these languages must have been originally united in one, whence they drew these common elements essential to them all; and, on the other, that the separation between them, which destroyed other, no less important, elements of resemblance, could not have been caused by any gradual departure, or individual development,—for these we have long since excluded,—but by some violent, unusual, and active force, sufficient alone to reconcile these conflicting appearances, and to account at once for the resemblances and the differences. It would be difficult, methinks, to say what further step the most insatiable or unreasonable sceptic could require, to bring the results of this science into close accordance with the scriptural account.

But to complete the history of this study, I must not omit the writings and opinions of several authors who have not entered into the line of demonstration I have till now followed, although their names have been occasionally introduced. I will lay before you, therefore, their positive conclusions, thus showing you how far they bear me out in the consequences I have drawn from their researches. I will divide them into two classes, the first whereof shall contain such as agree in acknowledging the original unity of all language.

The learned Alexander von Humboldt, to whom we owe so much valuable information regarding the languages and monuments of America, thus expresses himself upon this interesting point:—" However insulated certain languages may at first appear, however singular their caprices and their idioms, all have an analogy among them, and their numerous relations will be more perceived, in proportion as the philosophical history of nations, and the study of languages, shall be brought to perfection."*

Upon this important subject a most decisive testimony was given by the Academy of St. Petersburg, in the fifth volume of its memoirs.† This learned body was, probably, in this part of its labours, very much under the influence of Count Goulianoff, who was an enthusiast for the unity of languages, as demonstrated simply by similarity of words, without sufficient attention, often, to real identity, much less to the essential construction of the languages. He himself has sufficiently declared his views in his discourse on the Fundamental Study of Languages, from which I will extract one passage:—" La succession des faits antérieurs à l'histoire en s'effaçant avec les siècles, semble nuire à l'évidence du fait essentiel, savoir, celui de la fraternité des peuples. Or ce fait, le plus intéressant pour l'homme qui pense, s'établirait implicitement par le rapprochement des langues anciennes et modernes, considérées sous leur aspect originaire. Et si jamais quelque conception philosophique venait multiplier encore les berceaux du genre humain, l'identité des langues serait toujours là, pour détruire le prestige; et cette autorité ramènerait, je pense, l'esprit le plus prévenu."‡ A year later than this publication, he sent forth a prospectus of a work which was to prove the unity of languages.§ I know not whether it appeared, for the character of his researches is not such as to have induced me to inquire after it; but I fear there was too much promised in that prospectus, for the promises to have been kept. The decision of the Academy was, however, quite unreserved upon this point; for it maintains its conviction, after a long research, that all languages are to be considered as dialects of one now lost.

* Ap. Klaproth, "Asia Polyglotta," p. vi.
† See the "Bulletin Universel," 7e section, vol. i. p. 380.
‡ "Discours sur l'Etude Fondamentale des Langues:" *Paris*, 1822, p. 31.
§ The title of the work was to be: "Etude de l'Homme dans la manifestation de ses facultés."

And in the same class of writers must be reckoned the late State-councillor Merian, who has adopted the same conclusion, though not perhaps positively stated in his great work the *Tripartitum*. This consists of four folio volumes, published at Vienna between 1820 and 1823, and contains comparative tables principally of German and Russian words, but with an additional mass of incongruous materials from all other languages. For lexical comparison, the work no doubt has considerable value; but it must be owned that page after page has to be turned over, before anything like a tolerable resemblance can be discovered, in languages of different families. Be this as it may, the conclusion of his first Continuation, or second volume, sufficiently declares his sentiments upon the point now under consideration, for he thus writes:—" Those who doubt of the unity of language, after perusing Whiter, may read Goulianoff."*

Of the same school, but far superior in merit to the authors yet mentioned, is Julius Klaproth, whose name I have already more than once introduced. To few authors are we more indebted for curious information regarding the languages and literature of most Asiatic nations, and the geography of countries, else but little known. It must, however, be owned, that he is a bold writer, whose assertions should be received with some degree of caution: it would, indeed, have been difficult to unite perfect accuracy with the varied character of his researches. His great work on the affinity of languages, the *Asia Polyglotta*, published at Paris in 1823, consists of a large quarto of text, with a folio of comparative tables. In it he makes no secret of his complete disbelief in the Mosaic history of the dispersion; it is, he tells us, like many other things in the writings of western Asia, a mere story founded upon the

* "Tripart. seu de Analogia Linguarum Libellus, Continuatio:" *Vien.* 1822, p. 585. Whiter's work here alluded to is the "Etymologicum Universale."

F

significant name of Babylon.* He supposes mankind to have escaped from the deluge at different points, by climbing the highest mountains; and hence considers the various families of the human race, as propagated afterwards from so many centres,—in the Caucasus, the Himalaya, and the Altai mountains. Notwithstanding these inauspicious opinions, his results are in strict accordance with sacred history. He flatters himself that in his works " the universal affinity of languages is placed in so strong a light, that it must be considered by all as completely demonstrated." "This," he adds, " does not appear explicable on any other hypothesis, than that of admitting fragments of a primary language yet to exist, through all the languages of the old and new worlds."† And I think it must be owned, that in the numerous comparative lists given after his account of each language, though many examples may be slight and fanciful, abundance of resemblances may be discovered, sufficiently marked to justify the successful application of Dr. Young's calculus, if his theorem is to be allowed any value.

With greater pleasure still, I proceed to record the sentiments of the lamented Frederick Schlegel, a man to whom our age owes more than our children's children can repay—new and purer feelings upon art and its holiest applications; the attempt, at least, to turn philosophy's eye inward upon the soul, and to compound the most sacred elements of its spiritual powers with the

* "Die andere (Sprachverwandschaft) ist *postdiluvianisch*, und ihre Ursachen sind nicht so verborgen, so dass wir nicht nöthig haben den Thurm von Babel zu Hülfe zu nehmen, das, wie manches in den Schriften der Westasiaten, nur eine Erzählung zu seyn scheint, die zu einem Bedeutung habenden Namen erfunden ist."—S. 40, comp. S. 41.

† "Die allgemeine Sprachverwanschaft, mit der ich mich bei der Ausarbeitung dieses Werkes weit mehr beschäftigt habe, als es anfänglich mein Vorsatz war, ist durch dasselbe in ein so helles Licht gebracht worden, dass man sie als erwiesen anzunehmen gezwungen ist. Sie scheint nicht anders erklärbar als durch die Ueberbleibsel einer Ursprache, die sich in allen Mundarten der alten und neuen Welt Wieder finden."—Vorrede, S. ix.

ingredients of human knowledge; above all, the successful discovery of a richer India than Vasco de Gama opened unto Europe, whose value is not in its spices, and its pearls, and its barbaric gold, but in tracts of science unexplored, in mines long unwrought of native wisdom, in treasures deeply buried of symbolic learning, and in monuments long hidden of primeval and venerable traditions.

In the work which first turned the eyes of Europe to these important subjects (his little treatise, published in 1808, upon the language and wisdom of the Indians), he clearly lays down his opinion touching the original unity of all language. He rejects with indignation the idea that language was the invention of man in a savage and untutored state, brought to gradual perfection by the toil or experience of successive generations. He considers it, on the contrary, as a whole, with its roots and structure, its pronunciation and written character,* which was not hieroglyphic, but consisted of signs exactly expressive of the sounds that composed that early speech. He speaks not, indeed, of language as given to man by superior communication; but he considers the mind of man so to have been organized as necessarily to produce, on his first appearance, this well-ordered and beautiful structure, and thereby supposes its oneness and indivisibility.†

---

* The idea of writing having been a primeval art, and an essential part of language, taken in its completest sense, is not by any means confined to Schlegel. Not to mention the attempt of Count de Gebelin to prove the unity of all alphabets ("Monde Primitif," end of vol. iii.), or the still more learned and ingenious comparisons given by Paravey ("Essai sur l'Origine unique et hiéroglyphique des chiffres et des lettres de tous les peuples:" *Paris*, 1826), I will only mention two authors who agree in this opinion. Herder observes: "Les alphabets des peuples présentent une analogie encore plus frappante: elle est telle, qu'à bien approfondir les choses, il n'y a proprement qu'un alphabet."—Nouveaux Mémoires de l'Académie Royale, an 1781: *Berlin*, 1783, p. 413. Baron W. Humboldt seems to admit the same opinion, at the conclusion of his essay, "Ueber das Entstehen der grammatischen Formen:" *Berlin*, 1823.

† "Sprache und Weisheit der Indier," 1tes Buch, 5tes Kap. S. 64, comp. S. 60. These sentiments, expressed with the fervid eloquence

Nor did he alter his opinion by farther study; on the contrary, in his last beautiful work, his *cycnea vox et oratio*, which, as has been beautifully observed, closed his philosophical speculations with an expression of doubt,* for death found him watching by his night-lamp over the best interests of virtue, and, like the slayer of Archimedes, refused him time to work out his problem; in his *Philosophy of Speech* he considers language as an individual gift to man, and, consequently, in its origin only one. I cannot forbear making one quotation.

"With our present senses and organs, it is as impossible for us to form the remotest idea of that speech, which the first man possessed before he lost his original power, perfection, and worth, as it would be to reason of that mysterious discourse whereby immortal spirits send their thoughts across the wide space of heaven upon wings of light; or of those words, by created beings unutterable, which, in the unsearchable interior of the Deity, are spoken, where, as is in holy song expressed, depth called upon depth, that is, the fulness of endless love upon eternal majesty. When, from this unattainable height, we descend again into ourselves, and to the first man, such as really he was, the simple unaffected narrative of that book which contains our earliest records, that God taught man to speak, even if we go no further than this simple unaffected sense, will be in accordance with our natural feelings. For how could it be otherwise, or how could any other impression be made, when we consider the relation which God therein holds—of a parent, as it were, teaching her

---

which distinguishes all the philosophical speculations of their author, have been severely commented on by F. Wüllner, in his interesting work, "Ueber Ursprung und Urbedeutung der sprachlichen Formen:" *Münster*, 1831, p. 27. This author deduces all language from interjectional forms (p. 4).

* "Philosophische Vorlesungen insbesondere über Philosophie der Sprache und des Wortes:" *Wien*. 1830. The author expired while writing the tenth lecture; the last word of his manuscript was *aber*, but.

child the first rudiments of speech? But under this simple sense there lieth, as does through all that book of twofold import, another, and a far deeper signification. The name of any thing or living being, even as it is called in God, and designated from eternity, holds in itself the essential idea of its innermost being, the key of its existence, the deciding power of its being or not being; and so it is used in sacred speech, where it is, moreover, in a holier and higher sense, united to the idea of the Word. According to this deeper sense and understanding, it is in that narration shown and signified, according as I have before briefly remarked, that together with speech, intrusted, communicated, and delivered, immediately by God to man, and through it, he was installed as the ruler and the king of nature, yea, more rightly, as the deputed of God over this earthly creation, unto which office was his original destination."*

Such, then, is our first conclusion drawn from the writings of modern ethnographers, that the language of men was originally one; come we, therefore, to the second, which will much confirm it. How was this one language separated into so many strangely different?

I will first give you the authority of Herder, and, that he may not be suspected as a partial witness, I will premise that, in the very page I am about to quote, he is careful to inform us, that he considers the history of Babel as a "poetical fragment in the oriental style." First, then, he tells us, that "as the human race is a progressive whole, the parts whereof are intimately connected, so must language form, also, a united whole, dependent upon a common origin.... Having laid this down," he continues, "there is a great probability that the human race, and languages therewith, go back to one common stock, to a first man, and not to several

* P. 70. Perhaps this idea is borrowed from Herder, "Philosophy of History:" *London*, 1800, p. 89, though there only the capacity of speech, and not language, is mentioned.

dispersed in different parts of the world." This position he then proceeds to illustrate, by an inquiry into the grammatical structure of languages. His conclusions, however, do not stop here: he confidently asserts, that, from the examination of languages, the separation among mankind is shown to have been violent; not, indeed, that they voluntarily changed their language, but that they were rudely and suddenly (*brusquement*) divided from one another.*

To demonstrate the same conclusion, was the object of a series of papers, read in 1824 and 1825 to the Royal Society of Literature, by Mr. Sharon Turner. The learned author went into a minute analysis of the primary elements of speech; and concluded that the numerous evidences of attraction and repulsion between languages, left no alternative in explaining them, save the adoption of some hypothesis similar to the event recorded in Genesis. But I will not insist further on his testimony, the only one I have referred to, in this science, of an author expressly defending the Scripture narrative.†

More than once I have had occasion to quote the opinions of the learned Abel-Rémusat, a man who may justly be considered the reviver and great facilitator of Chinese literature, and who possessed at once a profound knowledge of the languages of eastern Asia, and a reflective philosophic mind. To me his memory must ever be joined in close association with the interest I feel in this science; for when young I had the pleasure of hearing his instructive conversation thereon

---

* *Ubi sup.* "Memoires of the Royal Acad." *Ber.* pp. 411-413.
† These papers are printed in the "Transactions of the Royal Society of Literature," vol. i. part 1: *London*, 1827, pp. 17-106. There are many inaccuracies in the examples given in these elaborate papers; and a system of philological principles is employed, which will not stand the tests universally admitted by continental linguists. No notice whatsoever is taken of the acknowledged division of families; the same word spelt differently, perhaps by writers of different countries, is repeated again and again, and some given which do not exist in the languages quoted.

with others learned as himself, but, like him, now no more:—

> "E quale il cicognin che leva l' ala
> Per voglia di volar, e non s' attenta
> D' abbandonar lo nido, e giù la cala ;
> Tal era io con voglia accesa e spenta
> Di dimandar, venendo infino all' atto
> Che fa colui ch' a dicer s' argomenta."*
> <div align="right">DANTE, " <i>Purgat.</i>" xxv.</div>

His work on the Tartar languages, though unfinished, is a mine of rare information upon many points besides its immediate subject; and is distinguished throughout by that power of simplification and analytical resolution, which seems to have been one of his peculiar faculties. In the long and diversified preliminary discourse, we have his sentiments clearly stated, touching the accordance of philological ethnography with the sacred narrative. For, after having expatiated on the manner in which linguistic pursuits may be brought to bear upon history, he thus concludes:—" It is then we should be able to pronounce with precision, what, according to the language of a people, was its origin, what the nations with which it has stood in relation, what the character of that relation was, to what stock it belongs; at least, until that epoch when profane histories cease, and where we should find among languages that confusion which gave rise to them all, and which such vain attempts have been made to explain."†

But, in fact, if once we admit the original unity of language, we can hardly account for its subsequent divisions without some such phenomenon. This has

---

* " Even as the young stork lifteth up his wing
   Through wish to fly, yet ventures not to quit
   The nest, and drops it ; so in me desire
   Of questioning my guide arose, and fell,
   Arriving even to the act that marks
   A man prepared for speech."—CARY'S *Translation.*
† " Recherches sur les Langues Tartares," vol. i. p. xxix.

been observed by the sagacious and learned historian Niebuhr, in one of those occasional excursions which we meet in his work, always indicative of the marvellous diversity of his pursuits, among which our science was particularly one. And I quote the following passage the more willingly, because in the first edition (I believe the best known in England, through the able translation made of it shortly after its appearance) a very different sentiment occupies its place. "This fallacy," he writes in his third edition, "escaped detection among the ancients, probably because they admitted several primitive races of mankind. They who deny these, and go back to a single pair, must, to account for the existence of idioms different in structure, suppose a miracle; and for those languages which differ in roots and essential qualities, adhere to that of the confusion of tongues. The admission of such a miracle offends not reason; since, as the remains of the ancient world clearly show, that, before the present, another order of life existed, so it is certainly credible that this lasted entire after its commencement, and underwent at some period an essential change."[*] And to this remark we may add, that if to account for different languages we must have recourse to so many independent races, we shall be driven to the necessity of admitting, not a few in distant quarters of the globe, but as many as there are idioms at present to all appearance unconnected,—that is, many hundreds; a consequence unphilosophical in its principle, for it goes at once to the extremest solution of a constant phenomenon; and still more unphilosophical in its application, for we must multiply the races almost in the inverse ratio of the numbers that compose them; for the smallest tribes and the most subdivided savage populations, exhibit, in the most marked manner, remarkable differences of language. Hence the interior of Africa,

---

[*] Niebuhr's Römische Geschichte, 3 Ausg. 1er Th. S. 60. Compare the English translation, 1828, p. 44. It is pleasing to see these changes, in spite of the author's declaration, p. xii.

or the unexplored tracts of Australia, may contain more races than the entire of Europe and Asia. But on this subject more will shortly have to be said.

I will conclude the testimonies of ethnographers by that of Balbi, the diligent and learned author of the "Atlas Ethnographique du Globe." This work consists of charts classifying languages according to ethnographic *kingdoms*, as he calls them; which are followed by comparative tables of elementary words in every known language. The accompanying volume of introduction contains a vast collection of valuable and interesting information on the general principles of the science. In compiling this work, Balbi not only had access to every class of information actually before the public, but received most important assistance from the ablest ethnographers in Paris. It must be therefore interesting to know what has been the impression produced upon the mind of one who has thus gone over the entire field of ethnographic science, and has heard the opinion of those who have devoted their lives to its cultivation. From my personal intercourse with him, I can say that he is far from thinking that the researches of linguists have in the least wise tended to impeach the veracity of the sacred historian. Nor is this opinion unrecorded in his work; for in his first chart he thus expresses it:—"The books of Moses, no monument, either historical or astronomical, has yet been able to prove false; but with them, on the contrary, agree, in the most remarkable manner, the results obtained by the most learned philologers, and the profoundest geometricians."*

Such, then, appears to be the twofold result of this study, once perhaps a dangerous pursuit, now lending a valuable and ever-growing evidence to the narrative of Scripture. Languages gradually forming themselves into groups, and those groups daily tending to approximate and claim mutual relationship, assuredly afford the best proof of a former point of departure, and serve to

---

* "Atlas Ethnographique du Globe," par Adrien Balbi : *Paris* 1826. Mappemonde Ethnog. i.

divide the human race into certain great characteristic families, whose further subdivision enters into the province of history. Like those grouped but disunited masses which geologists consider as the ruins of former mountains, we see in the various dialects of the globe the wrecks of a vast monument belonging to the ancient world.* The nice exactness of their tallies in many parts, the veins of similar appearance which may be traced from one to the other, show that they have been once connected so as to form a whole; while the boldness and roughness of outline at the points of separation, prove that it is no gradual devolution, no silent action, which hath divided, but some violent convulsion which hath riven them in sunder. And even such positive conclusions you have seen drawn by the most learned ethnographers.

There is still one branch of our science which seems without the pale of all that has been hitherto expounded; and it would be unjust to pass it over in silence. All the history of this study, so far as I have given it, appears to apply almost exclusively to the old world, where civilization must have done much towards assimilating forms and amalgamating dialects; whereas, in the interior of Africa, and still more strikingly in the western hemisphere, the theory of language seems to refuse submission to the principles we have established, and the endless variety of tongues involves in painful mystery the origin of the population.

The number of dialects spoken by the natives of America, is indeed almost incredible. Choose any tract of the old world where you think most languages spoken, then select an equal space at random in any district of America peopled by native tribes, and the latter will assuredly give a greater number of various tongues.† I have been myself a witness to such anxiety

---

* See D'Aubuisson, "Traité de Géognosie;" *Stras.* 1827, tom. i. p. 227.

† See Humboldt's "Essai Politique sur la Nouvelle Espagne;" *Par.* 1825, tome ii. p. 352.

on this subject, in persons of great learning and good understanding, that they refused credit to Humboldt's assertions regarding the number of American languages, rather than admit what they deemed an almost insuperable objection to the Scripture narrative. For we cannot suppose each of these tribes, speaking a language totally unintelligible to its neighbours, to be lineally descended from one formed at the dispersion, without allowing the strange anomaly, that, of the human families then formed, such countless, yet such insignificant tribes should have wandered to that distance. No wonder, therefore, that the unbelievers of the last century should have taken a shorter method to solve this problem, by asserting that America had its own population independent of that in the older continent.*
Here, too, the friends of religion came early forward, and, as too often has happened, with crude hypotheses and groundless theories, as to the source of the American population, and the means whereby it was transported into that country. Campomanes patronized the Carthaginians, Kircher and Huet the Egyptians, De Guignes the Huns, Sir William Jones the Indians, and many American antiquaries the ten tribes of Israel.

We have now only to examine what light ethnography has been able to throw upon this question, and how far the solutions it presents accord with the gratifying results obtained in other quarters of the globe. The first step towards establishing a connection between the inhabitants of the two continents, was attempted by the followers of what we have named the lexical school, and consisted of the comparison of words in American dialects with terms found among the nations of northern and eastern Asia. Smith-Barton was the first who made any progress in this attempt, and his labours were incorporated, in a very extended form, in an essay by Vater, first published in 1810, and afterwards republished

---

* See Ballet's "Réponses Critiques:" *Besançon*, 1819, vol. ii. p. 51.

in his *Mithridates*.* The results of their labours I will give in the words of a competent judge:—" Investigations made with the most scrupulous exactness, in following a method till then not used in the study of etymologies, have proved the existence of a few words common to the vocabularies of the two continents. In eighty-three American languages examined by Messrs. Barton and Vater, one hundred and seventy words have been found, the roots of which appear to be the same; and it is easy to perceive that this analogy is not accidental, since it does not rest merely upon imitative harmony, or on that conformity of organs which produces almost a perfect identity in the first sounds articulated by children. Of these one hundred and seventy words which have this connection, three-fifths resemble the Mantchou, the Tongouse, the Mongul, and the Samoyed; and two-fifths the Celtic and Tchoud, the Biscayan, the Coptic, and the Congo languages. These words have been found by comparing the whole of the American languages with the whole of those of the old world; for hitherto we are acquainted with no American idiom which seems to have an exclusive correspondence with any of the Asiatic, African, or European tongues."†

Malte-Brun endeavoured to advance a step further, and to establish what he calls a geographical connection between the American and Asiatic languages. After a minute investigation, his conclusions are these:—that tribes connected with the Finnish, Ostiack, Permian, and Caucasian families, passing along the borders of the Frozen Ocean, and crossing over Behring's Straits, spread themselves in very different directions towards Greenland and Chili: that others, allied to the Japanese, Chinese, and Kourilians, proceeding along the coast, penetrated to Mexico;‡ and that another colony, related

---

* " Untersuchung über Amerikas Bevölkerung aus dem alten Continente:" *Leipz.* 1810. "Mithrid." 3 Th. 2 Abth. p. 340.

† Alex. von Humboldt, "Views of the Cordilleras," Eng. trans. vol. i. p. 19.

‡ Humboldt thinks the Tolteks, or Azteks, who colonized Mexico,

to the Tungooses, Mantcheous, and Mongols, passed along the mountain-tracts of both continents, and reached the same destination. Besides these, he supposes several smaller emigrations to have borne over a certain number of Malay, Javanese, and African words.* However limited the comparison thus made may appear, it has been admitted, as you have seen, by the sagacious traveller I have quoted, and also by Balbi, as sufficient to prove a resemblance between the languages of the two continents, too marked to be the result of accident.

Still I will own that I consider these results as but little worth; both because the resemblances are very slight, and too anomalous to be of much service, and because the very authors who give them, consider these migrations as simple additions to a population already existing, and merely as modifying agents in the formation or alteration of the indigenous languages.† They have therefore, if satisfactory, only this value—that they authorize us to conjecture that the original population reached the western hemisphere by the same road which subsequent emigrations held. Hence I am not surprised that a similar attempt, made still later by Siebold, to connect, through their respective vocabularies, the Japanese and the Moscas, or Muyscas, a large American nation between Macaraïbo and Rio de la Hacha, should have been pronounced unsuccessful by the committee appointed in 1829 to examine it, on behalf of the Paris Asiatic Society.‡

But there are conclusions drawn by ethnographic science, from the observation both of local and general

were the Hiongnoos, who are said in the Chinese annals to have emigrated under Puno, and to have been lost in the north of Siberia.—"Essai Polit." p. 350. See also Paravey, "Mémoire sur l'origine Japonaise, Arabe, et Basque des peuples du plateau de Bogota:" *Par.* 1835.

* Tableau de l'enchaînement géographique des langues Américaines et Asiatiques, "Géographie Univ.:" *Par.* 1821, tome v. pp. 227, *seqq.* comp. p. 211.

† Vater, p. 338. Malte-Brun, p. 212.

‡ Mémoire relatif à l'origine des Japonaise, "Nouveau Journal Asiatique," Juin, 1829, p. 400.

phenomena, which bear most materially upon this point, and have completely removed all the difficulties arising from the multiplicity of American languages. And first, the examination of the structure pervading all the American languages, has left no room to doubt that they all form one individual family, closely knitted together in all its parts by the most essential of all ties—grammatical analogy. This analogy is not of a vague, indefinite kind, but complex in the extreme, and affecting the most necessary and elementary parts of grammar; for it consists chiefly in the peculiar methods of modifying conjugationally the meanings and relations of verbs, by the insertion of syllables; and this form led the late W. von Humboldt to give the American languages a family name, as forming their conjugation by what he termed *agglutination*. Nor is this analogy partial, but it extends over both great divisions of the new world, and gives a family air to languages spoken, under the torrid and arctic zones, by the wildest and by the more civilized tribes. " This wonderful uniformity," says one writer, " in the peculiar manner of forming the conjugations of verbs from one extremity of America to the other, favours in a singular manner the supposition of a primitive people, which formed the common stock of the American indigenous nations."[*] Another remarks, that the most natural conclusion to which we can come, upon seeing such an extraordinary affinity between languages so many hundreds of miles asunder, is, " that there is a divergence from one common centre of civilization in all."[†]

Secondly, the more attention is paid to the study of the American languages, the more they are found to be subject to the laws of other families, inasmuch as this one great family tends every day to subdivide itself into large groups, having closer affinities with themselves than with the great division of which, in their turn, they

---

[*] Malte-Brun, p. 217, comp. p. 213.
[†] Vater, p. 329.

form a part. Thus, it had been early observed by the missionaries, that certain languages were considered keys to other dialects, so that whoever possessed them, easily made themselves masters of the others. This remark is, I remember, somewhere made by Hervas, and subsequent researches have amply confirmed it. Hence Balbi, in his *Tableau* of the American languages, has been able to divide them into certain great provinces, holding within them numerous dependencies.

Thus, therefore, is the objection to the unity of the American nations, drawn from the multiplicity of their languages, satisfactorily removed, by the very study within which it had arisen; and with it the difficulty of their belonging to a common stock with the inhabitants of the older world. But the collection and comparison of facts connected with linguistic researches, have led to a further, and equally satisfactory result; for you will see that we yet have to account for the dissimilarity of dialects spoken by nations and tribes bordering on each other, and composed of trifling numbers. Now, it has been observed, that this is a phenomenon noways peculiar to America, but common to all uncivilized countries. Had we no other criterion of unity of origin but language, we should perhaps be under difficulties in examining this point. But another science, whereof we shall treat next time, and which will greatly confirm the conclusions I am drawing, is able to fix characteristics, whereby the connections of tribes in unity of race may be easily determined. And yet it is found, that in instances, where no doubt can exist of savage hordes having been originally united, there has sprung among them so endless and so complete a variety of dialect, that little or no affinity can be therein discovered. And hence we have, as it were, a rule, that the savage state, by insulating families and tribes, and raising the arm of each one ever against its neighbours, has essentially the contrary influence to the aggregating, unifying tendencies of social civilization; and necessarily introduces a jealous diversity, and unintelligible idioms, into the jargons which hedge round the independence of different hordes.

Nowhere has this disuniting power been more attentively examined than among the tribes of Polynesia. "The Papuans, or Oriental negroes," says Dr. Leyden, "seem to be all divided into very small states, or rather societies, very little connected with each other. Hence their language is broken into a multitude of dialects, which, in process of time, by separation, accident, or oral corruption, have nearly lost all resemblance."* "Languages," says Mr. Crawfurd, "follow the same progress. In the savage state they are great in number, in improved society few. The state of languages on the American continent, affords a convincing illustration of this fact; and it is not less satisfactorily explained in that of the Indian islands. The negro races who inhabit the mountains of the Malaya peninsula, in the lowest and most abject state of social existence, though numerically few, are divided into a great many distinct tribes, speaking as many different languages. Among the rude and scattered population of the island of Timor, it is believed that not less than forty languages are spoken. On Ende and Flores we have also a multiplicity of languages; and among the cannibal population of Borneo, it is not improbable that many hundreds are spoken."† The same facts may be observed in relation to the tribes of Australia, who belong to the same race, by examining the list of words peculiar to different tribes, which Captain King has given us.‡ The greatest dissimilarity exists among them; some, however, as the equivalents for *eye*, pervade them all, and occasionally, as in the terms for *hair*, tribes immediately in contact differ essentially, and yet are found respectively to agree with other islands far removed. Now, if these causes so act elsewhere, they must be far

---

* "Asiatic Researches," vol. x. p. 162.
† "History of the Indian Archipelago," vol. ii. p. 79.
‡ "Narrative of a Survey of the Intertropical and Western Coasts of Australia:" London, 1826, vol. ii. Append.

more powerful in America; for there, as Humboldt has well observed, "the configuration of the soil, the strength of vegetation, the apprehensions of the mountaineers, under the tropics, of exposing themselves to the burning heat of the plains, are obstacles to communication, and contribute to the amazing variety of American dialects. This variety, it is observed, is more restrained in the savannas and forests of the north, which are easily traversed by the hunter, on the banks of great rivers, along the coast of the ocean, and in every country where the Incas had established their theocracy by force of arms."*

Thus, then, I think, that, in this department of its researches, ethnography will be found to have done its duty, by first reducing the immense number of American dialects into one family, and then accounting, by analogy, for their extraordinary multiplicity. But, as the course of lectures I have sketched out will not bring us again into this interesting quarter of the globe, I will draw a little further on your kind indulgence, while I touch upon a few evidences of the connection between the inhabitants of the two worlds, so to supply the defects of our ethnographic acquaintance with their idioms.

First, we have the traditions of the Americans themselves, which describe them as a migratory people, proceeding southward from the north-west. The Tolteks, then the seven tribes as they are called, the Checheneks, and the Azteks, are all represented in Mexican history, as successive nations arriving in Anahuac or Mexico. In the hieroglyphic picture exhibiting the migrations of this last people, they are represented, according to Borturini, as crossing the sea, probably the Gulf of California, a circumstance which can leave no doubt respecting the course they held. These traditions further record the arrival of later settlers, who greatly advanced the civilization of those countries. Manco Capac is the most celebrated among them, as being the founder of the dynasty and religion of the Incas. A

---

* "Views of the Cordilleras," vol. i. p. 17.

fanciful writer has seized upon this circumstance, and built upon it a complete history of a conquest of Peru and Mexico by the Monguls.* He supposes Mungo Capac to have been the son of Kublai, the Mongul emperor, grandson of Genghis Khan, who was sent by his father with a great fleet against Japan. A storm dispersed the fleet, so that it returned not home any more; and this author imagines it to have been driven on the coast of America, where the commander made himself chief. Ingenious as this may be, and even probable, the evidence brought to establish it appears very unsatisfactory. Many analogies may doubtless be found between the Peruvians and Monguls, but they may easily be explained from other sources. However, chronological data, the nature of the religion they established, and the monuments they erected, leave no room to doubt, that Thibet or Tartary was the original country of Mungo Capac's emigration.

Secondly, the computation of time among the Americans, affords too marked a coincidence, in matters of mere caprice, with that of eastern Asia, to be purely accidental. The division of time into greater cycles of years, again subdivided into smaller portions, each whereof bears a certain name, is, with trifling difference, the plan followed among the Chinese, Japanese, Kalmucks, Monguls, and Mantcheous, as well as among the Tolteks, Azteks, and other American nations; and the character of their respective methods is precisely the same, particularly if those of the Mexicans and Japanese be compared. But a comparison of the zodiac, as existing among the Thibetans, Monguls, and Japanese, with the names given by this American nation to the days of the month, will, I think, satisfy the most incredulous.

* Ranking's "Historical Researches on the Conquest of Peru and Mexico, &c., in the 13th century, by the Mongols, accompanied with elephants:" *Lond.* 1827. The spirit of system occasionally betrays the ingenious author into a mistake. Thus, p. 419, he refers to Humboldt as an authority for a Tartar inscription said to have been found in Narraganset Bay; whereas Humboldt, in the very place, rejects the story as more than doubtful.

The identical signs are, the tiger, hare, serpent, ape, dog, and bird, in all which it is plain there is no natural aptitude that could have suggested their adoption in both continents. This strange coincidence is still further enhanced by the curious fact, that several of the Mexican signs, wanting in the Tartar zodiac, are found in the Hindoo Shastras, exactly in corresponding positions. These are no less arbitrary than the former; being a house, a cane, a knife, and three foot-prints. But to do justice to this subject, it would be necessary to enter into much minuter details.*

Lastly, were everything else wanting, the clear traditions so vividly preserved among the Americans of man's early history, of the flood, and the dispersion, so exactly conformable to those of the old world, must remove every hesitation regarding their origin. The Azteks, Mitteks, Flascalteks, and other nations, had innumerable paintings of these latter events. Tezpi or Coxcox, as the American Noah is called, is seen floating in an ark upon the waters, and with him his wife, children, many animals, and several species of grain. When the waters withdrew, Tezpi sent out a vulture, which, being able to feed on the carcases of the drowned, returned no more. After the experiment had failed with several others, the humming-bird at length came back, bearing a green branch in its little beak. In the same hieroglyphic painting, the dispersion of mankind is thus represented. The first men after the deluge were dumb; and a dove is seen perched upon a tree, giving to each a tongue; the consequence whereof is, that the families, fifteen in number, disperse in different directions.† This coincidence, which reminds me that I am still indulging in digression, would alone be sufficient to establish a link of close connection between the nations of the two continents. But, in fact, so numerous, so extraordinary, and so minute, are the resemblances

---

* See the comparative plates, &c., in the 2nd vol. of the "Views of the Cordilleras."
† Humboldt, *ib.* pp. 65, 66.

between them, that in a publication of which I must say a few words, two long and elaborate dissertations have been inserted, to prove that Jews first, and then Christians, colonized America.*

The work to which I allude is the truly royal collection of Mexican monuments, published by Lord Kingsborough, a treasure of materials for such as dedicate themselves to their study. It seems impossible to look through these splendid volumes, without being struck with the varied character of art therein exhibited. The hieroglyphic figures representing the human form in squat and distorted proportions, have nothing in common with the sculptured reliefs. Here we have tall figures standing in warlike attitudes; there, females sitting cross-legged upon double-headed monsters, with children in their arms, their necks surrounded by strings of pearls, their heads crowned with conical and fretted head-dresses, sometimes formed of animals; in another place we meet the tortoise, the sacred emblem of India; in another we see the serpent winding round the tree, or men threatened to be swallowed by misshapen monsters; so that we imagine ourselves to be examining the sculptures of some Indian cavern, or ancient pagoda.† And I would add, that the type of countenance in these sculptures is no way American, but strongly recalls to mind the early Indian manner. Then we have another class of monuments, equally distinct, and seeming to harmonize with Egyptian art. We have pyramids constructed upon the same model, and apparently for the same purposes; we have figures closely wrapped up, so that only the feet below, and the hands at either side, appear, as in Egyptian statues: while the head-dress surrounds the head and drops down at each side, pushing forward enormous ears;

---

* The Antiquities of Mexico, published by A. Aglio, vol. vi. pp. 232-409, and 409-420.

† See vol. iv. part i. fig. 20, 36; 27, 28, 32: Specimens of Mexican sculpture, in possession of M. Latour Allard, at Paris, fig. 15, part iii. fig. 8.

besides other kneeling figures, where this attire is still more marked; so that, as Enea Quirino Visconti observed, they might have been copied from the portico at Dendara, whose capitals they exactly resemble. In figures, too, of this class, the physiognomy is by no means the same as in the former, but of a character more suiting the style of art.*

Who shall solve this riddle for us, and say whether these resemblances are accidental, or produced by some actual communication? Assuredly this is yet a land of mystery and clouds, and much study is yet requisite, to clear up anomalies, to reconcile contradictions, and place our knowledge upon a stabler footing. We cannot even remove difficulties of this nature nearer our own time; we cannot, for instance, explain how, as Muratori has proved, Brazil wood should be entered among the taxable commodities, at the gates of Modena, in 1306; or how Andrea Bianco's map, preserved in St. Mark's Library at Venice, and constructed in 1436, should place an island in the Atlantic, with the very name *Brasile*. How much more must we be involved in difficulties, when we attempt to unravel the intricacies of primeval records, or reconstruct an early history from a few fragmentary monuments?

And, in conclusion, I would remark, that many other problems there are, in the history of languages, which enter into the mysteries of nature, and have their solution involved in those hidden laws of her constitution, that form her links with the moral ordinance of the world. For, it might be asked, how is it that languages so easily sprung up in early ages, which till now have remained unchanged; or rather, how were their first families so soon divided into dialects, essentially fixed and independent, while in the progress of time mankind have formed little more than dialects of these provincial idioms or manifest derivations, hardly any further prolific? For, within a very short period after

* See *ib.* p. i. fig. 1, *seqq.* 48. Latour's mon. fig. 8, 14, &c.

the dispersion, must the Sanskrit, the Greek, and the Latin, or, at least, its parent-tongue, have separated from one another, and received their marked characteristic forms; and in the Semitic family the separation must have been equally early. Now, as well might we ask, why the oak, only near its roots, sends forth huge gigantic branches, each whereof shall of itself seem large enough to form another tree, and have its own dominion of boughs, and its own crown of yearly shoots, while later it can only put forth a punier and less vigorous offspring, wherein the generating virtue seems almost exhausted. And truly there is a sap in nations as well as in trees, a vigorous inward power, ever tending upwards, drawing its freshest energies from the simplest institutions, and the purest virtues, and the healthiest moral action. While these form the soil wherein a people is, as it were, deeply rooted, its powers are almost boundless; and as these alter and become exhausted, it likewise will be weakened, and decay. Assuredly, there was a vigour in the human mind, as compared with ours, gigantic, when the Homeric songs were the poetry of the wandering minstrel, when shepherd-chiefs, like Abraham, could travel from nation to nation, and even associate with their kings, and when an infant people could imagine and execute monuments like the Egyptian pyramids.

And if of nations we so may speak, what shall we say of the entire human race, when all its energies were, in a manner, pent up in its early and few progenitors; when the children of Noah, removed but a few generations from the recollections and lessons of Eden, and possessing the accumulated wisdom of long-lived patriarchs, were marvellously fitted to receive those strange and novel impressions, which a world, just burst forth in all its newness, was calculated to make; yea, when they, themselves an infant race, struggling on one side against the ravages of the late disaster, and on another, against the luxuriency of its renovating influence, must have felt within themselves a boundless energy in thought and action, a quickness of apprehension, a richness of contrivance, and a might in execution, equal to the crisis, and such as later generations could never want? And from minds thus subject to such peculiar impressions, alive to such unmodified feelings, and so strongly compelled to note their action, the first coinage of language must have received an impress and an image bolder and more indelible than after-times could have communicated, when the early springs of vigorous action had been impaired, or had ceased to act.

But we are not, I think, to imagine that Divine Providence, in distributing to different human families this holy gift of speech, had no farther purpose than the material dispersion of the human race, or the bestowing on them varied forms of utterance: there was doubtless therein a deeper and more important end—the sharing out among them of the intellectual powers. For language is so manifestly the embodying power, the incarnation, so to speak, of thought, that we can almost as easily imagine to ourselves a soul without a body, as our thoughts unclothed by the forms of their outward expression. And hence these organs of the spirit's conceptions must, in their turn, mould, control, and modify its peculiar character, so that the mind of a nation must necessarily correspond to the language it possesses.

The Semitic family, destitute of particles and grammatical forms suited to express the relations of things, stiffened by an unyielding construction, and confined by the dependence of words upon verbal roots, to ideas of outward action, could not lead the mind to abstract or abstruse ideas; and hence its dialects have been ever adapted for the simplest historical narratives, and for the most exquisite poetry, where mere impressions or sensations are felt and described in the most rapid succession; while not a school of native philosophy has arisen within their pale, not an element of metaphysical thought occurs in their sublimest compositions. Hence are the deepest revelations of religion, the awfullest denunciations of prophecy, the wisest lessons of virtue, clothed, in Hebrew, under imagery drawn from outward nature. And in this respect, the author of the Koran necessarily followed the same course.

But to the Indo-European was given a wonderful suppleness in expressing the inward and outward relations of things, by flexion in its nouns, by conditional and indefinite tenses in its verbs, by the tendency to make or adapt innumerable particles, but principally by the powerful and almost unlimited faculty of compounding words; joined whereunto is the facility of varying, inverting, and involving the construction, and the power of immediately and completely transferring the force of words, from a material to a purely mental representation. Hence, while it is a fit instrument for effecting the loftiest designs of genius, it is no less powerful in the hands of the philosopher; and in it, and by it, have arisen those varied systems, which, in ancient India, and in later Greece, and in modern Germany, have attempted to fathom the human understanding, and analyze to their primitive elements the forms of our ideas.*

And do you not see in all this, a subserviency to still nobler designs, when, in conjunction with these reflections, you look back at the order observed by God in the manifestation of His religion? For so long as His revelations were rather to be preserved than propagated, while His truths regarded principally the history of man and his simplest duties towards God, when His law consisted of precepts rather of outward observance than

---

* As an illustration of these remarks, I may say that, in our times, the transcendental philosophy could hardly have risen in any country except Germany, whose language possesses the characteristics of the family more than any other, and could most easily permit or suggest the using of the first pronoun objectively—a violence too great, in other European languages, for them to have first devised it. In Latin, for instance, where there is no article, it is almost impossible to express it; nor could one using that language have conceived such an idea.

inward constraint, while the direction of men was managed rather by the mysterious agency of seers into futurity, than by the steady rule of unalterable law, the entire system of religion was deposited in the hands of that human family whose intellectual character and language were admirably framed for clinging with tenacity to simple traditions of early days, and for describing all that was on the outside of man, and lent themselves most effectually to the awful ministry of the prophet's mission.

But no sooner is a mighty change introduced into the groundwork of His revelation, and the faculties unto which it is addressed, than a corresponding transfer manifestly takes place in the family whereunto its ministration and principal direction are obviously committed. The religion now intended for the whole world, and for each individual of the human race, requiring in consequence a more varied evidence, to meet the wants and satisfy the longings of every tribe and every country and every age, is handed over "to other husbandmen," whose deeper power of thought, whose ever eager impulse to investigate, would more easily discover and bring to light its inexhaustible beauties; who would search out its connections with every other order of truth, every other system of God's dispensation; thus ever bringing forth new motives of conviction, and new themes of praise. And in this manner Divine Wisdom, while it hath made the substance of religion one and immutable, hath yet in a manner tied its evidences to the restless wheel of man's endeavour, and mingled them with the other motives of his impelling desires: that so every step made in the prosecution of sound study and humble inquiry, may give them also a new advance, and a varied position; on which the reflecting mind may dwell with surpassing admiration. And how this hath happened with the science of Ethnography, I trust you have now sufficiently seen.

LECTURE THE THIRD;

ON THE

NATURAL HISTORY OF THE HUMAN RACE.

PART I.

HISTORY of this Science.—Division of Human Families among the Greeks.—Aristotle's Classification.—Who are his Egyptians?—Proofs that they represent the Negro race; the Scythians and the Thracians are Germanic and Mongul tribes.—Later writers.—System of Camper explained; its difficulties.—Blumenbach's System of Classification.—Division into three primary, and two secondary Families: first, by the form of the skull; secondly, by the colour, hair, and iris.—Geographical distribution of families.—Distinction between Tartars and Monguls.—Labours of Dr. Prichard.—Opposers of the unity of the human race; Virey, Desmoulins, Bory de Saint Vincent; Theory of Lamarck. RESULTS.—I. Remote examination of the subject by analogy of plants and animals.—Examples of varieties in these of a similar character to those observable in man. II. Direct examination of phenomena on a small scale.—Tendency of one family to produce varieties possessing the characteristics of another.—Examples of more extraordinary peculiarities springing up among men.—Reflections on the identity of moral feelings in all races, as applicable to the proof of their common origin.

IF St. Paul warns us to avoid perplexing ourselves with vain and endless genealogies, it might be thought that the study whereon we are now entering, belongs to the forbidden class. For, assuredly, the attempt to trace out the course and origin of each variety in the human species, back to one common progenitor, must seem an almost hopeless task; when we consider how the investigation it requires has been involved in numerous and complicated questions, by the contradictory statements of writers, and by the conflicting principles on which it has been conducted. Still, the successful results of the science last discussed, may well encourage us to undertake the examination of this its sister science—the history of the human race. It may, indeed, be said, that their objects are very nearly the same, even so far that a common name might perhaps be given them, descriptive of their object, with a distinctive epithet to mark the processes whereby they seek to attain it. And if the former was rightly called *philological*, this might be not unaptly styled *physiognomical Ethnography*.

The former has already brought us to the satisfactory conclusion, that so far as languages in their comparative bearings may be heard in evidence on the subject, the entire human race formed originally one family, or, in the words of the sacred penman, " were of one lip and one speech.". But, if great difficulties had to be overcome for the vindication of this scriptural assertion, arising from the great variety of idioms which now divide the tribes of earth, a stronger and more complicated one yet remains, striking more directly at the unity of the human race, and its origin from one stock. This consists in the consideration of those physical differences that distinguished the human form, in various regions of the globe.

The Word of God hath always considered mankind as descended from one parent, and the great mystery of redemption rests upon the belief that all men sinned in their common father. Suppose different and unconnected creations of men, and the deep mystery of original sin, and the glorious mystery of redemption, are blotted out from religion's book. Is it not then important to answer their reasoning, who maintain it is impossible to reduce the many varieties of human families into one species, or trace them to one common progenitor; who assert that natural history doth show such deeply-intrenched divisions between the physical characteristics of different nations, as that one could never have been derived from the other; and that no conceivable action of causes, either instantaneous or progressive, could have ever altered the European's shape or colour into the negro's, or caused "the Ethiopian to change his skin," and produce the Asiatic race? And how shall this confutation be obtained? Assuredly by no other means than I have already suggested to you, and intend often to inculcate and exemplify—by the deeper study of that very science which has engendered the objection—by the collection of yet better evidence than has already been produced—and by a well-digested classification of phenomena, whence satisfactory conclusions may be drawn.

This task, pursuant to my engagements, I enter upon this morning. I will premise an historical view of this science, dwelling, perhaps, more fully than may appear consistent with my plan, upon the earliest stages of its history, for motives which will easily be seen; I will then endeavour to classify and arrange the conclusions which the study in its present state may justly warrant us to draw, supporting them with such additional illustrations as I have been able to collect; and then will leave you to compare these conclusions with the history of the human race delivered to us in Genesis.

The mention of this sacred record brings before my mind, with regret, a passage, which being, as it were, preliminary to the very subject I am going to handle, and presenting a direct contradiction to what I have just asserted, I may not in silence pass over. The "Mosaic account," says a learned writer, "does not make it quite clear that the inhabitants of the world descended from Adam and Eve. Moreover, the entire or even partial inspiration of the various writings comprehended in the Old Testament, has been, and is, doubted by many persons, including learned divines, and distinguished oriental and biblical scholars. . . . . To the grounds of doubt respecting inspiration, which arise from the examination of various narratives, from knowledge of the original and other oriental languages, and from the irreconcilable opposition between the passions and sentiments ascribed to the Deity by Moses, and that religion of peace and love unfolded by the Evangelists, I have only to add, that the representations of all the animals being brought before Adam in the first instance, and, subsequently, of their being all collected in the ark, if we are to understand them as being applied to the living inhabitants of the whole world, are zoologically impossible." The first assertion in this quotation is supported in a note, by citing the passages where it is said, " God created man, male and female," and again (chap. v.), " in the day that God created man, male and female He created them." These passages the author supposes to refer to a different creation from that of Eve.* I am sorry to offer any comment upon this passage, because its author, I am sure, no longer holds the opinions he here incautiously expressed. But the value of the work itself, as a great collection of important facts, connected together by very learned observations, will continue to give it weight, and insure it the perusal of the young. And therefore I will venture to make a few remarks upon the theological portion of the argument. The author's conclusions from the investigation of the science, are perfectly in accordance with the inspired narrative, and therefore it is doubly a pity that he should have gone out of his way to show that the contrary opinion might be held, for anything which the Scriptures teach. It was not, perhaps, to be expected from him, that he should be acquainted with the labours of theologians; but the appeal to them warrants us in looking into their opinions. Now, taking one of the rashest and boldest interpreters that modern Germany has produced, we should find even him vindicating the different texts quoted by our author from all charge of

* Lectures on Physiology, Zoology, and the Natural History of Man : *Lond.* 1819, p. 248.

contradiction. I allude to Eichhorn, who, upon grounds solely philological, seems to have satisfactorily proved, what Astruc had conjectured in the last century, that the book of Genesis is composed of several distinct documents, which Moses has plainly incorporated into his work, clearly distinguishable, not only by their definite and complete form, but by the use of peculiar words; as, for instance, the word Jehovah, which is totally absent from one, and invariably found in another. Thus, the first chapter, where we are told that "God created man, male and female," without giving the details of his creation, always calls the Almighty by the name of *Elohim*, or simply God. But the fourth verse of the second chapter begins, manifestly, a new narrative or document, having a particular title: "These are the generations of the heavens and the earth," in other words, "this is the history of the creation of heaven and earth,"* entering into the details of paradise and man's creation, and distinguishable throughout by the constant use of the title of *Jehovah*, till its end with the fourth chapter. In the fifth, we have the return of the same document given in the first, or else another, in which Jehovah is not used, and where, again, man is said to have been created, male and female. Now, this being the hypothesis or system of the most "learned divine" who rejects inspiration, this divine thereby no less overthrows the scriptural deduction of a separate creation of man, besides that of Adam. For the texts quoted are shown to be only different descriptions of the same event. With the other objections drawn against inspiration, from the "examination of the various narratives, from the knowledge of the original and other oriental languages, and from the irreconcilable opposition" between the God of Moses and the Christian religion, it would be out of place now to

---

* All who are conversant in scriptural science are aware of the correspondence of these two expressions—histories being called genealogies, from their being prefaced by such documents. See Gen. vi. 9, and Mat. i. 1.

engage; and it is not, perhaps, very clear in what sense the learned writer's words are to be taken. Having been at some pains to make myself acquainted with " the original and other oriental languages," anyways applicable to the study of Scripture, I have not discovered that any " grounds of doubt, respecting inspiration," have arisen from this knowledge. But pass we on to more pleasant occupation.

The more marked divisions of the human race are so striking to the eye, that it was impossible for them to escape the notice of the ancients. No one, for instance, could avoid being struck with the difference in features, colour, and hair, between the European and the negro. Aristotle appears to have recorded the classification prevalent in earlier and in his own times, when he tells us, that the older physiognomists decided of a person's character by the resemblance of his features to " those of nations who differ in appearance and manners, as the Egyptians, Thracians, and Scythians."* As these races, or rather their characteristics, must be considered as compared to another, from which, as from a type or standard, they variously differ, which doubtless was the Grecian form, we have here a division of mankind into four distinct classes, or races, as we now call them. No attempt, as far as I am aware, has been made to investigate this point more minutely, and yet it is not without its importance. For, besides thus giving the very foundation or first step in the history of a science every day growing in interest and importance, we may, perhaps, gather some facts useful towards examining the changes which time has introduced into the nations occupying particular tracts of country; and for these reasons, even at the risk of deviating, for a moment, from the popular form I wish to preserve in these lectures, I will enter at some length into the discussion.

---

* Διελόμενοι κατὰ τὰ ἔθνη, ὅσα διέφερε τὰς ὄψεις, καὶ τὰ ἤθη, οἷον Αἰγύπτιοι, καὶ Θρᾶκες, καὶ Σκύθαι.--Physiognomic. cap. i. Opp. Par. 1619, tom. i. p. 1169.

The first race, or distinctly characterized class of men, which Aristotle, after the older physiognomists, here mentions, is the Egyptian. By this there can be no doubt that he means the negro race; for, besides the impossibility of his omitting this in speaking of the varieties in the human species, in another place he clearly confounds the two; saying, "that persons who are very dark are also timid, being referred to the Egyptian and Ethiopian race."* Again, on another occasion, he asks the question, why the Egyptians and Ethiopians have crooked legs and distorted feet? to which he answers, that this arises probably from the same cause as gives them both woolly hair—that is, the heat of their climate.†

Here, then, arises a complicated and interesting inquiry—Were the ancient Egyptians really so formed upon the negro type, that the two could be confounded together? The testimony of Aristotle is undoubtedly strong in favour of the affirmative, and becomes doubly so from the agreement of almost all the classics, especially that of the sagacious and accurate Herodotus. For, speaking of the Colchi, he says they are proved to be descendants of the Egyptians, ὅτι μελάγχροές εἰσὶ καὶ οὐλότριχες,‡ "because they are black and woolly-headed." Here, as in the philosopher, we have the two most definite characteristics of the negro race attributed to the Egyptians.

Blumenbach, whose name I shall often have to mention with praise, has manifestly a favourite theory regarding the physiognomy of the Egyptians. In his invaluable "Decads of Skulls," he first hinted that it is impossible to suppose, during so many ages of embalming, no variety in the national type.§ In 1808,

---

* Οἱ ἄγαν μέλανες δειλοί. ἀναφέρεται ἐπὶ τοὺς Αἰγυπτίους, καὶ Αἰθίοπας.—Ib. cap. vi. p. 1180.

† Διὰ τί οἱ Αἰθίοπες καὶ οἱ Αἰγύπτιοι βλαισοί εἰσιν: . . . δηλοῦσι δὲ καὶ αἱ τρίχες· οὐλοτέρας γὰρ ἔχουσιν.—Problem. Sec. xiv. 4, tom. ii. p. 750.

‡ Lib. ii. § civ. tom. i. p. 157, ed. Lond. 1824.

§ Decas collectionis suæ craniorum diversorum gentium illustrata: Götting. 1790, p. 14.

he more clearly expressed his opinion, that monuments prove the existence of three distinct forms or physiognomies among the inhabitants of Egypt.* Three years later he entered more fully into this inquiry, and gave the monuments which, he thought, bore him out in his hypothesis. The first of these he considers to approach to the negro model, the second to the Hindoo, the third to the Berber, or ordinary Egyptian head.† But I think an unprejudiced observer will not easily follow him so far. The first head has nothing in common with the black race, but is only a coarser representation of the Egyptian type; the second is but its mythological or ideal purification. To make out this system from monuments, two things appear wanting: first, that instead of single representations, which may be called only sporadic or casual, classes of monuments should have been pointed out, wherein the different characters are preserved, for occasional deviations from the ordinary course are to be found in every law; secondly, that some chronological relation be established between the different classes, so to prove that the change which he supposes, occurred at different epochs in the national features. Neither of these points, however, has been attempted.

All the remains of the Egyptians oppose the statements of the classics I have quoted. For as to their colour and hair, nothing can be more clearly represented than they are on their monuments. We always see the bodies of the natives painted of a red or tawny colour, with long flowing hair, where the head-dress allows it to be seen; while we often see the negroes represented beside them, by a jet black colour, frizzled hair, and perfect negro features, precisely as they really are at the present day.‡ But we have still more precious

* Specimen historiæ naturalis antiquæ artis operibus illustratæ: *Ibid.* 1808, p. 11.
† "Beiträge zur Naturgeschichte," 2ter Th. *Gött.* 1811. "Dreyerley National Physiognomie unter den alten Ægyptern," p. 130.
‡ See the coloured plates in Hoskins's "Travels in Ethiopia."

monuments than these painted representations, in the very mummies themselves, the skulls of which, as Mr. Lawrence observes, invariably have the European form, without a trace of the negro shape.* And as to the hair, we may give, for a general description, the account given by M. Villoteau of the hair of a mummy opened under his direction: "Les cheveux étaient noirs. . . . bien plantés, longs, et divisés en nattes retroussées sur la tête."†

It is not easy to reconcile the conflicting results thus obtained from writers and from monuments, and it is no wonder that learned men should have differed widely in opinion on the subject. I should think the best solution is, that Egypt was the country where the Greeks most easily saw the inhabitants of interior Africa, many of whom doubtless flocked thither and were settled there, or served in the army as tributaries or provincials, as they have done in later times; and thus they came to be confounded by writers with the country where alone they knew them, and were considered a part of the indigenous population. Some such hypothesis must be adopted to reconcile writers among themselves; for Ammianus Marcellinus writes that the Egyptians were only dark and blackish, "homines Ægyptii plerumque subfusculi sunt et atrati."‡ Thus much, however, is perfectly certain, that by the Egyptian variety, which he places first among those of the human species, Aristotle means the black or negro race.

The next upon his list are the Scythians; and Hippocrates in like manner mentions them as possessing characteristics common to all their tribes except one, no less marked and distinctive on the one side, than those of the Egyptians on the other.§ Though ancient Scythia

---

* "Lectures," p. 345.

† Ap. De Sacy, "Relation de l'Egypte, par Abd-Allatif:" *Paris*, 1810, p. 269.

‡ Lib. xxii. in fine; in "Scriptor. Hist. Rom.:" *Heidelb.* 1743, tom. ii. p. 518.

§ Ὅτι πολὺ ἀπήλλακται τῶν λοιπῶν ἀνθρώπων τὸ Σκυθικὸν γένος, καὶ

occupied the country now in great measure peopled by tribes belonging to what is called the Mongul race, whom the ancient Scythians greatly resembled in the nomadic form of their lives, we cannot for a moment suppose that a tawny or olive-coloured race would be placed by writers like Aristotle and Hippocrates, as the variety contrasting with the Greek in an opposite direction from the negro. There can be no doubt but the Scythians mentioned by Aristotle, in his classification of the human races, were the Germanic tribes, which were found scattered over the whole of Scythia. This country, as described by Herodotus, is not, like the Scythia of Ptolemy, confined to northern Asia, but also comprehended Dacia, Mœsia, and all the country north of Thrace.* Now there can be no question but the inhabitants of these regions were Germanic; for besides their representation on monuments, the descriptions given of them by Ovid in his exile, present all the traits of the ancient Germans. Thus their hair is described as yellow or light-coloured:

> " Hic mea cui recitem nisi flavis scripta Corallis,
> Quasque alias gentes barbarus Ister habet.' †

And as always unshorn:

> " Mixta sit hæc (gens) quamvis inter Graiosque Getasque,
> A male pacatis plus trahit ora Getis,
> Vox fera, trux vultus, verissima Martis imago,
> Non coma, non ulla barba resecta manu."‡

Ovid, too, it need scarcely be noted, speaks in almost every page of his place of exile as Scythia.

ἔοικεν αὐτὸ ἑαυτέῳ, ὥσπερ τὸ Αἰγύπτιον.—De Aere, Locis, et Aquis, ed. *Genev.* 1657, tom. i. p, 291.

* See lib. iv. § xcix. p. 327.

† "Epist. de Ponto," lib. iv. ep. ii. 37. The Coralli seem to be confounded with the Getæ, on comparing ep. viii. 83, with x. 2. A fanciful etymologist might consider them as the ancestors of the Kouriliana.

‡ "Trist." lib. v. eleg. vii. 11. Lucan (lib. i.), speaking of a German tribe, says—
"Et vos crinigeros bellis arcere Chaycos."

But thus far we hardly needed proof. It is far more important to note that Herodotus, with his usual accuracy, has clearly distinguished two races as occupying the wide regions of Asiatic Scythia—the Germanic, according to the ancient classification, and the Mongul. For, he tells us, that above the Sarmatians, and consequently, as Breiger well observes, about the territory of Astrakan, on the Jaik,* there lived a tribe called the Budini, "a great and numerous nation, with eyes exceedingly blue, and red hair."† Here, then, we have a Scythian tribe, with all the characteristics attributed by the ancients to the Germanic nations.‡ But, in another place, Herodotus describes the Agrippæi, no less a Scythian people, with very different traits. "They are said," he writes, "to be bald from their births, both males and females, with flat noses and large chins."§ Their manners, he adds, are perfectly harmless and innocent. Now compare these marks with the characteristics of the Mongul race, and you will at once see how accurate Herodotus is, and how certainly the same race of nomads, as now, partly occupied the northern tracts of Asia in his time. Blumenbach gives us the following distinctives of the Mongul family:—a flat nose (*nasus simus*), corresponding to the σιμοί of Herodotus, and a rather prominent chin (*mentum prominulum*, γένειον μεγάλον).‖ But what are we to say to the baldness from birth? Is it to be accounted a fable; seeing that the judicious father of profane history, whose correctness every new research confirms, is careful

---

* "Commentatio de Difficilioribus quibusdam Asiæ Herodoteæ." Prefixed to the cited edition, p. clxxxiv.
† "Βουδῖνοι δὲ ἔθνος ἐὸν μέγα καὶ πολλὸν, γλαυκόν τε ἰσχυρῶς ἐστὶ καὶ πυρρόν.—Melpom. § cviii. tom. i. p. 327. Cf. § xxi. p. 292.
‡ See them collected by Corringius, "De habitus corporum Germanorum antiqui et novi causis, liber singularis:" *Frankfort*, 1727, with a voluminous commentary by Burggraff, pp. 29–100.
§ "Ἄνθρωποι λεγόμενοι εἶναι πάντες φαλακροὶ ἐκ γενεῆς γινόμενοι, καὶ ἔρσενες, καὶ θήλεαι ὁμοίως, καὶ σιμοὶ, καὶ γένεια ἔχοντες μεγάλα.—*Ib.* § xxiii. p. 293.
‖ "De Generis Humani Varietate nativa:" *Götting.* 1705, p. 179.

to qualify his assertion by an expression of doubt? λεγόμενοι, he says, είναι πάντες φαλακροί,—they are *said* to be all bald. I might answer, that Blumenbach, in another place, describing the hair of different races, gives that of the Monguls as *rarus*—thin, or, as Virey expresses it, *clair-semé*.* But I think this difficulty is still better removed by what Pallas relates of the Calmucks:—" Ils rasent la tête à leurs enfans mâles, dès la plus tendre enfance;" and again, " les hommes ont tous la tête rasée."† By this striking custom we may explain how Herodotus, speaking of the Agrippæi, should often call them by no other name than the *bald people*— φαλακροί τουτοί.‡

This mixture of tribes probably gave rise to the confusion sometimes observable in ancient writers, when they characterize the Scythians: for they blend together features which could not well have belonged to one race, but appear taken from both parts of the population. Such, at least, appears to be the case in the two principal physiognomical writers of antiquity, Adamantius and Polemon. I will confine myself to the former, as the latter is nothing more than his transcriber. Adamantius, therefore, who professes to follow Aristotle, like him speaks of the Scythians and Ethiopians as of the extremes of the human race.§ Now, in another place, he gives us the characteristics of nations near the north, and of those under the torrid zone, meaning, therefore, probably, those whom he had before designated as Scythians and Ethiopians. Of the former he says: " Generally speaking, the inhabitants of the north are well-formed, *xanthous*, fair, with soft

---

* "De Generis Humani Varietate nativa :" *Götting.* 1795, p. 166. Virey, " Histoire naturelle du Genre Humain :" *Bruxell.* 1827, vol. i. p. 411.
† " Voyages en différentes provinces l'Empire de Russie :" *Par.* 1788, tom.i. pp. 502, 503.
‡ *Ubi sup.* §§ xxiv. xxv. pp. 293, *seqq.*
§ " Physiogn." l. i. "Scriptores Physiognom. Veteres :" *Altemb.* 1780, p. 318. "Polemon." *Ibid.* p. 173. Adamantius, however, there clearly distinguishes the Egyptian from the Ethiopian features.

hair, blue eyes, and flat noses; have thick legs, loose flesh, and large paunches."* It is evident that this description in great part applies to some Germanic nation, with the exception of the flat nose, loose flesh, and obesity, which seem to have been borrowed from the description of some Mongul tribe; though the last of these characteristics could only apply to a few, as the Kirghis or Bashkirs.†

This dispersion of Germanic tribes over the whole of Scythia, appears to me a very interesting fact; and after having thus endeavoured to trace them by the aid of Greek writers, it was a great satisfaction to me to find the fact confirmed by a lamented orientalist, from sources of a different class. "How much soever this assertion may appear a paradox," says Abel-Rémusat, "I think it will be proved that the family of the Gothic nations once occupied large tracts of Tartary; that some of its branches inhabited Transoxana, and even reached the Altai mountains; and that they were well known to the people of eastern Asia, who could not fail to be struck with the singularity of their languages, their light hair, blue eyes, and white complexions; traits particularly remarkable in the midst of men dark-coloured, and with brown eyes and dark hair, who have in the end occupied their place. When I shall have given the proofs I have collected, it will be seen whether my assertion is too rash."‡ These proofs he did not, I believe, live to publish; but the learned and sagacious Ritter has most satisfactorily unravelled the complicated history of the population of central

---

* *Ὡς δὲ πολὺ οἱ μὲν ὑπὸ τῇ ἄρκτῳ οἰκοῦντες, εὐμήκεις εἰσί, ξανθοὶ λευκοὶ τὰς κόμας, ἀπαλότριχες, γλαυκοί, σιμοί, παχυσκελεῖς, περιπληθεῖς σαρκὶ λαγαρᾷ, προγάστορες.*—Lib. ii. § xxiii. p. 409. In my translation, I have inserted a comma after λευκοι, and erased it after κομας; first, because otherwise there is either a useless repetition or a contradiction as to the colour of the hair, already expressed by the epithet ξανθοὶ; secondly, because in the corresponding passage of Polemon, the entire number τας—γλαυκοι is omitted, as he says, λευκοί, σιμοί, &c.—Lib. i. § iii. p. 181.

† Pallas, *ubi sup.* p. 496.

‡ "Recherches sur les Langues Tartares," p. xlv.

Asia, so entangled by the confusion of names transferred from one nation to another. He considers tribes of the Indo-European or Indo-Germanic race, to have been the first inhabitants of the central plateau of Asia, who are represented by all Chinese writers as having red hair and blue eyes. In the second century before Christ, some remains, which had been driven westward by the Hiong-nu, were still in force on the shores of Lake Bhalkush, and the river Hi, under the name of Ui-siun, or U-siun; but being afterwards weakened, they were driven to the west in the fourth century, and probably fell into the stream of northern inundation, then beginning to move towards the south.*

But what I wish principally to conclude from this lengthy disquisition is, that with this mixture of tribes among the Scythians, we cannot doubt but it was the Germanic family which Aristotle and Hippocrates had in view, when they described the Scythians as differing by their fairness from the Greeks, as much as did the Ethiopians by their dusky hue. And, in fact, the Latin writers, to whom the Germans were more familiarly known than to the Greeks, contrast them with the Ethiopians, as though they too formed the opposite extremes of the human family. "The colour of the Ethiopian," says Seneca, "is not singular among his countrymen, nor is red hair tied up in a knot a peculiarity among the Germans."† Martial says, in like manner,

"Crinibus in nodum tortis venere Sicambri
Atque aliter tortis crinibus Æthiopes."‡

The third race of men enumerated by Aristotle, consists of the Thracians. It is, I think, still more difficult to decide whom he means to characterize by this name;

* "Die Erdkunde in Verhältniss zur Natur, und zur Geschichte des Menschen," 2 Th. ii. Buch. Asien, 1 Band: *Berl.* 1832, pp. 431-435.
† "De Ira," lib. iii. c. xxvi. ‡ "Spectacul." lib. Epig. iii.

though it is evident that he must mean a nation having peculiar distinctives in colour and feature, sufficient to mark them when mixed with the other races he has described. This would naturally lead us to conjecture that in his classification they correspond to the olive or Mongul race, the only one wherewith he must have been acquainted, that finds no place in his enumeration. In this conjecture I feel confirmed by the following considerations.

First, as Aristotle is guided chiefly by colour, in his distribution of mankind into races, and the two classes which we have examined give us the extremes, this must represent an intermediate colour, differing however from the Grecian complexion. But there is a passage in Julius Firmicus, overlooked by the commentators of Aristotle, which gives us the same ternary division, with the colours of each race. "In the first place," he writes, "speaking of the characters and colours of men, they agree in saying,—if by the mixed influence of the stars the characters and complexions of men are distributed; and if the course of the heavenly bodies, by a certain kind of artful painting, form the lineaments of mortal bodies—that is, if the moon makes men white, Mars red, and Saturn black— how comes it that in Ethiopia all are born black, in Germany white, and in Thrace red?"* By this it would appear, that the copper or olive colour was the characteristic of the Thracian family, and consequently that it corresponded to what we now should call the Mongul race.

Secondly, Homer has described the Thracians as ἀκρόκομοι,† or as having their hair only on the crown of

---

* "Primum itaque de moribus hominum coloribusque conveniunt dicentes : Si stellarum mixturis mores hominibus, coloresque distribuuntur, et quasi quodam picturæ genere, atque artificio, stellarum cursus mortalium corporum lineamenta componunt ; hoc est, si ☽ fecit candidos, ♂ rubros, ♄ nigros ; cur omnes in Æthiopia nigri, in Germania candidi, in Thracia rubri procreantur?"—Astronomicon, lib. i. c. i. ed. *Basil.* 1551, p. 3.

† "Iliad," Δ 533.

the head. This seems opposed to the description given us of the Grecian and Germanic fashion, which rather cherished an abundant growth of hair; but is a very striking characteristic of Kalmuck costume, wherein, as in that of many other Mongul nations, the head is shaved, and only a tuft or tress of hair is left on the crown.*

Thirdly, we may strengthen this conjecture from another passage in Aristotle, where he observes that one nation among the Thracians is so rude, as not to go, in their arithmetic, beyond the number four.† Upon this assertion, besides deducing therefrom that the Thracians were not one nation, but a collection of tribes, I will remark, that a similar ignorance is said to have been discovered among people of the Mongul race, as, for example, the Kamstchatkadales. Indeed, it is difficult to suppose that Pelasgic or Germanic tribes, who are proved, by the conformity of their numerals with those of southern Asia, to have separated from them after that system had been framed, and a certain civilization prevailed, should have fallen into such a state of miserable barbarism.

I might add other reflections, such as the prevalence of *shamanism* in the religion of Thessaly, and the origin of horsemanship, attributed in fable to the same country; both points indicating a relationship with the race now occupying northern and central Asia. Nor need I observe that the boundaries between that country and Thrace are so badly defined, as to be often neglected or overlooked by ancient writers. Probably, therefore, mixed with the population of Thrace, were wandering tribes of the olive or copper-coloured race, whom Aristotle and Julius Firmicus justly placed in a distinct class.

But assuredly I have dwelt too long upon this early period in the history of our science, led away by the unfrequented state of the path I have pursued: nor dare

---

* Pallas, *ubi sup*. p. 502.
† Problem. sec. xv. 3, tom. ii. p. 753.

I flatter myself that, in this instance at least, I have verified the poet's opinion:

> —— τὰ μακρὰ τῶν σμικρῶν λόγων
> Ἐπίπροσθέν ἐστι, καὶ σαφῆ μᾶλλον κλύειν.*

For many ages, the same obvious classification of mankind, formed upon the prevalent complexion in different parts of the world, was followed without much discrimination; so that the human race might be considered as divided, like the earth which it inhabited, into three classes or zones; the very white occupying the colder regions, the black possessing the torrid, and the fair the temperate region. Such, for instance, is the division adopted by the Arabic historian Albulpharaj.† In the last century, this simple arrangement was modified till it assumed the form of a complicated system, in consequence of the discovery of many intermediate shades in the colour of nations, not easily to be introduced into that threefold division. Leibnitz, Linnæus, Buffon, Kant, Hunter, Zimmerman, Meiners, Klügel, and others, proposed different classifications based upon the same principle, which, as this is now universally rejected, possess but little interest, and are not easy to remember.

The first who proposed a new basis for this important study, was Governor Pownall, who, though he adopted colour as the ground of his classification, yet suggested the propriety of attending to the form of the skull in the various families of mankind.‡ But Camper has the merit of having first devised a rule by which the heads of different nations might be mutually compared, so as to give definite and characteristic results.

Camper enjoyed peculiar advantages for this undertaking, from having united two sciences not often pursued by the same individual—a perfect and practical

---

* Euripid. "Orest." 640.
† "Historia Dynastiarum:" *Oxf.* 1663, p. 3.
‡ "New Collection of Voyages:" *Lond.* 1767, vol. ii. p. 273.

PLATE 1 — Page 115.

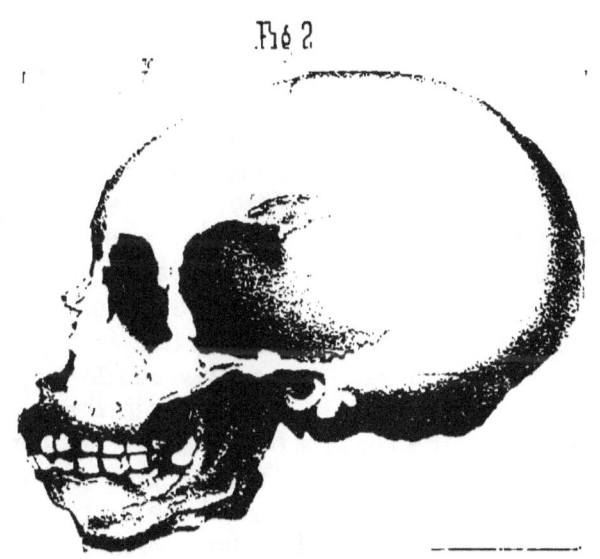

Fig 2.

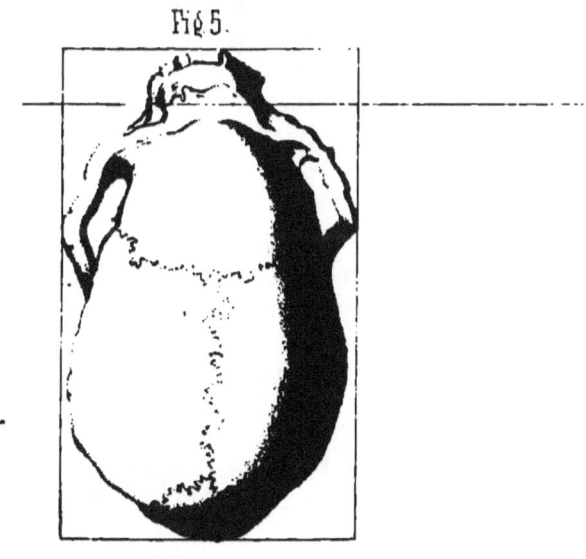

Fig 5.

knowledge of art, and an extensive acquaintance with physiology and comparative anatomy. It was seeing how imperfectly the best artists, whom he copied, had caught the features and form of the negro, that led him to examine what were the essential peculiarities of his configuration.* He then extended his researches to the heads of other nations, and discovered, as he supposed, a canon or rule by which they might be measured, with certain and regular results. This rule consists in what he calls the facial line, and is applied as follows:—The skull is viewed in profile, and first a line is drawn from the entrance of the ear (the *meatus auditorius*) to the base of the nostrils; then a second, from the most prominent point of the forehead to the extreme border of the upper jaw, where the teeth are rooted (the alveolar process of the superior maxillary bone). It is evident that an angle will be formed at the intersection of these two lines, and the measure of that angle, or, in other words, the inclination of the line from the brow to the jaw, gives what is called the facial line, and forms in Camper's system the specific characteristic of each human family.† By inspecting the drawings (Pl. 1), you will easily perceive the application of this rule. From them it appears that the facial angle, in the baboon nearest approaching the human shape, is of about 58 degrees (fig. 1); that in the negro and Kalmuck it measures 70° (fig. 2); and in the European, 80° (fig. 3). The ancients, who doubtless perceived this increase of the angle in proportion to the advance in the intellectual scale, went beyond the line found in nature, and in their sublimer works have ventured to give an overhanging swelling prominence to the forehead, which increases the facial angle to 95° or even 100°.‡ This fact Blumenbach has very positively denied,

---

* "Dissertation physique de M. Pierre Camper, sur les Différences réelles que présenteut les traits du visage chez les hommes de différens pays," &c.: *Utrecht*, 1791, p. 3.
† *Ibid.* p. 35.
‡ See Camper's second plate, figures 3 and 4, and pp. 42 and 55. Roman art has the smaller, Grecian the larger of these two angles.

saying that all those representations of ancient art which gave such an angle are not correct copies.* But I think whoever will examine the heads of Jupiter in the Vatican Museum, particularly the bust in the large circular hall, or the more defaced heads of the Elgin marbles, will be satisfied that Camper is accurate in this respect.

To this system of measurement proposed by him, Blumenbach has brought more serious objections. He observes that even Camper himself admits a great vagueness in fixing the origin of his lines: but principally he objects that it is a measurement totally inapplicable to those races or families whose more marked distinctive consists in the breadth of the skull rather than in the projection of its upper portion.†

It is to this sagacious and assiduous physiologist that we owe the system of classification now almost universally followed, and the principles by which it is conducted. His museum contains the most complete collection in existence of skulls belonging to members of almost every nation in the globe. Not content with the results given him by their study, he has collected from every branch of natural science, and from every department of literature, whatever can throw light upon the history of the human race, and account for the varieties it contains. His works are, in fact, a storehouse from which all must draw; and the most voluminous works upon this study which have appeared since his time, have done, and can do little more than confirm, by additional evidence, what he had already proved.

Blumenbach's classification is determined primarily by the form of the cranium, and secondarily by the colour of the hair, skin, and iris.

It may at first appear to you that an acquaintance

---

* " Specimen Historiæ Naturalis antiquæ artis operibus illustratæ." *Gotting.* 1808, p. 13.
† " De Generis Humani Varietate nativa;" *Gött.* 1795, p. 200.

with the anatomy or construction of the skull is necessary for rightly comprehending his system. This, however, is not the case; for a very few observations, with a drawing before us, will soon convey all the information necessary on this subject. You have only to pay attention to the following particulars. The head or skull, when viewed from above, presents more or less an oval form, smoothly rounded at the back, but rough and less regular in front, in consequence of the bones of the face. If we examine these, we shall see that they project in different degrees, and may be divided into three portions: first, the forehead, which may be more or less depressed; then the bones of the nose; and below these the jaws, with the respective teeth. Particular attention, too, must be paid to the manner in which the *malar*, or cheek-bones, are connected with the *temporal*, or bones at the ears, by means of an arch called the zygoma, so formed as to allow strong muscles to pass under it, and be fixed to the lower jaw. (See fig. 5.)

Now, Blumenbach's rule consists precisely in viewing the skull as I have described it, and attending to the particulars I have mentioned. He places it in its natural position upon a table, and then looks upon it from above and behind; and the relative forms and proportions of the parts thus visible, give him what he calls the vertical rule, or *norma verticalis*. Following this, he divides the entire human race into three principal families, with two intermediate ones. The three leading divisions he calls the Caucasian, or central; secondly, the Ethiopian; and thirdly, the Mongul, or two extreme varieties. By inspecting the drawings made from his works, you will instantly perceive their characteristic differences. In the Caucasian, or, as others have called it, the Circassian variety (fig. 4), the general form of the skull is more symmetrical, and the zygomatic arches enter into the general outline, and the cheek and jaw-bones are concealed entirely by the greater prominence of the forehead. From this type

H 2

the other two depart in opposite directions, the negro by its greater length and narrowness, the Mongul by its excessive breadth. In the negro's skull (fig. 5), you see the remarkable lateral compression of the fore part of the skull, by which the arches aforesaid, though themselves much flattened, yet come to protrude much beyond it; and you will observe that the lower part of the face comes forward so much beyond the upper, that not only the cheek-bones, but the whole of the jaw, and even the teeth, are visible from above. The general surface of the skull is also remarkably elongated and compressed.

The Mongul cranium is distinguished by the extraordinary breadth of its front, in which the zygomatic arch is completely detached from the general circumference; not so much, as in the negro, on account of any depression in this, as from the enormous lateral prominence of the cheek-bones; which, being at the same time flat, give the peculiar expression of the Mongul face. The forehead, too, is much depressed, and the upper jaw protuberant, so as to be visible when viewed in the vertical direction. (Fig. 6.)

Between the Caucasian variety and each of the two others, is an intermediate class, possessing, to a certain degree, the distinctives of the extremes, and forming a transition from the centre to them. That between the Caucasian and negro families is the Malay; the link between the former and the Mongul is the American variety.

Besides this great and primary characteristic, there are others of a secondary, though not less distinguishable nature: they consist in the complexion, hair, and eyes of the different races. The three principal families are distinguished by as many different colours; the Caucasian by white, the negro by black, and the Mongul by the olive or yellow complexion: the intermediate races have also intermediate hues, the Americans being copper-coloured, and the Malays tawny.

The colour of the hair and of the iris follows that

of the skin in a sufficiently obvious manner. Even in the fair or Caucasian race, to which we belong, persons with very fair or ruddy complexions have always the hair red, or light-coloured, and the eyes blue or of a light shade; and this has been called the *xanthous* variety of the white race. In persons with a brown skin, the hair is invariably black, and the eye darker; and these are called the *melanic* variety. This conformity of colour in these different parts, was well known to the ancients, who observed it strictly in their personal descriptions. Thus Ausonius, in his Idyll on Bissula, who belonged to the first class, says of her:

———"Germana maneret
Ut facies, oculos cærula, flava comis."

And in another fragment he gives her the corresponding complexion:

"Pumiceas confunde rosas, et lilia misce,
Quique erit ex illis color aëris ipse sit oris."*

So Horace describes a youth of the second variety:

"Et Lycum nigris oculis, nigroque
Crine decorum."†

From these remarks you will easily understand, that in both the negro and Mongul races, in which the skin is dark, the hair will be black and the eye dark. The hair, too, besides its colour, has a peculiar character in each race; in the white race it is flexible, flowing, moderately thick, and soft; in the negro, very thick-set, strong, short, and curly; in the Mongul, stiff, thin, and straight.

In every one of these races, there springs up occasionally a variety which ought to be mentioned, and which appears, in the human species at least, to bear a morbid character. I allude to *albinos*, or persons in

* "Idyll." vii. 9, et Fragm. annex.
† "Od." lib. i. 32.

whom the skin is of a dazzling whiteness, with hair excessively light, and almost colourless, and red eyes. These, too, are peculiarly sensitive, and can bear but little light; so that albinos are vulgarly supposed to see in the dark: they are, also, generally very feeble in health and intellect. They are to be found in every country: in a village a few miles distant from this city (Rome) is a highly-respectable family, in which several of the children belong to this class. The sagacious Arabic physician, Abdollatiph, mentions one whom he saw among the Copts, as a natural curiosity.* Mr. Crawfurd throws discredit on Sonnerat's description of the Papuans of New Guinea, because he says that their hair is of a brilliant black, or fiery red.† Sonnerat, however, seems to have had in view some albinos, whose hair, among the blacks, assumes a sandy or reddish colour. Even in Africa, among the darkest race, they are far from uncommon, and form, of course, a much stronger contrast, by their snowy whiteness, with the ebony hue of their neighbours.‡

I pass over many other minor distinctives of these human races, such as the direction of the teeth, the stature and form of the body; and proceed to trace for you the geographical limitations of each great family.

The Caucasian comprehends all the nations of Europe, excepting the Laplanders, Finlanders, and Hungarians; the inhabitants of Western Asia, including Arabia, Persia, and upwards, as far as the river Oby, the Caspian Sea, and the Ganges; and those of Northern Africa.

The negro race comprises all the remaining inhabitants of this last-named quarter of the globe.

* "Among the wonders of nature of this time, is to be reckoned that a child was born with white hair; which did not resemble the greyness of old age, but rather approached to a red."—De Mirabil. Ægypti: *Oxon.* 1800, p. 278.
† *Ubi sup.* p. 27.
‡ See a minute description of a white negro from Senegal, in the "Description de la Nigritie, par M.P.D.P." *Amst.* 1789, p. 60.

The Mongul race embraces all the nations of Asia not included in the Caucasian or Malayan varieties, and takes in the European tribes excluded by the former, as well as the Esquimaux in North America.

The Malayan embraces the natives of the peninsula of Malacca, and of Australia and Polynesia, distinguished in ethnography by the name of the Papuan tribes.

Finally, the American includes all the aborigines of the new world, excepting the Esquimaux.

I must observe, that considerable confusion and perplexity exists regarding the name and extent of what, after Blumenbach, I have called the "Mongul race." Blumenbach gives several reasons for rejecting the old name of "Tartar," which is, however, still retained by many writers on the subject. It is not easy, indeed, to unravel the genealogy of the tribes which have been confusedly called by the two names, nor to establish the limitations of the different races into which they run. I will, however, try to explain it as far as possible. The Turks are often called Tartars, and the invaders of Western Asia, under Tschingis Khan, are sometimes called Tartars, and sometimes Monguls. The Mantchous are equally subject to vague classification.

Historically; the Turks, Tartars, and Monguls, are perfectly distinct nations. According to Ritter, who has, certainly, most profoundly examined all questions of geographical history, the first of these, under the name of Hiong-nu, occupied all the north of China; they separated into two kingdoms in the first century, disappeared from history in the fourth, recovered their dominion in the following, and later, were swept away by the irresistible power of Tschingis Khan, and so received the name of "Tartars," which they consider a reproach. The Tartars, or Tata, as they are called by Chinese historians, and Monguls, were also distinct nations, or rather, perhaps, tribes of one nation; their own origin being, according to Abulghazi,* from two brothers, who bore those names. In the eleventh century they formed two of four tribes settled in the Inschan mountains, near the Hoang-ho river. Tschingis Khan, being born of a Mongul father, and a Tata mother, united the two, and gave the united nation the name of "Monguls;" but his chief officers and nobles being Tartars, they were more generally known by this name, which is commonly used in popular history.†

Philologically considered, they are classified together by Abel-Rémusat, who devoted a great portion of his life to the study of their languages. In his classical work upon them, he comprises under this name the Turks, Tartars, Mantchous, and Monguls, whom he considers only a branch of the Tartars.‡ In like manner, Klaproth and Balbi classify the language of these nations in one general division.§

Physiognomically viewed, there is, as I before observed, considerable difference of opinion. What we now call Turks, or the Osmanlis, undoubtedly belong to the Caucasian race, as do the Turcomans, or wandering tribes north of Persia. According to Virey, the Tartars, upon physiognomical grounds, belong to the same family as the Monguls, of which they form only a subdivision.‖ Lacepède is extremely confused in his account, and first unites the Turks and Laplanders in one family, with the greater part of the Tartars, as members of the Caucasian race, then throws into the other "the Tartars, properly called the Monguls."¶ Blumenbach clearly distinguishes the two, referring

---

* "History of the Monguls," p. 27.
† Ritter, "Erdkunde in Verhältniss sur Natur und zur Geschichte des Menschen," 2 Th. ii. Buch, Asien, 1 Band, pp. 241-283. Dr. Prichard considers the Turks and Tartars as historically one race.— "Researches," vol. ii. p. 283.
‡ "Recherches," &c. Discours prélim. p. xxxvii.
§ Klaproth, "Asia Polyglotta," p. 255. Balbi, "Atlas Ethnog." No. viii.
‖ *Ubi sup.* p. 413.
¶ "Dictionnaire des Sciences naturelles," tom. xxi. art. Homme, p. 385.

the Tartars to the Caucasian family, although he acknowledges, that, through the Kirghis, they run insensibly into the Mongul variety. Dr. Prichard makes the same distinction, but supposes that this resemblance never occurs without an intermixture of blood.* The same seems to be the opinion of Pallas, who observes, that "the Monguls have nothing in common with the Tartars, except their nomadic or wandering life, and some resemblance of language. The Monguls," he continues, "differ as much from the Tartars, as the negroes from the Moors, in customs, political institutions, and features." But he likewise acknowledges that the Monguls have, by their emigrations and wars, communicated their features to the above-named, and other Tartar tribes.† This explanatory digression, concerning these nations, will not be without its use in what I have later to discuss: I shall, on the contrary, have occasion to refer to it for very important conclusions.

Before quitting this historical portion of my subject, it would be unjust not to mention a national writer, who has most ably and learnedly collected into one work all the historical and physical facts which can any way throw light upon the natural history of mankind. He examines each nation, or family of nations, distinctly, and from the observations of travellers and historians, endeavours to trace them from their original seats, and connect them with their cognate tribes. He is perhaps, too, the first writer who attempted to connect this science with the philological researches which formed the subject of our last lectures. If I had to find any fault, it would be, that the learned author does not draw consequences sufficiently definite and decisive from the mass of facts which he has collected: that the preliminary or introductory portion of the work is so far separated from

---

* "De Gener. Humani Variet." p. 306. Researches, *ibid*.
† *Ubi sup.* p. 486.

the particular data to which its principles are to be applied, that a reader, giving only ordinary attention to the book, will not easily seize the important conclusions which it has a right to suggest. It will, however, be difficult for any one in future to treat of this theme, without being indebted to Dr. Prichard for a great portion of his materials.

Having thus enumerated the authors, and explained the systems, which appear most deserving of our notice, as ranged on the side of truth, it is fair to state who are our opponents, and what are their views of this science. They are to be found chiefly among French naturalists, who, unfortunately, are yet, in part at least, unreclaimed from the sceptical theories of the last century. Voltaire, in fact, was one of the first to observe, that " none but a blind man can doubt, that the whites, negroes, albinos, Hottentots, Laplanders, Chinese, and Americans, are entirely distinct races."* Desmoulins, in an Essay, which, to the credit of the Académie des Sciences, was rejected by that learned body, asserts the existence of eleven independent families of the human race.† Mons. Bory de Saint-Vincent goes farther still, and increases the number to fifteen, which are again considerably subdivided. Thus the Adamic family, or the descendants of Adam, constitute only the second division of the Arabic species of man, the *homo Arabicus;* while we, the English, belong to the Teutonic variety of the Germanic race, which is again but the fourth fraction of the *gens braccata*, or small-clothes-wearing family of the Japhetic species, the *homo Japheticus*, who is divided into the above mentioned class and another, somewhat more elegantly cognizanced, namely, the *gens togata*, or cloaked family ‡

---

* " Histoire de Russie sous Pierre le Grand," c. 1.
† " Histoire Naturelle des Races Humaines."
‡ " Dictionnaire classique d'Histoire Naturelle," tom. viii. *Par.* 1825, pp. 293 and 287. The Japhetic man is himself only a division of the Leiotric or close-haired race. The unity of origin of the fifteen races is denied, p. 331.

Virey belongs to the same school; though his works are even more revolting, from the light and wanton manner in which the most delicate points of morals and religion are handled throughout. Not content with attributing to the negro a different origin from the European, he goes so far as almost to suspect a certain fraternity between the Hottentot and the baboon.* But on this subject Lamarck has gone much farther, and attempted to point out the steps whereby nature proceeds, or, in former times, did proceed, towards gradually developing one class of beings from another, so as to establish a graduated chain, not of simultaneous, but of successive links; and thus produced in the end the human species, by a metamorphosis, the inverse indeed, but not for that the less marvellous, of what we read in ancient fable. The two volumes of his *Philosophie Zoologique* are entirely directed to support this degrading theory; the first, to prove how man's bodily organization sprung from a casual though natural modification of the ape; the second, to show that the spiritual prerogatives of the human mind are but the extension of the faculties enjoyed by brutes, and only differ in quantity from their reasoning powers.† Lamarck assumes, upon slight and ill-supported grounds, that because we see in nature an existing gradation of organized beings, there must also have been a successive development, whereby animals of one class might rise into another; inasmuch as any animal, being driven, by its wants, to new or peculiar habits, thereby acquires the variation of organization necessary for them, although

* Op. cit. tom. ii. p. 157.
† "Philosophie Zoologique; ou, Exposition des considérations relatives à l'histoire naturelle des animaux, par J. B. Lamarck:" *Paris*, 1830. See, for this point particularly, tom. ii. p. 445. I may here observe, that Steffens denies altogether the existence of a graduated scale of beings, inasmuch as, to support it, according to him, the lowest animals should come next to the most perfect plants, whereas the links between the two orders possess the lowest qualities of each, as polypi, infusoria, algæ, &c.; the organization of all which, whether in reference to the vegetable or animal kingdom, is of the lowest kind.—Anthropologie, ii. Buch, p. 6.

generations must persevere in their exercise before the effect is perceptible. Thus, for instance, a bird is driven by its wants to take to the water, and either swim or wade; its successors do the same; in the course of many generations, the outstretching of its claws produces a web between them, and it becomes a regular waterfowl; or it extends its limbs to walk in deeper places, and gradually its legs are prolonged to the length of the crane's or the flamingo's.* These two agencies combined, new wants, and the tendency of nature to meet them, conspired to make man out of the baboon. One race of these, probably the Angola Orang, from some unrecorded reason, lost the habit of climbing trees, or holding by their hind as well as by their fore limbs. After thus walking on the ground for many generations, the former changed into a shape more suited to their habits, and became feet, and they gradually acquired the habit of walking erect. They now no longer needed their jaws for cropping fruit or for fighting with one another, having their fore feet or hands now disposable for these purposes; and hence, by degrees, their snouts shortened, and their face became more vertical. Advancing still further in this road to humanization, their grin subsided into a courtly smile, and their jabbering resolved itself into articulate sounds. "Such," he concludes, "would be the reflections which might be made, if man were distinguished from animals only by the character of his organization, and if his origin were not different from theirs."† Unfortunately, however, his second volume disposes of any other proof that man had a different origin. I hardly need detain you to confute this scheme; I will content myself with remarking, that the experience of thousands of years has abundantly disproved it. How comes it that we

---

* Tom. i. p. 249. If some birds, he says (p. 251), which swim, have long necks, as the swan and goose, it is from their custom of plunging their heads in the water to fish. Why, then, we may ask, has not the same habit produced a like effect in the duck or teal?
† Page 357.

can discover no instance of any such developments as Lamarck assumes, during this long period of observation? The bee has been striving without intermission in the art of making its sweet confection, since the days of Aristotle; the ant has been constructing its labyrinths, since Solomon recommended its example: but from the time they were described by the philosopher and the sage, till the beautiful researches of the Hubers, we are certain that they have not acquired a new perception, or a new organ for these purposes. Egypt, which, as the learned commission of French naturalists well observed, has preserved for us a museum of natural history, not only in its paintings, but in the mummies of its animals, presents us every species, after three thousand years, perfectly unchanged. What striving has there not been in man, and is there not particularly now, after new resources, after new powers, and after a greater range in the use of his senses! and yet, alas! not the sprouting of a new limb, not the expansion of a single organ, not the opening of a single new channel of perception, begins as yet to give us hope, after many thousands of years, that we shall yet reach a higher step in the scale of progressive improvement, or recede somewhat farther from our consanguinity with the chattering ape.*

It is now time to proceed, from the history and principles of this study, to its discoveries and results. In making you acquainted with these, and with their bearing upon what religion teaches regarding the origin of mankind, I will follow what appears to me the simplest and most satisfactory method. I will condense these results into a compendious essay upon the subject, bringing together the observations and discoveries of modern authors, interspersed with such facts as I have myself collected, and freely communicating my own

---

* See a very full confutation of Lamarck's system in Lyell's "Principles of Geology," vol. ii. p. 18: *Lond*. 1830. Lamarck, however, denies that his theory is at all affected by the animals found in Egypt, tom. i. p. 70.

reflections. By this means, I hope to put you in possession of all that can interest you on this important, but yet not perfectly elucidated, subject.

The great problem to be solved is, How could such varieties as we have seen, have taken their rise in the human species? Was it by a sudden change, which altered some portion of one great family into another; or are we to suppose a gradual *degradation*, as naturalists call it, whereby some nations or families passed gradually through successive shades, from one extreme to the other? And, in either case, which is to be considered the original stock? It must be owned, that the present state of this science does not warrant us in expressly deciding in favour of either hypothesis, nor, consequently, in even discussing the last consequence. But, independently of this, it has arrived so far as to leave no reasonable room to doubt the common origin of every race.

For, I think we may say, after looking through all that has been done in this yet infant science, that the following points, embracing all the elements of the problem, have been satisfactorily solved. First, that accidental, or, as they are called, sporadic varieties, may arise in one race, tending to produce in it the characteristics of another; secondly, that these varieties may be perpetuated; thirdly, that climate, food, civilization, &c., may strongly influence the production of such varieties, or at least render them fixed, characteristic, and perpetual. I say that these points, if proved, embrace all the elements of the proposed problem, which is, " *Could* such varieties as we now see in the human race, have sprung up from one stock?" For if this is demonstrated, we have removed the grounds whereon the adversaries of revelation deny the unity of origin which it teaches. And, moreover, every sound philosopher will, if unobjectionable, prefer the simpler to the more complex hypothesis. In treating these points, it will be almost impossible to keep them completely unmixed, especially the two first; but no inconvenience will, I trust, result from their running into one another.

The ground, before closing directly with the inquiry, is in general prepared, by writers on this science, by examining the laws which nature has followed in regard to the lower orders of creation. To begin, for instance, with plants, every observation leads us more and more to the conclusion, that each species takes its rise from some common centre, whence it has gradually been propagated. The observations made by Humboldt and Bonpland in South America, by Pursh in the United States, and by Brown in New Holland, have furnished Decandolle with sufficient materials to attempt with success a geographical distribution of plants, showing the centre whence each probably proceeded. He has enumerated twenty botanical provinces, as he calls them, inhabited by indigenous or aboriginal plants. It is not, therefore, wonderful, that when America was first discovered, not a single plant should have been there found which was known in the old world, except such as could have had their seeds transmitted through the waters of the ocean. In the United States, out of 2,891 species of plants, only 385 are found in Northern Europe; and out of 4,100 species discovered in New Holland, only 166 are common to our countries; and of these many have been planted by the settlers.* This shows at once the tendency of nature to simplicity and unity in its origin of things; while the varieties that spring up in the vegetable world, under the influence of outward circumstances, demonstrate the existence of a modifying influence in constant action.

But the analogy between animals and man is closer and more applicable. The physical organization of

* See Lyell's able chapter on this subject, vol. ii. p. 66; and Prichard, vol. i. c. 2, sec. 2, p. 23. For the points of resemblance in the organization of plants and animals, see Camper's dissertation on that subject, "Oratio de Analogia inter Animalia et Stirpes." *Gröning.* 1764.

both classes of animated beings is so similar, the laws whereby their individuals and their races are preserved are so identical, their subjection to the laws of morbid influences, to the operation of natural causes, and, under the different names of domestication and civilization, to the agency of artificial combinations, is so analogous, that we have almost a right to argue from the one's actual, to the other's possible, modifications.

Now, it is certain and obvious, that animals, acknowledged to form one species, under peculiar circumstances, divide into varieties as distinct as those observable in the human species. For instance, as to the shape of the skull, those of the mastiff and Italian greyhound differ from one another far more than those of the European and negro: and yet, every criterion which can be given of species, will comprehend the two extremes, between which a chain of intermediate gradations can be clearly established. The skull, too, of the wild boar, as Blumenbach has observed, does not differ less from the tame swine's, its undoubted descendant, than those of any two human races from one another.* In every species of domestic cattle, varieties as striking will be found.

Changes in the colour and structure of the hair, are no less ordinary and remarkable. All the fowls in Guinea, and the dogs, too, according to Beckman, are as black as the inhabitants.† The ox of the Roman campagna is invariably grey, while in some other parts of Italy the breed is mostly red; swine and sheep are also here chiefly black, while in England white is their prevailing hue. In Corsica, horses, dogs, and other animals, become beautifully spotted, and the carriage-dog, as it is called, belongs to that country. Many writers have attributed to particular rivers the quality of giving colour to the cattle on their banks. Thus Vitruvius observes that the rivers of Bœotia, and the

---

* Op. cit. p. 80.
† "Voyage to and from Borneo:" *London*, 1718, p. 14.

Xanthus near Troy, gave a yellow colour to their herds, whence the river Xanthus took its name.* Mr. Stewart Rose, in his *Letters from the North of Italy*, says, that a similar quality is attributed to the Po, at the present day.† And many of you will here probably remember the white herds of the beautiful Clitumnus, as described by the poet:

> "Hinc albi, Clitumne, greges, et maxima taurus
> Victima, sæpe tuo perfusi flumine sacro,
> Romanos ad templa Deûm duxere triumphos."‡

The texture of the hair undergoes similar changes. Every attempt to produce wool in the West Indies has, I believe, failed, because sheep, if transported thither, entirely lose their wool, and become covered with hair.§ This is the same in other hot climates. "The sheep in Guinea," says Smith, "have so little resemblance to those in Europe, that a stranger, unless he heard them bleat, could hardly tell what animals they were, being covered only with light brown and black hair, like a dog:" so that a fanciful writer observes: "here the world seems inverted, for the sheep are hairy, and the men woolly."‖ A similar phenomenon

---

* "Sunt enim Bœotiæ flumina Cephysus et Melas, Leucaniæ Crathis, Trojæ Xanthus, &c. . . . . cum pecora suis temporibus anni parantur ad conceptionem partus, per id tempus adiguntur eo quotidie potum, ex eoque, quamvis sint alba, procreant aliis locis leucophæa, aliis pulla, aliis coracino colore. Igitur quoniam in Trojanis proxime flumen armenta rufa, et pecora leucophæa nascuntur; ideo id flumen Ilienses Xanthum appellavisse dicuntur."—Architect. l. viii. c. iii. p. 162, edit. De Laet. *Amst.* 1649. In the notes to this passage are added confirmatory authorities from Pliny, Theophrastus, Strabo, &c.; some evidently run into fable. Aristotle, "De Historia Animal." l. iii., gives the same etymology of the river Xanthus.

† "Letters from the North of Italy:" *Lond.* 1819, vol. i. p. 23. The idea of the natives is, "that not only the indigenous beasts are white (or, to speak more precisely, cream-coloured), but that even foreign beeves put on the same livery on drinking the Po."

‡ Virgil, "Georg." ii. 146.
§ Prichard, *ib.* p. 226.
‖ Smith, "New Voyage to Guinea:" *Lond.* 1745, p. 147. "New General Collection of Voyages and Travels," vol. ii. : *Lond.* 1745, p. 711.

occurs in the country round Angora, where almost every animal, sheep, goats, rabbits, and cats, are covered with a beautiful long, silken hair, so celebrated in Oriental manufactures. Other animals are subject to this change; for Bishop Heber informs us, that "dogs and horses carried into the hills from India, are soon covered with wool, like the shawl-goats of that climate."*

And if we look to the general form and structure of animals, we shall find them subject to the greatest variations. None shows this more clearly than the ox, simply because on none have art and domestication been tried to a greater extent. What a contrast there is between the slow, massive, long-horned animal, which traverses the Roman streets, and the small-headed, clean-limbed breed, which an English farmer most prizes! According to Bosman, "European dogs soon degenerate to a strange degree on the Gold Coast: their ears grow long and stiff, like a fox's, to the colour of which animal they also incline; so that they grow very ugly in three or four years, and in. as many broods their barking turns to a howl or yelp." Barbot says, in like manner, that the native "dogs are very ugly, being much like our foxes, with long upright ears; their tails long, small, and sharp at the end, without any hair, having only a naked, bare skin, either plain or spotted, and never bark, but only howl. The blacks call them *cabre de matto*, which in Portuguese signifies a wild goat, because they eat them, and value their flesh beyond mutton."† Thus it appears that climate or other local circumstances have the effect, in this instance, of reducing, in a few generations, a breed of animals brought from another country, to the same condition as the native race, so as to be quite distinct, and hardly traceable to its original stock. The camel likewise presents an example of extraordinary modifica-

---

* "Narrative of a Journey through the Upper Provinces of India," 2nd edit. : *Lond.* 1828, vol. ii. p. 219.
† "New Collection of Voyages," &c., p. 712.

tions. "In some caravans which we passed," says a late traveller, "were camels of a much larger kind than any I had ever seen before, and as different in their forms and proportions from the camel of Arabia, as a mastiff is from a greyhound. These camels had large heads and thick necks, from the under edge of which depended a long, shaggy, dark-brown hair; their legs were short, their joints thick, and their carcasses and haunches round and fleshy, though they stood at least a foot higher from the ground than the common camels of the Arabian desert."* And, speaking of this animal, I may observe, that its great characteristic, the hump upon its back, which in the Bactrian variety is doubled, is supposed by some naturalists to be an accidental deviation from the original type, arising from a sebaceous or fatty deposit in the cellular tissue of the back, in consequence of exposure to heat; just like the hunch on the zebu or Indian ox, or the tail of the Barbary and Syrian sheep, or the similar formation on the loins of the Bosjman Hottentots.†

These examples, in which I have rather sought to add to those adduced by others, than to repeat what have been already collected, prove that sporadic, or accidental, varieties, may not only be produced, but, what is much more to our purpose, may be propagated among animals. Nor would it be difficult to multiply instances of this last fact; for the great dissemination of albino animals, as white rabbits, or cream-coloured horses, which probably rose originally from disease, proves how well such casual varieties may be reproduced. But Dr. Prichard gives one example, which is very remarkable, that of a breed of sheep reared, within a few years, in England, and known by the name of the *ancon* or otter breed. It sprang up from an accidental variety, or, we may say, deformity, in

---

* "Travels in Assyria, Media, and Persia," by J. S. Buckingham, 2nd edit.: *Lond.* 1830, vol. i. p. 241.
† Levaillant, "Second Voyage," tom. ii. p. 207. Virey, tom. i. p. 218.

one animal, which communicated its peculiarities so completely to its progeny, that the breed is completely established, and promises to be perpetual; indeed, it is highly valued on account of the shortness of its legs, which does not allow it easily to get through fences.* It is well known, also, that the breed of cattle which produced the enormous Durham ox, was artificially produced, by crossing it with such as seemed to present fine points of every sort, the basis being the kyloe, or small Highland breed; and all the cattle that arrive at any extraordinary dimensions, are connected with this race.

The reasonings sanctioned by these facts, present a strong ground of analogy, applicable to the human species; nor is it easy to see why varieties as great may not have been produced, and transmitted by descent, among men, as among inferior animals. For it thus appears certain, that diversities, equally affecting the form of the skull, the colour and texture of the hair, and the general form of the body, do arise among animals of one stock; further, it seems proved that such differences may originally spring from some casual variety, which, owing to peculiar circumstances, becomes fixed and characteristic, and transmissible by descent. May we not, then, consider it as highly probable, that, in the human species, the same causes may similarly operate, and produce no less lasting effects? And that such variations as appear within it, being no more asunder from one another, than such as in the brute creation have been noted, require no more violent or extraordinary agency to account for them? But let us now come nearer to the point, and take the matter more closely in hand.

It seems, then, to me clear, that in each family, or race, of the human species, there are occasionally produced varieties tending to establish within it the characteristics of some other. For example, red hair is

* Vol. ii. p. 550.

considered almost exclusively confined to the Caucasian family; yet individuals exist in almost every known variety with this peculiarity. Charlevoix observed it among the Esquimaux, Sonnerat among the Papuans, Wallis among the Tahitans, and Lopes among the negroes.* This is no more surprising than that amongst us individuals should be found with frizzled hair; and, I think, those who have paid attention to such things, will have often observed in such persons a tendency towards some other characteristics of the Ethiopian family, as a dark complexion and thick lips. In the specimens of craniums published by Blumenbach, from his Museum, there is one of a Lithuanian, which, viewed in profile, might well be mistaken for a negro's.† But the most curious example which I have met of sporadic tendency to produce in one human race the characteristics of another, is in a recent traveller, almost the first who explored the Hauran, or district beyond the Jordan. He writes as follows:—"The family residing here (at Abu-el-Beady) in charge of the sanctuary, were remarkable for having, with the exception of the father only, negro features, a deep black colour, and crisped hair. My own opinion was, that this must have been occasioned by their being born of a negress mother, as such persons are sometimes found among the Arabs, in the relation of wives or concubines; but while I could entertain no doubt, from my own observation, that the present head of the family was a pure Arab of unmixed blood, I was also assured, that both the males and females of the present and former generations were all pure Arabs by descent and marriage, and that a negress had never been known, either as a wife or slave, in the history of the family. It is certainly a very marked peculiarity of the Arabs that inhabit the valley of the Jordan, that they have flatter features, darker skins, and coarser hair, than any other tribes; a peculiarity rather attributable, I

---

* Blumenbach, p. 169.
† " Decades Craniorum," dec. 3a, pl. xxii. p. 6.

conceive, to the constant and intense heat of that region, than to any other cause."* If all the facts and circumstances here given can be considered sufficiently verified, we have certainly a very striking instance of approximation in individuals of one family, to the distinctives of another, and of these distinctives being transmitted by descent.

There are, indeed, examples of much more decided and stranger varieties arising among men, than what constitute the specific characteristics of any race, and of such being continued from father to son;—such varieties as would have made the problem in hand far more difficult to solve than at present it is, had they sprung up in a distant quarter of the globe, and been extended to any considerable population. The most remarkable of these is doubtless what has been traced through three generations in the family of Lambert, commonly known by the name of the *porcupine-man*. The founder of this extraordinary race was first exhibited as a boy by his father in 1731, and came from the neighbourhood of Euston Hall, in Suffolk. Mr. Machin in that year described him in the *Philosophical Transactions*, as having his body covered with warts as thick as packthread, and half an inch long: the name, however, is not given.† In 1755, he was again exhibited with the forenamed title, and was described by Mr. Baker, in a paper purporting to be a supplement to the former. But what is important is, that, being now forty years of age, he had had six children, every one of whom, at the same period, nine weeks after birth, had presented the same peculiarity; and the only surviving one, a boy eight years old, was exhibited with his father. Mr. Baker gives a drawing of the boy's hand, as Mr. Machin had before of his father's.‡ In

---

* Buckingham's "Travels among the Arab Tribes:" *London*, 1825, p. 14.
† "On an uncommon Case of a distempered Skin," by John Machin, "Philosophical Transactions," vol. xxxvii. for 1731-2, p. 299.
‡ *Ibid.* vol. xlix. p. 21.

1802, the children of this boy were exhibited in Germany, by a Mons. and Mde. Joanny, who pretended that they belonged to a race found in New Holland, or some other very remote place. Dr. Tilesius, however, examined them most minutely, and published the most accurate account we have of this singular family, with full-length figures of the two brothers, John, who was twenty-one, and Richard, who was thirteen years of age.* Their father, the boy of Mr. Baker's narrative, was still alive, and was gamekeeper to Lord Huntingfield, at Heaveningham Hall, in Suffolk. Upon being shown the drawing of his hand in the *Philosophical Transactions*, they both instantly recognized it by the peculiar button at the wrist.† Tilesius's description, from page 30 to the end of his work, is most minute, and corresponds exactly with that given of their progenitors. The whole of the body, excepting the palms of the hands, the soles of the feet, and the face, was covered with a series of horny excrescences of a reddish brown, hard, elastic, and about half an inch long, which rustled against one another, when rubbed with the hand. I do not know to what I can compare the appearance of this singular integument, as given in Tilesius's plates, better than to a collection of basaltic prisms, some longer, some shorter, as they are generally grouped in nature. Once a year this horny clothing was shed, and its falling off was accompanied with some degree of uneasiness; it yielded also to the action of mercury, which was tried for the purpose; but in both cases it gradually returned after a very short period.‡ The conclusions which Mr. Baker draws from this extraordinary phenomenon, are very just, and have still greater weight now, that it has been reproduced in another generation, and in two distinct instances. "It appears, therefore," says he, "past

---

* "Ausführliche Beschreibung und Abbildung der beiden so genannten Stachelschweinmenschen, aus der bekannten englischen Familie Lambert." *Altenburg*, 1802, fol.
† Page 4.
‡ "Philosophical Transactions," vol. xlix. p. 22.

all doubt, that a race of people may be propagated by this man, having such rugged coats or coverings as himself; and if this should happen, and the accidental origin be forgotten, 'tis not impossible they might be deemed a different species of mankind: a consideration which would almost lead one to imagine, that if mankind were produced from one and the same stock, the black skin of the negroes, and many other differences of a like kind, might possibly have been originally owing to some such accidental cause."[*]

Another more common variety which runs in entire families, consists in supernumerary fingers. In ancient Rome it was designated by a peculiar name; and the *Sedigiti* are mentioned by Pliny and other eminent authors. Sir A. Carlisle has carefully traced the history of one such family through four generations. Its name was Colburn, and the peculiarity was brought into the family by the great-grandmother of the youngest examined; it was not regular, but only attached to some children in each generation. Maupertius has mentioned other instances in Germany; and a celebrated surgeon at Berlin, Jacob Ruhe, belonged to a family with this peculiarity by the mother's side.[†]

Thus far, then, we have proved, both from analogy and from direct examples: first, that there is a perpetual tendency, I might say a striving, in nature, to raise up in our species varieties, often of a very extraordinary character, sometimes approximating, in a marked manner, to the peculiar and specific distinctives of a race different to that in which they arise; and secondly, that these peculiarities may be communicated through successive generations, from father to son. A strong presumptive evidence is thus obtained, that the different families or races among men, may owe their origin to some similar occurrence; to the casual rise of a variety which, under the influence of favourable circumstances—the isolation, for instance, of the family in which it began, and its

[*] "Philosophical Transactions," vol. xlix. p. 22.
[†] *Ibid.* vol. civ. 1814, part i. p. 94. Prichard, vol. ii. p. 537.

consequent intermarriages—became fixed and indelible in succeeding generations.

But you will ask, Have we any instance of whole nations having been so changed? or, in other words, have we any example of these two deductions in operation on a larger scale? To answer this question, you will allow will be closing at once with all the difficulties of the subject; and I know not where I shall better be able to interrupt the handling of this matter, than at the point we have now reached.

In treating of this science, we are unfortunately precluded from using a series of arguments, which greatly affect its results—those moral resemblances between men of every race, which could hardly be found among creatures of independent stock. I have entirely omitted, as unnecessary, the usual discussions of zoologists and physiologists, as to what is sufficient or necessary to constitute distinctness of race. For I think that, passing over the technicality of such an inquiry, as unfit for our purpose, we are safe in considering animals of different species, when we discover in them habits and characters, if I may use the expression, of a totally different nature. The wolf and the lamb are not more distinguished from one another by their outward covering, and their different features, than by the contrast between their dispositions. And if this should appear to you like a comparison of extremes, I will say that the rude ferocity of the wolf, and the prowling cunning of the fox,—the gregarious and tumultuary aggression of the one, and the solitary pilfering of the other,—more clearly serve to classify them to our minds, than the difference of their forms. Now, if we look at man in the most dissimilar states of social life, however brutalized or however cultivated, we shall certainly find that there is an approximation of feeling, a similarity of affections, and a facility of adaptation, which clearly shows that the faculty corresponding to the instinct of animals, is identical through the entire race. The Mohawks and Ossages, the inhabitants of the

Sandwich or the Pellew Islands, by short intercourse with Europeans, especially when brought into our countries, have learnt to adapt themselves to all the proprieties of life as understood by us, and formed attachments and friendships of the most affectionate nature, with men of another race. The difference of organization in animals is always connected with their difference of character; the groove which any single muscle makes upon the bones of the lion, shows its habits and nature; the smallest bone in the antelope exhibits a reference to its timid and fugitive disposition. But in man, whether for generations he have dozed away his days, like a listless Asiatic on the corner of his divan, or, like an American hunter, has for ages tired the wild deer in the trackless forest by his restless chase, there is nothing in his organization to show, that, through custom or education, he might not have exchanged one occupation for another,—nothing to prove that nature intended him for either state.

On the contrary, the similarity of moral attributes; the enduring power of domestic affections; the disposition to establish and maintain mutual interest; the common feelings regarding property and the methods of protecting it, notwithstanding occasional deviation; the accordance upon the leading points of the moral code; and, more than all, the holy gift of speech, which secures the perpetuation of all other human characteristics, prove that men, wherever situated, however degraded they may now appear, were certainly destined for the same state, and consequently therein originally placed. And this consideration ought surely to possess great weight towards establishing in man, as its parallel one does in other animals, an identity of origin.

This reasoning is of course opposed to the popular theory of ordinary philosophers; that the natural progress of man is from barbarism to civilization, and that the savage must be considered the original type of human nature, from which we have departed by gradual efforts. But the reasoning I have pursued; the reflection that nature, or rather its Author, will place His creatures in the state for which He intended them; that, if man were formed in body, and endowed in spirit, for a social and domestic life, he can have been no more cast originally into a desert or a forest, savage and untutored, than the sea-shell can have been first produced on the mountain's top, or the elephant been created amidst the icebergs of the pole; this reflection must exclude the idea that the savage state is any but a degradation, a departure from the original destiny and position of man. Such is the view taken by the learned Frederick Schlegel, in a valuable work, which I am glad to see a respected and learned friend of mine has at length presented to our countrymen in their own tongue: and I hope he will receive such encouragement in his undertaking, as may lead him to complete the task, by translating the later works of that philosopher.

"When man," says he, "had once fallen from virtue, no determinable limit could be assigned to his degradation, nor how far he might descend by degrees, and approximate even to the level of the brute; but as from his origin he was a being essentially free, he was in consequence capable of change, and even in his organic powers most flexible. We must adopt this principle, as the only clue to guide us in our inquiries, from the negro, who as well from his bodily strength and agility, as from his docile and, in general, excellent character, is far from occupying the lowest grade in the scale of humanity, down to the monstrous Patagonian, the almost imbecile Peshwerais, and the horrible cannibal of New Zealand, whose very portrait excites a shudder in the beholder. So far from seeking, with Rousseau and his disciples, for the true origin of mankind, and the proper foundations of the social compact, in the condition even of the best and noblest savages, we regard it, on the contrary, as a state of degeneracy and degradation."*

* "Philosophy of History," translated by J. B. Robertson, Esq. *London*, 1835, vol. i. pp. 48, 49.

This, assuredly, is more consoling to humanity than the degrading theories of Virey or Lamarck; and yet there is immixed therewith some slight bitterness of humiliation. For, if it was revolting to think that our noble nature should be nothing more than the perfecting of the ape's maliciousness, yet is it not without some shame and sorrow that we see that nature anywhere sunk and degraded from its original beauty, till men should have been able plausibly to sustain that odious affinity? Yet may this be of "sweet use" to us, in checking that pride which the superiority of our civilization too often excites, by recalling to our minds, that, if we and the lowest savage are but brethren of one family, we are, even as they, of a lowly origin, and they, as we, have the sublimest destiny; that, in the words of the divine poet, we are all equally

> ——" worms, yet made at last to form
> The wingèd insect imped with angel plumes
> That to heaven's justice unobstructed soars."*

And some such composition, some such scheme of being, whereby the twofold alliance of man to a superior and an inferior world, should be shown, some such variety of state, as might prove the existence of conflicting powers, of one which calleth him upwards by the expansion of his faculties, and of one which weighs him towards the enjoyment of the mere animal life, seems natural and necessary for his complex being. For thus, to conclude with the eloquent words of a triuy Christian philosopher, " man stands as a living individuality, composed of nature and spirit, of outward and inward being, of necessity and freedom; to himself a mystery, to the world of spirits an object of deep thought, of

---

* " O superbi cristiani, miseri lassi,
Che della virtù della mente infermi
Fidanza avete ne' ritrosi passi,
Non vi accorgete voi che noi siam vermi
Nati a formar l' angelica forfalla,
Che vola alla giustizia senza schermi ?"—*Purgat.* x.

God's almightiness, wisdom, and love, the perfectest witness. Veiled round by his corporeal nature, he sees God as at a distance, and is as certain of his existence as the heavenly spirit,—the son of revelation, and the hero of faith, who is weak, and yet strong, poor, and yet possessor of the highest empire of love divine."[*]

[*] Pabst, "Der Mensch und seine Geschichte:" *Vienna*, 1830, p. 50.

LECTURE THE FOURTH;

ON THE

NATURAL HISTORY OF THE HUMAN RACE.

PART II.

RESULTS.—Application of Linguistic Ethnography to this Study.—Proof that nations shown to be of a common stock by their languages, have deviated from the family type: in the Mongul race, and in the Caucasian.—Origin of the negro race: Climate an insufficient cause.—Collection of facts to prove a change to the black colour possible: the Abyssinians, Souakin Arabs, Congoese, Foulahs, &c.—Apparent example of actual transition. Objections answered.—Effects of civilization: Selluks, Monguls, Germans.—Modification and suspension of causes formerly in action.—Connections of the different races: internal division into graduated shades of difference in each; Polynesians, Malays, inhabitants of Italy.—On the type of national art.—Reflections applicable to the Christian Evidences, in reference to the authenticity of the Gospel, and the perfection of our Saviour's character.

IN my last lecture, I contented myself with the analogies which seemed to bear upon the subject of our inquiry, and endeavoured to prove, both from parallel phenomena in the lower departments of organized creation, and from the deviations occasionally observed in our own species, that a strong probability existed in favour of the varieties found in the human race having all sprung up from the same stock; and I promised, on our next meeting, forthwith to close with the question, and treat of it more directly. I wish, therefore, to prove, that a transition must, some time or other, have taken place in entire nations, from one family to another. And to effect this purpose, I must call in the assistance of a new test, for which our two first conferences will have prepared you—the comparative study of languages.

I suppose no one has yet doubted, or is likely to doubt, that nations speaking languages with a strong affinity between them, must originally have been united somehow together. Even those who deny the common origin of the human race, allow that identity or similarity, and, particularly, strong grammatical affinity, of language, between nations however distant, cannot be the result of chance, but proves some real connection of origin, or early relationship. This, even if it had not been mathematically proved by Dr. Young, as, on a former occasion, I showed you, is self-evident; for the relationship which I exposed to you between some languages, the Sanskrit, for instance, and Greek, cannot possibly have been the result of accident. Hence, if two nations speak, and have spoken, as far as history can reach, dialects of the same tongue, we must conclude them to have had a common origin; unless one of them, at least, can be shown to have changed its language, an hypothesis always requiring the strongest evidence; for experience proves the extraordinary tenacity with which even small communities keep hold of their original language. The *Sette Comuni*, a small German colony established, beyond the reach of historical documents, in the north of Italy, the Greeks of Piana dei Greci, near Palermo, the Flemish clothiers in Wales, settled there for many centuries, all retain dialects, more or less impure, of their mother tongue, and afford some of the many proofs which might be brought, how difficult it is to root out any language.

Having thus established one fixed and unalterable element, it affords a certain test whether the other has remained unchanged; or, to speak more plainly, if identity of speech infallibly proves two nations to have been originally one, and yet they differ from one another in physical characteristics, to such an extent as to be now classified in different races, these characteristics must

K

thereby be proved liable to change, for one of the nations must have lost its original type. Now I think it can be proved, that the boundaries of the twofold classification of men, according to language, and according to form and feature, no longer coincide; and as they must have once run together, and as that of language has remained unvaried, we must conclude that the other has undergone a change. Nay, I think we shall be able to go even farther; for while no instance has yet been brought, nor ever will nor can be, of any people, either by gradual transition, or by voluntary impulse, transferring its language from one family to another, we may perhaps surprise nature in her other order of classification, at the moment of effecting a transition from one family to another, by discovering examples of an intermediate state between any two, or of the processes whereby it has sometimes been produced.

In treating of the affinity of languages, I pointed out a remarkable connection, solidly demonstrated, between Hungarian and the languages of northern Europe, the Finnish, Lapponian, and Esthonian; and an inspection of the ethnographic map will show you how it is placed, like what geologists call outliers of peculiar strata, as a mass detached from the group to which it really belongs. But this relationship is still more extensive, and includes the Tchermisses, Votiaks, Ostiaks, more properly called As-jachs, and Permians, tribes now inhabiting the banks of the Oby, or even more eastern parts of Siberia.* But while no one doubts that all these tribes compose only one family, their physical traits are singularly distinct. They are all, indeed, remarkable for very low stature; but while several of these Uralian or Tschudish tribes, as the Laplanders, Tchermisses, Woguls, and Hungarians, have black hair and brown eyes, others, as the Finns, Permians, and As-jachs, have all, according to

---

* These languages form the Uralian family, in Balbi's ethnography, "Atlas Ethnogr." No. xv. See the ethnographic chart prefixed to this work.

Dobrowsky, red hair and blue eyes.* And this, too, appears worthy of observation, that as all these tribes belong to Blumenbach's Mongul family, so do we find the characteristics of this less plainly marked as we recede from its great seat, and those of the Germanic branch of the Caucasian family become prevalent as we approach its geographical centre. Here, then, assuredly, one portion or the other of the family must have varied from its primitive type, so as to overstep, to a certain degree, the boundary of the race to which it may be supposed to have belonged.

Another change may be, perhaps, traced in the same family. You doubtless remember, that, at our last meeting, I entered into rather a detailed explanation of the relation in which the Tartars and Monguls stand to each other, and I observed, that the best and most modern writers on the classification of languages, Abel-Rémusat, Balbi, Klaproth, and Pallas, place the two languages in the same family. I observed, also, that their own traditions represent them as descended from two brothers, and that in the eleventh century they formed two of a community of four cognate tribes. All this would surely seem to indicate a common origin, as far as it is traceable by historical, traditionary, and philological arguments. And yet it cannot be doubted, but that the extremes of the two nations, or families, are as dissimilar as possible, and that the Tartars belong to the Caucasian race.* It has been sometimes said, that the Turks owe their fine forms and heads to their great mixture of Circassian blood, introduced by their captive wives from that country. But this theory, which has been applied to other similar cases, can hardly be supported, if we consider that such an infusion of foreign blood could never reach the great mass of the nation, but must be confined to the rich, who alone could well be subject to the operation of this cause. I will show you later, that ages and ages of intermarriages

---

* Prichard, vol. ii. p. 266. † See page 122.

have not been able to obliterate the characteristic traits of the two nations anciently occupying Italy. But, besides this, we may observe, that the Osmanlis or Turks presented the same features, before the luxurious reason assigned could well have been in very active operation.*

But further, I before observed that some Tartar tribes, as the Kirghis, approach so nearly to the Mongul type, as to form a sort of intermediate step between them. This, again, Dr. Prichard attributes to intermarriages; but it would, I think, be difficult to establish the existence of this cause.

In Blumenbach's collection of skulls, we have one of a Yakut Tartar, which has all the characters of the Mongul race.† This may be only an individual case: but Dobell seems to allow that this tribe of Tartars approximate somewhat to the Monguls; for he observes, "There are credible proofs to adduce of their being descended from the Monguls, but their most probable origin is Tartar. . . . . A Yakut's features, and the expression of his countenance, partake more of the Tartar than of the Mongul race."‡

The race to which we belong presents a similar phenomenon. Whatever hypothesis we may choose to adopt, the prevalence of a language essentially the same from India to Iceland, proves the intermediate nations to be of common origin. Yet the inhabitants of the Indian peninsula differ from us in colour and shape, so materially as to be classified in another race. Klaproth, to account for this circumstance, imagines

---

* At least, if we suppose the custom to have begun only after the consolidation of Turkish power. An old historian thus describes Mohammed the Great, first emperor of the Turks : " His complexion was Tartar-like, sallow, and melancholy, as were most of his predecessors, the Othoman kings ; his looks and countenance sterne, with his eyes piercing, hollow, and a little sunk into his head ; and his nose so high and crooked, that it almost touched his upper lip."— Knolles " History of the Turks," 5th edit. p. 433.

† " Decad. i. Cranior." pl. xv. p. 10.

‡ " Travels in Kamtschatka and Siberia :" *Lond.* 1830, vol. ii. pp. 13, 14.

that the Indo-Germanic nations were saved from the Deluge on two chains of mountains, the Himalaya and the Caucasus. From the former, according to him, descended the Indians to the south, and the Goths to the north; from the other came the Medes, Persians, and Pelasgians. He then supposes the dark complexion of the Hindoos to have been produced by intermixture with a dusky race, who were there before them, having been saved from the same scourge upon the mountains of Malabar.* But all this is pure conjecture, without the slightest foundation either in history or in local tradition; and has been devised simply to escape from the difficulty, which is more easily met by allowing that a nation may change its characteristics, so as to pass into a different family from what its language proves was its original stock.

These examples will, however, by no means satisfy you that the two extremes, the black and the white race, can ever have been one: for the red or tawny cannot be considered an intermediate step, and we must look for examples of direct transition from one extreme to the other: and this assuredly is the hardest knot we have to untie in this inquiry. I will not speak of the great discussions held by many authors as to the original colour of the human race; many, as Labat, considering it to have been red;† either because the name of the first man signifies, in Hebrew, that colour, or, as Bishop Heber conjectures, because undomesticated animals tend towards it.‡ Blumenbach supposes the original colour was white; and if I might venture to give an argument in favour of this opinion, I should say that every

---

* "In Indien hat sich derselbe ganz mit früheren dunkelfarbigen Bewohnern vermischt, und seine Sprache herschend gemacht, dabei aber seine charakteristischen physischen Kennzeichen eingebüsst. Die brauen oder negerartigen Urbewohner von Indien retteten sich wahrscheinlich, zur Zeit der Noahischen Fluth, auf die hohen Gebirgen von Malabar, und den Ghauts."—Asia Polygl. p. 43.
† See Labat, "Nouvelle Relation de l'Afrique:" *Paris*, 1728, tom. ii. p. 257.
‡ *Ubi sup.* vol. i. p. 69.

departure from this hue bears the mark of an excess, or of a morbid affection. Alpinus has proved that the seat of the negro's colour is not in the outward skin, which is in him as colourless as in us, but in the fine tissue situated under it, and known in anatomy by the name of the tissue or net of Malpighi.* This tissue in the black is the seat of a dark pigment, and in the albino is said to be filled with cysts or small bags, containing a white substance which gives their peculiar colour: though Buzzi, in his account of the examination of an albino after death, says he could find no trace of the tissue at all.† It would appear, therefore, that the white, placed between two contrary deviations, should be the natural or normal state.

The ancients took the simple expedient of attributing the negro's colour to the action of the sun. That climate taken in reference to its progressive degrees of heat, has an influence on the tint of the skin, is so far true, that we see a certain ratio exist between the two. Generally speaking, the whitest races are nearer the pole, and the darkest are more under the influence of tropical heat: and between these two extremes we may trace many intermediate steps, as from the Dane to the Frenchman; after whom may come the Spaniard or Italian, then the Moor, and so the Negro.‡ But this endeavour to establish a chain of graduation in colour, has to encounter two serious difficulties. First, in all these degrees, the tint is too evidently the result of an outward action upon the skin, the effects whereof can be moderated or suspended by precautions against heat. The Moorish females who keep the house, are almost perfectly white; but the negro child begins to become black when ten days old, however it may be sheltered from the heat; the action, therefore, in the first case is

---

* "De Sede et Causa Coloris Æthiopum:" *Leyd.* 1738.
† "Opere Scelte:" *Milan*, 1784, tom. vii. p. 11.
‡ Such seems to be the opinion maintained by Dr. Hunter, "Disputatio inauguralis quædam de hominum varietatibus, et harum causis exponens:" *Edinb.* 1775, p. 26.

merely from without, while in the other it consists in the development of some internal principle. Secondly, directly opposed to this theory of considering different degrees of darkness a series of transitions from the white to the black, are the startling facts, that the same race preserves its hue without sensible variation under the most distant latitudes, and that under the same latitude the most singular varieties occur apparently in the same race. Of the first, the Americans afford a most singular example. Whether on the frozen banks of the Canadian lakes, or on the burning Pampas of the southern peninsula, hardly a shade of difference can be discovered in the complexion of the native Indians: the same copper colour distinguishes all the tribes. Of the second we have a no less striking exemplification in the east.

"The great difference in colour between different natives," says Bishop Heber, describing his first arrival at Calcutta, "struck me much; of the crowd by whom we were surrounded, some were black as negroes, others merely copper-coloured, and others little darker than the Tunisians whom I have seen at Liverpool. Mr. Mill, the principal of Bishop's College, who had come down to meet me, and who has seen more of India than most men, tells me that he cannot account for this difference, which is general throughout the country, and everywhere striking. It is not merely the difference of exposure, since this variety of tint is visible in the fishermen, who are all naked alike. Nor does it depend on caste, since very high caste Brahmins are sometimes black, while Pariahs are comparatively white."* This last observation, if it can be completely depended upon, is of great importance. For, as we shall see on a future occasion, Heeren and others, guided by the division into castes, have imagined that India was peopled by two distinct nations, one of whom, having conquered the other, reduced it to a state of inferiority and

---

* Vol. i. p. 9.

dependence; which hypothesis would be completely demonstrated, if a difference of complexion were distinguishable between the high and low castes.

Thus far, you see, I have only thrown doubts on the processes imagined to explain the black colour of the negro: for though I think it depends upon climate, certainly no theory has been yet discovered to account for its origin. Our science is yet young, and we must content ourselves with collecting facts and drawing their natural inferences. It is therefore to these we must appeal; and they will suffice to prove that such a change may have taken place, though whether by accident or gradual deviation, we know not. I will submit such as I have noticed to your consideration.

The natives of Abyssinia are perfectly black, and yet certainly belong by origin to the Semitic family, and, consequently, to a white race. Their language is but a dialect of that class, and its very name intimates its having come across the Red Sea. Hence, in Scripture, the term *Cush* applies equally to them and to the inhabitants of the other side; and neither in features, nor in the form of the skull, do they any way resemble the negro. You may easily satisfy yourselves, either from portraits, or from living individuals, that, save in colour, their faces are perfectly European. Here, then, a change has taken place, though we know not how.

Another and more striking example we have in the intelligent and accurate traveller, Burckhardt. The town of Souakin, situated on the African coast of the Red Sea, lower down than Mecca, contains a mixed population, formed, first of Bedouins or Arabs, including the descendants of the ancient Turks, and secondly of the townspeople, who are either Arabs from the opposite coast, or Turks of modern origin.* The following is his account of the two classes. Of the first he says: " The Hadherebe or Bedouins of Souakin have exactly the same features, language, and dress, as the

* "Travels in Nubia," 2nd edit. p. 391.

Nubian Bedouins. In general, they have handsome and expressive features, with thin and very short beards. Their colour is of the darkest brown, approaching to black; but they have nothing of the negro character of countenance."* The others, who are descended entirely from settlers from Mosul, Hadramout, &c., and from Turks sent thither by Selim, upon his conquest of Egypt, have undergone the same change. " The present race," says Burckhardt, " have the African features and manners, and are in no way to be distinguished from the Hadherebe."† Here, then, we have two distinct nations, Arabs and Turks, in the course of a few centuries, becoming black in Africa, though originally white.

Captain Tuckey, speaking of the natives of Congo, says that they "are evidently a mixed nation, having no national physiognomy, and many of them perfectly south European in their features. This, one would naturally conjecture, arises from the Portuguese having intermarried with them, and yet there are very few mulattoes among them."‡ This observation completely overthrows that conjecture, even if admissible on other grounds; for an entire nation's physiognomy could never have been entirely changed by a few settlers. In the general observations on Captain Tuckey's voyage, collected from the scientific men and officers who accompanied him, we are informed that " their features, though nearest to those of the negro tribe, are neither so strongly marked nor so black as the Africans in general. They are not only represented as being more pleasing, but also as wearing the appearance of great simplicity and innocence."§

There are many nations, not only along the coast, but in the very heart of central Africa, who are perfectly

* Page 395.
† Page 391. As the Hadherebe have not, according to the first quotation, the negro countenance, I suppose by features we must understand only colour.
‡ " Narrative of an Expedition to explore the River Zaire :" *Lond.* 1818, p. 96.
§ *Ibid.* p. 374.

of a glossy black without a sign of negro features. Among them are the Foulahs, whom Park describes as "not black, but of a tawny colour, which is lighter and yellower in some states than in others. They have small features, soft silky hair, without either the thick lips or crisp wool which are common to other tribes."* Jobson describes them as "of a tawny colour, with long black hair, not near so much frizzled as that of the negroes."† Of the Yoloffs Mr. Moore writes, "that they are much blacker and handsomer than either the Mandingoes or Flups, not having the broad noses and thick lips peculiar to those nations, and that none of the inhabitants of those countries come up to the Yoloffs for blackness of skin and beauty of features." The writer from whom I quote adds, that travellers do not always distinguish the Yoloffs, with the same accuracy as Mr. Moore, from the Mandingoes and other flat-nosed blacks among whom they are mixed; and, in another place, describing the Mandingoes, he says, "that they are as remarkable for thick lips and flat noses, as the Yoloffs and Foulahs are for handsome features."‡ Now this is quite contrary to the account given by later travellers; for Caillié thus describes the inhabitants of Timbuctoo:—"They are of the ordinary size, well made, upright, and walk with a firm step. Their colour is of a fine deep black; their noses are a little more aquiline than those of the Mandingoes, and, like them, they have thin lips and dark eyes."§ This contradiction is, however, of small moment: for any way, it is evident that the black colour has no necessary connection with the negro feature, but that two races or varieties exist, equally black, but belonging, by the more important characteristic of the shape of the skull and features, to different families. Blumenbach has, indeed, remarked, in vague terms, the existence of these two classes in

* Sumner's "Records of Creation:" 2nd edit. vol. i. p. 380.
† "New General Collection of Voyages," *ut sup.* p. 262.
‡ *Ibid.* pp. 255, 266.
§ "Travels through Central Africa:" *Lond.* 1830, vol. ii. p. 61.

Africa, the one negro in every respect, the other black, but with handsome and perfectly European features; but he calls them all indiscriminately Ethiopians, and has made no provision for a distinct classification.*

This difference will perhaps appear more remarkable, if I am correct in another observation. I think we shall in general find, that those tribes which are described as not having the negro features, but only the black colour, are raised a degree in civilization above their neighbours, and profess some religion claiming a revelation—as the Abyssinians a very corrupt Christianity, the natives of Congo some remnants of it, and all others the Mohammedan religion; whereas, those that have the negro characteristics to their fullest extent, as the Dahometans, Caffres, or Hottentots, are in the lowest state of moral and physical degradation, and profess some miserable system of fetichism or idolatry. Now, if craniology have any foundation—and even its warmest opponents must, I think, allow regarding it Bossuet's axiom, that " every error is a truth abused"—the depression of forehead, and compression of temples, which is the negro distinctive in Blumenbach's system, would be precisely indicative of that degraded condition. And thus we should have two distinct causes: features would depend upon civilization, and colour mainly upon climate.

For, regarding the influence of the latter, this extraordinary circumstance, that *every* nation, however various, that is found in the torrid climate of Africa—taking climate in its widest sense, as including the character of the tracts inhabited—should have put on the sun's dusky livery, seems to warrant the conclusion, that this characteristic is attributable to the region which they all inhabit. The effect may not proceed from the direct outward action of the sun's rays; but as it has been proved by Le Cat, Camper, and Lawrence,† that

---

* "Decas Cran." i. p 23.

† Le Cat, "Traité de la Couleur de la Peau humaine," *Amst.* p. 130; Camper, "Dissertat. physique," p. 16; Lawrence, "Lectures on Physiology," &c. p. 522. It is a phenomenon observed mostly in females during gestation.

the skin of the fairest European may, under certain circumstances, become as black as a negro's, over the whole, or a great part, of the body, so may we suppose that the principle which causes this change, and which is evidently inherent in the white, may, under the influence of peculiar climate, be brought into activity, and rendered perpetual by descent.

And, before leaving the soil of Africa, I will give an example of what may be, perhaps, considered a state of transition. Burckhardt has described the savage population of Mahass, as having characteristics intermediate between those of the negroes and the Nubians: " In colour they are perfectly black, their lips are like those of the negro, but not the nose or cheek-bone."*

Opposed to these facts, others may indeed be brought, which are often popularly cited. It is observed, that the descendants of French, English, and Portuguese settlers on the coast of Africa, have remained unchanged after many generations, while the negroes in North America, after several centuries, are still negroes.†
And, to add a new example, Burckhardt twice mentions the descendants of Bosnian soldiers, left by Selim in Nubia, who yet retain the features, though they have forgotten the language, of their native country.

Much of this, or all, may be true; but what does it prove, when placed by the side of the facts I have quoted? Why, only, that the operation of causes is yet unknown to us; that we cannot discover the law whereby nature acts; that there are two series of facts, each true, but neither confuting the other. I wish only to show that the observation of modern philosophers tends to demonstrate that such a change *may* have taken place, not that it *must* take place. One instance is sufficient to prove the first assertion, whereas it might require some thousands to demonstrate the second.

---

* *Ubi sup.* p. 53.
† " Description de la Nigritie," *ut sup.* p. 56. Labat, tom. ii. p. 255.

But let us enter more minutely into the objection. We are credibly informed, that, in some parts of India, the descendants of Europeans long ago settled there, have totally changed their colour, though, of course, not their features. "It is remarkable, however, to observe," says an author, whom I have already often quoted, "how surely all these classes of men" (Persians, Greeks, Tartars, Turks, and Arabs), "in a few generations, even without any intermarriage with the Hindoos, assume the deep olive tint, little less dark than the negro, which seems natural to the climate. The Portuguese natives form unions among themselves alone, or, if they can, with Europeans. Yet the Portuguese have, during a three hundred years' residence in India, become as black as Caffres. Surely this goes far to disprove the assertion which is sometimes made, that climate alone is insufficient to account for the difference between the negro and the European. It is true, that in the negro are other peculiarities, which the Indians have not, and to which the Portuguese colonist shows no system [*symptom?*] of approximation. . . . . But, if heat produces one change, other peculiarities of climate may produce other and additional changes; and when such peculiarities have three or four thousand years to operate in, it is not easy to fix any limits to their power."*
This reasoning is, indeed, defective, inasmuch as the negro features were fixed as early as the days of Herodotus or Homer, or even much earlier, as appears from Egyptian monuments; and climate will not account for the cases I have given, of tribes under the same latitude, and on the same soil, having totally different characteristics. But still the fact contained in this passage is valuable, as it shows that transition may take place from the white to the black colour.

In like manner, Long, in his *History of Jamaica*, and Edwards, in his *History of the West Indies*, have both remarked that the skulls of the white settlers in those

---

* Heber's "Narrative," vol. i. p. 68.

countries differ sensibly in shape from those of Europe, and approach to the original American configuration. Dr. Prichard likewise asserts, upon good authority, that the third generation of those slaves in the United States who live in houses, have little left of the depressed nose, and that their mouth and lips become more moderate; while their hair grows longer at each succeeding generation. The field slaves, on the contrary, retain much longer their original form.* Caldani has given an instance of a black shoemaker, who, having been brought very young to Venice, had so far changed his colour, as to be no darker than a European affected with a slight jaundice; and in this case he speaks from personal observation.†

The important remark I just quoted from Dr. Prichard, is highly interesting; and will, I doubt not, be much farther confirmed by accurate observation. It brings me back to the consideration of the influence exercised by civilization upon the characteristics of a race. Cuvier has noticed that servitude or domestication is the most powerful agent yet discovered for producing modifications in animals, and the greatest variety yet obtained was produced by its means.‡ Civilization comes nearest to this agent in man, and must be even stronger, from its moral influence. There is no doubt, but the mode of life, the food and comforts, and the degree of mental culture enjoyed, produce a strong and permanent effect on different nations. A late traveller in Syria has noted the great difference observable between the Bedouins and the Fellahs of the Hauran. The first, or wandering Arabs, ever exposed to hardships and the fatigues of a roaming active life, are slightly-shaped, and have a small face and thin beard. The

---

* Vol. ii. p. 565.
† "Institutiones Physiologicæ, auctore L. M. Caldanio:" *Ven.* 1786, p. 151.
‡ In his "Discours préliminaire." See likewise Blumenbach, in his chapter entitled "Ausartung des vollkommensten aller Hausthiere, des Menschen," in his "Beyträge zur Naturgeschichte," i. Th. *Götting.* 1790, p. 47.

latter, or sedentary Arabs, are stout and large, have a strong beard, but want the keen looks of their brethren of the desert. Yet there can be no question but that these two classes are in reality only one nation, speaking the same language, and inhabiting the same climate. What, then, causes the difference between them? No doubt their different modes of life: for this accurate observer adds, that till the age of sixteen no difference can be perceived between them.* In another work he says that equal difference is to be seen in their dispositions.†

Mr. Jackson notes the same difference between the Arabs who inhabit towns in Morocco, and the Bedouins who dwell in tents. " The Selluks of Haha," says he, " are physiognomically distinguishable from the Arabs of the plains, and even from the Selluks of Susa, though in their language, manners, and mode of living, they resemble the latter."‡ Nay, even among the Bedouins themselves, Volney has observed that a marked difference is discernable between the people and their sheikhs or princes, who, being better fed, are taller, stouter, and better-favoured than their poorer subjects, who subsist on six ounces of food a day.§ Foster has remarked a similar distinction in Tahiti. " The common people," says he, " who are most exposed to the air and sun, exert their strength in agriculture, fishing, paddling, building houses and canoes, and are stinted in their food, are blacker, their hair more woolly and crisp, their bodies low and slender. But their chiefs and arees have a very different appearance. The colour of their skins is less tawny than that of the Spaniard, and not so coppery as that of an American; it is of a lighter tint than the fairest complexion of an inhabitant of the East-India Islands.

* Burckhardt's "Travels in Syria." Not having at hand the English edition, I translate from the German version: *Weimar*, 1823, i. Th. p. 456.
† " Notes on the Bedouins and Wahabees :" *Lond.* 1830, p. 104.
‡ " An Account of the Empire of Morocco :" *Lond.* 1811, p. 18.
§ " Voyage en Egypte et en Syrie :" *Par.* 1787, tom. i. p. 359.

From this complexion we find all the intermediate hues, down to a lively brown, bordering upon black. A few have yellowish, brown, or sandy hair."* Kotzebue, and other later navigators, have made the same observation; but it seems clear that the Yeris, or noble race of the Sandwich and other Polynesian islands, are really a distinct tribe from the common people."†

Both Pallas and Klaproth have expressed an opinion, that the Mongul complexion seems to depend much upon the habits of that race. The children and women are remarkably white; smoke and exposure to the sun give the men their yellow tint.‡ Though much might be urged against this hypothesis, it may serve to draw more attention to the bearing which habits and civilization may have upon the characteristics of different races. With the same view, I would notice the remarkable alteration which has occurred in the Germanic family. For we have seen that its traits were once so marked, that it was made to constitute one of the great and most strongly-characterized divisions of the human species, forming, to the eye of the Greek, a perfect contrast with the swarthy hue of the Ethiopian. Yet these distinctives, if not totally effaced, are now become so faint, as to be hardly traceable; doubtless through the influence of civilization, and the assimilation of that nation's manners to those of others belonging to the same family.

Perhaps the most extraordinary illustration of the permanent influence of habits upon the different races, may be drawn from the teeth. Blumenbach has observed that the teeth of man show him manifestly to be an omnivorous animal. But in some nations,

---

* "Observations made during a Voyage round the World :" *Lond.* 1778, p. 229. See also the son's "Voyage round the World," 1777, vol. i. p. 305.

† Kotzebue's "New Voyage round the World :" *Lond.* 1830, vol. ii. p. 58.

‡ Pallas, *ubi sup.* Klaproth, "Voyage au Caucase," tom. i. p. 73.

probably from the use of food requiring great mastication, the incisors become blunt and rounded, and the canine teeth are undistinguishable from the grinders. This is the case with many, perhaps most, Egyptian mummies, and with the Greenlanders and Esquimaux, who eat their meat uncooked, with most extraordinary contortions of jaw.*

These examples may suffice, instead of many, to show what an important element difference of habit is; for nature, always tending to adapt her laws to particular circumstances, where the general harmony will not be disturbed, seems, after a time, to perpetuate varieties produced by this accidental cause.

There are many other physiological observations and objections connected with the unity of origin in the negro and white races, which I pass over, as they are hardly of a nature to be interesting to you.† I will

---

* "De Generis Humani Varietate," pp. 27, 224.
† I will simply mention in a note one argument, both as a sample of the strange expedients to which recourse has been had by writers on these subjects, and because I am not aware that any one has taken the trouble to answer it. I allude to Virey's objection to unity of race, drawn from Fabricius's accurate observations on the *pediculus nigritarum*, as the parasite insect of the negro has been scientifically called, as specifically distinct from all others; so that, according to him, the black race which it accompanies must have been also distinct from the beginning (tom. i. p. 391). In reply to this, I will content myself with saying, that there are other instances of a parallel nature, where we cannot account for the existence of the smaller tribes of animals before their present seats and nourishment existed. For instance, the *tinea*, or moth, which attacks dressed wool, never touches it when it is unwashed; where did it exist before wool was washed and combed? Are we to consider washed and unwashed wool two different species, because the same animal will not live in both? The larva of the *oinopota cellaris* will live nowhere but in wine or beer; another insect described by Reaumur now disdains all food but chocolate. (See Kirby and Spence's "Introd. to Entomology," 4th edit. vol. i. pp. 384-388.) How or where did these little creatures live, before what is now their exclusive nourishment was manufactured? for no one will suppose that these substances were ever found ready-made by the hand of nature. These cases are exactly parallel to the one objected; but there is an instance perfectly similar, of an insect which produces disease in tame swine, but is never found in the wild, though acknowledged to be the original stock. "Der Finnenwurm

therefore at once proceed to sum up the results of this study as briefly as possible. I have endeavoured to connect and lay before you, what I think may be considered its admitted results, imperfect as it yet remains. We have seen it well established: first, that among animals acknowledged to be of one species, there have arisen varieties similar to those in the human race, and not less diverse from one another. Secondly, that nature tends, in the human species, to produce varieties in one race approaching to the characteristics of the others. Thirdly, that sporadic varieties, of the most extraordinary sort, may be propagated by descent. Fourthly, that we can find sufficient proofs in the languages and the characteristics of larger bodies, or entire nations compared, of their transition from one race to another. Fifthly, that though the origin of the black race is yet involved in mystery, yet are there sufficient facts collected to prove the possibility of its having arisen from another, particularly if, in addition to the action of heat, we admit that of moral causes acting upon the physical organization.

And here I will remark, that we are often precipitate and unjust, in judging of the past by causes now in action. It is indeed true that nature is constant and regular in her operations; but if in the short course of our experience, or that of past observers, no variation may have been noted in the uniformity of her workings, it is that the little segment of her duration's cycle, over which we and they have travelled, is but as a straight line, an infinitesimal element, whose curvature can only appear, when referred to a much larger portion of her circumference. That besides the partial laws with which we are acquainted, there have been others once

---

in Schweinfleisch," says Blumenbach, "ist, in seiner Art, ein eben so vollkommenes Thier als der Mensch. Nun aber findet sich, so viel bekannt, dieses Thier blos beym zahmen Hausschwein, und niemahlen hingegen bey der wilden Sau, von der doch jenes abstammt." (Beyträge zur Naturgeschichte, i. Th. p. 30.) See also some curious remarks on this subject by Tilesius, in the "Mémoires de l'Académie de St. Pétersbourg," tom. v. 1815, p. 402.

most active, whose agency is now either suspended or concealed, the study of the world must easily convince us. There were times within the verge of mythological history, when volcanos raged in almost every chain of mountains; when lakes dried up, or suddenly appeared, in many valleys; when seas burst over their boundaries, and created new islands, or retired from their beds, and increased old continents; when, in fine, there was a power of production and arrangement on a great, magnificent scale, when nature seemed employed not merely in the yearly renovation of plants and insects, but in the procreation from age to age of the vaster and more massive elements of her sphere; when her task was not confined to the embroidering the meadows in spring, or to the paring away of shores by the slow-eating action of tides and currents, but when she toiled in the great laboratories of the earth, upheaving mountains, and displacing seas, and thus giving to the world its great indelible features. And how are we to account for this, but by supposing in nature a twofold action, one regular from the beginning, and uniform to the end, the other a mysterious slow-moving power, which, though revolving on the same plane, travels over it with an imperceptible motion, proportioned to the wants of the entire system? And in other cases, and on a smaller scale, such should seem to be the course of nature. In the child, the circulation of the blood, the absorbing and digestive operations, all the functions of life, are the same as in the man; with variations only as to degree of activity, they commence with being, and are regular through its duration. But in its earlier stages there is, besides, a plastic virtue at work within us, traceable to no law of necessity, having no clear dependence on the general course of the ordinary vital powers, which gives growth and solidity to the limbs, characteristic shape to the features, gradual development and strength to the muscles; then to all appearance sinks into inertness and ceases to act, till age seems once more to call the extraordinary laws into activity, to efface the impression, and undo the work of their earlier operations. And, in like manner, we must allow that, in the world's infancy, besides the regular ordinances of constant and daily course, causes necessary to produce great and permanent effects may have had a power, now no longer wanted, and consequently no longer exercised; that there was a tendency to stamp more marked features upon the earth and its inhabitants, to produce countries as well as their vegetation, races as much as individuals.

There are instances certainly as yet discoverable, of a twofold action of one cause, upon a smaller and a greater scale. An epidemic disease, for instance, besides its particular action upon individuals, runs a similar course, only referable to large communities or aggregations of men, or even to the entire human race: is first slight in its public infliction, then increases, and so by contrary gradations yields to nature or art, and wears itself away; even in such sort, that, at the period or crisis of greater fatality, the lot of each patient shall seem rather to depend upon some mysterious law, which connects him with the infected community, than upon the individual circumstances of his peculiar case. And, in a somewhat similar manner, we may say, that the daily and yearly courses of nature, which appear so identical throughout, are yet but components of a much longer period, at the end of which an action, now so small as to be invisible, will, by the aggregation of its effects, appear great and important, and seem to have been produced by laws, now hidden in the complex machinery of the universe.

And, to apply still further the illustration I before gave; when any part of the human system has been so far altered, that the power which acted in its infancy again is needed, though apparently suspended, there are hidden resources which recall it into action; so that, when any portion of the bony structure has been removed, there is again wrought, to reproduce it, that marvellous weaving which shoots its threads, like a crystallization, from point to point, and then stretches across it a firm and solid texture, just as occurred many years before in childhood. And just so do we see, that when, by accidental circumstances, nature can be brought back to her primitive position, she resumes her primitive action, and renews the laws she had held suspended. The production of coral reefs, and, from them, islands, in the South Sea, which soon receive a population from distant points, shows us, in that last corner, to which she seems to have withdrawn her creative powers, how she once prepared new habitations for man; the incredible scale on which the inhabitants increase on such occasions, far beyond the calculations of modern statistics, proves what powerful energies she exerted when wanted to propagate the human race. An island first occupied by a few shipwrecked English in 1589, and discovered by a Dutch vessel in 1667, is said to have been found peopled, after eighty years, by 12,000 souls, all the descendants of four mothers.* Acosta, writing the natural history of New Spain, within a hundred years of its discovery, tells us, that there were, even earlier, " men who had 70,000 or 100,000 sheep, and that, even then, were many who had as many; which in Europe would be considered great riches, but there, is only moderate wealth." And yet, not one of these animals existed in the country before its discovery, and the breed was propagated entirely from those imported by the Spaniards. The same is to be said of horned cattle; yet such was their increase, that, in his time, they went roaming in herds of thousands over the plains and mountains of Hispaniola, and were the property of whoever chose to hunt them down with houghing-knives (*desjarretoderas*), and cut them down; and so profitable was this chase, that, in 1585, the fleet brought over from that island 35,444 hides, and from New Spain 64,350; showing an increase quite beyond all ordinary calculation.†

* Bullet, "Réponses critiques :" *Besanç.* 1819, vol. iii. p. 45.
† Acosta, "Historia natural y moral de las Iudias:" *Barcelona*, 1591, fol. 180.

Such examples, to which I might add many others, seem to show the existence of hidden resources in nature, never called forth, save in her infant state. And it surely cannot be unphilosophical to suppose, that impressions, meant to be characteristic and permanent, were then more easily communicated, and more indelibly stamped. We need not, with Carové, have recourse to the hypothesis that the black colour of the negro was the mark set upon Cain, and that it was continued after the Deluge in the family of Japhet, whom he supposes to have married into that stock.* The admission of such an hypothesis gains us but little, for we have still the colour of the Americans and Malays to account for. But it is much more simple to allow, that one individual, or one family, placed in favourable circumstances, may have given rise to peculiarities, which, in consequence of intermarriages, and the continued operation of the same circumstances, may have become enduring.

But we, too, indulge here in conjecture. I am willing to own it; for though sufficient has been said, to prove that our science already can refute all solid objection to the unity of race in the human species, although the admitted facts which I have laid before you, may show that there is no impossibility of one family having sprung up from the other, yet we must own that the methods whereby nature has proceeded are yet a mystery; so that the philosopher must be content with conjecture, and honestly confess:

Οὐκ οἶδ' ἀκριβῶς εἰκάσαι γε μὴν πάρα.†

Nor can such conjectures be refused as rash and unwarrantable, so long as the fact which they are directed to account for, is certain and incontestable.

And I will conclude the evidence upon this subject by once more recapitulating the connections of the

---

* "Kosmorama, eine Reihe von Studien zur Orientirung in Natur," &c., *Frankf.* 1831, p. 65. He does indeed suppose them to be of a mixed race, between the Sethites, represented by Shem, and the Cainites, continued in Japhet.
† Eurip. "Rhes." Act ii. 280.

different races, and the insensible shades whereby they seem to blend one into another.

The white race, which, of course, I consider the central one, connects itself with the Mongul through the Finns and As-jachs, who have its complexion, hair, and iris; likewise through the Tartars, who insensibly pass though the Kirghis and Yakuts into the Mongul race; and thirdly, through the Hindoos, who communicate with us through the Sanskrit language. With the negro race it is connected through the Abyssinians, who have a Semitic language and European features, and through the Arabs of Suakin, who resemble the Noubas; then come the natives of Mahass, then the Foulahs and Mandingoes, and so forward to the Congoese, the complete negroes, and the Hottentots. These last are again closely allied to the mountaineers of Madagascar; they to those of Cochin-China, the Moluccas, and Philippine Islands, in all which are a race of black woolly-headed mountaineers, differing in language from the other natives. These again join the New Hollanders, and the natives of New Caledonia and the New Hebrides, who are farther connected by similarity of customs, religion, and partly by physical traits, with the New Zealanders, and other natives of Polynesia; and so, in fading tints, till we almost return to the Asiatic families.

The population of these islands deserves a more particular attention. I have observed, that through the innumerable islands of Polynesia, there are two distinct tribes or families. Forster, in fact, proves this point incontestably. While the inhabitants of Tahiti and New Zealand, the Marquesas, Friendly, and Society Islands, speak but dialects of the same language, as is proved by his comparative tables, those of the New Hebrides, especially Mallicollo, New Caledonia, and Tanna, speak barbarous dialects, quite distinct, and, to all appearance, unconnected. Their physical characteristics are likewise very different, approaching, as I have intimated, to the negroes of the more western islands. But what I wish principally to remark is, how the tribes belonging to the first race, the unity of which no one will deny, have varied, on one side, in form and complexion, to such an immense extent, and how those of the other have likewise departed so much from their original type, that the two have blended together, so as to be hardly distinguishable, excepting by their languages. "Each of the above two races," says Dr. Forster, "is again divided into several varieties, which form the gradations towards the other race; so that we find some of the first race almost as black and slender as some of the second; and in this second race are some strong athletic figures, which may almost vie with the first."* Thus, in the same race, while some are hardly distinguishable from a negro tribe, allied through inseparable links to the negroes of Africa, others depart so far from it, as to approximate in symmetry of form in the body and skull, as well as in colour, to the natives of Europe. And in these gradations we trace a corresponding scale of civilization. "The natives of some of the islands in the South Sea," says Mr. Lawrence, speaking of the form of the skull, "are hardly to be distinguished, in countenance and head, from Europeans." And again: "The inhabitants of these islands, from New Zealand on the west to Easter Island, contain a race of much better organization and qualities. In colour and features, many of them approach to the Caucasian variety; while they are surpassed by none in symmetry, size, and strength."† Dr. Prichard reasons very forcibly upon this gradation within the race or family. "If," says he, "we view these races (the Papuan and Polynesian) together, they appear to furnish sufficient proof, that the utmost physical diversities presented by the human frame in different nations, may and do arise from a uniform stock. They enable us to produce actual facts,

---

* "Observations," &c., p. 228. See the comparative table, p. 284. There are several important coincidences, however, between the dialects of the two families, as well as of both with Malay.
† "Lectures on Physiology," pp. 382, 571.

as examples of this deviation. We cannot, indeed, go back all the steps at once, but we can go the whole of the way by degrees. If a few of the fairest New Hollanders were separated from the community, and placed on an island by themselves, they would form a race of lighter colour than the New Zealanders. Under favourable circumstances, would not this stock deviate into still lighter shades, as the race of New Zealand, or its kindred in the Society Isles, has done?"* I must not pass over the singular custom prevalent, not only throughout these islands, but among the Hottentots in Africa, the Guaranos of Paraguay, and the Californians in America—that of amputating the little finger of one or both hands, in token of mourning for the death of a relation,† a custom so singular, that we can hardly conceive it to have sprung up spontaneously in such distant parts.

The existence of such gradations, almost from one extreme to the other, in the same race, is not peculiar to these tribes. The Malays exhibit a similar variety. "The complexion," says Mr. Crawfurd, "is generally brown, but varies a little in different tribes. Neither climate nor the habits of the people seem to have anything to do with it. The fairest races are generally towards the west, but some of them, as the Batteeks of Sumatra, upon the very Equator. The Javanese, who live most comfortably, are among the darkest people of the Archipelago; the wretched Dayaks, or cannibals of Borneo, among the fairest."‡ This difficulty of accounting for such diversities, is rather favourable than opposed to the consequences we have been drawing; for, the fact being thus established, that in a race acknowledged to be one, such varieties have sprung up, the difficulties of tracing them to a uniform cause, only show that there are agencies which we have not yet discovered, or a complication of causes whose elements

* Vol. i. p. 488.
† Forster (G.) "Voyage round the World," vol. i. p. 435.
‡ "History of the Indian Archipelago," vol. i. p. 19.

L

we have not yet mixed in the prescribed proportions, so as to understand its action. And the more we extend the potency of nature, beyond our comprehension, the more easily we justify the production of inexplicable phenomena.

In the family to which we belong, the same series of modifications exists; we have therein varieties which, if not so strongly marked, appear just as indelible; yet no one would maintain that each sprung from an independent stock. The Jew is at this day perfectly distinguishable from the Europeans that surround him, though West and other eminent artists have found it impossible to characterize him by any particularly distinctive traits.* The Gipsies I may here likewise mention as an instance of a tribe, which, proved by its language to be of Indian origin, has lost much of its original configuration, and particularly the olive colour of its country, by living in other climates. But the Germanic tribes may yet be distinguished by feature from the Greeks, and these again from

> —— "The Celtic race,
> Of different language, form, and face,
> A various race of man;"

as their own northern bard has somewhere called them. It is in vain for these subdivisions to blend by every civil and moral union; they will continue, like the united waters of the Rhone and Saone, to flow together in one stream, but with distinguishable currents.

Thus are even the smallest varieties, once produced, never again obliterated; and yet not therefore are they marks of independent origin. Even families may transmit them, and the Imperial house of Hapsburg has its characteristic feature. And whence arises this indelibility, by natural processes, of varieties by natural processes introduced? This should seem to be one of the mysteries of nature, that we may on anything

---

* See Camper, "Dissert. physique," p. 21.

compel her to place her signet; but we know not how again to force it off. Man, like the magician's half-skilled scholar, so beautifully described by the German poet, possesses often the spell whereby to compel her to work, but has not yet learnt that which may oblige her to desist.

The country and city where we now are, suggests an application of what we have just discussed, to researches both useful and amusing. Dr. Edwards, in a French work, *on the Physiological Characters of the Human Races, considered in their relation to History*, has given a very interesting hint for the prosecution of this study.*
He was struck, at some market in the south of France, by observing two distinct characters in the heads of the country people, each referable to an individual type; and he paid particular attention to the prevalence of either, in his tour through Italy, and everywhere observed the one to predominate over the other. The one he considered the Gaulish type, the other the Roman. As the model of the former he proposes the features of Dante, too well known to all my hearers to require any description. I am sure no one can pay attention to the countenance prevalent in different parts of Italy, without noticing how often this form recurs in Tuscany and in Upper Italy, while in Rome and the southern provinces it is of very rare occurrence. It gives, however, no type of the Roman face and head. To find this, we must not allow ourselves to be led away by popular representations. There are some quarters of Rome where the descendants of the ancient inhabitants are supposed yet to remain; and travellers have often written, that the countenance of the population beyond the Tiber exactly resembles that of the Roman soldiers upon the column of Trajan, and other ancient monuments.

Supposing these to be sufficiently distinct, or sufficiently well copied, to allow the making of such a comparison, I should say it was one of the worst criterions

---

* Paris, 1829.

possible. For a slight acquaintance with Roman art will satisfy any one, that, on historical monuments, where no portrait is intended, all the figures are formed upon the Grecian model, and can give no clue towards ascertaining the physiognomy of the ancient inhabitants. But look at the sarcophagi on which the busts of the deceased are carved in relief, or raised from their reclining statues on the lid, or even examine the series of imperial busts in the Capitol, and you cannot fail to discover a striking type, essentially the same, from the wreathed image of Scipio's tomb, to Trajan or Vespasian; consisting in a large and flat head, a low and wide forehead, a face, in childhood, heavy and round, later, broad and square, a short and thick neck, and a stout and broad figure; a type totally at variance with what we find generally considered as the Roman countenance. Nor need we go far to find their descendants; they are to be met every day in the streets, principally among the burgesses or middle class, the most invariable portion of every population. The contrast between the true features of the Romans, and their ideal type in art, is nowhere, perhaps, so clearly observable as in the sculptures of Titus's arch. The various soldiers represented on each side, are so exactly like one another, that, were they not sculptured in stone, we might suppose them to have been all cast in one mould. The entire profile, particularly in the half-open mouth and lips, shows the existence of a rule or model, from which the artist might not depart. But with these the emperor in his chariot contrasts in the strongest manner: his whole shape is formed on another type; and. though the features are quite effaced, sufficient remains of the outline to show the full heavy face and bulky head of a true Roman.

These remarks may lead us to a great caution, in judging of characteristic forms, from works belonging to the higher departments of art. No nation long possesses the art of representation, without forming to itself an ideal, abstractive type; and the caution to be used, should, necessarily, be doubled, where the arts and their types were borrowed. Even the Egyptians had their ideal beauty, as well as the Greeks; and Champollion, to the horror of pure classical artists, used to descant in raptures on the elegance of feature and form in some Egyptian statues. And he must have seemed right to those, who would consider them as the perfection of those principles which guided the genius of one people, necessarily keeping within the national type of living forms, and led to one of the earliest manifestations of art. It was by not sufficiently attending to these considerations, that Blumenbach, as I observed in my last lecture, imagined, that in Egypt there must have been different races of men; whereas the solitary specimens he brings of various physiognomies, only seem to mark the difference between a ruder and a more ideal period of style. On another occasion, he seems to fall into a similar error. The heads on the Athenian tetradrachmas have nothing in common, according to him, with works of the age of Pericles, and approach in features to the Egyptian model.* But if, on the other hand, we compare them with the Ægina marbles,† we shall discover a striking similarity of character; they have all the leer, or laughing expression, so peculiar to those early works. Yet will no one suspect them of being anything but purely Grecian. Indeed, far as they are removed from the perfect works of a later period, they show how soon a uniform rule or model is introduced into art, and becomes its necessary principle. Cockerell has remarked that, in the Ægina marbles, "a canon of proportion, and a system of anatomical expression, are observable throughout:"‡ and

---

* Specimen Historiæ naturalis antiquæ artis operibus illustratæ :" *Götting.* 1808, p. 11.
† The collection of statues which adorned the Temple of Jupiter Panhellenius, in the island of Ægina; and which, having been restored in a most masterly manner by Thorwaldsen, at Rome, form the principal ornament of the splendid Glyptotheca at Munich.
‡ In the "Journal of Science and the Arts," vol. vi. 1819, p. 338.

Thiersch has approved of Wagner's observation, that though art in other respects improved, and every grace of form was introduced into that school, the countenances remained unchanged.* And so, in fact, not only in the school of Ægina, but in every other Grecian school, from the hasty etchings on the Grecian, or, as they are called, Etruscan, vases, to the sculptures of the Parthenon, there is manifestly one rule or ideal principle of the beautiful, which never can be mistaken; and there can be no doubt but that the abstract form was derived from the national features, of which it may be considered the purified representation. And thus, in some respects, where art is indigenous and national, it may be indirectly of use towards representing to us, even in its heroic or mythological figures, the character of the people.

And, having wandered thus far, step by step, from the subject of our inquiry, allow me to proceed a little farther in pursuit of a moral application, which these remarks have suggested, and which may perchance lead us back once more unto our theme. As no nation or race of men could ever have gone out of their own physical characteristics for their type of ideal perfection, in the beauty of form; as the Egyptian never could, by any abstraction, have generated a style of art, in which the colour, shape, and features of his divinity should be purely European; nor the Greek have given to his hero the tawny hue, narrow eyes, and protruding lips of the Egyptian—for each to the other must have seemed deformity—so could neither they, nor the men of any other nation, have framed to themselves an ideal type or canon of moral perfection of

---

* "Von der Minerva an bis zum letzten der Krieger sehen sich alle ähnlich, und scheinen insgesammt leibliche Brüder und Schwestern zu seyn, ohne den geringsten Ausdruck von Leidenschaft. Zwischen Siegern und Besiegten, zwischen Gottheit und Menschheit, ist nicht der geringste Unterschied zu bemerken."—Ueber die Epochen der bildenden Kunst unter den Griechen, 2e Abhandlung: *Munich*, 1819, p. 59.

character, which arose not from what, to them, seemed most beautiful and perfect. A Hindoo cannot conceive his Brahman saint, other than as possessing in perfection the abstemiousness, the silence, the austerity, and the minute exactness in every trifling duty which he admires, in different degrees, in his living models. Plato's Socrates, the perfection of the philosophical character, is composed of elements perfectly Greek, being a compound of all those virtues which the doctrines of his school deemed necessary to adorn a sage.

Now this hath often appeared to me the strongest internal proof of a superior authority stamped upon the Gospel history, that the holy and perfect character it portrays, not only differs from, but expressly opposes, every type of moral perfection which they who wrote it could possibly have conceived. We have, in the writings of the Rabbins, ample materials wherewith to construct the model of a perfect Jewish teacher; we have the sayings and the actions of Hillel and Gamaliel, and Rabbi Samuel, all perhaps in great part imaginary, but all bearing the impress of national ideas, all formed upon one rule of imaginary perfection. Yet nothing can be more widely apart than their thoughts and principles, and actions, and character, and those of our Redeemer. Lovers of wrangling controversy, proposers of captious paradoxes, jealous upholders of their nation's exclusive privileges, zealous, uncompromising sticklers for the least comma of the law, and most sophistical departers from its spirit, such mostly are those great men—the exact counterpart and reflection of those scribes and Pharisees, who are so uncompromisingly reproved, as the very contradiction of Gospel principles.

How comes it that men, not even learned, contrived to represent a character every way departing from their national type—at variance with all those features which custom and education, and patriotism, and religion, and nature, seemed to have consecrated as of all most beautiful? And the difficulty of considering such a character the invention of man, as some have impiously imagined, is still further increased by observing how writers recording different facts, as St. Matthew and St. John, do lead us, nevertheless, to the same representation and conception. Yet herein, methinks, we have a key to the solution of every difficulty. For if two artists were commanded to produce a form embodying their ideas of perfect beauty, and both exhibited figures equally shaped, upon types and models most different from all ever before seen in their country, and, at the same time, each perfectly resembling the other, I am sure such a fact, if recorded, would appear almost incredible, except on the supposition that both had copied the same original.

Such, then, must be the case here: the Evangelists, too, must have copied the living model which they represent; and the accordance of the moral features which they give him, can only proceed from the accuracy with which they have respectively drawn them. But this only increases our mysterious wonder. For, assuredly, he was not as the rest of men, who could thus separate himself in character from whatever was held most perfect and most admirable by all who surrounded him, and by all who had taught him; who, while he set himself far above all national ideas of moral perfection, yet borrowed nothing from Greek, or Indian, or Egyptian, or Roman; who, while he thus had nothing in common with any known standard of character, any established law of perfection, should seem to every one the type of his peculiarly beloved excellence.* And truly, when we see how he can have been followed by the Greek, though a founder of none among his sects,—revered by the Brahman, though preached unto him by men of the fishermen's caste,—worshipped by the red man of Canada, though belonging to the hated pale race,—we cannot but consider him as destined to break down all

---

* Διάφοροι δὲ φύσεις βροτῶν
Διάφοροι δὲ τρόποις· ὁ δ' ὀρθὸς
Ἐσθλὸν σαφὲς αἰεί.—*Euripid. Iphigen.* 559.

distinction of colour, and shape, and countenance, and habits; to form in himself the type of unity, to which are referable all the sons of Adam, and give us, in the possibility of this moral convergence, the strongest proof that the human species, however varied, is essentially one.

LECTURE THE FIFTH;

ON

THE NATURAL SCIENCES.

PART I.

CONNECTION of the Natural Sciences with the preceding topics. MEDICINE.—Applied in Germany to the denial of our Saviour's resurrection.—General remarks upon the utility of discussing such objections.—The reality of our Redeemer's death, and consequently the truth of his resurrection, vindicated by physicians, upon medical grounds: Richter, Eschenbach, the Gruners.—Translation of an Arabic narrative of a crucifixion.

GEOLOGY.—Classification of systems.—*First:* Systems professedly framed to defend Scripture.—Older theories of the earth: Penn, Fairholme, Croly.—Defects of such systems. *Secondly:* Systems opposed to Scripture: Buffon, and other French writers. *Thirdly:* Purely scientific researches.—Example of objection from a particular case; Brydone on the lavas of Jaci Reale: confuted by the observations of Smyth, Dolomieu, and Hamilton.—Points of contact between Geology and the Sacred Narrative. The *Creation.*—Pre-existence of a chaotic state; doctrine of successive revolutions: found in all ancient cosmogonies, and in the Fathers of the Church. —Fossils; early speculations regarding their origin: Cuvier's discoveries.—Constancy and regularity of the cause employed in such revolutions.—Elie de Beaumont's theory of the elevation of mountains: its accordance with Scripture.—Theory of the days of creation being periods.—Opinions of modern foreign geologists on the harmony between the Mosaic creation and geological observations.

"IN all pursuits," says the amiable philosopher Fronto, "I think it better to be wholly ignorant and unskilled, than half-learned and half-expert. Philosophy, too, they say, it is better never to have touched, than to have but partially tasted; inasmuch as those become most malicious, who, pausing in the porch of science, turn away without proceeding further."* Nothing has proved the accuracy of these observations so well, as the connection between the natural sciences and revealed religion. It has been the malice of superficial men, who had not patience or courage to penetrate into the sanctuary of nature, that has suggested objections, from her laws, against truths revealed. Had they boldly advanced, they would have discovered, as in the cavern-temples of India and Idumea, that the depths which serve to conceal her darkest mysteries, may the soonest be changed into fittest places for profound adoration.

The natural sciences, of which we have now to treat, are usually connected with religion by forming the basis of what is called " natural theology," that is, by giving strong demonstration of the goodness and wisdom of God, in the works of creation, and thus showing the existence of a regulating providence in the construction and direction of the universe. The very character of the course of lectures which I have undertaken to deliver, forbids me to enter upon the consideration of this connection: and, even if want of abundant materials for my definite undertaking, had inclined me to wander into this ground, I should have found myself deterred by the detailed and interesting, as well as learned and able, manner, in which that branch of religious science has of late been treated in the Bridgewater publications. If, therefore, we confine ourselves, according to our engagement, to the connection between science and *revealed* religion, we shall find that the study of which I last discoursed, may

---

* "Omnium artium, ut ego arbitror, imperitum et indoctum esse præstat quam semiperitum et semidoctum. Philosophiæ quoque disciplinas aiunt satius esse nunquam attigisse quam leviter et primoribus ut dicitur labiis delibasse; eosque provenire malitiosissimos, qui in vestibulo artis obversati, prius inde averterint quam intraverint."—Ad M. Caes. lib. iv. ep. 3, *Romæ*, 1823, p. 94.

appear very naturally to lead us into the consideration of the alliance, if any exists, between philosophical pursuits and the facts communicated in the inspired pages. For we may truly say, that, in attempting to establish the unity of the human race, we found ourselves involved in a variety of physiological speculations, and had to unravel the action of natural causes upon the physical organization of man. This would seem to conduct us into the department of medicine; and however strange it may appear to you, it is through this study that I mean to lead you into the natural sciences.

You will probably ask, what light the progress of medicine can throw upon the truths of religion. Not much, perhaps, if we consider it as an aggregate of principles, varying in different schools, as a succession of theories, most conflicting among themselves, and not often referred to any illustration of sacred doctrines. But, in particular cases, in the examination of individual facts, where science has been first invoked by the adversaries of revelation, a fuller and more learned discussion, based exclusively upon scientific principles, has done the work of confutation much more effectually, and much more satisfactorily, than mere theology could have achieved it. I will select one example, in which superficial medical observation has been applied to the denial—and, afterwards, more solid learning to the complete vindication, of an important portion of the Christian evidences.

I must, however, premise some observations, which may apply to other cases, in future lectures, as well as to the one in hand. Is it useful, it may be asked, or is it wholesome, to bring before you objections against sacred and solemn truths, which have never been proposed to you, and of which you, perhaps, are ignorant? Would it not be better to waive illustrations of my theme, that tend to make you acquainted with religious discussions, or free-thinking assertions, broached in foreign countries, but totally excluded from your own?

Were I addressing an illiterate assembly, or were these lectures directed to the instruction of those who have not travelled—I will not say, out of their own country, but—out of their own literature, I own I might be inclined to avoid the mooting of such dangerous inquiries. Or, were the rationalist philosophy of the Continent of that seductive kind, which ensnares the dallying imagination, or catches the unwary and casual inquirer, I should feel it a duty to close, rather than to open, any avenue, which could lead into its enchanted gardens. But the case is far otherwise in both regards. For, in the first place, all know in general, that many such strange opinions and fond objections have been made by the pretended philosophers of France or Germany; and any one, however superficially acquainted with the history of literature in these two countries, during the last fifty years, is familiar with the names of those who have laboured in the unholy work. Now, I apprehend that there is more danger in the vague impression, that learned and able men have rejected Christianity, as irreconcilable with their scientific discoveries or meditations, than in the particular examination of the grounds on which they specifically based their rejection. An able critic has observed, that it was a pity the writings of Julian the Apostate were lost, as it would have been interesting to see what so learned and ingenious a man could object to Christianity. This species of conjecture, and of longing regret, is a thousand times more mischievous than the works themselves could possibly have been: for from the specimens of Julian's reasoning, preserved by St. Cyril, it clearly appears that his objections must have been of the most flimsy description. Thus, then, when I lay before you objections of freethinkers, wherewith you were previously unacquainted, and, with them, the satisfactory answers, whereby they have been met, and repelled, I trust I shall be much diminishing, rather than increasing, the uneasiness, which ill-defined and shadowy apprehension of danger must often produce. Nor can

M

I fear that any one will be easily lead, by what I shall say, to any dangerous prying into forbidden pursuits; for the authors with whom I shall mostly deal, are such as require a very determined scholar to grapple with them, and a sterner motive, whether good or evil, than curiosity, to insure perseverance in their perusal.

This much premised, I return to observe, that the point to which I alluded as attacked, by superficial inquiries, upon medical grounds, is no other than the truth of our Saviour's resurrection. You are of course aware, that as St. Paul holds this for one of the principal grounds of our faith, without which his preaching would be vain, so have the enemies of Christianity, in ancient and modern times, left no art untried to shake this foundation-stone of our belief. Every apparent contradiction in the narrative of the apostles, has been eagerly seized upon to disprove it; but the most direct way in which it has been attacked, of old, and in later ages, is by endeavouring to throw doubts upon the reality of our Saviour's death. From the earnestness with which St. John seems to dwell upon the last events of his life, and the strong asseverations wherewith he declares himself to have witnessed the piercing of his side,* it would clearly appear, that already, in his time, this solemn and important event had been called in question. I will not for a moment dwell on the coarse and revolting blasphemies of some writers in the last century, who unfeelingly and impiously charged our Blessed Redeemer with feigning death upon the cross;† such monstrous impiety carries confutation in its own absurdity. But modern unbelievers, who will not venture to deny the virtue and holiness of Christ, while they reduce his miracles to mere natural events, have chosen a more artful way of accounting for his resurrection, by imagining that, upon medical grounds, he

---

* John, xix. 34, 35; coll. 1 John, v. 8. See the Bishop of Salisbury's letter to the Rev. T. Benyon, 1829, p. 26.
† For a confutation of this impiety, see Süskind's "Magazin für Christliche Dogmatik," 9 Heft, p. 158.

could not have died upon the cross, but must have been taken down while in a state of asphyxia or trance. Paulus, Damm, and others, adopt this opinion, and support it by much specious reasoning. It is certain, they say, that, according to the testimony of Josephus and other ancient writers, persons crucified lived for three, or even nine days upon the cross: and hence we find that the two who shared our Saviour's sentence were not dead at evening, and that Pilate would not believe that he could so soon have expired, without the centurion's express testimony.* But, on the other hand, nothing is more probable than that fatigue, mental anguish, and loss of blood, should have produced exhaustion, syncope, or trance; in which state our Blessed Redeemer is placed at the disposal of his faithful friends, who medicate his wounds with spices, and leave him to repose in a quiet and well-sheltered sepulchral chamber. There he soon recovers from the state of suspended animation, and returns to his friends. As to the vigilance of his eager enemies, it is said that there are other instances of that being eluded; as in St. Paul, who was left for dead, after having been stoned at Lystra; or St. Sebastian, who was cured by the Christians after he had been shot with arrows. The piercing of our Saviour's side with a lance, is got rid of by saying that the verb used in the Greek (νυττειν) signifies rather to prick, or superficially wound, than to pierce the body! And thus, according to them, nothing occurs in the history of his passion to account for death.

Had theologians been left to themselves to answer this specious and superficial reasoning, no doubt their own science would have been fully equal to the task. They could have pointed out sufficient errors in the statements, and an abundant liberty in the assumptions, of these writers, to confute them most satisfactorily.

* See Justius Lipsius, "De Cruce," lib. ii. c. 12; Josephus, "Cont. Apion." p. 1031.

But it was much more fitting that the very science which had been enlisted in opposition to religion, should be brought in to throw off from itself the odious imputation, and take the charge of finally confuting the objections pretended to be brought from its own principles.

Several eminent writers had occupied themselves with the physiology of our Saviour's passion, if we may so express ourselves, before this method of attacking it had been resorted to; such were Scheuchzer, Mead, Bartholinus, Vogler, Triller, Richter, and Eschenbach. But a much fuller and more scientific investigation has been since made by the two Gruners, father and son; the latter of whom first wrote under the direction, and by the advice of the former. These different authors have collected all that medical analogies could furnish towards establishing the character of our Saviour's sufferings, and the reality of his death.

They have shown that the torments of crucifixion in themselves were fearful, not merely from the outward wounds inflicted, and from the painful posture of the body, or even from the gangrene which must have ensued from exposure to the sun or heat, but also from the effects of this position upon the circulation, and other ordinary functions of life. The pressure upon the main artery or aorta, must, according to Richter, have impeded the free course of the blood; and, by disabling it from receiving all which was furnished by the left ventricle of the heart, must have prevented the blood from the lungs being returned. By these circumstances, a congestion and effort must have been produced in the right ventricle, " more intolerable than any pain, and than death itself." " The pulmonary and other veins and arteries about the heart and chest," he adds, " by the abundance of blood flowing thither, and there accumulating, must have added frightful bodily suffering to the anguish of mind, produced by the overpowering burthen of our sins."* But this general

* Georgii G. Richteri "Dissertationes Quatuor Medicæ :" *Götting.* 1775, p. 57.

suffering must have made a relative impression upon different individuals: and, as Charles Gruner well observes, the effect it produced upon two hardy and hardened thieves, brought out fresh from prison, must naturally have been very different from that on our Saviour, whose frame and temperament were of a very opposite character; who had been previously suffering a night of tortures and restless fatigue; who had been wrestling with mental agony till one of the rarest phenomena had been caused—a bloody sweat; who must have felt to the most acute degree of intensity all the mental aggravation of his punishment, its shame and ignominy, and the distress of his holy mother, and few faithful friends.* And to these he might have added other reflections; as that our Saviour was evidently weakened beyond other persons in similar circumstances, seeing he was not strong enough to carry his cross, as criminals led to execution were always able to do; and, if the men whom we are answering suppose our Lord to have fallen into a trance from exhaustion, they have manifestly no right to judge from other cases, for in them even this did not occur. The younger Gruner goes minutely into all the smallest circumstances of the passion, examining them as objects of medical jurisprudence, and particularly takes cognizance of the stroke inflicted by the soldier's lance. He shows the great probability of the wound having been in the left side, and from below, transversely upwards; he demonstrates that such a stroke, inflicted by the robust arm of a Roman soldier, with a short lance, for the cross was not raised much from the ground, must, in any hypothesis, have occasioned a deadly wound.† Up to this moment, he supposes our Saviour may have been still faintly alive; because, otherwise, the blood would not have flowed, and because the loud cry which he uttered is a symptom of syncope from too great a

* Caroli Frid. Gruneri "Commentatio Antiquaria Medica de Jesu Christi morte vera non simulata:" *Halæ*, 1805, pp. 30-36.
† Pages 40-45.

congestion of blood about the heart. But this wound, which, from the flowing of blood and water, he supposes to have been in the cavity of the chest, must, according to him, have been necessarily fatal.* His father, Christian Gruner, goes over the same ground, and answers, step by step, the additional objections of an anonymous impugner. He shows that the words used by St. John, to express the wound inflicted by the lance, are often used to denote a mortal one,† he proves that, even supposing the death of Christ to have been in the first instance apparent, the infliction of even a slight wound would have been fatal, because in syncope or trance arising from loss of blood, any venesection would be considered such;‡ and that, in fine, so far from the spices or unguents used in embalming, or the close chamber of the tomb, being fitting restoratives to a person in a trance, they would be the most secure

---

* Page 37. Tirinus and other commentators, as well as many physicians, Gruner, Bartholinus, Triller, and Eschenbach, suppose this water to have been lymph from the pericardium. Vogler, "Physiologia Historiæ Passionis," *Helmst.* 1693, p. 44, supposes it to have been serum separated from the blood. But from the manner in which St. John mentions this mystical flow, and from the concurrent sentiment of all antiquity, we must admit something more than a mere physical event. Richter observes, that the abundant gush of the blood and water, "non ut in mortuis fieri solet, lentum et grumosum, sed calentem adhuc et flexilem, tamquam ex calentissimo misericordiæ fonte," must be considered preternatural, and deeply symbolical. (P. 52.)

† "Vindiciæ Mortis Jesu Christi veræ." *Ibid.* p. 77, *seqq.* A consideration not noticed by any of these authors, seems to me to decide the point of the depth of the wound, and place beyond doubt that it could not be superficial, but must have entered the cavity. Our Saviour distinguishes the wounds in his hands from that of his side, by desiring Thomas to measure the former by his finger, and the latter by the insertion of his hand. (John, xx. 27.) This, therefore, must have been of the breadth of two or three fingers on the outside. But for a lance, which tapered very gently from the point, to leave a scar or incision on the flesh of such a breadth, at least four or five inches must have penetrated into the body, a supposition quite incompatible with a superficial or flesh-wound. Of course this reasoning is with those who admit the entire history of the passion and subsequent appearance of our Saviour, but deny his real death : and such are the adversaries of the Gruners.

‡ Page 67.

instruments for converting apparent into real death, by suffocation.* To which, we may add Eschenbach's observation, that there is no well-recorded instance of syncope lasting more than one day, whereas, here it must have lasted three;† and also that, even this period would not have been sufficient to restore to strength and health, a frame which had undergone the shattering tortures of crucifixion, and the enfeebling influence of syncope from loss of blood.

I cannot omit, on this occasion, a case which may confirm some of the foregoing observations; the more so, because, never having been translated into any European language, it is not likely to come in the way of many readers who take an interest in these investigations. I allude to an account of a crucified Mameluke, or Turkish servant, published by Kosegarten from an Arabic manuscript, entitled *The Meadow of Flowers, and the Fragrant Odour.* The narrative, after quoting the authorities, as is usual in Arabic histories, proceeds as follows: " It is said that he had killed his master, for some cause or other; and he was crucified on the banks of the river Barada, under the castle of Damascus, with his face turned towards the east. His hands, arms, and feet, were nailed, and he remained so, from mid-day on Friday, to the same hour on Sunday, when he died. He was remarkable for his strength and prowess; he had been engaged with his master in sacred war at Askalon, where he slew great numbers of Franks; and when very young he had killed a lion. Several extraordinary things occurred at his being nailed, as that he gave himself up without resistance to the cross, and without complaint stretched out his hands, which were nailed, and after them his feet; he in the meantime looked on, and did not utter a groan, or change his countenance or move his limbs." Thus we see a person, in the flower of his age, remarkable

---

* Page 70. Charles Gruner, p. 38.
† " Scripta Medico-biblica:" *Rostoch*, 1779, p. 128.

for his hardihood and strength, inured to military fatigue, nay, so strong, that we are told in another part of the narrative that "he moved his feet about, though nailed, till he loosened the fastenings of the nails, so that, if they had not been well secured, in the wood, he would have drawn them out;" and yet he could not endure the suffering more than eight and forty hours. But the most interesting circumstance in this narration, and the illustration of the scriptural narrative I had principally in view, is the fact, not I believe mentioned by any ancient describer of this punishment,—that the principle torture endured by this servant was that of thirst, precisely as is intimated in the Gospel history.* For the Arabic narrator thus proceeds:—" I have heard this from one who witnessed it —and he thus remained till he died, patient and silent, without wailing, but looking around him to the right and to the left upon the people. But he begged for water, and none was given him; and the hearts of the people were melted with compassion for him, and with pity on one of God's creatures, who, yet a boy, was suffering under so grievous a trial. In the meantime the water was flowing around him, and he gazed upon it, and longed for one drop of it . . . and he complained of thirst all the first day, after which he was silent, for God gave him strength."†

What I have said may suffice to show, how our neighbours on the Continent have directed their medical pursuits to the vindication and illustration of the word of God. There are many other points well worthy of similar attention, many which would well

---

* John, xix. 28. The very fact of drink being prepared proves this circumstance.
† Kosegarten, "Chrestomathia Arabica:" *Lips.* 1828, pp. 63-65. There is a little circumstance mentioned in the course of this narrative, which may serve to illustrate what is related of Absalom's hair, 2 Sam. xiv. 26, observing that, according to one opinion, the weight is another expression for the value. "He was the most beautiful of youths, and most fair of countenance, and had the longest hair, the value of which was some thousands of dirhems." (P. 65.)

repay the study of a learned physician, who should feel inclined to dedicate some portion of his abilities and experience to the defence or ornament of religion. I will notice one which seems to me to invite such study, as I know I have the honour to reckon among my audience more than one fully competent for the undertaking. The subject to which I allude is the attempt made by Eichhorn to explain the sudden blindness of St. Paul, when going to Damascus, and his recovery through the ministry of Ananias, by natural and medical considerations. He has collected a number of medical cases, for the purpose of proving, that it was no more than an amaurosis, caused by lightning, and curable by means of the simplest character, such as even the imposition of hands upon the head!* Of course this absurd, as well as impious, hypothesis, may be met upon obvious grounds: as the very circumstance recorded, that Ananias told Saul he was come to restore his sight, proves that he trusted not to natural remedies; for, granting that amaurosis *may* accidentally be cured by such simple means, assuredly the most skilful oculist would not venture to predict their efficacy, or rely upon their certainty. But, at the same time, it would be still more satisfactory to see this history vindicated, as doubtless it may be, by the very science through which it has been attacked; and to have something written in confutation of Eichhorn's denial of this miracle, of the same nature as we have seen done in contradiction to the blasphemies of Schuster and Paulus.

It would not be difficult to establish links between the science I have just treated of, and the one on which I next shall enter, that is, Geology. Chemistry, for instance, which presents many analogies to both, might furnish us several interesting applications. But I pass them over, both because they are probably better known, and because the abundance of materials lying

---

* In his "Allgemeine Bibliothek," vol. iii. pp. 13, *seqq.*

before us will not allow us time for less important topics. I hasten, therefore, forward, to as rapid a view as I can give, of the connection between Geology and Sacred History.

Geology may truly be called the science of nature's antiquities. Fresh and young as this power may look to us, and ever vigorous in all her operations—free from all symptoms of decay as her beauty and energy may appear—yet hath she, too, her olden times, her early days of rude contention and arduous strivings, and then, her epochs of calmer subsidence, and gentler rule. And the legends of all these she hath written upon monuments innumerable, scattered over the boundless tract of her supreme dominion, in characters which the skill of man hath learned to decipher. She has her pyramids in those mountain-cones of disputed formation, which rise in every continent—her mighty aqueducts in the majestic rivers which bestride, as it were, large territories—now sinking into the depths of earth, now flowing in peaceful streams to the reservoirs of the vasty deep; her landmarks and local monuments, to note the times and places of her victories over art, or of her defeats by a stronger energy than her own; her cameos and sculptured gems, in the impressions, upon stone laminæ, of insects or plants; and we have but even now discovered her cemeteries, or *columbaria*, in those curious caverns, wherein the bones of early generations lie inurned, yea, embalmed, by her preserving hand, with evidences and proofs of when they lived, and how they died. And even beyond those times, we may go back to her cyclopean monuments, her fabulous ages of

"Gorgons and hydras and chimeras dire,"

when the huge *saurians* and *megatheria* disported in giant proportions over sea and land, and find, to our astonishment, all that a nightmare fancy might have dreamt of their shapes, recorded in sure representations upon unerring monuments.

Of all sciences, none has been more given up to the devices of man's heart and imagination than geology; none has afforded ampler scope for ideal theories, and brittle, though brilliant, systems, constructed for the most conflicting purposes. In enumerating the various theories of the earth, as they are called, which have been framed during the last two centuries, we may conveniently divide them into three classes.

The first should embrace those who assumed the Mosaic cosmogony or creation, and the deluge, as demonstrated points, and conducted their studies primarily with a view of reconciling actual appearances with these events. In the earlier works of this, as of every other class, there is, naturally, more of imagination and ingenuity, than of solidity or research. The older theorists hardly deserve to be dwelt upon; Burnet and Woodward, and Whiston and Hooke, and many others, may deserve praise for their zeal in the cause of religion, but can receive but little for real services in its behalf. Nothing was easier than to show how the world was first created, and how it was destroyed by a deluge, when all the agents employed were pure suppositions, or fictions of the author's imagination. Burnet supposed a brittle crust to have formed the earth's original surface, and a change to have taken place, about the era of the deluge, in the direction of its axis; this imaginary change, which has been sufficiently disproved by modern astronomers, freed the imprisoned waters from their frail bondage, and made them overflow the earth. Whiston was still more poetical. He supposed our earth to have roamed, for ages, through space,

> "A wandering mass of shapeless flame:
> A pathless comet;"—BYRON.

till, at the period of the Mosaic creation, its course was bridled in, and it was reclaimed from its vagrant state, to begin the peaceful revolutions of a planet. But, then, what occurred so soon to interrupt it, in its orderly career, at the deluge? Another comet is at hand, let loose by almighty vengeance upon the wicked world:

> "Down amain
> Into the void the outcast world descended,
> Wheeling and thundering on : its troubled seas
> Were churned into a spray, and, whizzing, flurred
> Around it like a dew."—Hogg.

In this state it bore down upon our little globe, caught it up in its watery atmosphere, and at once drowned and demolished it.

Truly, theories such as these, which caused Voltaire, in his scoffing mood, to say that "philosophers put themselves, without ceremony, in the place of God, and destroy, and renew, the world after their own fashion," materially hurt, instead of assisting, the cause of religion. For De la Beche has observed, that, when a river grows impetuous in its course, and threatens an inundation, they are the bridges which men have thrown over it, that they may pass it in safety, or the drains they have constructed to turn it into useful purposes, which give its waters a dangerous accumulation, and, by opposing a frail bar, impart to them, when this is broken, a more fearful rush;[*] and so may we here say, that the artificial means thus taken to pass unhurt over what were deemed the dangers of this study, and to apply it to profitable ends, did rather give those dangers a greater power: and, as Dr. Knight observes, when they were overthrown by the advance of science, seemed to entail some disgrace upon the subjects they pretended to illustrate.[†]

I am unwilling to say anything of living authors, where blame must almost seem to be cast upon labours directed by a zealous love of religion, and for the most

---

[*] "A Geological Manual," 3rd edit. 1833, p. 65.
[†] "Facts and Observations towards forming a New Theory of the Earth:" *Edinb.* 1819, p. 262. See also Conybeare and Phillips's "Outline of the Geology of England:" *Lond.* 1822, p. xlix. And the "Correspondance particulière entre M. le Dr. Telier et J. A. De Luc:" *Hanov.* 1803, p. 161.

disinterested purposes. But I am sure that the cause of religion is no way served by crude theories, or the rejection of facts repeatedly demonstrated. I shall have to allude, though very briefly, to the warm attacks made by Mr. Granville Penn upon Dr. Buckland's discoveries and observations regarding the antediluvian remains of bone-caverns; it is impossible not to be struck with the manner in which he seizes hold of secondary or inconsiderable circumstances and inferences, and denies, through them, the more general and important results. Mr. Fairholm follows much the same process: for instance, before observations had been well collated, some geologists had considered the *mastodon* a native exclusively of America; the discovery of its bones in Europe is enough, according to him, to overthrow the whole system of fossil animals.* If we reason that there are extinct species of animals, because the huge bones of the *saurians*, or the capricious skeletons of the *pterodactyli* have no parallel in the known modern world, all this is inconclusive; because we have not yet explored all the rivers in the interior of Africa, and, consequently, know not but these animals may exist in their vicinity!†

But while upon this theme, and while alluding to authors who reject all geological facts and principles, and then pretend to reconcile geology with the Mosaic history; who severely reprove geologists for framing any theory in their science, and then fashion to themselves *two*, one of geology, and another of the inspired narrative; I cannot pass over one writer, who, perhaps, of all others the most visionary, partly by declamation, more by distortion, chiefly by perversity of reasoning, attacks this study as essentially antichristian, and

---

* "We know that, in America, the remains of both the Mastodon and Mammoth are constantly discovered on the same soils. This circumstance would, of itself, be sufficient to destroy the whole theory of geologists, who confine the Mastodon to America."—"A General View of the Geology of Scripture:" *Lond.* 1833, p. 368.
† Page 366.

consigns all foreign geologists, at least, to the anathema of true believers. I allude to Dr. Croly's *Divine Providence*, a book which seems to assume, that Christianity was undemonstrated, till the author discovered the marvellous parallelism between Abel and the Waldenses, Enoch and the Bible ("the two witnesses in sackcloth!"), Constantine and Moses, the relics of the Apostles and the two golden calves, Ezra and Luther, Nehemia and the Elector of Saxony.* Surely, one so visionary, and one, moreover, who had been sufficiently courageous to add another baseless theory to the shivered fragments of preceding apocalyptic interpretations, should have paused before he scoffed at a science because of the many systems imagined by its cultivators. To detail the various inaccuracies, philological and physical, in the declamations of this writer,†—to expose the false views which he gives of the tendencies of geology, especially on the Continent,‡—to confute,

---

* "Divine Providence; or, the Three Cycles of Revelation:" *Lond.* 1834. Compare the preface with these strange comparisons, pp. 549, 571, 581, &c.

† For instance, p. 95, after Granville Penn, Dr. Croly denies that the *days* of creation can mean anything but the space of twenty-four hours; because, among other reasons, the Hebrew word יוֹם *yom*, comes from the verb *yama* (*ferbuit*). There is no such a verb in Hebrew (consult Winer's Lexicon, p. 406); neither if there were, could it be root to the other. In Arabic, there is a cognate verb, وَمَى *wama*, (ferbuit *dies*), "*the day* was hot:" but surely the simple term *day*, could in no language be derived from the idea of a *hot day*. To prove that the word day could not symbolically signify a longer term, because literally it means the period of light, "the time between two sunsets," is surely an error in logic : you might as well say that night cannot mean death, because it signifies the time between sunset and sunrise. I do not advocate the prolongation of the days to periods; but I think it very wrong to call men infidels for doing so, when only such erroneous grounds are given to the contrary. The terms used to express the sun's standing still, are just as literal and express as those used in the history of creation; yet no one hesitates to take them figuratively, because demonstrated laws of physics compel us to do so.

‡ Dr. Croly always affects to speak against *foreign* geology; and even in a note contrasts with it the conduct of the English Geological Society, p. 108. And yet he must have known that all eminent English geologists concur in the opinions he so severely denounces, of great revolutions prior to that of the deluge.

particularly, the unjust and unjustifiable criticism he passes on the views and reasonings of the learned Dr. Buckland, would require not much time, but more than the work deserves. The charge of infidelity, whether against a large class of men, or against particular writers, is easily made; it resembles, in our days, the vague outcry of treason or suspicion, which, in times of commotion, will bring down, without examination, popular indignation or vengeance upon the most innocent: and I know not if there be a worse class of slander than that which endeavours to affix the most odious of stigmas upon any one, who shall dare to think differently from ourselves upon matters indifferent.

But if we feel inclined to speak severely of those who have been builders of systems without foundations, but with correct motives at least, we must not forget that another class too has been guilty of no less, or rather of far greater, extravagance, without even this ground for extenuation of censure. I allude to those whose theories were framed in direct opposition to the inspired records. The last century produced plenty such in France; and one in particular, which, if not intended, was at least conceived, by too many admirers, to be in conflict with the Mosaic narration. I mean Buffon's, who, in his celebrated *Epochs of Nature*, published in 1774, repeated and illustrated the *Theory of the Earth*, which he had produced twenty-six years before.* All that brilliancy of imagination, charm of style, and decision of tone, could do in favour of any theory, this one certainly possessed. "He came forward," says Howard, "no longer to give a bold conjecture on the formation and theory of the universe, but with pretended proofs in hand, to evince not only the possibility, but, on most points, the necessary truth, of his former assertions. This was no longer in the style of a man who offers his

---

* Rousseau was among those who placed Buffon's system in opposition to the scriptural account, and gave it the preference.—See De Luc, " Discours Préliminaire," in his " Lettres sur l'Histoire Physique de la Terre:" *Paris*, 1798, p. cx.

conjectures to the world, but in the magisterial and dictatorial tone of one who is perfectly sure of whatever he advances."* The basis of his theory was, that the earth had originally been a mass of fire, heated to an almost incredible degree, and that it has been gradually cooling till our own times; so that at each appropriate stage in this process, it produced the plants and animals suited to each degree of warmth. It cannot be necessary to enter into any explanation of the dissension which now exists concerning the grounds of this theory; that is, as to whether a process of gradual cooling is going on in the earth. M. Arago contends, upon observation, that the exact accordance of climate, so far as we can reason between ancient and modern times, will not allow the admission of this supposition. And he argues from elements which a French philosopher at the time of Buffon would, I think, have hardly ventured to use, without consenting to incur the ridicule of being too credulous. For, with the books of Moses in his hand, he shows that the seasons in Palestine correspond now exactly to what they were in his time, as to order of succession and power of production; and he thence concludes that no alterations of climate can possibly have occurred.† To which reasoning, perhaps, it might be objected, that a gradual change of climate, by degrees almost imperceptible, except at long intervals, might produce a corresponding modification in the habits, if one may so speak, of plants and vegetables. Connected with this subject, and bearing in an interesting manner upon geological facts, is the question of central heat, which has been treated with great mathematical accuracy and learning by Fourrier and Poisson, the former maintaining the existence of a radiating heat in the interior of the earth; the other, while he admits the experimental facts, denying the conclusions. But any

---

* Howard's "Thoughts on the structure of the Globe:" *London*, 1797, p. 286.
† "Annuaire du Bureau des Longitudes," for 1834.

discussion of this question would lead us too far from the matter in hand.

From the time of Buffon, system rose beside system, like the moving pillars of the desert, advancing in threatening array; but, like them, they were fabrics of sand; and, though in 1806 the French Institute counted more than eighty such theories hostile to Scripture history, not one of them has stood till now, or deserves to be recorded.

The third and most important class of geologists comprises those, who, without positively constructing theories, have been content to collect phenomena, and to classify and compare them. And geology, in this its true sense, owes its origin and principal development to Italy. Brocchi, in a preliminary discourse to his *Conchiologia fossile subapennina*, has done ample justice to his country, by describing a series of geological writers, principally treating of fossils, such as no other country can produce. It would be tedious to enumerate them; though later I may have to allude to some of their amusing speculations. Suffice it for the present to say, that throughout their works there appears a fear of pushing their conclusions too far; a sort of lurking apprehension, that if bold consequences were drawn from their opinions, they might be found at variance with more important truths. Of this uneasiness, the writings of Moro, Vallisnieri, and Generelli, would furnish ample proofs.

It is not, however, to be understood, that in this class are to be comprehended writers *indifferent* to the bearings of their science upon religion; on the contrary, in it are to be placed its most zealous upholders, and those who have really served it most effectually, although they have carefully refrained from constructing formal theories of the earth. Thus, De Luc, who, through the course of a very long life, never lost sight of the Scripture narrative, has been a most valuable collector and collator of facts. The researches of Dolomieu, Cuvier, Buckland, and innumerable others, whose judgment you shall hear in their proper places, have been conducted without any spirit of system, and yet have proved most favourable to the cause of truth.

While science is in the hands of men thus persuaded of the certainty of those great leading facts which are enrolled in the sacred account of the world's early history, assuredly the writers, whom I have quoted as hostile to this study, should have little cause to fear. So long, indeed, as phenomena are simply recorded, and only the natural and obvious consequences drawn from them, there can be no fear that the results of the study may prove hostile to religion. How much wiser was the counsel of Gamaliel, and how applicable to those who impugned these pursuits:—" Refrain from these men and let them alone: for if the work be of men, it will fall to nothing; but if of God, ye are not able to destroy it."* If the representations they have given of nature are the fictions of men, they cannot stand against the progress of science; if they truly picture the work of God, they must be easily reconcilable with his revealed manifestations.

Before entering directly upon the greater conclusions of this science, I will stop to notice an instance of one of those popular objections raised, upon a specious reasoning, from ill-observed facts, which, for a time, was again and again repeated, and produced no inconsiderable impression. Brydone, in his *Tour in Sicily*, wrote as follows:—" What shall we say of a pit they sunk near to Jaci, of a great depth? They pierced through seven distinct lavas, one over the other, the surfaces of which were parallel, and most of them covered with a thick bed of fine rich earth. Now," says he (the canon Recupero), " the eruption that formed the lowest of these lavas, if we may be allowed to reason from analogy " (that is, allowing two thousand years for a stratum of lava to be covered with vegetable mould), " must have flowed from the mountain at least

* Acts v. 38, 39.

fourteen thousand years ago. Recupero tells me he is exceedingly embarrassed by these discoveries, in writing the history of the mountain. That Moses hangs like a dead weight upon him, and blunts his zeal for inquiry, for that really he has not the conscience to make his mountain so young as that prophet makes the world. What do you think of these sentiments from a Roman Catholic divine? The bishop, who is strenuously orthodox, for it is an excellent see, has already warned him to be upon his guard, and not to pretend to be a better natural historian than Moses; nor to presume to urge anything that may in the smallest degree be deemed contradictory to his sacred authority."*

It is difficult to say where to begin in answering this absurd statement, whether with the scientific, or with the moral delinquencies 'it heaps together. Some writers believed this story, and give the canon credit for profound experience and learning in this matter, and thus were seduced by the first class of errors: others, like Dr. Watson, while they rejected the reasoning pursued, did not spare either the poor ecclesiastic or his bishop, for their respective conducts.† Both classes were equally wrong; for, in the first place, it does not take two thousand years, nor two hundred, to cover lava with what, to unskilful observers, will appear earth; secondly, the strata of Jaci Reale are not covered with vegetable mould; thirdly, the canon Recupero never asserted what Brydone has put into his mouth, nor drew any such consequences.

The first point has been placed beyond doubt, by a scientific observer, who surveyed the coast of Sicily, by order of the British Government:—"The practice,"

---

* "A Tour through Sicily and Malta:" *London*, 1773, vol. i. p. 131.
† "I will not add more upon this subject, except that the bishop of the diocese was not much out in his advice to Canon Recupero, to take care not to make his mountain older than Moses; though it would have been fully as well to have shut his mouth with a reason, as to have stopped it with the dread of an ecclesiastical censure."—Two Apologies, 1816, p. 156.

says Captain Smith, " of estimating the ages of lava by the subsequent progress of vegetation, is founded on a fallacious theory; as that progress must depend on their local situation, their porosity, and their component parts. Nor is more dependence to be placed on the alternate strata of lava and earth, as a shower of ashes, assisted by filtration of rain, soon forms a stratum of earth resembling argil. Some of the volcanic masses of the Æolian islands, that have existed beyond the reach of history, are still without a blade of verdure; while others, in various parts, of little more than two hundred years' date, bear spontaneous vegetation; and the same is seen on two lavas of Ætna near each other; for the one of 1536 is still black and arid, while that of 1636 is covered with oaks, fruit trees, and vines."* Sir W. Hamilton has made the same remark upon the lava currents which have passed over Herculaneum, the period of whose destruction is so well known in history. " The matter which covers the ancient town of Herculaneum," he says, " is not the produce of one eruption only; for there are evident marks that the matter of six eruptions has taken its course over that which lies immediately above the town, and was the cause of its destruction. These strata are either of lava or burnt matter, with veins of good soil betwixt them."*

The second and third points were sufficiently made good by Dolomieu, who vindicated the canon's character, while he established, by personal observation, that no vegetable mould whatever exists between the lava beds of Jaci Reale. These are his words: " The canon Recupero deserves neither the praises which have been bestowed on his science, nor the doubts raised against his orthodoxy. He died without any other annoyance than that inflicted on him by Brydone's work. He could not understand for what end this stranger, to whom he had been kind, should endeavour to excite

---

* " Memoir on Sicily and its Islands :" *London*, 1821, p. 164. See also Knight, " Facts and Observations," p. 264.

† " Philosophical Transactions," vol. lxi. p. 7.

suspicions concerning the correctness of his belief. This simple man, who was very religious, and sincerely attached to the faith of his fathers, was far from admitting, as evidence against the book of *Genesis*, pretended facts which are false, but from which, even if true, nothing could have been concluded. Vegetable earths, between the several beds of lava, do not exist; and the argillacious earths which are sometimes there, may have been placed there by means quite independent of the antiquity of Ætna."* I will only add to this satisfactory confutation, from my own personal knowledge, that Swinburne's statement is incorrect, that Recupero was deprived of his benefice, and otherwise persecuted, in consequence of Brydone's statement. His character was too well known at home to be injured by such calumny; and in fact, after its publication, he received a pension from the government, which he enjoyed till his death.† You will farther see, in its proper place, how, even if vegetable mould did exist between many successive layers of lava, no conclusion could thence be drawn in reference to the period of the present order of things.

Still we cannot too harshly censure the cruelty of the slanderer, who could thus requite kindness by a groundless aspersion, necessarily tending to bring suspicion, if not even ruin, upon the person whom he called his friend. And, at the same time, this may serve as an example of the crude and ill-directed speculations, to which a superficial and unscientific observer may bring himself and others.

And after so long a preamble, come we now to see, in what way the doctrines of geology bear upon the inspired records, and how far the phenomena, observed by men upon whose accuracy we may rely, are in accordance with their artless narrative.

The first point of contact between this study and the Mosaic history, is the creation of the world. Dr. Sumner thus briefly enumerates the questions whereon

* "Mémoire sur les Isles Ponces:" *Paris*, 1788, p. 471.
† "Journal des Savans," 1788, p. 457.

the connections between the two may be discussed:
"The account in Genesis may be briefly summed up in these three articles: first, that God was the original creator of all things; secondly, that at the formation of the globe we inhabit, the whole of its materials were in a state of chaos and confusion; and thirdly, that at a period not exceeding 5,000 years ago (5,400)—whether we adopt the Hebrew or Septuagint chronology is immaterial—the whole earth underwent a mighty catastrophe, in which it was completely inundated, by the immediate agency of the Deity."[*]

Some writers have attempted to read the days of creation step by step in the present appearances of the world, and to give a history of each successive production, from light to man, as recorded upon the face of the globe All this, however laudable in its object, is not certainly satisfactory in its results. The first portion of my task, therefore, shall be rather negative than positive—an attempt to show you that the startling discoveries of modern science no ways clash, or stand at variance, with the Mosaic narrative.

And, in the first place, the modern geologists must, and gladly will, acknowledge the accuracy of the statement, that after all things were made, the earth must have been in a state of chaotic confusion; in other words, that the elements, which later were to combine in the present arrangement of the globe, must have been totally disturbed, and probably in a state of conflicting action. What the duration of this anarchy was, what peculiar features it presented, whether it was one course of unmodified disorder, or was interrupted by intervals of peace and quiet, of vegetable and animal existence, the Scripture has concealed from our knowledge: while it has said nothing to discourage such investigation as may lead us to any specific hypothesis regarding it. Nay, it would seem as though that indefinite period had been purposely mentioned, to leave

---

[*] "Records of Creation," vol. ii. p. 344.

scope for the meditation and the imagination of man. The words of the text do not merely express a momentary pause between the first fiat of creation, and the production of light; for the participal form of the verb, whereby the Spirit of God, the creative energy, is represented as brooding over the abyss, and communicating to it the productive virtue, naturally expresses a continuous, not a passing action. The very order observed in the six days' creation, which has reference to the present disposition of things, seems to show that divine power loved to manifest itself by gradual developments, ascending as it were, by a measured scale, from the inanimate to the organized, from the insensible to the instinctive, from the irrational to man. And what repugnance is there in the supposition, that from the first creation of the rude embryo of this beautiful world, to the dressing out thereof with its comeliness and furniture, proportioned to the wants and habits of man, it may have also chosen to keep a similar ratio and scale, through which life should have progressively advanced to perfection, both in its inward power, and in its outward instruments? If the appearances discovered by geology shall manifest the existence of any such plan, who will venture to say that it agrees not, by strictest analogy, with the ways of God, in the physical and moral rule of this world? Or who will assert that it clashes with his sacred word, seeing that in this indefinite period, wherein this work of gradual development is placed, we are left entirely in the dark? Unless, indeed, with one now enjoying high ecclesiastical preferment, we suppose allusion made to such primeval revolutions, that is, destructions and reproductions, in the first chapter of Ecclesiastes;* or with others we take the passages wherein *worlds* are said to have been created in their most literal sense.†

---

* "Ricerche sulla Geologia:" *Rovereto*, 1824, p. 63.
† Heb. i. 2. In like manner one of the titles of God in the Koran is, رب العالمين —the Lord of the worlds.—*Sura* i.

It is indeed singular that all ancient cosmogonies should conspire to suggest the same idea, and preserve the tradition of an early series of successive revolutions, whereby the world was destroyed and renewed. The institutes of Menu, the Indian work most closely agreeing with the Scripture narrative of the creation, says: " There are creations also and destructions of worlds innumerable; the supremely exalted Being performs all this with as much ease as if in sport, again and again, for the sake of conferring happiness."*

The Burmese have similar traditions; and a scheme of their various destructions of the world by fire and water, may be seen in the interesting work of Sangermano, translated by my friend Dr. Tandy.† The Egyptians, too, have, by their great cycle, or Sothic period, recorded a similar opinion.

But I think it much more important and interesting to observe, how the early Fathers of the Christian Church should seem to have entertained precisely similar views; for St. Gregory Nazienzen, after St. Justin Martyr, supposes an indefinite period between the creation and the first ordering of all things.‡ St. Basil, St. Cæsarius, and Origen, are much more explicit; for they account for the creation of light prior to that of the sun, by supposing this luminary to have indeed before existed, yet so as that its rays were prevented, by the dense chaotic atmosphere, from penetrating to the earth; this was on the first day so far rarified as to allow the transmission of the sun's rays, though not the discernment of its disk, which was fully displayed on the third day.§ This hypothesis Boubée adopts as highly conformable to the theory of central heat, and the conse-

---

* "Institutes of Hindu Law:" *Lond.* 1825, chap. i. No. 80, p. 13, comp. No. 57, 74, &c.
† "A Description of the Burmese Empire," printed for the Oriental Translation Fund : *Rome*, 1833, p. 39.
‡ Orat. ii. tom. i. p. 51, ed. *Bened.*
§ "St. Basil Hexæmer," hom. ii. *Paris*, 1618, p. 23. "St. Cæsarius, Dial. i. Biblioth. Pat. Gallandi." *Ven.* 1770, tom. vi. p. 37. "Origen Periarch." lib. iv. c. 16, tom. i. p. 174, ed. *Bened.*

quent solution of substances in the atmosphere; which would gradually be precipitated as the dissolving medium cooled.* Nay, if Dr. Croly is so indignant at some geologists, for considering the days of creation indefinite periods, because according to its etymology the word used signifies "the time between two sunsets," what will he say to Origen, who in the passage I have alluded to, exclaims, " Who that has sense can think that the first, second, and third days were without sun, or moon, or stars?" Assuredly the time between two sunsets would exist most anomalously without a sun.

In making these remarks, I am not guided by a personal predilection for any system. I have no claim to be called a geologist; I have studied the science more in its history than in its practical principles; rather to watch its bearings upon more sacred researches, than from any hope of personally applying it. I will just now give you another method, whereby some able geologists think they prove the beautiful accordance of this study with Scripture. I do not pretend—it would be presumption in me to pretend—to judge between the two, or pronounce upon the reasons which each may advance. But I am anxious to show that there is plenty of room, without trenching upon sacred ground, for all that modern geology thinks it has a right to demand. I am anxious—and I trust the authorities I just now gave will secure that point—to show, that what has been claimed or postulated by it, has been accorded of old by ornaments and lights of early Christianity, who assuredly would not have sacrificed one tittle of scriptural truth.

But what, you will ask me, renders it necessary, or expedient, thus to suppose some intermediate period, between the act of creation, and the subsequent ordering of things as they now exist? According to my plan, it is my duty to explain this point, and I will endeavour to do so with all possible brevity and simplicity.

* " Géologie Elementaire à la portée de tout le Monde:" *Paris*, 1833, p. 37.

Within, comparatively, a few years, a new and most important element has been introduced into geological observation—the discovery and comparison of fossil remains. Every one of my hearers is doubtless aware, that, in many parts of the world, enormous bones have been found, which used to be considered those of the elephant—the *mammoth*, as it was called from a Siberian word, designating a fabulous subterraneous animal. Besides these and similar remains, vast accumulations of shells, and impressions of fishes in stones, as at Monte Bolca, have been at all times discovered, in every country. All these used formerly to be referred to the deluge, and quoted as evidence that the waters had covered the entire globe, and extinguished terrestrial life, as well as deposited marine productions upon the dry land. But perhaps you will hardly believe me when I say, that, for many years, the fiercest controversy was carried on in this country (Italy) upon the question, whether these shells were real shells, and had once contained fish, or were only natural productions, formed by, what was called, the "plastic power of nature," imitating real forms. Agricola, followed by the sagacious Andrea Mattioli, affirmed, that a certain fat matter, set in fermentation by heat, produced these fossil shapes.* Mercati, in 1574, stoutly maintained, that the fossil shells collected in the Vatican, by Sixtus V., were mere stones, which had received their configuration from the influence of celestial bodies;† and the celebrated physician Fallopio asserted, that they were formed, wherever found, by "the tumultuary movements of terrestrial exhalations." Nay, this learned author was so adverse to all idea of deposits, as boldly to maintain,

---

* "Agricola sognava in Germania, che alla formazione di questi corpi fosse concorsa non so qual materia pingue, messa in fermento dal calore. Andrea Mattioli addottó in Italia i medesimi pregiudizii."—Brocchi, Conchiologia Fossile Subapennina, tom. i. *Milan*, 1814, p. v.

† "Egli niega che le conchiglie lapidefatte sieno vere conchiglie; e dopo un lunghissimo discorso, sulla materia e sulla forma sostanziale, conchiude che sono pietre in cotal guisa configurate dall' influenza dei corpi celesti."—*Ibid.* p. viii.

that the potsherds, which form the singular mound, known to you all under the name of Monte Testaceo, were natural productions, sports of nature to mock the works of man.* Such were the straits to which these zealous and able men found themselves reduced, to account for the phenomena they had observed.

As a more accurate attention was paid to the order, and to the strata, in which the remains of animals were found, it was perceived, that there was a certain ratio existing between the two. It was, moreover, observed, that many of these remains lie entombed in situations which the action of the deluge, however violent and extensive, could never have reached. For, we must suppose this action to have been exercised upon the surface of the earth, and to have left signs of a disturbing and destructive agency; whereas, these remains were found below the strata which form the outermost rind of the earth's crust; and this reposed over them with all the symptoms of a gradual and quiet deposit. Again, if we consider these two observations in unison, supposing the whole to have been deposited by the deluge, we should expect to find them mixed in complete confusion: whereas, we discover that the lower strata, for instance, exhibit peculiar classes of fossils: then, those which are superimposed, are again pretty uniform in their contents, though, in many cases, they differ from the inferior deposits, and so forward to the surface. Which symmetry of deposition through each range, while it is dissimilar to the preceding one, supposes a succession of actions exercised upon varied materials, and not one convulsive and violent catastrophe. But this conclusion seems put out of doubt, by the still more unexpected discovery, that, while in moveable beds, or wherever the deluge can be supposed to have left its traces, we find the bones of animals belonging to

---

* "Concepisce più facilmente che le chiocciole impietrite siano state generate sul luogo, dalla fermentazione, o pure, che abbiano acquistato quella forma. mediante il movimento vorticoso delle esalazioni terrestri."—*Ibid.* p. vi.

existing genera; among the more deeply seated fossils such are never discovered. On the contrary, their skeletons give us a representation of monsters, whether considered in their dimensions or their forms, such as have not even analogous species now existing, and should seem to have been incompatible with the co-existence of the human race.

This latter consideration deserves some illustration, because it will introduce such as have not paid attention to this science, to some knowledge of its recent discoveries. They may, perhaps, wonder how, from a few fractured bones, any judgment can be formed of the animals to which they belonged. Some years ago the problem would have appeared absurd,—to reconstruct an animal from one of his bones; and yet we may truly say that it has been most fully solved. It may be, perhaps, unnecessary to observe, that so perfect is the individuality of each species of animals, that every bone, almost every tooth, is sufficiently characteristic to determine its shape. The careful study of these varieties, and the analogous results to which it always leads, were the bases on which the lamented Cuvier rested his extraordinary construction of this new science. The habits or characters of animals, as I once before had occasion to remark, impress their peculiarities upon every portion of their frames: the carniverous animal is not merely so in its fangs and its claws; every muscle must be proportioned to the strength and agility required for its method of living, and every muscle grooves the bones which it grasps, or under which it passes, with a corresponding cavity. Nothing can be more curious than the convincing, though unexpected analogies, by which Cuvier confirms his theory; for he shows a constant and ever proportioned relation between parts apparently unconnected, such as the feet and the teeth.

When, however, he first commenced the application of his principles of comparative anatomy to the broken remains of bones dug up in the limestone quarries of Montmartre, he soon discovered that they were referable to no species now inhabiting the globe. Yet so sure were the scientific principles which guided him, that he easily apportioned the bones to different animals, according to the various structure and size; and he pronounced them to represent animals of the *pachydermatous*, or thick-skinned class, and most closely allied to the tapir. He distinguished two genera, and discovered even several subdivisions, and gave them their appropriate names. The two genera he styled the *palæotherium* or ancient animal, and the *anaplotherium* or unarmed, from the circumstance of the one being distinguished from the other by a want of tusks. His results must not, however, be looked upon as mere conjectures: for when it happened, after he had constructed from such analogy the skeleton of any animal, that an entire skeleton, or any part not before possessed, was discovered, he was found to have been invariably right in his suppositions, and in no case, I believe, was it necessary to modify his conjectural restoration.*

In some instances, indeed, naturalists have been sufficiently fortunate to discover the spoils of these extinct monsters in such completeness, as to dispense with the toilsome process I have explained. Spain, for example, was early in possession of an almost complete skeleton of the *megatherium*, as it is now called, sent over from Buenos Ayres, in 1789, by the Marquis de Loreto; it was reunited in the cabinet of Madrid, and published in plates by Juan Bautista Bru. Other fragments, indeed a considerable portion of the bones, of the same animal, have been since brought over to England by Mr. Parish, and presented by him to the Royal College of Surgeons; and, fortunately, they serve, in a great measure, to fill up the defective parts of the

---

* See his principles in the "Extrait d'un ouvrage sur les espèces des quadrupèdes dont on a trouvé les ossemens dans l'intérieur de la Terre," p. 4; in his "Discours préliminaire, Recherches sur les ossemens fossiles," vol. i. p. 58. Published likewise separately. See also vol. iii, pp. 9, *seqq.* for the processes followed in the creation, as he calls it, of the new genera.

Madrid specimen.* We have thus an animal, with the head and shoulders of the sloth, yet with limbs and feet between the armadillo's and the ant-eater's. But, at the same time, it must have equalled the largest elephant in size, being thirteen feet long, and nine high.

Still more strange are the classes of animals allied to the *saurian,* or lizard tribe; the enormous dimensions, and almost chimerical shapes, of some among which, would hardly have been conceived by the imagination. The *megalosaurus,* as it has been justly named by Dr. Buckland, was at least thirty feet long; indeed, judging from a specimen found in Tilgate Forest, in Sussex, it seems, after making every deduction, to have attained the frightful length of sixty or seventy feet.† The *ichthyosaurus,* or fish-lizard, when discovered in parts, presented such strange incongruities, that its limbs could hardly be supposed to belong to the same animal. It was not till after repeated discoveries, that Conybeare and De la Beche produced an animal, with the head of a lizard, a fish's body, and four paddles instead of legs. The size of some of these monsters must have been enormous, as the specimens in the British Museum will satisfy any observer. Still more fantastical is the formation of the *plesiosaurus,* or, as it has been now more properly named, *enaliosaurus,* or sea-lizard, which, to characteristics similar to the others, joins a neck longer than that of any swan, at the extremity of which is a very small head.‡ In fine, not to detain you upon such mere illustrations, another far more extraordinary, and I might almost say fabulous, animal, has been discovered, to which the name of *pterodactylus* has been given by Cuvier, who first determined its character from a drawing by Collini, and had the satisfaction of afterwards seeing his decision confirmed by several

---

* See a plate showing the parts supplied by each, in the "Geological Transactions," New Series, vol. iii. 1835, plate xliv. with a minute description by Mr. Clift, p. 437.
† *Ibid.* vol. i. 1825, p. 391.
‡ See "Geological Transactions," vol. i. pp. 43, 103.

specimens. This he pronounces to have been the strangest animal of the ancient world: for it had the body of a reptile or lizard, with excessively long legs, manifestly formed, like the bat's, to expand a membrane, by which it was enabled to fly, a long beak, armed with sharp teeth; and it must have been covered neither with hair nor feathers, but with scales.*

These examples, out of many, may be sufficient to show you, that the species of animals found imbedded in limestone, or other rocks, have no corresponding types in the present world; and that, if we consider them in contrast with the existing genera, which are found in more superficial beds, we must conclude that they were not destroyed by the same revolution as swept the latter from the face of the earth, to be renewed from the specimens preserved by God's command.

Some naturalists have, in spite of the valuable use made, by our geologists, of fossil remains, even in the comparison of mineralogical strata, persisted in excluding them from geology, as foreign to the science.† But it is impossible to shut our eyes to the new light which these discoveries have shed upon its study, and, consequently, to neglect considering the relation in which the science, thus enlarged, stands to the scriptural account. So far, I think that, however negative our conclusion may appear, it is highly important; for the first step in the connection of any science with revelation, after it has passed through the tumultuary period of crude, conflicting theory, is, that it gives no result adverse to revelation. And this is, in fact, a positive confirmation. For, as I will more fully demonstrate in my concluding lecture, the beautiful manner in which the scriptural narrative, subjected to the examination of the most different pursuits, defies their power therein to discover any error, forms, in the

* "Ossemens Fossiles," vol. iv. p. 36; vol. v. part ii. p. 379. De la Beche, in "Geological Transactions," vol. iii. p. 217.
† As Dr. MacCulloch, in his "System of Geology, with a Theory of the Earth :" *London*, 1831, vol. i. p. 430.

aggregate of various examples. a strong positive proof of its unassailable veracity. Thus, here, had the Scripture allowed no interval between creation and organization, but declared that they were simultaneous or closely consecutive acts, we should, perhaps, have stood perplexed in the reconciliation between its assertions and modern discoveries. But, when, instead of this, it leaves an undecided interval between the two, nay, more, informs us that there was a state of confusion and conflict, of waste and darkness, and a want of a proper basin for the sea, which thus would cover first one part of the earth and then another; we may truly say, that the geologist reads in those few lines the history of the earth, such as his monuments have recorded it—a series of disruptions, elevations, and dislocations; sudden inroads of the unchained element, entombing successive generations of amphibious animals; calm, but unexpected subsidences of the waters, embalming in their various beds their myriads of aquatic inhabitants;[*] alternations of sea and land, and fresh-water lakes; an atmosphere obscured by dense carbonic vapour, which, by gradual absorption in the waters, was cleared away, and produced the pervading mass of calcareous formations; till at length came the last revolution preparatory for our creation, when the earth, being now sufficiently broken for that beautiful diversity which God intended to bestow on it, or to produce those landmarks and barriers which his foreseeing counsels had designed, the work of ruin was suspended, save for one more great scourge; and the earth remained in that state of sullen and gloomy prostration, from which it was recalled by the reproduction of light, and the subsequent work of the six days' creation.

But, I think, we may well say, that even on this first point of our geological investigation, science has gone farther than I have stated. For, I think, we are in a

---

[*] See this point beautifully treated by De la Beche, "Researches into Theoretical Geology:" London, 1834, chap. xli. p. 242.

fair way to discover so beautiful a simplicity of action in the causes which have produced the present form of the earth, and, at the same time, such a manifest approach to the progressive method manifested in the known order of God's works, as to confirm, if such a term may be used, all that he hath manifested in his own sacred word.

For when I have spoken of successive revolutions, destructions, and reproductions, I have meant not a mere series of unconnected changes, but the steady action of a single cause, producing most complete variations, according to established laws. And this, I may say, it is certainly the tendency of modern geology to establish. I have before slightly touched on the subject of central heat, or the existence of a principle of that power, in the interior of the earth; whether it arises from the former state of the globe, or from some other source, it matters not. That its action can be even now sufficiently violent to effect revolutions on our earth—great, if viewed in reference to particular tracts—in miniature, if compared to its primeval efforts, must be known, from observation, to most of you, who have visited the scenes of volcanic action. There, islands have been formed, and swallowed up again, hills have been raised, the cones of mountains broken down, the sea has altered its boundaries, and fruitful fields have been changed into black tracts of desolation. Suppose this power acting on a gigantic scale, not in one district, but over the entire world, now bursting out on one side, and now on the other; the effects must have been convulsive to a frightful degree, the disruptions must have been far more tremendous, and mountains may have been heaved up instead of hills, like Monte Rosso, which Ætna raised in 1669, or the sea may have invaded large territories, instead of small tracts of coast.

The observations of geologists go far towards proving the action of some such power, in the manner which I have described: Leopold von Buch first proved that mountains, instead of being the most immoveable and firm portions of the earth's structure, and existing previously to the softer materials which repose on their sides, have, on the contrary, been raised up through these, by an upheaving action from below. M. Elie de Beaumont has carried this observation so much farther, as almost to be considered the founder of the theory. One simple demonstration of it you will easily comprehend. If the various strata on the side of a mountain, though necessarily precipitations of a solution in water, instead of lying horizontally, as such precipitations must do, and consequently cutting the mountain's sides at angles, thus (*a* being the section of the mountain, and *b* representing the surrounding strata),

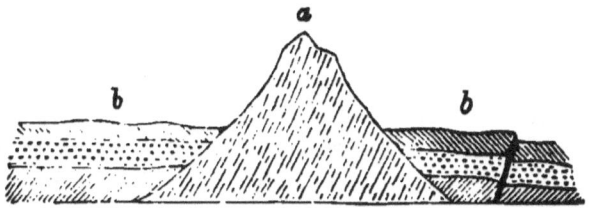

shall, on the contrary, lie parallel to its sides in this manner,

it is manifest that the mountains must have been thrust up through the strata already deposited. M. de Beaumont, by comparing the various strata thus perforated, as it were, by each chain of mountains, with those which lie in horizontal order, as if deposited after its elevation, endeavours to determine the period, in the series of primeval revolutions, when each was upraised.

And each of these *systems of mountains*, as he calls them, produced or accompanied some great catastrophe, destructive, to a certain extent, of the existing order of things.* This system of the French geologists has been confirmed and adopted by the scientific men of our own country. Professor Sedgwick and Mr. Murchison remark upon the phenomena observable in the Isle of Arran, that they seem to prove the great dislocations of the secondary strata to have been " produced by the elevation of the granite;" in which case, " the upheaving forces must have been in action some time after the deposition and consolidation of the new red sandstone."† But De la Beche is clearly of opinion that these successive elevations, indicative of the convulsions which disturbed the quiet action of sedimentary depositions, may be farther simplified, by reference to one cause, that is, the power of a great central heat, variously breaking the earth's crust, whether by the progress of refrigeration, as he supposes,‡ or as the author of the theory imagines, by volcanic action.

Now it seems to me that this theory, by its beautiful unity in cause and action, is in perfect accordance with all we know of the methods used by divine Providence, which establishes a law and then leaves it to act: so that the budding forth of mountain chains should be the well-timed effect of causes, constant in rule, though irregular in action; just as much as the putting forth of the new germ is the yearly consequence of the same action of heat, on the plant. But it seems, moreover, in the most striking harmony with the express declarations or explanations of the phenomena of creation recorded

---

* "Revue Française," May, 1830, p. 55. See also his MS. communications to De la Beche, in his Manual, pp. 481, *seqq*. Carlo Gemmellaro informs us, that, at the scientific meeting at Stuttgard, in 1834, he read a paper proposing a modification of the theory, and restricting the elevation of mountain chains to small spaces. "Relazione sul di lui viaggio a Stuttgard:" *Catania*, 1835, p. 12.
† "Geolog. Trans." vol. iii. p. 34.   ‡ Researches, p. 39.

in God's word. According to these we learn, that, to limit the ocean within its bed, " the *mountains ascend*, and the valleys descend, into the place which God has founded for them; he has placed (them) as a barrier which they (the waters) shall not pass, nor return to cover the earth."* Again, the formation of mountains is spoken of as distinct from that of the earth. " Before the mountains were brought forth, or the earth was born."† Another remarkable passage seems graphically to describe the effects of this consuming principle: " Fire shall be kindled in my wrath, and it shall burn into the lowest abyss (grave, or hell); it shall eat the earth and its produce, and shall burn up the foundations of the mountains."‡ In which description, as in most that extol either the glory or power, the munificence or the severity, of the Supreme Being, the figures are most probably drawn from his actual works; as Bishop Lowth has abundantly demonstrated.

But the discoveries of modern geologists have, as I have before suggested, also established a progressive series in the production of different races of animals, in evident accordance with the plan manifested to us in the six days' creation. Indeed, this approximation between the two has appeared to some so striking, as to lead them to abandon the method I have explained, for reconciling the inspired record and modern science, and induce them to maintain that the two are in far more perfect accordance than I have hitherto asserted. If you will not agree with them in their hypothesis, you will at least have an opportunity of seeing that " foreign geology" has no desire to destroy or controvert the Mosaic narrative.

Dr. Buckland truly observes, that learned men, upon grounds quite distinct from geology, have maintained the days of creation to signify long indefinite periods.§ With the plausibility of this supposition I have nothing

---

* Ps. civ. 8, 9. † Ps. xc. 2. ‡ Deut. xxxi. 22.
§ "Vindiciæ Geologicæ:" *Oxford*, 1820, p. 32.

to do; philologically or critically I perceive no objection to it; but I do not deem it absolutely required. Still, admitting the hypothesis before given, that all which modern science demands is granted in the intermediate space between creation and the present arrangement of the earth, some longer period may be required than a day, if we suppose the laws of nature to have been left to their ordinary course; for then, some longer interval would have been requisite for the plants produced to be decked out as we must suppose them, with flower and fruit, and grown to their complete perfection, when man was placed among them. But it might please God to bring them forth at once, in all their grandeur and beauty, from the first instant of their production.

Cuvier first remarked, that in the fossil animals of the primeval world, there was a gradual development of organization; inasmuch as the lowest strata contained the most imperfect animals, molluscs, and shell-fish; after which come crocodiles, saurians, and fish; last of all, quadrupeds, beginning with the extinct species whereof I have spoken."* Mr. Lyell, perhaps justly, denies the correctness of the consequence often drawn from this result, " that there is a progressive development of organic life, from the simplest to the most complicated forms;"† inasmuch as the discovery of one fish, or the bones of a saurian, among the shells, is sufficient to derange the scale. But this observation noways clashes with the view which I am going to state: since every subsequent examination has, as far as I know, tended to confirm this succession of animals. For instance, in the very minute tabular arrangement given by Mr. Mantell, of the organic remains of Sussex, we find in the alluvial deposits, the stag, and other such animals; and in the diluvial, the horse, ox, and elephant; after these, proceeding downwards, we have

* "Discours Prélim." p. 68.
† "Principles of Geology," vol. i. p. 145.

fish, and shells, and in some formations, tortoises, and the different saurians I have before described. The bones of, what he at first supposed to be, a bird, were discovered; but Professor Buckland considers it most probable that they belonged to a pterodactylus, or flying lizard.*

Assuming these premises, the authors, to whom I have alluded, suppose the days of creation to signify longer, and of course indefinite, periods; during which a certain order of animate beings existed; and they observe that the disposition of organic remains in strata, corresponds exactly to the order in which their respective classes are, in the Scripture record, said to have been produced. An anonymous writer, last year, published a comparative table of this conformity, following, on the one hand, Humboldt's valuable work on the superposition of rocks, and the acknowledged succession of organic fossils on the other. In the lowest, primitive, or as they are better called, unstratified rocks, as well as in the lowest order of the stratified, we have no traces whatsoever of vegetable or animal life; then we find plants mingled with fish, but more especially with shells and molluscs, as in the *grauwacke* group; thus indicating that the sea was the first to produce life, and bring forth its inhabitants; while the greater abundance of the inferior class, as shells, molluscs, &c., seems to indicate their prior existence to the more perfect tenants of the same element. Reptiles, or the monstrous creeping things, before described, and connected with the occupiers of the air, through the flying lizard, are the next that appear, and are no less justly classed by the inspired historian as marine productions. Now at length the earth produces life, and accordingly we next find the remains of quadrupeds, of species, however, in a great measure no longer existing. They are found only in the latest strata, superior to those

---

* "Geolog. Trans." vol. iii. pp. 200-216. Comp. Dr. Buckland, p. 220.

wherein the larger marine reptiles lie, such as the Paris fresh-water formation. Then at last come moveable beds, in which, as at our next meeting will be more fully shown, exist the remains of genera now inhabiting the earth. With the remains of each class are found sufficient marks of their having been swept from existence by some great catastrophe.*

This hypothesis and attempt to place in harmony the Jewish annalist with the modern philosopher, may appear to many deficient in the precision, requisite to establish so minute a parallelism. At any rate, it will serve to vindicate the cultivators of the science, from the reproach of being unconcerned about the connection their results may have with more sacred authorities. And I will add, moreover, that many among those on the Continent, so far from slighting the truth of that record, on the contrary, express a deep veneration for it, and their admiration of its wisdom, from seeing how their scientific pursuits do, in the manner I have rehearsed, appear to confirm it.

"We cannot too much remark," says Demerson, "this admirable order, so exactly according with the soundest notions which form the basis of positive geology. What homage ought we not to render to the inspired historian!"† "Here," exclaims Boubée, "we are met by a reflection which cannot fail to strike us. Since a book, written at a time when the natural sciences were so little advanced, contains nevertheless, in a few lines, the summary of the most remarkable consequences, at which it could not be possible to arrive otherwise than by the immense progress made in the eighteenth and nineteenth centuries; since these conclusions are connected with facts, which were neither known nor even suspected at that time, nor ever had been till our days, and which philosophers have ever considered contradictorily, and under erroneous points of view; since, in

---

* "Annales de Philosophie Chrétienne," Aug. 1834, p. 132.
† "La Géologie enseignée en 22 leçons, ou histoire naturelle du globe terrestre :" *Paris*, 1829, p. 408, comp. p. 461.

fine, that book, so superior to its age in scientific knowledge, is equally superior to it in morals, and in natural philosophy, we are obliged to admit that there is in that book something superior to man, something which he sees not, which he comprehends not, but which presses upon him irresistibly."*

Both the works which I have cited, are of a popular and elementary character, written designedly to instruct youth, and persons of an inferior education, in the outlines of the science. And on this account I quote them more willingly; because they serve to show how the tendency of this study, on the Continent, so far from being towards infidelity, is rather towards the confirmation, and even demonstration of Christianity; and how foreign geologists, instead of directing their pupils to contemn the sacred books, as irreconcilable with their new pursuits, do, on the contrary, strive to gain fresh motives of respect and admiration towards them, from the result of their researches. To the names already cited I might add many others, as D'Aubuisson, Chaubard, Bertrand, whose work, recently translated into English, has gone through six or seven editions in France, and Margerin, the outline of whose course, in the programme of the Université Catholique,† is eminently Christian.

These observations, too, must be doubly gratifying, when we consider the country whence they arise; that which for years supplied Europe with crude and illdigested materials, for unreflecting minds to object against religion. But to those who know the better spirit which is now fermenting in the warm blood of many among its youth, who are apprised of the genial ardour of true patriotism, which cheers them on in the holy desire to blot that stain from their country's scutcheon, and to raise her as much by the new glory she shall shed around the cause of religion, as she has

* "Géologie élémentaire à la portée de tout le Monde :" *Paris* 1833, p. 66.
† Paris, 1815, p. 57.

been shamed by her former enmity to it; to those who are acquainted with the sacred league tacitly existing among many, to devote their various and superior accomplishments and abilities to the defence, the illustration, and the triumph, of religion, under the secure guidance of the Church which they obey; to such as know these things, the authorities I have quoted are but small manifestations of a widely-extended feeling, mere leaves rising to the surface of the waters, to show the rich and luxuriant growth of vegetation, which their depths enclose.

And surely it must be gratifying thus to see a science, formerly classed, and not, perhaps, unjustly, among the most pernicious to faith, once more become her handmaid; to see her now, after so many years of wandering from theory to theory, or rather from vision to vision, return once more to the home where she was born, and to the altar at which she made her first simple offerings; no longer, as she first went forth, a wilful, dreamy, empty-handed child, but with a matronly dignity, and a priestlike step, and a bosom full of well-earned gifts to pile upon its sacred hearth. For it was religion which, as we saw at the commencement of this lecture, gave geology birth, and to the sanctuary she hath once more returned. And how, our next entertainment shall yet farther declare.

LECTURE THE SIXTH;

ON

THE NATURAL SCIENCES.

PART II.

SECOND point of contact between Geology and Scripture—the DELUGE.—1. Geological proofs of the existence of a Deluge—denudation of valleys; erratic block group; appearance of the Alps.—Huttonian theory.—Elie de Beaumont's application of his theory to the causes of the Deluge.—Animal remains: entire animals found in the North; Bone-caverns and osseous breccias. Objections.—2. Unity of the Deluge, proved by uniformity of effects. 3. Date of the Deluge. General impression produced from observation of facts.—Deluc's system of *chronometers.*—Deltas of rivers; progress of *dunes.* Judgment of Saussure, Dolomieu, and Cuvier.—Concluding remarks on the natural sciences.

IF we travel along some smooth and pleasant road, those objects which immediately surround us, shall seem to us adverse to our course, and moving in the opposite direction. And these are mostly works of the hands of man, the hedgerows, perhaps, which he hath planted, or the cottages and houses which he hath built. But if we cast our eyes beyond these, and gaze upon the handiwork of nature, upon the huge mountains which engird the horizon, or the majestic clouds which swim in the ocean of heaven, we shall see that they travel with us on our way, and that their course is onward, even as our own. And thus, methinks, it is with us in our pilgrimage towards truth. Men have hedged us round with the plantings of their own hands, or the devices of their own hearts; and if we look at these as we advance, we shall seem to be, as it were, in opposition and contradiction to the realities of things. But raise we our sight above and beyond these new and mortal creations, and when we shall contemplate and interrogate nature herself, in her primeval and enduring works, we shall find her, through them, travelling on the same road with us, and pointing towards the object of our desires.

Assuredly the science of geology hath already given you some proof, that so long as men piled up systems, they hindered those who would have gladly advanced towards the discovery of sacred truths; but that when the appearances of nature were fairly consulted, and simply delivered, they manifestly led to the wished-for conclusions. But, descending now to the second point to which I before alluded, as supposing a contact between sacred and profane researches, that is, the Deluge, I think you will find the usefulness of this science much more plainly manifested. It is evident, that if any traces of former events can be met upon the earth, it needs must be, that the last catastrophe which passed over its surface, hath left the clearest footmarks of its course. The short duration of the deluge, and the convulsive nature of its destructive action, would allow no leisure for the slow operation of successive deposits, but must have left traces rather of a disturbing than of a shaping power, of removal, dislocation, and transport, of a scooping and furrowing tendency, rather than of a formative and assimilating agency. We should expect to trace its course now, as we follow in summer that of a winter torrent, rather than as we discover the bed of a dried-up lake; by the fragments it tore from its banks, by the wearing action it exercised on the mountain's flank by the accumulation of loose materials, where its eddies were the strongest, perhaps by the fragments of more valuable spoil, by the remains of those plants and animals, which, as it burst over its ordinary limits, it swept from their natural haunts into its gulf. The universality of its action would produce such a uniformity in its effects, as would identify them through tracts placed at a considerable distance from one another; so that the ocean-torrent, issuing from the opened floodgates of the abyss, would mark its ravages in a similar direction in the American and in the European continent. It must be, doubtless, difficult to fix the era of such a scourge over tracts, which many centuries of vegetation have covered with their yearly tribute of decay; which the hand of man has industriously broken up, or otherwise altered; which the wearing and defacing corrosion of time has smoothened and disguised; and which a series of minor and local catastrophes have, from time to time, materially deranged. Yet, in spite of all these altering causes, there may be time-marks, either in the state of the ruins which the last devastation left, or in the effects of progressive agencies, which can only date from it, sufficient to guide us to, at least, a vague and approximating calculation of the epoch at which it occurred.

In examining the light which modern geology has cast upon these three points—the existence, the unity, and the date of a deluge, or devastation of the world by water—I shall chiefly follow, as my text, the summary given, in a few lines, by Dr. Buckland, at the conclusion of his *Vindiciæ Geologicæ*, and afterwards repeated in his *Reliquiæ Diluvianæ*.* Indeed, it will be this work which I shall have principally in my eye, in the compendious view I shall endeavour to present you, of what modern geology has decided regarding the physical evidences of this catastrophe.

The first phenomenon which, we may say, was justly observed and proposed, as giving proof of a sudden and complete inundation, such as the deluge supposes, is that which is known in modern works by the name of *valleys of denudation*. Catcott, in his work on the deluge, was the first to notice it; but it has received much more accurate attention since his time. By this term are

* "Vindiciæ," p. 36. "Reliquiæ," *Lond.* 1823, p. 226.

understood—valleys enclosed between hills, the strata of which correspond exactly, so that the valley has evidently been scooped out from their substance. To explain this by a familiar illustration: if you discovered, among the ruins of this city, fragments of wall, recurring at intervals, and standing in the same line, and if, upon minuter examination, you ascertained that the different portions were built of the same materials, in precisely the same order, so that, for instance, rows of brick, tavertine, and tufo, succeeded one another at equal intervals throughout, and with corresponding dimensions, assuredly you would conclude that the different fragments had originally formed one continuous wall, and that the breaches interposed were the result of time or violence. Precisely the same line of reasoning must lead us to conclude, that the valleys, which have manifestly cut the hills in two, have been excavated in them, by some agency equal to the effects. Dr. Buckland has been particularly successful in the examination of this appearance, on the coast of Devon and Dorset, of which he has given illustrative plates. From these, as well as from his description, it appears that the entire coast is cut by valleys running towards the sea, dividing the strata of the hills, so that they tally one with another. On the sides of these valleys are accumulations of gravel, manifestly deposited on the slopes of the hills, and at the bottom of the gorge, by the excavating cause. This cannot have been any agent now in operation, for no river runs through many of them; and in the gravel thus deposited are found the remains of animals, such as would be destroyed by a sudden flood in the present order of creation.* Similar examples might be brought from the essays of other geologists.

To this class of proofs I may refer another singular appearance, which seems attributable to the washing away, by water, of the sides of mountains. I allude to those huge pinnacles of granite, or other hard rock,

* "Reliquiæ," p. 247. "Geolog. Trans." vol. i. p. 96.

which seem to stand detached and insulated from the neighbouring mountains. Mount Cervin, in the Vivarais, presents a pyramid 3,000 feet high upon the loftiest Alps, and is thus commented on by Saussure:— "However keen a partizan I am of crystallization, it is impossible for me to believe that such an obelisk issued directly from nature's hand, in this shape. The surrounding matter has been broken off and swept away; for nothing is seen around it but other pinnacles, springing like it abruptly out of the ground, with their sides, in like manner, abraded by violence." At Greiffenstein, in Saxony, are a number of granitic prisms, standing upon a plain, and rising to the height of a hundred feet, and upwards. Each of these is again divided, by horizontal fissures, into so many blocks; and thus they present the idea of a great mass of granite, the connecting parts of which have been violently torn away."*

Another class of phenomena which gives the same results, may be justly comprehended in the term proposed by De la Beche, the *erratic block group*.† Dr. Buckland had before proposed a distinction between *alluvial* and *diluvial* formations; understanding by the former, those deposits which tides, or rivers, or other existing causes, make in their ordinary action, and by the latter, those which seem due to the agency of a more powerful cause, than any now at work,—such as a vast and overwhelming inundation. The constituents of this class may be reduced to two: first, deposits of sand or gravel, where no water now acts, or could well have acted, in the present order of things; and secondly, those larger masses, varying from some inches in diameter, to the weight of many tons, technically denominated *boulder stones*. These, when small, are generally intermixed with the gravel; but often they surprise us with their huge masses, standing insulated and alone,

---

* Saussure, "Voyage dans les Alpes," tom. iv. p. 414. Ure, "New System of Geology:" *Lond.* 1829, p. 370.
† Page 181.

on the side of a mountain, so as to verify the beautiful description of the poet:

> "As a huge stone is sometimes seen to lie
> Couched on the bald top of an eminence,
> Wonder to all who do the same espy,
> By what means it could hither come, or whence;
> So that it seems a thing endued with sense,
> Like a sea-beast crawled forth, that on a shelf
> Of rock or sand reposeth, there to sun itself."
> WORDSWORTH.

De la Beche has paid particular attention to the circumstances in which deposits of gravel occur, and shows them to be incompatible with the theory,—that actual causes have produced them. Thus, we often find that the strata have been broken into what is called a "fault," over which the transported gravel lies quiet and undisturbed, thus showing that a different action deposited it there, from that which caused the fracture of the strata. In like manner, wherever it has been possible to examine the ground under these deposits, we find the rocks, however hard, scored in furrows, as if a vast current, bearing heavy masses along, had passed over its surface. Upon these facts he reasons thus:— "Our limits will not permit greater details, which would require the necessary maps; but it would go far to support the supposition, that masses of water had passed over the land. Confining our attention to one district, it should be observed, that the dislocations are far greater, and the faults, evidently produced at a single fracture, far more considerable, than we can conceive possible from modern earthquakes. It is not, therefore, unphilosophical to infer, that a greater force, causing vibrations and fractures of the rocks, would throw a greater body of water into more violent movement, and that the wave or waves, bursting upon the land, or acting upon the bottom, at comparatively small depths, would have an elevation and destructive sweeping power, proportioned to the disturbing force employed.

"The next question that will arise is, are there any

other marks of masses of water passing over the land? To this it may be replied, that the forms of the valleys are gentle and rounded, and such as no complication of meteoric causes, that ingenuity can imagine, seems capable of producing: that numerous valleys occur on the lines of faults, and that the detritus is dispersed in a way that cannot be accounted for by the present action of mere atmospheric waters"*

Dr. Buckland has minutely traced the course of quartzose pebbles, from Warwickshire, to Oxfordshire and London, in such a manner as to leave no doubt, that they have been carried down by a violent rush of waters from north to south. For, when we first meet them, in the neighbourhood of Birmingham and Lichfield, they form enormous beds, subordinate to the red sandstone. Thence they have been swept downwards, chiefly along the valleys of the Evenlode and Thames, mixed with fragments of rock existing in Yorkshire and Lincolnshire, but nowhere *in situ* near the places where the pebbles are now found. The quantity decreases in proportion as we recede from their original bed; so that in Hyde Park, and the Kensington gravel-pits, they are less abundant than at Oxford. But these transported pebbles, being found on the heights which line these valleys, it would appear a natural conclusion, that the same cause which brought them hither, also excavated the valleys: though, according to the learned professor's supposition, rather in its retreat than in its first advance. The sufficiency of this one action to produce all the effects, affords, surely, a strong ground for adopting his hypothesis.†

De la Beche found on the top of Great Haldon-hill, about 800 feet above the sea, pieces of rock, which must have been derived from lower levels. "I there found," he adds, "pieces of red quartziferous porphyry, com-

---

* Page 184. In the first edition the learned author is more explicit, as he used the word "deluge," where now he has "masses of water," in the beginning of the second paragraph.
† "Reliquiæ," p. 249.

pact red sandstone, and a compact siliceous rock, not uncommon in the grauwacke of the vicinity, where all these rocks occur at lower levels than the summit of Haldon, and where certainly they could not have been carried by rains or rivers, unless the latter be supposed to delight in running up hill." Dr. Buckland collected, in the county of Durham, within a few miles of Darlington, pebbles of more than twenty varieties of greenstone rock and slate, which occur nowhere nearer than the lake district of Cumberland; and one block of granite in that town cannot have come from any nearer place than Shap, near Penrith. Similar blocks are found also on the elevated plane of Sedgfield, on the south-east of Durham. The nearest point from which these blocks and pebbles could have been derived, is the lake district of Cumberland, from which they are separated by the heights of Stainmoor; and if it be thought too great a difficulty to suppose them brought thence, the only choice is to give them a Norwegian origin, and suppose them transported from beyond the present sea. Mr. Conybeare has remarked, that it would not be difficult to collect almost a complete geological series of English rocks, in the neighbourhood of Market Harborough, or in the valley of Shipton-on-Stour, from the rolled fragments and boulders which there occur. Professor Sedgwick has observed, that the boulders accompanying the detritus, or gravel, in Cumberland, must come from Dumfriesshire, and consequently have crossed Solway Frith. Still more striking is the discovery of Mr. Phillips, that the *diluvium* of Holderness contains fragments of rocks, not only from Durham, Cumberland, and the north of Yorkshire, but even from Norway; and similar fragments of Norwegian rocks are said to exist in the Shetland Islands. The same writer gives a singular phenomenon of this sort. In the valley of the Wharf, the substratum of slate is covered with a stratum of limestone, on the top of which, 50 or 100 feet above, we find huge transported blocks of slate in great abundance; farther on the scars, to an elevation of 150 feet, the blocks are still more numerous. They appear to have been driven up, at a particular place, by a current, towards the north, and afterwards carried along the surface of limestone.* So that here we have a manifest deposition of limestone upon the slate, and then a violent transportation of blocks of this rock, over the surface of the deposit.

On the Continent, precisely the same appearances are observed. In Sweden and in Russia large blocks occur, with every evidence of their having been borne from north to south; Count Rasoumousky observes, that those between St. Petersburg and Moscow come from Scandinavia, and are disposed in lines from N. E. to S. W. The erratic blocks from the Duna to Niemen, are attributed by Professor Pusch to Finland, Lake Onega, and Esthonia: those of Eastern Prussia and part of Poland belong to three varieties, all found in the vicinity of Abo, in Finland.† In America, appearances are precisely the same. Dr. Bigsby, describing the geological appearances of Lake Huron, observes: " The shores and bed of Lake Huron appear to have been subjected to the action of a violent rush of waters, and floating substances rushing from the north. That such a flood did happen, is proved, not only by the abraded state of the surface of the northern mainland and scattered isles of the Manitouline range, but by the immense deposits of sand, and rolled masses of rock, which are found in heaps at every level, both upon the continent and islands; since these fragments are almost exclusively primitive, and can in some instances be identified with the primitive rocks *in situ* upon the northern shore; and since, moreover, the country to the south and west is secondary to a great distance, the direction of this flood from the north seems to be well attested."‡

It is just, however, to notice the hypothesis main-

* "Geol. Trans." vol. iii. p. 13.
† De la Beche, *ubi sup.* Buckland, "Reliquiæ," pp. 192, *seqq.*
‡ "Geolog. Trans." vol. i. p. 205.

tained with so much acuteness and learning by some very able modern geologists, that all these phenomena can be explained by causes actually in operation. Fuchsel was the first who made this assertion, which may be said to have afterwards formed the basis of the Huttonian theory. This, like many other philosophical sects, owes its celebrity more to its disciples than to its founder; and Playfair and Lyell have certainly done all, for its support, which a vast accumulation of interesting facts, and a most ingenious train of reasoning, can effect. The latter, in particular, must be acknowledged to have added immensely to the collection of geological observations. According to this theory, all valleys have been excavated by the rivers or rills which run through them; whatever requires a convulsive agent, is attributed to earthquakes, of the character and extent now witnessed; all transport of rocks or gravel may have been effected by tides, or rivers, or torrents, or floating icebergs. Opposed to this theory are, of course, the authors I have quoted, and most others of eminence in geology. Brogniart, for instance, confutes that portion of it which attributes so strong a cutting power to water, as to suppose deep glens and ravines to have been eaten through rock, by the action of a stream. The rich vegetation of mosses upon the surface of the rocks, at and below the water's edge, proves that the rock on which they grow, is not constantly worn away; for, if so, they must be as constantly swept away with their hard bed. The Nile and Orinoko, in spite of the immense force which their volume gives them, when they come to a barrier of rock which intercepts their course, so far from wearing it out, only cover it with a rich brown varnish of a peculiar nature.*
Greenough has observed, that the action of rivers tends rather to fill up than to excavate valleys, inasmuch as they rather raise their beds than dig deeper channels. For it is proved by observation, in digging pits by their

---

* "Dictiounaire des Sciences Naturelles," vol. xiv. p. 55.

sides, that the sedimentary deposit goes deeper than their beds. "The action of rivers," he continues, "may consist either in filling up or in scooping out; it cannot consist in both; if in scooping out, they have not formed those beds of gravel; if in filling up, they have not excavated the valley."* The transport of gravels and boulders to such immense distances, and such great heights, can no more be accounted for by existing causes. For it has been observed, that even rivers, unless exceedingly strong, do not carry their pebbles to any distance; as different parts of their course will be found paved with pebbles of various sorts. It has been thus calculated, that for any Alpine torrent to carry some of the blocks, scattered at the foot of that chain, we must give it such an inclination as would place its source above the line of the perpetual snows. The boulder rock, called Pierre-à-Martin, contains 10,296 cubic feet of granite; another, at Neufchatel, weighs 38,000 cwt. At Lage is a block of granite, called the Johannis-stein, twenty-four feet in diameter. An enormous boulder stone, on the shore of Appin, in Argyleshire, has been described by Mr. Maxwell as being a granitic compound, of an irregular form, but having its angles rounded with a vertical circumference of forty-two feet, and a horizontal one of thirty-eight. Numerous other granite boulders occur in the same part of Scotland, but no granite is there *in situ*, from which it can be derived.†

Before quitting this subject of rolled blocks, I must not omit the peculiar appearance they present at the Alps. This has been particularly examined by Elie de Beaumont and, later, by De la Beche. It is precisely what we should suppose would have been produced by the rush of a current of water through the valleys, bearing with it fragments of the mountains by which it

---

* "Critical Examination of the First Principles of Geology:" *Lond.* 1819, p. 139.
† "Geolog. Trans." vol. iii. p. 488.

passed, and filling up entire hollows with the ruins it bore down. Where an escarpment, or projecting ledge, obstructed it, it deposited a greater accumulation of materials; nearer the place whence the blocks were torn, they are larger, whereas they diminish in size, and become more worn by friction, as they recede.

The geologist whom I have so closely followed, puts the question, how far the distribution of blocks from the Alps may have been contemporaneous with the supposed transport of erratic fragments from Scandinavia? To this, after a preliminary caution, he replies, "that the blocks in both cases appear to a certain extent superficial, and uncovered by deposits which would afford us information respecting their difference of age; and that it is possible a great elevation of the Alps, and distribution of blocks on both sides of the chain, may have been contemporaneous, or nearly so, with a convulsion in the North."* In another work he enters somewhat more fully into the distinction between these two great distributions of blocks, the Alpine and the Northern, both of which he considers attributable to a comparatively recent period. "How far," he writes, "the events which have produced both accumulations of these blocks, may have been separated by time from each other, we know not; but we are certain that the geological epochs of both must have been very recent, since they both rest on rocks of little comparative antiquity." Afterwards, he infers, from the phenomena observed in Europe and America, that some cause, situated in the polar regions, has so acted, as to produce this dispersion of solid matter, over a certain portion of the earth's surface. We know of no agent capable of causing the effect required, but moving water.† This author considers, that the same simple cause proposed by M. de Beaumont, to account for all the preceding revolutions on the earth's surface, will likewise explain

* "De la Beche," p. 194.
† "Researches in Theoretical Geology," p. 390.

this latest one. An elevation of the land under the polar seas, would drive the ocean southward over the continents, with a force proportioned to the intensity of its action.

Here, once more, I must observe, that we have another proof, that, far from the tendency of many continental geologists being to incredulity, they, on the contrary, display an anxiety, so to frame their hypothesis, as that the Scripture narrative shall be embraced by it, and that their solution of the great geological problem shall in part be verified, by its including so great an historical fact, as is there recorded. For Elie de Beaumont observes, at the conclusion of his *Researches*, that the elevation of a chain of mountains, while it produced the violent effects he had described, on the countries in its immediate neighbourhood, would cause, in more distant ones, a violent agitation of the sea, and a derangement of their level; "events comparable to the sudden and passing inundation, of which we find an indication, with almost uniform data, in the archives of all nations." He then adds, in a note, that, looking at this historical event merely as being the last revolution on the surface of the globe, he should be inclined to suppose that the Andes were elevated at that period; and from their elevation, all the effects concurrently necessary to produce a deluge, might be explained.*

I come now to another great, and far more interesting, topic, but one on which I enter with considerable hesitation, in consequence of the various hypotheses, and conflicting opinions, connected with it—the remains of animals, discovered in different parts of the world, under circumstances extremely varied. I before observed, that, in the superior, or more moveable, strata, such as we may suppose to have been deposited during a temporary submersion of the earth under a violent

---

* *Ubi sup.* and "Annales des Sciences Naturelles," tom. xix. p. 232.

and impetuous rush of waters, are found the bones or bodies of animals, belonging, in most cases, to genera now existing, though in species sometimes differing from them. Judging by analogy, we should conclude that these were deposited in their present situations by the last convulsion which agitated the globe, since there is no trace of any other having passed over them; and it seems hardly possible to doubt, that water was the agent employed for preserving them in so remarkable a manner.

Dr. Buckland may be considered as having exhausted this subject, up to the period of his publication on diluvian remains; and the discovery, since his work, of later entombments, may seem, with a few exceptions of some moment, which I will presently notice, to have only presented repetitions of the phenomena he had observed, and confirmed many of his conclusions.

The remains of animals, superficially discovered, may be classified in three divisions: first, those which are found entire, or nearly so, in the northern regions, to which must be joined such as, from similarity of situation, are to be accounted for by a similar hypothesis; secondly, those found in caverns; thirdly, those which exist in what is called *osseous breccia*, or mixed with gravel or detritus, in the fissures of rocks.

In the first class, then, we may include, primarily, the carcases of elephants and rhinoceroses found in ice, or, perhaps, more properly, in frozen mud, in the northern latitudes. In 1799, Schumachoff, a Tungusian chief, observed a shapeless mass in the ice, on the peninsula of Tamset, at the mouth of the Lena; in 1804 it became detached, and fell on the sand. It was found to be an elephant, so entire, that the dogs, and even the men, partook of its flesh. The tusks were cut off and sold, and the skeleton, with some of the hair, was conveyed to the imperial museum at St. Petersburg, where it is still preserved. A rhinoceros, described by Pallas, in 1770, as discovered in the frozen mud on the banks of the

Viluji, was likewise covered with skin and hair.* The expedition of Captain Beechey into the north of Asia, has brought to light a number of similar discoveries, as the bones of these two animals have been there found in considerable numbers, encased in frozen sand.† The animals thus found, have been considered as belonging to different species from those now existing, chiefly in consequence of the hairy coat with which they were covered. Perhaps, however, the variety may go no further than is traceable in well-known animals, which in some countries have the skin quite, or nearly, bare, while in others they are shaggy—such as the dog, the hairless variety of which is well known. Mr. Fairholme has quoted a passage from Bishop Heber's narrative, showing the existence of some elephants covered with hair, in India, at the present day;‡ and maintains, that experience proves the tendency of the elephant to become hairy, in colder climates. However, placing this point aside, it cannot be doubted that these animals must have been surprised by some sudden overwhelming catastrophe, which destroyed and embalmed them in one and the same moment. It is quite foreign to our purpose to inquire whether these animals were inhabitants of the country where they now lie buried; and, if so, how they lived in so cold a climate; or whether, on the other hand, the climate has undergone a change. It does, indeed, seem most probable, that they lived and died where they now lie, instead of having been transported thither; and that the climate must have undergone such a modification, as renders it no longer a fit temperature for animals, which, before, could not only endure it, but found, in its vegetation, their necessary sustenance. This change, too, must have been so sudden, at least to all appearances, as to have allowed no time for decomposition; but a sudden

* See the "Mémoires de l'Academie Impériale de St. Petersb." vol. vii.
† See the Essay on this subject by Professor Buckland, at the end of Captain Beechey's narrative. ‡ *Ubi sup.* p. 356.

cold must have frozen the animals, almost as soon as dead. How all this can have happened, is a matter of system and conjecture; but assuredly it is nowise inconsistent with the idea of a scourge, intended not only to sweep all life from the earth, but also to complete the original curse, by causing such modifications of climate, or other influential agents on vitality, as should reduce the immense longevity of mankind, from the antediluvian to the patriarchal term.

Whatever difficulties, therefore, there may be yet unsolved in the class of phenomena I have explained, it is evident that, so far from standing in opposition to the character of the last great revolution, they appear, on the contrary, better explicable by admitting it, than by any other hypothesis. And hence Pallas owns, "that, until he had explored these parts, and witnessed such striking monuments, he never had persuaded himself of the truth of the deluge."*

The second class, comprising the bones of animals preserved in caverns, possesses greater interest than the first. To enumerate all the situations where these sepulchres of the early world are found, whether in England or on the Continent, would greatly exceed the limits I must keep; I will, therefore, content myself with giving you a general idea of them, from Buckland's accurate description. The one which first excited very general attention, was that of Kirkdale in Yorkshire. It was discovered in a quarry in 1821, and presented a very small opening, through which a man was obliged to creep. The floor was covered superficially with stalagmite, or the calcareous deposit formed by water, dripping from the roof. Under this was a rich loam or mud, in which were encrusted the bones of a variety of animals and birds. By far the greater quantity of teeth belonged to the hyæna, and among them were specimens indicating every age. In addition to these were bones of the elephant, rhinoceros, bear, wolf,

---

* "Essai sur la Formation des Montagnes."

horse, hare, water-rat, pigeon, lark, &c. Besides other evidences of this cavern having been the lair of hyænas through successive generations, the bones were almost, without exception, in a state of comminution, splintered and broken, with the exception of such hard solid bones as would best resist the action of the teeth. There were in fact toothprints, if I may say so, upon many of the bones, which were found exactly to correspond with the teeth of the hyænas discovered in the cave. By comparing these traces with the actual habits of these animals, by examining the extent and character of the accumulation, and taking into account the position and accessories of the cavern, Dr. Buckland comes to the interesting conclusion, that it must have been for ages the haunt of hyænas, which dragged in the bones of the animals they had slaughtered, and cranched them there at leisure; and that an irruption of water carried into the cavern the loam in which they now are imbedded, and which has preserved them from decay. Such a conclusion exactly accords with the character of the deluge.* This description may, in the main, be considered applicable to the other most celebrated caverns, such as those of Torquay, Gailenreuth, Külock, &c.; though it is observable, that in the German caverns the bones of bears chiefly predominate.

The facts expounded by Professor Buckland, are admitted by all to have been observed with scupulous exactness, and detailed with perfect impartiality: his reasoning, however, and conclusions, have not escaped criticism. Mr. Granville Penn, in particular, has attacked the whole of his explanation with considerable earnestness and ingenuity, and maintained that the bones must have been washed into the cavern by the flood, which caught them up in the neighbourhood, and forced them through the narrow opening in the cliff. As he, however, agrees in the most important points, that is, that here we have a strong evidence of

---

* "Reliquiæ," pp. 1-51.

the deluge, it is unnecessary to go into his arguments. It may be sufficient to say, that geologists have not been gained over by his reasoning: and that Cuvier, Brogniart, and others, have continued to retain Buckland's explanation.

But there is another more important question, which, perhaps, could not be so easily solved when the learned professor published his interesting account. Have human bones been discovered, so blended with the remains of animals, that we may conclude man to have been subject to the action of that catastrophe which swept these from existence? Certainly the instances which could come under his observation were such as to justify the conclusion to which he came, that wherever human bones had been discovered, mixed with those of animals, they had been introduced into the cavern at a later period. But there appear to be one or two instances rather varying in circumstances from these examples.

The cave of Durfort, in the Jura, was first visited in 1795, by M. Hombres Firmas, who did not, however, publish any account of it till he had examined it again, twenty-five years later. His essay appeared under the title of *Notices sur des Ossemens Humains Fossiles*. In 1823, M. Marcel de Serres published a more detailed account of it. The cavern is situated in a calcareous mountain, about 300 feet above the level of the sea, and entered by a perpendicular shaft 20 feet deep. Upon entering the cavern from this shaft, by a narrow passage, there is a space three feet square, containing human bones, incorporated, like the Kirkdale remains, in a calcareous paste.*

But a still more accurate observation, accompanied with the same results, has been made by M. Marcel de Serres, upon the bones found in the tertiary limestone at Pondres, and Souvignargues, in the department of

---

* "Granville Penn's Comparative Estimate of the Mineral and Mosaical Geologies," 2nd edit. 1825, vol. ii. p. 394.

the Hérault. Here M. de Cristolles discovered human bones and pottery, mixed with the remains of the rhinoceros, bear, hyæna, and many other animals. They were imbedded in mud and fragments from the limestone rock in the neighbourhood. Under this accumulation, in some places as thick as thirteen feet, is the original floor of the cavern. The human bones were found, on a careful analysis, to have parted with their animal matter, as completely as those of the hyæna which accompanied them. Both are equally brittle, and adhere as strongly to the tongue. To assure themselves of this point, MM. de Serres and Ballard compared them with bones extracted from a Gaulish sarcophagus, and supposed to have been buried fourteen hundred years; and the result was, that the fossil bones must be much more ancient.*

In this instance, however, the discovery of pottery makes it possible that the human bones may have been later introduced. For while, on the one hand, we cannot suppose men to have tenanted the same cavern with hyænas, on the other, we cannot imagine that these animals, however they might have indulged their bone-devouring propensities at the expense of man, would have introduced his pottery into their haunts, or tried their teeth upon it. Accident, therefore, or design, may have entombed some later inhabitant of the neighbourhood in the more ancient dwelling of the wild beast; though we must still account for the human bones being kneaded up in the same paste as the others. In either hypothesis, however, we have apparently a satisfactory proof, that a violent revolution, caused by a sudden irruption of water, destroyed the animals which inhabited the northern parts of Europe; and the corresponding phenomena in the southern parts, corroborated by similar discoveries in Asia and America, show that its influence extended farther still. In the middle of the last century, some human bones were said to have been found

---

* "Lyell," vol. ii. p. 225.

encrusted in a very hard rock, and were considered evidence of diluvial action.*

The third class of animal remains which I mentioned, consists of the osseous breccia, as it has been called, found generally in the fissures of rocks, or even in large caverns. It is formed of bones strongly cemented together, and with fragments from the surrounding rocks. De la Beche has minutely examined that which is found in the neighbourhood of Nice; and Dr. Buckland has collected particular details of that discovered at Gibraltar.† This species of incorporation is generally considered to have different dates, in different circumstances; but some of it may, perhaps, be pronounced as contemporary, in its formation, with the other deposits I have described.

And here I close the first part of my argument, or rather of my statements, regarding the latest conclusions of geology, on the subject of the last revolution, which disturbed the surface of the earth. But before proceeding farther, I must meet a difficulty which may easily be raised. There are many and very learned geologists, who attribute several of the phenomena I have described to older revolutions than the great cataclysm, or deluge, described in Scripture; nay, some perfectly sound writers distinguish the geological deluge from the historical, which they consider only a partial inundation;‡ and ascribe to the former all the appearances I have explained.

To these reflections I would variously reply. First, I would say, that the discovery of human bones must ultimately decide this point; for, if they can be proved to exist in similar situations, or under the same circumstances, as those of the animals in caverns, we must

---

* "A very curious and particular account of some skeletons of human bodies discovered in an ancient tomb, translated from the French; as also a circumstantial account of some petrified human bodies found last February standing upright in a rock:" *Lon.* 1760. See the letter at the end of the work.
† "Geolog. Trans." vol. iii. p. 173. "Reliquiæ," p. 156.
‡ "Boubée," p. 43, cf. p. 203.

P

assume the cause of their destruction to be what history describes. For if this, whether sacred or profane, represents men and animals as swept from existence by an inundation of waters, and if geology exhibits the effects of precisely such a catastrophe, and gives therewith evidence that no later revolution has happened, it would be most unphilosophical to disjoin the two. For their concurring testimony is like that of a written document, with a medal or other monument; just as the triumphal arch which commemorates Titus's victory over the Jews, by the representation of their spoils, though without a date, will be referred, by every sensible man, to the conquest, so minutely described by Josephus.

But suppose it should be *proved* that all the phenomena I have described belong to an earlier era, should I regret the discovery? Most assuredly not: for never should I fear, and, consequently, never should I regret, any onward step in the path of science. Should it be possible to discover an accurate system of geological chronology, and should any of these appearances be shown to belong to a remoter epoch, I would resign them without a struggle; perfectly sure, in the first place, that nothing could be proved hostile to the sacred record; and, in the second, that such a destruction of the proofs which we have here seen, would only be a preliminary to the substitution of others much more decisive. Who regrets, for instance, that Scheuchzer's *Homo diluvii testis*, or man who bore witness to the deluge, should have turned out to be only part of an animal of the salamander genus? He, indeed, thought it a most important proof; but surely no lover of truth can be sorry that it should have been detected, or can repine that its weak evidence should have been replaced by the co-ordinate facts which I have brought together. "The Christian religion," says Fontenelle, "has at no time needed false proofs to aid its cause; and this is still more the case now, from the care which the great men of this age have taken to establish it on its true foundations, with greater strength than the ancients had done. We should be filled with such a just confidence in our religion, as will make us reject false advantages, which another cause might not neglect."* Whatever we may think of the opinions of this writer, his judgment of our sincerity in that reliance which we place upon our cause, is perfectly correct. I will farther add, that I am only the historian of this and other sciences, viewed in reference to the Christian evidences; I have only, in general, to record the opinions of men learned in their respective pursuits, comparing the past with the present. The ground is constantly changing under our feet; and we should be contented with any science, if its progressive development shall be proved, by experience, favourable to a holier cause.

We come now to the interesting inquiry, how far geological phenomena tend to prove the oneness of this catastrophe; in other words, whether recent observations lead us to suppose a multiplicity of local inundations, or one great scourge, upon an awfully magnificent scale. Now, in answer to this, I will say that appearances indicate the latter case.

For, in the first place, you cannot have failed to remark, that in the sketch I gave you of the course which the rolled blocks and drifted matter must have taken, they present an almost uniform direction from north to south. The boulders of Durham and Yorkshire are from Cumberland, those of Cumberland from Scotland, those of Scotland from Norway. Pebbles from the same country are found in Holderness; and the valley of the Thames is supplied with them, disposed in the form of torrent beds, from near Birmingham. On the Continent it is the same; for the erratic blocks of Germany and Poland are traceable to Sweden and Norway. Brogniart has also remarked, that they run in parallel lines from north to south, sometimes slightly varying a little in direction, but always in the main

---

* "Histoire des Oracles," p. 4, ed. *Amst.* 1687.

presenting the appearance of having been borne downwards from the north by an overpowering current. You will remember, too, how Dr. Bigsby's observations showed him, that the detritus in North America came always from points farther to the north. In Jamaica, the same course seems observable. For De la Beche notices the great plain of Liguanea, upon which Kingston is situated, as being " wholly composed of diluvial gravel, consisting principally of the detritus of the Saint Andrew's and Port-Royal mountains, and evidently produced by causes not now in action, but derived from those mountains in the same manner, and probably at the same period, with the numerous tracts of European gravel, which have resulted from the partial destruction of European rocks." Now, these mountains are to the north of the plain. Again, the plain of Vere and Lower Clarendon is diluvial, and its materials seem derived from the trap districts among the St. John's and Clarendon mountains, which are situated towards the north.[*]

This coincidence of direction in the course pursued by the ocean-current in such remote parts of the world, whether we measure their distance from north to south, or from east to west, seems to indicate clearly the operation of a uniform cause. For, if we suppose the sea to have broken in upon the land at different periods, it might be at one time, for instance, the Baltic, at another the Mediterranean, at another the Atlantic; and in each case, the direction of the scourge, as evinced by its traces, would be naturally varied. Whereas, at present, not only is the admission of one only deluge the simplest, and, consequently, the most philosophical explanation of these constant and uniform phenomena, but a variety of such catastrophes can hardly be admitted, without supposing that each must have disturbed the effects of the preceding; so that we should have crossing lines of drifted matter, and varied directions in the rolled masses, to disturb every calculation. Yet nothing of this sort

---

[*] "On the Geology of Jamaica."—Geol. Trans. vol. ii. pp. 182, 184.

has been discovered in tracts hitherto explored; and, therefore, sound science should conclude that the cause was only one. Nor would this reasoning be much impaired, should subsequent investigation in more distant countries lead to different results. For we must naturally suppose that other oceans, besides the northern, were sluiced out upon the earth to produce its last great purgation; and from them the lines of drifted masses would point in another direction.

If the track of these transported materials show a uniform direction, we may expect the road over which they travelled to be worn in a corresponding manner. The first to notice this appearance, as I have already mentioned, was Sir James Hall, who observed, that in the neighbourhood of Edinburgh the rocks are marked with ruts or lines, apparently scooped out by the passage of heavy rolled masses, in the direction from east to west. Sir R. Murchison has minutely described the same appearance in the Brora district, in Sutherlandshire. "I remarked," he observes, "in my former paper, that these hills probably owe their origin to denudation; which supposition is now confirmed by the exposure on their surface of innumerable parallel furrows and irregular scratches, both deep and shallow— such, in short, as can scarcely have been produced by any other operation than the rush of rock-fragments transported by some powerful current. The furrows and scratches appear to have been made by stones of all sizes, which (with the occasional exception of lines slightly diverging, probably occasioned by the smaller pebbles coming forcibly in contact with the larger) preserve a general parallelism, with a direction from N.W. to S.E."* This coincidence is certainly remarkable, and leaves little room to doubt the unity of the cause, which produced such uniform results.

I will not dwell upon the coincidence of other appearances, as the similarity of distribution in the

* "Geol. Trans." vol. ii. p. 357.

diluvium, and its organic remains, in different parts of the world; for the remarks I have already made will suffice to show you, that the probabilities are greatly in favour of one single cause having produced them all. Neither shall I detain you upon another important conclusion, resulting manifestly from all that has been said, that the last inundation was not, like the supposed preceding ones, a long submersion under the sea, but only a temporary and passing flood, just such as the Scriptures describe it. That the land previous to it was, in part at least, the same as now, is apparent from the hyæna caverns: that it was only for a limited period under water, appears from the absence of all such deposits as suppose solution; for its sediment is composed of loose materials, gravels, breccias, and mingled *débris;* such as a river or sea, on a gigantic scale, might be supposed first to take up, and then to leave behind it.

We come at length to another still more interesting question: Does geology give any data towards ascertaining, with tolerable precision, the era of this last revolution? To this I think we may safely reply—and some of the authorities quoted expressly say it—that the general, and, if you please, vague impression produced upon accurate observers, by geological facts, is, that the last visitation is of comparatively modern date. The earth's surface presents the appearance of having been but lately moulded, and the effects of causes in actual operation appear but small, unless restricted to a very limited period. Thus, if we look at the trifling accumulation of rubbish or fragments, which surrounds the foot of lofty mountain chains, or at the small progress made by rivers in filling up the lakes through which they pass, in spite of the mud they daily and hourly deposit, we are necessarily driven to acknowledge, that a few thousands of years are amply sufficient to account for the present state of things.

But an attempt has been made to proceed in this investigation, with far more approximative accuracy, by measuring the periodical effects of such causes as I have incidentally mentioned, so to determine, with some precision, the length of time which must have elapsed since first they began to act. Deluc was the first who took some pains to observe and collect such data, to which he gave the name of *chronometers*. He has, indeed, been severely lashed for his attempt, by writers of an opposite school;* and yet it is but fair to remark, that his conclusions, and even in great measure their premises, were adopted by Cuvier, whose sagacity and immense geological knowledge few will attempt to impugn. It is, therefore, rather as admitted by him, than as proposed by the other, that I shall proceed briefly to lay before you the line of proof adopted in his system. The general results it is directed to afford are, first, that the present continents have not existed anything like the time supposed or required by the advocates of causes now in action; secondly, that whenever any accurate and definite measure of time can be obtained, it is nearly coincident with that which Moses assigns for the existence of the present order of things. Considering the immense distance of time to which we have to go back, there must be considerable discrepancies between the different dates; but they are not greater than the chronological tables of various nations, or even those of one nation as given by different authors, will exhibit.

One method of attempting to arrive at the date of our last revolution, is that of measuring the increase made by the deltas of rivers, that is, the land gained, at the mouths of rivers, from the sea, by the gradual deposit of mud and earth, which they bear along with them in their course. By examining history, we may ascertain the distance, at a given date, of the head of the delta from the sea, and thus with accuracy determine the annual increase. By comparing this with the whole extent of territory which owes its existence to the river, we should have an estimate of how long it has flowed through its present channel. But hitherto,

---

* "Lyell," vol. i. pp. 224, 300.

this measurement has been but vaguely taken, and consequently little more has been gained than a negative conclusion, opposed to the countless ages required by some geologists. Thus, the advance of the delta of the Nile is very sensible; for the city of Rosetta, which, a thousand years ago, stood upon the sea, is now two leagues distant from it. According to Demaillet, the cape before it was prolonged half a league in twenty-five years; but this must have been a very extraordinary instance. However, it is unnecessary to suppose so immense a distance of time, from which to date the commencement of this formation. The delta of the Rhone was proved by Astruc, by comparing its present state with the accounts of Pliny and Mela, to have increased nine miles since the Christian era. That of the Po was scientifically examined by M. Prony, by commission of the French government. You are most of you probably aware of the high embankments between which this river runs: and this engineer ascertained that its level is higher than the roofs of the houses of Ferrara, and that it has gained 6,000 fathoms on the sea since 1604, or at the rate of 150 feet a year. Hence Adria, which once gave its name to the Adriatic, is removed eighteen miles from the sea. These examples will not allow us to allot a very indefinite period to the action of these rivers. A stream carrying with it such enormous deposits, that their yearly increase may be almost called visible, could not have required so many thousands of years to reach its present level.*

According to Gervais de la Prise, the retreat of the sea, or extension of the land, by the depositions of the Orme, may be accurately measured, by monuments erected at different known epochs; and the result is, that these causes cannot have been in operation longer than six thousand years.†

---

* Cuvier, " Discours préliminaire," 3rd edit.: *Paris*, 1825, p. 144. Deluc, " Lettres à M. Blumenbach," p. 256; " Abrégé de Géologie :" *Paris*, 1816, p. 97.
† "Accord du Livre de la Genèse avec la Géologie :" *Caen*, 1803, p. 75.

A more interesting chronometer is that of *dunes*. By this term are signified heaps of sand, which first accumulate on the shore, and then are pushed forward, by the wind, upon the cultivated lands, so as to desolate and destroy them. They often rise to an almost incredible height, and drive before them pools of rain-water, the discharge of which into the sea they effectually cut off. Deluc paid particular attention to those on the coast of Cornwall, and has described many of them very minutely. Thus, one in the neighbourhood of Padstow threatened to swallow up the church, which it completely overhung, having reached the very roof; so that all access would have been prevented, but for the circumstance of the door being at the other end. Several houses had, however, been already destroyed in the memory of man.[*] In Ireland, these moving sands are not less destructive. The vast sand-plain of Rosapenna, on the coast of Donegal, was, little more than fifty years ago, a beautiful domain, belonging to Lord Boyne. A few years ago, the roof of the mansion-house was just above ground, so that the peasantry used to descend into the apartments, as into a subterranean; and now not the slightest trace of this is visible. But no part of Europe suffers so severely from this desolating scourge, as the department of the Landes, in France. It has buried fertile plains and tall forests under its irresistible course; not only houses, but villages, mentioned in the records of past ages, have been covered over, without chance of being ever more regained. In 1802, the pools invaded five valuable farms; and there are now, or were, at least, a few years ago, ten villages threatened with destruction by the shifting sands. One of these, called Mimisoa, had been struggling, when Cuvier wrote, for twenty years, against a dune, sixty feet high, with little chance of success.

Now, M. Brémontier studied this phenomenon with particular attention, for the purpose of submitting its

---

[*] "Abrégé," p. 102.

laws to calculation. He ascertained that these dunes advance from sixty to seventy-two feet a year; and then by measuring the entire space they have overrun, he concludes that their action cannot have commenced much more than 4,000 years ago.* Deluc had previously come to the same conclusion, from measuring those of Holland, where the dates of dykes enabled him to ascertain their progress with historical accuracy.†

I should be only repeating the same conclusions, were I to detail to you his researches into the increase of turf, or the accumulation of detritus at the base of hills, or on the growth of glaciers, and their accompanying phenomena.‡ I will therefore content myself with quoting the opinions of eminent observers of general geological facts, in favour of his conclusions.

"This observation," says Saussure, speaking of the devolution of rocks from the glaciers of Chamouny, "which accords with many others I shall make later, gives us reason to think, with M. Deluc, that the actual state of our globe is not as ancient as some philosophers have imagined it."§

---

* Cuvier, p. 161. See D'Aubuisson, "Traité de Géognosie:" *Strasb.* 1819, vol. ii. p. 468.
† "Abrégé," p. 100.
‡ Cuvier, p. 162. Knight's "Facts and Observations," p. 216. Deluc, "Traité élémentaire de Géologie:" *Paris*, 1809, p. 129; "Abrégé," pp. 116-134; "Correspondence particulière entre M. le Dr. Teller et J. A. Deluc:" *Hanov.* 1803, p. 161. A popular French writer on geology, speaking of the accumulations of detritus, brought down by glaciers, and deposited where they melt, known in French by the name of *murêmes*, thus concludes: "Their formation depending upon periodical and nearly constant causes, it is not difficult to calculate the time necessary for giving them the volume which we know them to possess; and as they certainly date from the commencement of the present order of things, they furnish a new method of arriving at an approximating knowledge of the time which has elapsed since the last cataclysm. This calculation leads still to the same result, and give us five or six thousand years at most, as the age of our world." He then proceeds, like Cuvier, to show how exactly these facts agree with the Mosaic records, as well as with the annals of every other ancient nation. Dr. Bertrand's "Revolutions of the Globe," English trans. 1835, p. 269. See above, p. 320.
§ "Voyage dans les Alpes," § 625.

LECTURE THE SIXTH. 251

Dolomieu writes as follows: " I will defend another truth, which appears to me incontestable, on which the works of M. Deluc have enlightened me, and of which I think I see the proofs in every page of the history of man, and wherever natural facts are recorded. I will say then, with M. Deluc, that the actual state of our continents is not very ancient."*

Cuvier has not only assented to these conclusions, but has laid them down in far more positive terms. " It is, in fact," he says, " one of the most certain, though least expected, results of sound geological pursuits, that the last revolution, which disturbed the surface of the globe, is not very ancient." And in another place he adds: " I think, therefore, with MM. Deluc and Dolomieu, that if there be anything demonstrated in geology, it is, that the surface of our globe has been the victim of a great and sudden revolution, of which the date cannot go back much farther than five or six thousand years."† And allow me to observe, that Cuvier intimates with sufficient clearness, that in his researches he has not allowed himself to be swayed by any wish to vindicate the Mosaic history.‡

I trust I have now said enough to satisfy you regarding the modern tendency of this science; and I doubt not but Dr. Buckland's expected treatise in the Bridgwater collection, although necessarily directed to show its connection with natural theology, will nevertheless throw farther light upon the topics I have discussed. I cannot here refrain from expressing a wish that the study of geology may soon enter into the course of education, as completely as the other physical sciences. It is while the memory is young and curiosity active, that the names of objects are most easily seized, so as to be firmly retained. Almost any district will present formations fit to exemplify the study; and its very

---

* " Journal de Physique:" *Paris*, 1792, part i. p. 42.
† " Discours," pp. 139, 282.
‡ Page 352.

pursuit, by requiring and encouraging actual and varied examination, gives a motive and a stimulus to exercise, which ensures health conjointly with improvement.

Many, I know, entertain the idea, that too minute an acquaintance with the material workings of nature, greatly weakens that more enthusiastic and poetic feeling, which the contemplation of her face excites, and thus produces a preponderance of a cold and scrutinizing, over a warm and admiring, disposition. Yet I know not how this can be, except from some defect in the method of communicating such knowledge. There can be no reason why the geologist should not stand enraptured on the mountain's brow, and first range, with a poet's eye, over the splendid scene of an Alpine valley, before he descends to study and classify the various rocks, which form its magnificent boundary. How should the comprehension of how nature works, be at all opposed to the perception of beauty in the results of her labours? On the contrary, it should seem as though the one must form a natural counterpart to the other. The skilful musician will, by casting his eyes over the written score, unravel in a moment its mazy movements, give to each note its harmonic power, and so combine them in his mind together, as thence to drink more music through his eyes than the untutored listener will enjoy, when he hears what has been written transformed into sound; and so may the learned in nature's laws measure her outward appearances by such just rule as must give him a truer perception of her charms, than the mere observer can ever attain. To the unpractised eye, the web which proceeds from the loom will appear exceeding beautiful, and in design most orderly, while the machine which produced it, seems a pile of confusion through its complicated wheels and pulleys; yet is it necessarily the type of what it brings forth, and the experienced artizan will perchance read in it, with equal admiration, the beautiful pattern it is calculated to work. And in like manner may the learned naturalist construct, from his knowledge of nature's processes, all those beautiful objects and scenes, which others cannot fancy unless they have actually beheld them. The observation of how the rolled masses are disposed in the gorges, and on the flanks of the southern Alps, must have led the discoverer to form in his mind a newer and a truer picture than a poet's imagination could have conceived, of the course pursued by the huge inundation which burst through them, tore down their sides, and rode in rude triumph, with their rough spoils, into the plains of Italy. The contemplation of volcanic effects by a scientific eye, which can distinguish the masses thrown up by explosion, from the rolling scum of the fiery torrent, and can note, as at Glen-Tilt, the strange and incomprehensible manner wherein the hardest granite, reduced into a vitreous fluid, has shot upwards into the superincumbent rock, and injected itself through its veins, and the accurate measurement of the causes proportioned to such mighty effects, would convey, we may suppose, the sublimest idea possible of the terrible action of that powerful element, unto whose scourge this globe is yet in doom reserved.

It would, of course, be impossible to bring every branch of the natural sciences so completely into contact with sacred studies, as these whereof we have treated, nor can it be necessary to do so. For there is one way in which they all can be made subservient to the interests of religion, by viewing them as the appointed channels by which a true perception and estimate of the divine perfections are meant to pass into the understanding; as the glass wherein the embodied forms of every great and beautiful attribute of the Supreme Being may best be contemplated; and as the impression upon the mind of the great seal of creation, whereon have been engraven, by an Almighty hand, mystical characters of deepest wisdom, omnipotent spells of productive power, and emblems most expressive of an all-embracing, all-preserving love. And even as the engraver, when he hath cut some way into his gem, doth make proof thereof upon the tender wax; and, if he find not the image perfect, is not thereby disheartened, so long as it presents each time a progressive approach to its intended type, but returns again and again unto his peaceful task; so if we find not that, at once, we bear upon ourselves the clear and deep impress of this glorious signet, must not we fear to proceed with our labours, but go on, ever striving to approach nearer and nearer the attainment of a perfect representation. A few years will probably bring forward new arguments for the great facts whereof we have treated, which will render all that you have heard but of small value. Those that come after us will, peradventure, smile at the small comprehension granted to our age, of nature and her operations:—we must be content, amidst our imperfect knowledge, with having striven after that which is more full.

For, if the works of God are the true, though faint, image of himself, they must, in some way, partake of his immensity; and, as the contemplation of his own unshadowed beauty will be the unsating, everlasting food of unembodied spirits, so may we say that a similar proportion hath been observed between the examination of his image reflected on his works, and the faculties of our present condition; inasmuch as therein is matter for meditation ever deeper, for discovery ever ampler, for admiration ever holier. And so God, not being able to give to the beauties of his work that infinity which is reserved to the attributes they exhibit, has bestowed upon them that quality which best supplies and represents it; for, by making our knowledge of them progressive, he has made them inexhaustible.

LECTURE THE SEVENTH;

ON

EARLY HISTORY.

PART I.

CONNECTION of this subject with the preceding.—INDIANS: Exaggerated ideas regarding their Antiquity.—Their *Astronomy*. Bailly's attempt to prove its extraordinary antiquity. Confutation by Delambre and Montucla. Researches of Davis and Bentley. Opinions of Schaubach, Laplace, and others.—*Chronology*. Researches of Sir W. Jones, Wilfort, and Hamilton. Attempts of Heeren to fix the commencement of Indian History. Discoveries of Colonel Tod.—OTHER ASIATIC NATIONS. Latest researches into the early history of the Armenians, Georgians, and Chinese.

AFTER having thus ascertained, as far as we may, when was first constructed and adorned this theatre, upon which have been acted all the great scenes of human life, it may seem superfluous to interrogate those who have trod its stage, how long it is since they commenced their varied drama of war and peace, of barbarism and civilization, of rude vices and of simple virtues. For, in Nature, whom we have hitherto consulted, there is no pride, no desire, and no power, to represent herself other than in reality she is. But if we ask the oldest nations when they sprang up, and when they first entered on the career of their social existence, there arise instantly, in the way of a candid reply, a multitude of petty ambitions, jealousies, and prejudices; and there intervenes between us and the truth a mist of ignorance, wilful or traditional, which involves the inquiry both in mystery and perplexity, and leaves us to find our way by the aid of the most uncertain elements, with the constant danger of most serious error.

There have been, moreover, learned and acute investigators, who, having peculiar ends to gain in their researches, have allowed themselves to be borne away by these representations,—have admitted as history what was only mythological fable,—have calculated upon dates, which were the purest fiction; and, not granting to the Jewish books the authority which they allowed to the Indian Vedas, or the Egyptian lists of kings, have most inconsistently condemned our sacred records, because they imagined, at first sight, that they agreed not with those of other nations. Fortunately, however, we have discovered methods which they knew not; we have learned to cross-question nations in their early history; we have accustomed ourselves to pore, with lawyer-like skill, over worn-out documents, till we have made out their value, or detected their flaws; we have lost the relish for sarcastic disquisition, that levity in examination which could give a witticism the force of an argument, and have learnt to love a sober and solemn mood in every office of science,—to prefer the real to the brilliant,—fact to theory,—and patient, plodding comparison to vague analogies.

The preference to which I have alluded, as given by learned and able men, to any document discovered in distant lands, over those which Christianity received from the Jewish people, is assuredly one of those many facts which, combined, establish a strange phenomenon of the human mind, the extravagant love of the wonderful in all that is out of our reach, and the desire of disparaging that which we possess. I have at home an Arabic manuscript, professing to give, among other very miscellaneous matter, an account of the principal cities of the world; and, of course, Rome could not be well excluded from the number. But, alas! not the charmed city of the wildest romance, not the fabulous splendour of the eastern Iram, not the dreamy imaginings of the most visionary Utopian, ever were planned with such a noble contempt of the possibilities of human wealth, as this sober representation of the Eternal City! It is described as a city of some sixty or eighty miles in length, through which flows the majestic river called the Romulus, over which are several hundred bridges of brass, so constructed that they may be removed upon the approach of an enemy; the gates of the city are numerous, and all of the same materials; a minute description is given of the dimensions and riches of many churches, among which, unluckily, St. Peter's is omitted; and the author has been careful to note how many gates of brass, and how many of silver; how many columns of marble, how many of silver, or of gold, each of them contains. Strangely absurd as this may seem, it is but a faint parallel of what well-educated Europeans have indulged in, when first describing the historical and scientific wealth of eastern nations, then comparatively but little known amongst us. There were to be found astronomical processes of the most refined character, requiring observations at epochs incalculably remote one from the other; there were periods or cycles of time, necessarily framed when the state of the heavens was countless ages younger than at present; there were books manifestly written many thousand years before the West gave any signs of human life; there were monuments obviously erected ages before the desolating flood is said to have swept over the face of earth; there, in fine, were long lists of kings, and even of dynasties, well attested in the annals of nations, which must reach back far beyond the epoch assigned, in the comparatively modern books of Moses, to the creation of the world!

And now, what has become of all these wonders? Why, you, who have seen, can transmute the Arab's fancies into their vulgar realties, the mighty Romulus into the yellow Tiber, the brazen gates into wooden portals, the gold and silver into stone and marble; and you have perhaps trotted round the huge city in your morning ride. And so I trust will you be able to treat the no less baseless visions of philosophical romance; after we shall have visited, to-day and at our next meeting, the countries where all those scientific and literary marvels were said to exist, you will, I trust, be convinced, that those are but as other lands, confined like ourselves within reasonable limits of duration; that the stream of their traditions bears down with it its due proportion of rubbish and defilement; that the precious materials, whereof their monuments and temples were said to be composed, are but the ordinary substance of which all things human must consist. But in both cases the truly valuable has been overlooked. The Arab was not refined enough to understand the treasures of art which we here possess, and which are far more valuable than gates of silver or pillars of gold; and the vain philosophers of the last century were too blind, or rather blinded, to examine the real wealth which the East was opening to their industry, in the confirmation of primeval truths, in the illustration of holier pursuits, and in the field of ethnographical and moral knowledge which it affords.

Opposed, however, to what I have said on the tendency of men to despise what they hold in the hand, and to exaggerate what is far removed, are the very objects of which I am going to treat. For, while amongst us there seems to be this strange propensity; while any discovery at variance with Scripture is eagerly seized upon by many,—of which we shall have yet plenty of examples, if the past lectures have not given enough—while there is an unnatural value set upon anything brought to light which seems to clash with some assertion of the sacred text; the nations of the East so jealously cling to their sacred books, and so pertinaciously reject every fact which may prove them wrong; the Chinese, and the Indians, and the ancient Egyptians, have been ever so attached to the unerring accuracy of their respective records, that we must seek some other explanation than a natural cause for the ease wherewith ours are so often abandoned. Nay, I believe, that had the book of Moses not been preserved by Christianity, but discovered for the first time among the Jews of China, or by Dr. Buchanan among those of Malabar,* they would have been received as a treasure of historical and philosophical knowledge, by those who have, under the present circumstances, slighted and blasphemed them.

It is not my intention, of course, to go over the ground, which has been completely drained of its interest by older writers, such as the antiquity of the Chaldeans or Assyrians, and the objections drawn in former times from the fragments of Berosus or Sanconiathon. They belong to the class of mere dry chronology, without a particle of historical interest,—they have been exhausted by many popular writers,—and they may be said to have been abandoned by the school which used to give them some value. I will, therefore, at once proceed to a country, the early history of which possesses much stronger claims to our attention, and will afford a strong illustration of the principle I have chiefly in view, through this course of lectures.

The peninsula of India should seem to be the field especially delivered by Providence to the cultivation of our countrymen, and ought certainly to possess a peculiar interest for us. Nor could anything have happened more opportunely for the wants of the human mind, than the discovery of its literary wealth. The taste of Europe, which the political and religious convulsions of the sixteenth and seventeenth centuries had driven to seek delight and food in the recollections of ancient classical lore, had almost begun to pall with the sweet but unvaried repast; the stream of newly-discovered authors, which, for a time, flowed from the young press, had ceased its refreshing supplies; every manuscript had been collated, every accent adjusted, every debateable letter made the theme of learned essays; we longed, if

---

* Where copies of the Pentateuch were really found.

possible, for something quite original, and able to rouse and stimulate our languishing appetite. Arabia and Persia had been tried in vain. Mohammedanism sat as an incubus on all their religious literature—their exquisite poetry was too sensuous to satisfy the intellectual demands of European refinement, and their history was too limited, too modern, and too well known, from its connections with our own, to excite any powerful interest. Whatever our anticipations of India may have been, they have been more than surpassed. We appear, on a sudden, introduced to the very fountains of ancient philosophy, to the laboratories of those various opinions which formed the schools of the West; to the nursery of our race, where the first accents of our language are preserved in their simplest forms; to the very oracle or sanctuary of all ancient heathen worship,—to the innermost chamber of all mystic lore and symbolical religion. Here everything bears the stamp of aboriginal freshness and simplicity; and we feel, that whether we examine the philosophical meditations of its sages, or the early and mythological annals of its history, we are perusing the results of native genius, and the uninterpolated records of national traditions.

But we must not allow our feelings to carry us too far, nor allow ourselves to be dazzled by the novelty of the scene, to an exaggeration of its real beauties. As well might the naturalist, upon witnessing the gigantic growth of the African or American forests, compared with the pigmy stature of our trees, calculate that, if the oak has required its hundreds of years to reach its strength, they must have been rooted for thousands in the soil, as the philosopher conclude, that so many ages must have been requisite to give to the systems of science which we there find their consistency and consolidation, anterior to the appearance of philosophy in the West. There are other elements to be calculated besides time: there is, in the one instance, the succulent vigour of the soil, and the ripening energies of the climate; and, in the other, the complex action of physical and moral influences, caused by an early settlement in a congenial country, by the fortunate preservation of earliest recollections, and a peaceful state amidst objects which draw the mind to contemplation.

I fear I have allowed my thoughts to ramble from reflection to reflection, without sufficient regard to the more important and substantial entertainment which you require at my hand; and I therefore proceed at once to my task. I have not to consider the Indians to-day in reference to their literature, but only to their history. And this I will divide into two parts. First, I will trace the history of inquiry into the antiquity of their scientific knowledge, particularly their astronomy; for this has been one of the most alarming topics in the hands of men hostile to religion. Then I will trace for you a brief sketch of the researches made into their annals, and the success experienced in unravelling the perplexities of their political history.

The first man of any reputation in science, who gave an unnatural antiquity to the astronomical discoveries of the Hindoos, was the unfortunate Bailly. During his life he possessed, at least amongst less profound mathematicians, a very brilliant reputation; but he was infected with all the defects of his time,—a love of bold and startling hypothesis, splendidly supported by ingenious and diversified arguments. "It was not for learned men that he wrote," says Delambre; "he aspired to a more extensive reputation. He yielded to the pleasure of entering into the lists with Voltaire; he revived the old romance of the Atlantis; he had a good many readers, and that ruined him. The success of his first paradox led him to create others. He devised his *extinct nation,* and his *astronomy perfected in mythological times;* he made everything bear upon this favourite idea; and was not very scrupulous in his choice of means to give colour to his hypothesis."* In his History of Ancient Astronomy, he started the theory

---

* "Astronomie du Moyen Age:" *Par.* 1809, p. xxxiv.

here alluded to. By analyzing the astronomical formulas of the Hindoos, as far as known through the imperfect communications of Le Gentil, he concluded that they must be based upon actual observations, but that the present state and character of the Indians will not allow us to consider them their original discoveries. He consequently treats the actual astronomy of that country as only fragments and wrecks of an earlier and far more perfect science; and adding to those conjectures others of another class, based upon surmises, allegories, and obscure hints, he brings out his celebrated theory, that a nation, which has long disappeared from the world, existed many ages ago, in the north of Asia, from which all the learning of the southern peninsula was derived. The Indians, he says, formed, in his opinion, a fully constituted nation from the year 3553 before Christ; and this is the reduced state of their dynasties. It is astonishing, he adds in another place, to find among the Brahmans astronomical tables which are five or six thousand years old.* I will give you one specimen of his reasoning in favour of the northern origin of astronomy. The Chinese have a temple dedicated, it is said, to the northern stars; and it is called "the palace of the great light." It contains no statue, but only an embroidered drapery, on which is inscribed, "To the spirit of the god Petou." The Petous are, he says, according to Magelhaens, the stars of the north. "But may not this temple be dedicated to the *aurora borealis?* It would appear that the name of 'palace of the great light' would suggest that conjecture. Why should they have made a divinity of the northern stars, rather than of those of any other quarter? They have nothing remarkable, whereas the phenomena of the aurora borealis, those crowns, those rays, those streams of light, appear to have something in them quite divine." This conjecture is then confirmed by another of M. de Mairan, that Olympus was the seat of the

* "Histoire de l'Astronomie ancienne:" *Par.* 1775, pp. 107, 115.

Grecian gods, because that mountain was particularly seen surrounded by the northern lights. But then the aurora borealis is not at all remarkable in China; for in thirty-two years, Father Parennin never saw anything worthy of the name. "We therefore see," thus he concludes, "in this species of worship, rendered to the northern lights, and to the stars of the north" (here the two objects before exchanged are artfully united), "a very strong trace of the superstition of an earlier period, and of the anterior seat of the Chinese in a more northern climate, where the phenomenon of the aurora borealis, being more extended and more frequent, must have made a more lively impression!"*

Is this science, or is it romance? is it history or vision? Even Voltaire, with all his love for the new and the rash, could not stomach this creation of a new people, and this attribution of the origin of astronomy, which all the world thought, must have required bright skies and mild climates, to the country of almost perpetual snows and hazy mountains; and he addressed to Bailly several letters, written with all that levity of tone, and carelessness about the truth or falsehood of the matter, which characterizes all his works. He merely seems anxious not to give up the Brahmans, whom he had taken under his especial protection, or sacrifice his own favourite theories on the historical antiquity of the Indians. "Nothing ever came out to us from Scythia," he writes, "except tigers who have eaten up our lambs. Some of these tigers, it is true, have been a little astronomical, when they have gained leisure, after sacking India. But are we to suppose that these tigers came forth from their lairs, with quadrants and astrolabes? . . . Who ever heard of any Greek philosopher going to seek science in the country of Gog and Magog?"†
In his answers, Bailly enters fully into the explanation and grounds of his theory. It is, I must own, almost nauseous to read the terms of fulsome compliment in

* Page 101.
† "Lettres sur l'Origine des Sciences:" *Lon.* and *Par.* 1777, p. 6.

which he addresses the superficial master of infidelity. "The Brahmans," he replies to these observations, "would be, indeed, proud, if they knew they possessed such an apologist. More enlightened than they can ever have been, you possess the reputation which they enjoyed in antiquity. Men go now to Ferney as they used to Benares; but Pythagoras would have been better instructed by you; for the Tacitus, the Euripides, and the Homer of the age, is, by himself, worth all that ancient academy." "If the immortal songs of the Grecian bard no longer existed," he writes in another place, "M. de Voltaire, after having described the combats and triumphs of the good Henry, would have conceived how Homer wrote the Iliad, and deserved his fame."* But, passing over these disgusting flatteries, I need only say that, in this work, Bailly sums up and presents in a more popular form, the arguments produced in his more scientific work in favour of his primeval people, source of all human science.

Still, he was not contented; and he undertook the more formidable task of verifying mathematically the Indian calculations, and reducing to the test of rigid formulas, the astronomical processes, and results contained in the statements of travellers and missionaries. It would be foreign to my plan, and could hardly be interesting to you, to follow him step by step in this toilsome undertaking. I will content myself, therefore, with giving you a slight idea of his method and results.

Three sets of astronomical tables had been made known in Europe; one of these was manifestly borrowed from another of the number, and, therefore, Bailly excludes it. The other two profess to have different dates, the one 1491 of our era, the other 3102 before it. Bailly proceeds to establish that it was exceedingly improbable, that the Indians borrowed their date from other nations, because in their methods they differ

---

* Pages 16-207.

essentially from them. He concludes that both the periods must have been fixed by actual observation; inasmuch as the account given of the heavens at each is accurate. The places of the sun and moon are given, for the early period, with a correctness that could not be obtained by calculating from our best tables; there is mention of a conjunction of all the planets, and the tables of Cassini prove that such a conjunction occurred about that period, though Venus was not in the number.* All these particulars, which I have very unscientifically stated, are apparently established by rigid calculation, through the course of his work.

Such was the specious theory of this unfortunate man. In his earlier work, he had imagined the scientific researches of his extinct nation to be antediluvian, and supposed the Indians, Chaldees, and others, to be the races who inherited the broken fragments of early science, after the great catastrophe.† In this, however, no notice is taken of that hypothesis, but the astronomy of India is treated as an indigenous invention; or, at least, Bailly contents himself with attempting to demonstrate that the supposed date of that early observation in India must be correct. It was not, however, long before, among his own scientific countrymen, he found an adversary fully equal to the task of confuting his romantic theory. Delambre, in his *History of Ancient Astronomy*, was necessarily led to treat of the supposed observations of the Hindoos; and, without entering into any very profound mathematical examination of the processes and formulas so extolled by his fellow-academician, laid open, one by one, the inaccuracies committed by him in the statement of the question, and his gratuitous assumption of the data on which he conducted them. He shows that there is no ground on earth to admit the truth of the supposed observations; but approves of the solutions given by

---
* "Traité de l'Astronomie Indienne et Orientale :" *Par.* 1787, xx. *seqq.*
† "Histoire de l'Astronomie," p. 89.

the English writers, of whom I shall presently speak.*

We may, perhaps, allow that the tone in which Delambre conducts his confutation of Bailly, is not such as would greatly delight an admirer of his dreams. For throughout there is but little respect shown to the science or to the character of that philosopher; not only the correctness of his mathematical inductions, but the fairness of his statements, is constantly called in question. It was in our country that Bailly found a champion to undertake his defence. Between the epoch at which Bailly wrote, and the time when Delambre confuted him, much important light, as I have hinted, had been thrown on the question; and the publication of a valuable collection of Indian mathematical treatises by Mr. Colebrooke, gave an opportunity to the *Edinburgh Review* to exalt the antiquity of Hindoo science, and censure the conduct of Delambre. The occasion, I think it must be owned, was a strange one; for Colebrooke's work affords strong presumptive grounds for supposing the comparatively modern origin of mathematics in India. For he gives us, in his valuable *Notes and Illustrations to his Preliminary Discourse*, a list furnished by the astronomers of Ujjayani to Dr. Hunter, of their most celebrated astronomical writers, and the oldest of these is Varaha-Mihira, whom they place in the third century of the Christian era. But of him there is nothing known; whereas another astronomer of the same name is very celebrated, and him Colebrooke shows to have lived, as is stated in Dr. Hunter's table, about the latter end of the sixth century. He quotes, it is true, more ancient treatises, called the five Siddhantas; but there is time enough for these to have existed and become old before his age, without arriving at any very extraordinary antiquity.† In like manner, Brahmegupta, one of the

---

* "Histoire de l'Astronomie ancienne :" *Par.* 1817, pp. 400, *seq.*
† "Algebra, with Arithmetic and Mensuration, from the Sanscrit :" Lon. 1817, pp. xxxiii., xlviii. But see Bentley's "Historical View of the Hindoo Astronomy :" *Lond.* 1825, p. 167.

oldest mathematical writers extant, some of whose treatises Mr. Colebrooke published in this collection, cannot be considered older than the seventh century; nay, this sagacious and critical orientalist, after showing the probabilities in favour of Aryabhatta's being the father and founder of Hindoo algebra, proceeds to establish his antiquity; and concludes that he flourished "as far back as the fifth century of the Christian era, and perhaps in an earlier age." He was thus nearly contemporary with Diophantus; though Mr. Colebrooke thinks he was superior to the Greek mathematician, in having methods of solving complicated equations, which the other did not possess.* These statements and acknowledgments of so competent a judge as Colebrooke, could not have been well supposed to form a good foundation for an assertion of the Hindoo claims to great antiquity in astronomical renown. But the reviewer, admitting all these facts, boldly asserts that we must by no means consider Aryabhatta as the inventor of his methods, but admit that many ages must have elapsed between their first invention and his improvements.† Though the writer confesses that Bailly was inaccurate, from want of local knowledge, from too great confidence in his informers, and from the spirit of system which carried him away, he still maintains that not only is the originality of Hindoo science quite vindicated by Mr. Colebrooke's publication, but that all must now confess that science to be only a wreck of what flourished in the Indian peninsula when the Sanskrit was a living language, or, perhaps, " some parent language, still more ancient, sent forth those roots which have struck with more or less firmness into the dialects of so many and so remote nations, both of the East and of the West."‡ A conclusion which would lead us back far beyond all reach of history, and pretty nearly to what Bailly would have desired.

As the name of Delambre was mentioned somewhat

---

* Page x.   † " Edin Rev." vol. xxix. p. 143.   ‡ Page 163.

invidiously, with a charge of undue severity upon the memory of his brother academician, the learned astronomer lost no time in replying to the reasonings, as well as the censure of the reviewer; and an opportunity was afforded him by the publication of his work on the *Astronomy of the Middle Ages*. In his preliminary discourse, he examines in detail the different grounds for admiration proposed by the anonymous critic; and concludes that, although the Indians may have now been shown to have acquired a certain degree of skill in solving algebraical problems more remarkable for their ingenuity than for their utility, nothing has been yet done to prove them possessed of anything approaching to a correct and scientific knowledge of astronomy.*

If I have dwelt at some length upon the opinions of Delambre, it would not be fair to omit the concurrence in the same sentiments, of another celebrated historian of mathematical science, who wrote, too, while his country was still more under the influence of that philosophical school to which Bailly had unfortunately attached himself. I allude to Montucla, who, with the utmost impartiality, addresses himself to the task of examining the grounds assigned by Bailly for the excessive antiquity of the Hindoo astronomy. He analyzes, for instance, the great period of the Cali-Yuga, consisting of 4,320,000 years, and finds that if divided by 24,000, it gives as quotient 180; which gives rise to a suspicion that this period is only the half of another composing the product of 24,000 by 360. Now, as the Arabs consider 24,000 years the term in which the fixed stars, by their progressive movement, would make one complete revolution, it would appear that, having borrowed this idea from them, the Indians made their great period equivalent to a year of 360 days, the primitive length of the year, each day of which consists of one complete revolution of the

---

* "Histoire de l'Astronomie du Moyen Age:" *Par.* 1819, p. xxxvii.

heavens. This he confirms from similar calculations among the Arabs; and this, among others, is a reason for his concluding that, so far from Indian astronomy boasting such wonderful antiquity as his ill-fated countryman had imagined, it was borrowed from the inhabitants of western Asia.*

But it is fair to turn to the labours of our countrymen in this branch of astronomical history. Mr. Davis was the first, as Colebrooke has remarked, to give an accurate account of Hindoo astronomy from native treatises. Montucla had observed that the Surya Siddhanta, an astronomical work supposed to have been inspired, would be a precious acquisition; "but who," he adds, " will ever force these mysterious men to communicate it?"† It is precisely from this very work that Mr. Davis drew his materials; and he states that he found no jealousy on the part of the Brahmans in either communicating the book, or assisting to explain it. The object of his researches was merely to discover the processes or formulas by which the Hindoos calculate their eclipses; and thus far he may appear to throw little or no light upon the subject of our inquiry. But still it is manifest, from his preliminary remarks, that he considers the remote periods assumed by the Hindoos as the bases or points of departure to their calculations, to have been assumed arbitrarily by a retrograde computation, and not selected, as Bailly fancied, by actual observation.‡

Mr. Bentley, however, must be acknowledged to have most earnestly and most successfully studied this and other important works of Indian astronomy, with a view to determine the true antiquity of the science: and with his researches, which extend over a long period of time, I shall close this portion of my task. His first essay upon this subject appeared in the sixth volume of the *Asiatic Researches.* It may be divided into two parts. In the first, he examines the astrono-

---

* "Histoire des Mathématiques :" *Par.* n. vii. tom. i. p. 429.
† Page 443.
‡ "Asiatic Researches," vol. ii. p. 228, ed. *Calcutta.*

mical methods of the Indians, and shows how easily a European unacquainted with them might fall into grievous error in assigning their date. He then proceeds to investigate the age of the Surya Siddhanta, to which the Brahmans modestly give an age of sundry millions of years. "The most correct and certain mode of investigating the antiquity of Hindoo astronomical works," he writes, "is by comparing the positions and motions of the planets computed from them, with those deduced from accurate European tables. For it must be obvious, that every astronomer, let the principle of his system be what it will, whether real or artificial, must endeavour to give the true position of the planets in his own time; or, at least, as near as he can, or the nature of his system will permit; otherwise his labour will be totally useless. Therefore, having the positions and motions of the sun, moon, and planets, at any proposed instant of time, given by computation from any original Hindoo system; and having also their positions and motions deduced from correct European tables for the same instant; we can from them determine the points of time back, when their respective positions were precisely the same in both."* Mr. Bentley proceeds to apply this simple rule. He takes his data, on the one side, from the Indian treatise, and on the other from Lalande's Tables; and by finding the number of years requisite to give the erroneous results deducible from the former, he discovers different periods of 600, 700, and 800 years, as having elapsed from the time it was composed. But not so content, Mr. Bentley gives strong reasons to conclude that its author was Varaha, whose disciple, Sotanund, is known to have lived about 700 years ago, a period corresponding with the mean given by the deductions from the Surya Siddhanta itself.†

The critical periodical, which I before mentioned as having so earnestly defended Bailly's fanciful theories,

---

* Page 564.
† Page 573. This, however, has been denied by Mr. Colebrooke, in his 'Algebra."

was thereby only following up the views it had taken in its first number, of Mr. Bentley's labours. To the severe and studied attack which it made upon the essay I have quoted, he answered in a strong and clear manner, in the eighth volume of the *Researches ;** but I pass over this paper, because he has since given a more enlarged and corrected, and far more valuable explanation of his views: and this I proceed to mention. In the very year that Mr. Bentley published his *Historical View of the Hindoo Astronomy*, the learned Ideler complained at Berlin, that no one had as yet been found, who united together a competent knowledge of the Sanskrit language and of astronomy.† In this instance, however, these two acquirements seem to have been combined with that firmness of purpose and eagerness of inquiry, which were necessary for directing them in their troublesome undertaking; and probably, the severity wherewith their possessor had been treated for his first attempt nerved him to the task, and materially forwarded the researches which they were intended to impede.

In this work, Mr. Bentley, after a preface, in which he confirms his former assertions regarding the Surya Siddhanta by new calculations, treats systematically of the different epochs into which Hindoo astronomy may be divided. He establishes eight distinct ages or periods in his history, each of which he endeavours to define and fix by astronomical data. The first operation in any system of astronomy, must be the division of the heavens; without which all astronomical determinations would be impracticable. The earliest Indian division is into Lunar mansions, formerly 28, and now 27 in number. While history places this operation at a period between 1528 and 1375, B.C, the astronomical data mentioned in conjuction with it, exactly coincide. For the place of the equinoxial and solstitial points gives

---

* Pages 193, *et seqq.*
† "Handbuch der Mathematischen und Technischen Chronologie:" *Berlin*, 1825, vol. i. p. 5.

the year 1426 B.C.; and the singular mythology of the operation, which states the planets to have been born from different daughters of Daksha, when reduced to the astronomical language of occultations of the moon in the respective lunar mansions, gives precisely the same period, 1425 B.C.* Now, if this calculation is correct, we have undoubtedly a date for the preliminary operation of Hindoo astronomy, quite within the range of probability. The next observation on record, Mr. Bentley places in 1181 before the Christian era; when the sun and moon were in conjunction, and the astronomers found that the colures had fallen back 3° 20′ from their position at the former observation. This consists of the giving proper names to the months; the conditions of which decide the period.

The next important era, which is decided by the astronomical data it supposes, is the age of Rama, whose exploits form the noblest theme of Indian poetry. "The Ramayuna," or epic poem which celebrates him, gives a minute description of the heavens at his birth, and upon his reaching his twenty-first year; and the result is, that such a state could only have occurred about 961 years before Christ.† There is, too, I may remark, in his history, a passage minutely corresponding with the battle of the gods and giants in Greek mythology.

I will not follow Mr. Bentley through the later stages of his course; because all that we can possibly desire is gained in the first. It matters little to us, that the Hindoos should place the ages of their astronomers back in absurd antiquity; that Garga and Parasara should be said by them to have lived and written 3,100 years before Christ; so long as it can be proved that the science, in which they were manifestly proficients, did not commence its preliminary observations till many centuries later. But it is just to say, that the Vasishta Siddhanta, and the Surya Siddhanta, which the Hindoos

* Page 4. † Page 15.

used to date at some million or two of years back, have been brought down, by his computations, to the tenth or eleventh century of the Christian era.

There is one Indian legend of considerable importance, the age of which Mr. Bentley endeavours to decide by astronomical computation; that is, the story of Krishna, the Indian Apollo. In native legends he is represented as an Avatar, or incarnation of the Divinity; at his birth, choirs of Devatas sung hymns of praise, while shepherds surrounded his cradle; it was necessary to conceal his birth from the tyrant Cansa, to whom it had been foretold that the infant should destroy him. The child escaped, with his parents, beyond the coast of Yamouna. For a time he lived in obscurity; but then commenced a public life, distinguished for prowess and beneficence; he slew tyrants and protected the poor; he washed the feet of the Brahmans, and preached the most perfect doctrine; but at length the power of his enemies prevailed, he was nailed, according to one account, to a tree by an arrow, and foretold before dying, the miseries which would take place in the Cali-Yuga, or wicked age of the world, thirty-six years after his death.* Can we be surprised that the enemies of Christianity should have seized upon this legend as containing the original of our gospel history? The names Christ and Krishna, perverted by some of them into Khristna, were pronounced identical, and the numerous parallelisms between their histories declared too clearly defined to permit any doubt respecting their being one and the same individual.† The ease with which the first explorers of Indian letters allowed themselves to be borne away by their enthusiasm, towards ascribing extravagant antiquity to everything they found, came in here to aid these bold assertions. For

---

* See this legend in Paulinus, a S. Bartholomæo "Systema Brahmanicum:" *Rome*, 1802, pp. 146, *seqq.* Creuzer's "Religions de l'Antiquité," par Guigniaut, tom. i. *Par.* 1825, p. 205.

† Volney's "Ruins, or Meditations on the Revolutions of Empires:" *Par.* 1820, p. 267.

Sir W. Jones, who was considered an infallible authority in all such matters, and whose judgment certainly deserves due consideration, had pronounced it quite certain " that the name of Krishna, and the general outline of his history, were long anterior to the life of our Saviour, and probably to the time of Homer." Hence, acknowledging the impossibility of so many casual coincidences, in the two lives or histories, he conjectures that the points of minute resemblance were engrafted, in later times, from spurious gospels, upon the original legend.* Maurice, in like manner, admits its antiquity, and meets its difficulties in a manner still less qualified to assist an adversary of Christianity, by considering it a remnant of an ancient primeval tradition, concerning the future coming of a redeemer, who was to be truly an Avatar, or incarnation of the Deity.†

Now, it is to the examination of the age when this godlike hero lived, that Mr. Bentley has applied astronomical calculation. For he diligently sought out, in the notices regarding him, some data upon which to base an inquiry into the era of his life; and after finding all these too scanty, though it was stated that the celebrated astronomer Garga assisted at his birth, and described the state of the heavens at that interesting moment, he was fortunate enough to procure the *Janampatra* of Krishna, which contains the position of the planets at the time of his birth. From computation, grounded upon European tables, reduced to the meridian of Ujein, it appears that the heavens can only have been as there described on the 7th of August, A.D. 600.‡ Mr. Bentley therefore concludes that this legend was an artful imitation of Christianity, framed by the Brahmans for the express purpose of withholding the natives from embracing the new religion, which had begun to penetrate to the uttermost bounds of the East.

* " Asiatic Researches," vol. i. p. 273.
† " History of Hindostan :" *Lond.* 1824, vol. ii. p. 225.
‡ Page 111.

It may probably happen that many will not agree with this writer in some of his opinions; and I must say that, without more positive proof, I cannot go to the lengths he does upon many particular points. But still, to his demonstration of the modern date assignable to Indian observations and Hindoo astronomical works, he certainly has the suffrages of the best modern mathematicians. Not to mention Delambre, who considered his paper on the age of the Surya Siddhanta as quite satisfactory, we have the opinion of Schaubach, who maintains all the knowledge possessed by the Hindoos, in astronomy, to be derived from the Arabs, and, consequently, to belong rather to modern than to ancient science.* Laplace, whose name will surely be respected by every astronomer of modern times, far beyond that of the overrated Bailly, whose friend and warm admirer he was, thus expresses himself upon this matter: "The origin of astronomy in Persia and India is lost, as among all other nations, in the darkness of their ancient history. The Indian tables suppose a very advanced state of astronomy; but there is every reason to believe that they can claim no very high antiquity. Herein I differ, with pain, from an illustrious and unfortunate friend." This expression clearly shows, that it was from no leaning towards our cause that Laplace decided against the claims of Sanskrit astronomy. After these remarks, he proceeds to a detailed examination of the point, which, I am sure, I have quite often enough repeated, whether the observations placed by the Indian tables as bases for their calculations, 1,491 and 3,102 years before the Christian era, were actually ever made; and concludes that they were not, and that the tables were not grounded upon any true observation, because the conjunctions which they suppose cannot have taken place. "The same results," he concludes, "are obtained from the mean motions

---

* In the Baron de Zach's "Monatliche Correspondenz," Feb. and March, 1813.

assigned by them to the moon, in reference to its perigee, its nodes, and the sun; which, being more accelerated than they are according to Ptolemy, indicate that they are posterior to that astronomer. For we know from the theory of universal gravitation, that these three movements have been accelerated for a great number of years. Thus the results of this theory, so important for lunar astronomy, serve also to elucidate chronology."* To these testimonies we may add that Dr. Maskelyne, personally communicated to Mr. Bentley,† of Heeren,‡ Cuvier,§ and Klaproth, who thus writes:—" Les tables astronomiques des Hindous, auxquelles on avait attribué une antiquité prodigieuse, ont été construites dans le septième siècle de l'ère vulgaire, et ont été postérieurement reportées par des calculs à une époque antérieure."‖

After these confirmatory authorities, in addition to the opinions of the older French mathematicians before cited, we may reasonably doubt whether any other champion will arise to defend the excessive antiquity of Indian astronomical science. It will be difficult, at any rate, to reinstate its pretensions in such a position as shall threaten a conflict with the Mosaic chronology. There are other branches of Indian learning, which must appear to you deserving of equal investigation, such as the age of the sacred and philosophical writings, to which such absurd antiquity was attributed by some men a few years back; but as it is my intention, in pursuance of my promise, to dedicate a special discourse to Oriental Literature, I shall reserve to it what appears to me most important on this head. I will, therefore, pass from the astronomy to the history of

---

* "Exposition du Système du Monde," 6th ed.: *Bruxelles*, 1827, p. 427.
† Preface, p. xxv.
‡ "Ideen über die Politik, Handel, und Verkehr der alten Völker,' 4th ed. 1 Th. 3 Abtheil, p. 142.
§ Cuvier, "Discours prélim." 8vo. *Par.* 1825, p. 238.
‖ "Mémoires relatifs à l'Asie;" *Par.* 1824, p. 397.

the Indians, and see if it can, any more than the other, pretend to rival in age the records of the Pentateuch.

It was, indeed, only to be expected that the national ambition, which led to extravagance in fixing an epoch for the rise of science, should have suggested a corresponding remoteness of time for the governments under which it flourished. One fiction necessarily supposed the other; and when Oriental nations set about giving a mythological era to their origin and early history, they do not stop at trifles, or allow themselves to be restrained by the European rule of attending to probabilities. A million of years are as soon invented as a thousand; very few kings are required to fill them with their reigns, if you give them a gross of centuries apiece; and your readers will believe it all, if you can only get them over the first step, that of believing the kings to have been descendants of the sun and moon, or some such unearthly progenitors. We cannot indeed help pitying those who have been deceived into the belief of such absurdities; but I think we must also be inclined to extend our compassion to those who first attempted to analyze the mass of fable presented to us by Indian history, and to separate the few grains of truth which lay concealed in this Augean confusion.

Sir W. Jones led the way in this, as in most branches of Indian research. He took, for the groundwork of his inquiries, the genealogical lists of kings, extracted from the Puranas, by the Pundit Rhadacanta; and sat down to the task of unravelling their history, with a determination not to be swayed by any consideration, however sacred, towards an unfair decision. "Attached," he writes, "to no system, and as much disposed to reject the Mosaic history, if it be proved erroneous, as to believe it, if it be confirmed by sound reasoning, from indubitable evidence, I proceed to lay before you a concise account of Indian chronology, extracted from Sanskrit books."* He soon, however, discovered that

* "On the Chronology of the Hindoos."—Asiatic Researches, vol. i. p. 11.

he had to deal with the high-born races before alluded to, which claimed exemption from all the laws which limit the duration of mortal dynasties. Yet, nothing daunted by this appalling discovery, which would have driven a less enthusiastic inquirer to despair, he attempts to account for these absurdities, and to reconcile all contradiction. He draws up tables of kings, and assigns dates to them, according to the most plausible conjectures he can devise. The result of these very unsatisfactory labours, you shall hear in his own words:— "Thus," he concludes, "have we given a sketch of Indian history, through the longest period fairly assignable to it; and have traced the foundation of the Indian empire above 3,800 years from the present time."* Taking, therefore, even from a most prejudiced investigator, the extent to which the annals of Hindoostan can possibly be stretched with any regard to plausibility, we have the establishment of a government in that country no earlier than 2,000 years before Christ, the age of Abraham, when the book of Genesis represents Egypt as possessing an established dynasty, and commerce and literature already flourishing in Phenicia.

Sir W. Jones was followed by Mr. Wilfort, who endeavoured to reduce to something like order the dynasties of Maghada, given in the Puranas.† Hamilton succeeded him in the same course;‡ but both these patient investigators found themselves checked at every step, by wilful misrepresentations or blundering contradictions. The first of these writers is an unfortunate example of the extent to which Pundits will carry their impositions, and, consequently, a proof of how far we are to trust them in those passages of their books which would carry us back to unreasonable antiquity. For Mr. Wilfort found that a most confidential man,

---

* Page 145.
† "On the Kings of the Maghada."—Asiatic Researches, vol. ix. p. 82.
‡ "Genealogies of the Hindoos extracted from their sacred Writings:" *Edinb.* 1819.

employed by him, at considerable expense, to assist him in his labours, did not hesitate to erase and alter passages in his most sacred books; and even, when he found that the originals would have to be collated to verify his extracts, went so far as to compose thousands of verses to screen himself from discovery.* Mr. Wilfort found, in reference to our subject, that these holy men of India had no scruple about inventing names, to insert between those of more celebrated heroes, and defended their conduct on the ground that such had ever been the practice of their predecessors. Now, after all due abatements and allowances have been made, we shall find but sorry materials left wherewith to construct any certain, or even probable history. For the two authors I have mentioned have only, in the end, produced a series of personages, for whose real existence we have no better authority than poems and mythologies.

" In that case," says a sagacious writer, who, however, is rather inclined to overrate than to depress the antiquity of Hindoo literature, " they are of no more authority than the generations of heroes and kings among the Helleni; and the tables so published hold the same rank in Indian mythology which those of Appollodorus do in the Grecian. We cannot expect to find in them any critical or chronological history; it is one by poets composed, and by poets preserved; and, therefore, in this respect a poetical history, without being on that account entirely a fictitious history."† " The chronology and history of the Hindoos," writes another, " are in general as poetical and ideal as their geography. In this people, the imagination prevails over every other faculty."‡ In fact, Klaproth places the commencement

---

* " Asiatic Researches," vol. viii. p. 250.
† " Es ist eine von Dichtern behandelte, und durch Dichter erhaltene (Geschichte); also in diesem Sinne eine Dichter-Geschichte, ohne das sie deshalb eine gänzlich erdichte Geschichte zu seyn braucht."—Heeren, *ubi sup.* p. 242.
‡ Guigniaut on Creuzer, *ubi sup.* tom. i. 2de partie, p. 585.

of true chronological history in India in the twelfth century of our era.*

Heeren, however, has taken considerable pains to trace the Hindoos back to their earliest institutions, and reconstruct their earliest political state. He enters at length into proofs that the caste of Brahmans are a different nation or tribe from the inhabitants of the peninsula, and follows their march from their supposed mountain-seats in the north, along a line marked by temples in the south. He cites the authority of travellers to prove that they are of a lighter complexion than men of the other castes; an assertion which, you will remember, is at variance with the observations of other travellers, whom I quoted to you, in treating of the varieties in the human species. However, I do not see any strong objection to this hypothesis, which alone seems to account for the absolute sway of the Brahmans over the bulk of the nation.† And, after all, though this supposes a very remote period (for the oldest accounts of India show this system to have been firmly grounded in their times), it does not lead us to any definite result.

The war between the Coros and Pandos, the Greeks and Trojans of Sanskrit poetry, appears to him to afford, in its historical basis, evidence of a very early political organization in the regions of the Ganges. But so far, again, we have only great antiquity—no decisive chronological epoch. And in reference to this event, it is consistent to remark, that it is so essentially connected with the history of Krishna, that if Mr. Bentley's theory regarding this be correct, the other must share its fate, and be reckoned a modern invention.

However, Heeren applies himself patiently to the task of arranging and reconciling the various fragments which remain of the early annals; he endeavours to discover what were the earliest states, and the contemporary dynasties which possessed them; but the results

* *Ubi sup.* p. 412. † *Ubi sup.* p. 257.

at which he arrives, after his long investigation, through which I have no wish to lead you, is such as need not alarm the most timid believer. "From all the foregoing considerations," he writes, "we may conclude the region of the Ganges to have been the seat of considerable kingdoms and flourishing cities, many centuries, probably even 2,000 years, before Christ."* Such, then, are his conclusions. Instead of the six thousand years before Alexander, attributed by some writers, on the credit of Arrian, or the millions deduced from the fables of the Brahmans, we have, as Jones and others had conjectured, the age of Abraham, as the earliest historical epoch of an organized community in India.

After having thus, and at some length, carried you through the history of Indian chronology during the last forty years, it would be both a grievous omission, and a violence to my feelings, to pass over without due notice the labours of one whom I have the honour to count among my audience, and whose presence it might be thought should have made me shrink from speaking on researches which he may be said to have completed. I am sure that no one can peruse the two splendid volumes on the *Annals and Antiquities of Rajasthan*,† without feeling that their author has been able to bring to researches apparently exhausted, a stock at once of new materials and of superior sagacity, by which he has thrown considerable light, not only upon the subject which occupies us now, but likewise on those which have preceded it. And if we descend to the later periods of history, he has certainly been sufficiently fortunate to find a vast unoccupied tract to explore, in the annals of those states which he has been the first to describe. He has thus been able to combine, what few discoverers before him have had the

---

* Page 272.
† By Lieut.-Col. James Tod. *Lond.* vol. i. 1829, vol. ii 1832. Since these lectures were delivered, death has robbed our literature of this learned, diligent, and amiable man.

good fortune to unite, new events with a new field, the varied drama of a history hardly known, with a theatre decked out in the most gorgeous scenery which nature can give, and with the most sumptuous monuments that eastern art could add. Whether we consider the geographical, the historical, or the artistic additions to our knowledge of India communicated in this work, or the interest of the personal narrative it contains, we may safely, I think, rank it among the most valuable, as well as among the most beautiful works upon eastern literature.

Colonel Tod has certainly gone farther than any of his predecessors in correcting and arranging the lists of Indian dynasties. He shows that there is a general conformity between the genealogies produced by Jones, Bentley, and Wilfort, and such as he himself had collected from different sources; and as there is sufficient discrepancy among them to warrant their being derived from various originals, he concludes, not improbably, that they have some foundation of truth. The two principal races, as I before observed, are those of the Sun and Moon; and it is remarkable, that the number of princes in the two lines, through the entire descent, preserves a tolerable proportion. Now, assuming Boodha to be, what seems not unlikely, the regenerator of mankind after the Deluge, as he is the beginning of the lunar line of princes, we should have, according to the genealogical tables, " fifty-five princes from Boodha to Crishna and Youdishtra" (I quote Colonel Tod's own words); "and, admitting an average of twenty years for each reign, a period of eleven hundred years; which being added to a like period calculated from thence to Vicramaditya, who reigned fifty-six years before Christ, I venture to place the establishment in India proper of these two grand races, distinctively called those of Soorya and Chandra, at about 2,256 years before the Christian era; at which period, though somewhat later, the Egyptian, Chinese, and Assyrian monarchies are generally stated to have been established, and about a century and a half after that great event, the Flood."* Thus far, certainly, there is nothing to excite a moment's uneasiness; and if we take the chronology of the Septuagint, which many moderns are disposed to follow, we have even an ampler period between that scourge and the epoch here allotted to the establishment of these royal houses.

What may serve to confirm this calculation, is the uniformity of other results obtained by a similar process.

But the most original, and doubtless most valuable of Colonel Tod's discoveries in the Hindoo annals, consist in the historical connections which he seems clearly to have established between the early Indians and those tribes towards the west, which, we before saw, exhibited a common origin, through the evidences of comparative philology. He shows, in the first instance, that the Hindoos themselves establish the birthplace of their nation towards the west, and probably in the region of the Caucasus. But at different periods those tribes which remained in that portion of Asia, and had received the name of Scythians, seem to have become the invaders of the new settlements of their brethren, and to have considerably modified Indian manners and religion, at the same time that they gave rise to some of the most distinguished lines of kings. About 600 years before Christ, we have notice of an irruption of those tribes into India, which is nearly contemporary with a similar invasion, from the same quarter, towards Asia Minor, the north of Europe, and eastward as far as Bactria, where they overthrew the Greek dominion. The ancient Getæ are to be discovered in the Jits of modern India, where they are spread from the mountains of Joud to the shores of the Mekran, and yet follow the same nomadic form of life which they did in their more northern latitudes. The Asi of ancient history are probably the Aswa race of

* Vol. i. page 37.

India.* After establishing these resemblances in name, the learned writer proceeds to trace such points of similarity between the inhabitants of the north and the present occupiers of the Rajasthan, in dress, in theogony, in warlike customs, in religious forms and civil observances, as cannot leave any reasonable doubt regarding the affinity of the two races.† Whether the hypothesis be well sustained, that these resemblances arise from a subsequent invasion, or whether they are remains of a primary affinity, may be, I think, a matter of free discussion. And whether some of the etymologies can be maintained I have reason to doubt; for I fear in some places the resemblance of names is not sufficiently confirmed by historical data to warrant our conclusion of identity of objects. But all these are considerations of secondary importance; quite enough has been done by my learned friend to satisfy us of the earlier connection between the tribes that yet occupy Scandinavia, and those which still hold dominion in India. And this will afford grounds for several reflections.

For you will perceive how, on several occasions, besides my principal object of tracing the bearings of scientific researches upon sacred truths, I have endeavoured to call your attention to the light which one pursuit casts upon another. And, so here, I wish you to note how our former inquiries seem to receive striking illustration from these totally different researches, yet so as to confirm still farther the evidence they gave in favour of the inspired narrative. Thus we found that every new step in the comparative study of languages, brought us nearer to a positive demonstration, that mankind were originally one family; and the investigation of the early history of nations, assisted by the observation of their manners, religions, and habits, brings us to precisely the same conclusion. Nor is this confined merely to the members of the same

---

* Page 63. † Pp. 65-80.

ethnographic family, such as the Germans and Indians; but Colonel Tod has certainly pointed out such curious coincidences between the origin assigned to their respective nations by the Monguls and Chinese, and the early mythological annals of the Indians, as seem to place us, in the historical investigation of their common origin, much in the same position as the discoveries of Lepsius and others do in respect of the ethnographical inquiry, that is, in the possession of strong probability that families of men, now completely distinguished by different languages, may be shown to have been originally one. In each science, perhaps only one step has been made, but that is so successful as to augur still fuller and more satisfactory discoveries. And if the common origin of these nations can be historically established, we have a strong proof that some great and unknown cause must have acted to give each of them a language so essentially peculiar and distinct.

Again, by these researches we have it still farther proved, that climate or some other cause may change the outward habit and physiognomy of a people. For, taking the learned writer's hypothesis to its full extent, and supposing the race now occupying the Rajasthan to be a northern tribe, who invaded it from the north only 600 years before Christ, indeed to be a portion of that nation which, about the same period, took possession of Jutland, we have it shown how two colonies of the same tribe may, in the course of some centuries, have acquired the most different physical characteristics; the one receiving the fair and xanthous traits of the Dane,—the other, the dusky hue of the Indian. But, if we do not go so far, and only suppose the resemblances of names and manners to be traces of a primeval affinity, we may still draw a similar conclusion, varying only in a comparative vagueness of date, that the Getæ of Scythia formed the fairest of the Caucasian race, while those of Hindoostan rank among the darkest of the Mongul. This reflection, too, will go far to overthrow Heeren's hypothesis of the existence of two different races in the Indian peninsula, discernible at this day by variety of colour, and constituting the Brahman and the inferior castes.

The complete resemblance between the mythological systems of India, Greece, and Scandinavia, obvious not merely in the characters and attributes of their respective deities, but even in their names and in the minutest circumstances of their legends, is a discovery which belongs to the earlier history of these studies. Sir W. Jones, Wilfort, and others, in the last generation, had abundantly established this point. The last-mentioned writer also renewed with elaborate care the old hypothesis, that a close affinity existed between the ancient worshippers of the Nile and the Ganges; but, unfortunately, the circumstances I have already detailed regarding him, have cast a damp upon the interest which his researches must have otherwise excited. Colonel Tod has, however, added many interesting points of resemblance to those which we already possessed, between the mythologies of the two countries. I will content myself with alluding to his description of the festival of Gourè, as kept with great solemnity in Mewar, and to the remarks which he has added as a commentary upon it.* Here, then, again, we have an accession of strength to those reasons which would lead us to suspect affinity between two nations belonging to different families, according to their philological distribution.

This growing accumulation of proof in favour of the common origin of nations, drawn from researches which have no natural direction to its discovery, must greatly strengthen our confidence in the usefulness of every study, when reduced to proper harmony with its sister sciences, and made to advance with them at an even pace.

After having thus seen the chronology of India brought down to reasonable limits, and new analogies discovered, in its early history, with the origin of other

* Page 570.

nations, there can be little to detain us amidst the inhabitants of Asia. No other people of that continent has afforded scope for such assiduous investigation, partly because none has materials of equal interest to stimulate the industry of scholars, partly because our connection with that country has given us greater opportunities of cultivating the language in which its records are written. But that I may not appear uncourteous to other nations, and that no suspicion may arise that their annals are not so easily dealt with as those which I have discussed, I will briefly give you the opinion of one or two writers who have, in our time, taken pains to unravel their native chronologies.

Klaproth, in an essay several times reprinted by him, in various forms and languages, has attempted to fix the dates for the commencement of certain and of doubtful history, in different Asiatic nations, following chiefly their own historians.* He soon disposes of all Mohammedan kingdoms, which have no early history except what they borrow from Moses, or engraft upon a Jewish stock. Even the Persian annals can hardly go back beyond the accession of the Sassanides to the throne in 227. Cyrus appears in them as an heroic or mythological person; before him we have the dynasty of the Pishdadians, a region of mere fable;† and it is a dispute among the learned, whether Gustasp, the contemporary of Zerdusht, or Zoroaster, is the Hystaspes of history, or a sovereign coeval with Ninus,‡ or, in fine, the Median Cyaxares.§

---

* "Examen des Historiens Asiatiques," first published in the "Journal Asiatique," Sep. and Nov. 1823; then reprinted in his "Mémoires relatifs à l'Asie," vol. i. p. 389, which I shall refer to in the text. The essay re-appeared, under the title of "Würdigung der asiatischen Geschichtschreiber," in his "Asia Polyglotta," pp. 1–18.

† Hyde, "De Religione veterum Persarum," p. 312. Von Hammer, "Heidelberg Jahrbücher," 1823, p. 86. Guigniaut, *ubi sup.* p. 668.

‡ Rhode, "Die heilige Sage . . . der alten Baktrer, Meder und Perser:" *Frankf.* 1820, pp. 152, *seqq.* Volney, "Recherches nouvelles sur l'Histoire ancienne:" *Par.* 1822, p. 283.

§ The opinion preferred by Tychsen, "Comment. Soc. Goetting." vol. xi. p. 112, and Heeren, "Ideen," i. Th. i. Abth. p. 440.

In much the same condition are those Christian nations whose history, comparatively modern, has fallen into the hands of the clergy, the natural annalists of a less refined people. These would, of course, reject those crude legendary traditions which form the remote history of pagan nations, whom they would not wish any longer to resemble, by descent, from unclean and impious deities; and they would seek to substitute such early records as the inspired writings afforded them, in their room. This we find to be actually the case with the Georgians and Armenians. The first portion of their annals is drawn from the Bible; they endeavour to find their forefathers in that storehouse of primeval history, the book of Genesis; they next fill up a long space with accounts gleaned from foreign historians, and, at last, attach to them their own meagre narratives, too modern to trouble the most delicate sensitiveness, on the score of revelation. The earliest period to which anything among them pretending to the name of history can reach, is, according to Klaproth, two or three centuries before Christ.*

But we still have China to dispose of; and surely it, at least, must be excepted from the remarks which I have made; for it possesses a native literature of great antiquity, and pretends to be the first or primary nation of the globe. We all know, too, that it carries back its annals to a very formidable age; and it might be expected, that as much attention should be devoted to its claims as we have bestowed on its rivals in India. I will, however, content myself with laying before you, in a few words, the conclusions to which Klaproth came, from the study of its authors, to which he was principally devoted; and I can assure you, that you will have the decision of a judge by no means disposed to second our desires, by depreciating the glories of the Chinese.

According to him, therefore, the earliest historian of

---

* Page 412.

China was its celebrated philosopher and moralist, Confucius. He is said to have drawn up the annals of his country, known under the name of Chu-King, from the days of Yao, till his own times. Confucius is supposed to have lived about four or five hundred years before Christ, and the era of Yao is placed at 2,557 years before the same era. Thus, then, we have upwards of 2,000 years between the first historian and the earliest events which he records. But this antiquity, however remote, did not satisfy the pride of the Chinese; and later historians have prefixed other reigns to that of Yao, which stretched back to the venerable antiquity of three millions two hundred and seventy-six thousand years before Christ.

That you may estimate still more accurately the authenticity of the Chinese annals, I must not omit to state, that two hundred years after the death of Confucius, the Emperor Chi-Hoangti, of the dynasty of Tsin, proscribed the works of the philosopher, and ordered all the copies of them to be destroyed. The Chu-King, however, was recovered, in the following dynasty of Han, from the dictation of an old man, who had retained it by memory. Such, then, is the origin of historical science in China; and in spite of all due veneration for the great moralist of the East, and of respect for his assertion, that he only wrought on materials already existing, Klaproth does not hesitate to deny the existence of historical certainty in the Celestial Empire, earlier than 782 years before Christ, pretty nearly the era of the foundation of Rome, when Hebrew literature was already on the decline.*

The Japanese, in historical knowledge, are but the copiers of the Chinese. They, too, pretend to their millions of years before the Christian era. But the first

* Page 406. Abel-Rémusat is disposed to allow Chinese history to reach back to the year 2200 before Christ, and plausible tradition to go as far back as 2637. Even this antiquity presents nothing formidable to a Christian's convictions.—"Nouveaux Mélanges Asiatiques," tom. i. p. 61: *Par.* 1829.

portion of their annals is purely mythological; the second presents us with the Chinese dynasties as reigning in Japan; and it is not till the accession of the Daïri to the throne, only 660 years before Christ, that any dependence can be placed upon their records.*

In glancing back over the chronology of the different nations of which I have treated, you cannot help being struck with the circumstance, that every attempt has failed to establish, for any of them, a system of chronology derogatory to the authority of the Mosaic records. In most of them, even when we have granted a real existence to the most doubtful portions of their history, we are not led back to an epoch anterior to what Scripture assigns for the existence of powerful empires in eastern Africa, and enterprising states on the western coast of Asia.

The learned Windischmann, whom I feel a pride in calling my friend, admits the entire period of Chinese history allotted by Klaproth to the uncertain times, and shows its agreement with another form of computation, drawn from the cycles of years adapted by the Chinese; and the result is a sufficiently accurate accordance between the date assigned to the foundation of the Celestial Empire by Fo-hi, or Fu-chi, whom some have even supposed to be Noah, the time of the Deluge, according to the Samaritan Pentateuch, and the beginning of the Indian Cali-Yuga, or iron age.† The philosophical Schlegel not only concurs in the same view, but approves also of Abel-Rémusat's idea, that the written Chinese character must be 4,000 years old; "this," he observes, "would bring it back within three or four generations from the Deluge, according to the vulgar era,—an estimate which certainly is not exaggerated."‡

Even in India, you have seen authors, like Colonel

---

* Page 408.
† "Die Philosophie im Fortgang der Weltgeschichte," 1 Th. 1 Abtheil: *Bonn*, 1827, p. 18.
‡ "Philosophy of History," vol. i. p. 106, Robertson's transl.

Tod, assuming, almost without limitation, the chronological tables of the country, and yet coming pretty exactly to the same period for the commencement of its history. Surely a convergence like this must have force of proof with the most obstinate mind, and produce conviction, that some great and insuperable barrier must have interposed between nations and any earlier definite traditions, at the same time that it allowed some faint rays of recollection to pass, of the original state and happier constitution of the human race. A sudden catastrophe, whereby mankind were, in great part, though not totally, extinguished, presents the most natural solution of all difficulties; and the concurrent testimony of physical phenomena, with the silent acknowledgment of the vainest nations, must assuredly shield, from every attack, this record of our inspired volume.

There is yet another nation, whose history is perhaps more interesting than any which we have discussed; but it will afford us sufficient matter for another meeting.

LECTURE THE EIGHTH;

ON

EARLY HISTORY.

PART II.

EGYPTIANS.—1. *Historical Monuments.* Mystery of their Monuments.—Excessive Antiquity ascribed to the Nation.—The Rosetta Stone.—First Researches into the Egyptian Characters on it, by Akerblad and De Sacy, Young and Champollion.—Hieroglyphic Alphabet.—Opposition raised.—Applications of the Chronology discovered through it to the illustration of Scripture by Coquerel, Greppo, and Bovet.—Inedited Letter by Champollion on this Subject.—Rosellini; his Series of Egyptian Kings;—their Coincidence with those of Scripture.—Vindication and Illustration of a Prophecy in Ezechiel.
2. *Astronomical Monuments.* Zodiacs of Dendera and Esneh. Absurd Antiquity ascribed to them. Discoveries of Mr. Bankes, MM. Champollion and Letronne. Proved to be purely Astrological.—Commentary on some Observations in the British Critic.

FROM the soil of Asia, over which late we strayed, fruitful in every science, and varied by the display of every degree in cultivation, from the restless nomade, or the untamed mountaineer, to the luxurious Persian, or the polished Ionian, we have now to turn to a country whereon nature seemeth to have set the seal of desolation physical and moral. One redeeming spot alone of Africa has been the seat of an indigenous civilization, a native dynasty and a domestic class of monuments; and the valley of the Nile appears rightly placed in such a geographical situation as almost detaches its inhabitants from the degraded tenants of the wilderness, and links them with the more favoured regions of the East.

At every period, this extraordinary nation has interested the attention of the learned. Its origin seemed to have been a problem to itself, and consequently to all others. The mysterious allegories of its worship, the dark sublimity of its morality, and, above all, the impenetrable enigma of its written monuments, threw a mythological veil over its history. The learned approached it, as if in the most obvious facts they had to decipher a hieroglyphic legend; and we were inclined to look upon the Egyptians, as a people, which, even in its more modern periods, retained the shadowy tints and ill-defined traits of remote antiquity, and which might consequently boast an existence far beyond the reach of calculation. We were almost tempted to believe them when they told us, that their first monarchs were the gods of the rest of the world.

When, after so many ages of darkness and uncertainty, we see the lost history of this people revive, and take its stand beside that of other ancient empires; when we read the inscriptions of its kings, recording their mighty exploits and regal qualities, and gaze upon their monuments, with the full understanding of the events which they commemorate, the impression is scarcely less striking to an enlightened mind, than what the traveller would feel, if, when silently pacing the catacombs at Thebes, he should see those corpses, which the embalmer's skill has for so many ages rescued from decay, on a sudden burst their cerements, and start resuscitated from their niches.

While such a darkness overhung the history of Egypt, it is no wonder that the adversaries of religion should have retreated within it, as a stronghold, and eagerly attacked her from behind its shelter. They collected together the scattered fragments of its annals, just as Isis did the torn limbs of Osiris, and tried to reconstruct, by their re-union, a favourite idol, a chronology of countless ages, totally incompatible with that of Moses.

Volney had no hesitation in placing the formation of sacerdotal colleges in Egypt, 13,300 years before Christ, and calling that the second period of its history!* Even the third period, in which he supposes the temple of Esneh to have been built, goes as far back as 4,600 years before that era; somewhere about what we reckon the epoch of creation! But the mysterious monuments of Egypt formed the most useful intrenchments for these assailants. They called upon those huge and half-buried colossal images, and those now subterraneous temples, to bear witness to the antiquity and early civilization of the nation which erected them; they appeal to their astronomical remains, to attest the skill, matured by ages of observation, of those who projected them. More than all, they saw in those hieroglyphic legends the venerable dates of sovereigns, deified long before the modern days of Moses or Abraham; they pointed in triumph to the mysterious characters which an unseen hand had traced on those primeval walls, and boasted that only a Daniel was wanted that could decipher them, to show that the evidences of Christianity had been weighed and found wanting; and its kingdom divided between the infidel and the libertine! Vain boast! The temples of Egypt have at length answered their appeal, in language more intelligible than they could possibly have anticipated; for a Daniel has been found in judicious and persevering study. After the succession had been so long interrupted, Young and Champollion have put on the linen robe of the hierophant; and the monuments of the Nile, unlike the fearful image of Sais, have allowed themselves to be unveiled by their hands, without any but the most wholesome and consoling results having followed from their labour.

The history of the discovery to which I allude, is not perhaps difficult to unravel; but it is by no means easy to allot to each claimant his share of merit. There certainly were approximating steps in the researches of

---

* "Recherches," vol. ii. p. 440.

sagacious antiquaries, before the announcement of a complete system of hieroglyphic literature flashed upon Europe. It is more than probable that Champollion would not so easily have attained it, had not the way been pioneered before him; but still the step which he at once made, from the conjectural course and detached applications which others had pursued before him, to a general system, at once applicable to any case,—and yet more, the public interest which his publication drew upon the study, making it pass from the hands of a few profound scholars, into the general literature of the day,—are grounds which he might well advance for being considered the discoverer, or restorer, of hieroglyphic learning.

In the last century, Warburton, and after him, Zoega, had conjectured that the hieroglyphics in reality represented letters, but neither could pretend to have verified the opinion by any practical observation. In fact, it was not even known with accuracy what the language of ancient Egypt was. Jablonsky had made it extremely probable that it was the same as the Coptic, or modern ecclesiastical language of the same country; for he had sufficiently explained from this the Egyptian names and words which occur in the Old Testament.* But, if any doubt existed regarding this matter, it was completely removed by the learned Quatremère, in his interesting work on the language and literature of Egypt,† wherein the identity, or close affinity, of the ancient and modern languages was amply demonstrated. One great obstacle, therefore, to the deciphering of ancient Egyptian inscriptions was removed, supposing them to be composed of alphabetical characters. It is just, also, to observe, that before the discovery which dimmed the glory he would otherwise have received from his

---

* "Opuscula quibus lingua et antiquitas Ægyptiorum, difficilia LL. SS. loca illustrantur:" *Lugd. Bat.* 1804.
† "Recherches sur la Langue et la Littérature de l'Egypte:" *Par.* 1808.

further researches, Champollion was one of the first and most assiduous to gather information from Coptic literature, upon the geography and history of ancient Egypt.*

When the language is known, or may be probably conjectured, in which inscriptions are written, there are certain rules whereby they may be reduced to intelligible characters. The great difficulty is to know where to begin, for the first step must be conjectural. Thus it was, for instance, with the arrow, or nail, or wedge-headed inscriptions of Persepolis, which had perplexed the learned world since they were first made known by Niebuhr, till they were almost simultaneously deciphered by Saint Martin, in Paris, and Grotefend, at Vienna. The process followed by the former was exceedingly simple and obvious. The language, he supposed, would be Persian, and the ancient dialect is sufficiently known in the modern and in the Zend, to give him some lever wherewith to commence his work. He selected an inscription, from its form and position manifestly historical; and assuming that in any such, if in honour of a Persian monarch, the title of "King of Kings" would be found, he turned his attention to two words or groups of letters placed together exactly similar, except that the termination of one was sufficiently varied to give ground for supposing that it was the plural of the other. Having by this means acquired the power of the letters which composed these two words, he applied them to a proper name, which nearly resembled them, and thus was in possession of the name of Xerxes, which does, in reality, bear an affinity in sound to the old Persian title of King.† The groundwork was thus laid, and by applying the letters gradually discovered to other words wherein they occurred in conjunction with others unknown, these, in their turn, yielded to his investigation, and placed him in possession of his alphabet.

The process pursued in the examination and discovery

* "L'Egypte sous les Pharaons:" *Par.* 1814.
† "Journal Asiatique," tom. ii. 1833, pp. 75, 79.

of hieroglyphics was precisely similar. The difficulty, as I before hinted, was where to begin; but fortunately a plausible conjecture, which, as in the other instance, proved well grounded, gave a firm foundation to the entire system of discovery. You cannot have failed to observe, how, on all Egyptian monuments, certain groups of hieroglyphics are inclosed in an oblong frame, or parallelogram, with rounded corners. It had long been conjectured, with great appearance of plausibility, that these distinguished hieroglyphics expressed proper names; and nothing was wanting to begin the work upon them; for proper names could never be well expressed in any language by emblems, but must be somehow composed of *phonetic*, or sound-expressing characters. This is the case even in Chinese; where the language is ideographic, or representative of objects or ideas, yet is reduced to the necessity of adopting a different system for words which represent neither, but only an artificial combination of sounds denoting a person or place. If, therefore, it could be once possible to know a single name contained in one of these squares, the decomposition of it into its primary elements or letters, would give the nucleus of an alphabet, which might be easily extended.

All this reasoning is extremely simple, and though, in detailing it, I am rather giving you a restrospective view of acts and their consequences, than a line of argument, distinctly and systematically planned beforehand, it may serve to show you by what consistent and well-warranted steps the entire investigation proceeded. These were not, indeed, the work of one man, nor of one country; and so far from any rivalry or jealousy being felt by learned men on different sides of the channel, about the apparent appropriation of each other's literary discoveries, I think it should be matter of congratulation to observe, how two nations, after having fought bravely for the time-worn spoils of Egypt, have been led to sit down together in peace and harmony around them, for their illustration; and if the mutilated fragment of the Rosetta stone has been to us a military trophy, it has been to our neighbours the monument of a more glorious conquest over the darkest mysteries of a hidden art.

This celebrated stone is, at present, an irregular block of basalt, smooth on one side, and may be considered the foundation-stone of this important study; as all discoveries in it owe their origin and strength to the first elements of knowledge which it supplied. This almost shapeless mass, which a few years ago would have been thrown aside into the lumber-room of the Museum, is now one of the most valuable monuments of our national collection, and was originally discovered by the French expedition in digging the foundation of a fort near Rosetta. It contains three inscriptions, one in Greek, another in hieroglyphics, and a third in an intermediate alphabet, which in the Greek legend is called *enchorial*.[*] It was evident from this, that each inscription contained nearly the same sense, and that each was probably a version of the others. Here there was some hope of a discovery in the unknown, from its being joined, as in equation, with the known. The Greek inscription contains proper names, so must the other two; but in the first instance, probably from considering the task as hopeless, the hieroglyphic inscription hardly obtained attention from the learned, who rather applied themselves to the study of the *enchorial*, or, as it has since been called, *demotic* legend. Perhaps I should observe, that the language so called was the vernacular dialect of Egypt, the Coptic, and that the alphabet used in it is a linear one, formed, however, undoubtedly, through several gradations, from the hieroglyphic.

The illustrious Silvestre de Sacy was the first to make any interesting discovery on this subject. He observed that the letters or symbols used to express the proper

---

[*] This custom of polyglott inscriptions, intended only for one country, which might be frequented by strangers, illustrates and explains the reasons of Pilate's commanding a trilingual inscription to be placed over our Saviour's cross.

names, in the *demotic* character, were grouped together, so as to have the appearance of being letters; and by comparing different words, wherein the same sounds occurred, he found them represented by the same figure; and thus he extracted from them the rudiments of a demotic alphabet, which was further illustrated and extended by Akerblad at Rome, and Dr. Young in England. All these researches and partial discoveries occurred as early as 1814, and by no means close the history of the demotic literature of Egypt. Dr. Young, who truly deserves the title of the father of this portion of Egyptian studies, pushed them forward to the almost complete formation of the current alphabet, and was aided in his researches by some most extraordinary combinations of circumstances.

Thus, for instance, a copy of a demotic manuscript, brought to Europe by Casati, was placed in his hands by M. Champollion at Paris, in 1822, because it seemed to bear considerable resemblance to the preamble of the Rosetta stone. Champollion had already deciphered the names of the witnesses who signed it, for it seemed to be a deed. It so happened that after Dr. Young's return to England, Mr. Grey placed at his disposal a Greek papyrus, which he had purchased at Thebes, together with others in Egyptian characters. The very same day he proceeded to explore this treasure, and, to use the Doctor's own expression, he could scarcely believe that he was awake and in his sober senses, when he discovered it to be nothing less than a translation of the very manuscript which he had procured at Paris; and it actually bore the title of "a copy of an Egyptian writing." "I could not, therefore, but conclude," he says, " that a most extraordinary chance had brought into my possession a document which was not very likely, in the first place, even to have existed, still less to have been preserved uninjured for my information, through a period of near two thousand years; but that this very extraordinary translation should have been brought safely to Europe, to England, and to us, at the very moment that it was most desirable to me to possess it, as the illustration of an original which I was then studying, but without any other reasonable hope of being fully able to comprehend it; this combination would, in other times, have been considered as affording ample evidence of my being an Egyptian sorcerer."*

But I have pursued farther than was necessary the history of this secondary branch of Egyptian discovery, which is interesting from the influence it had on the deciphering of hieroglyphical legends. Here also Dr. Young decidedly took the first step, however imperfect it may be considered. He conjectured that the frames which occurred in the inscription of Rosetta included the name of Ptolemy, and that another, in which was inscribed a group, with what he considered justly the sign of a feminine, contained that of Bernice. This conjecture was correct; but it must be allowed that the principle on which it was maintained could hardly be called a preliminary step to the discoveries of Champollion. For, as he observes, Dr. Young considered each hieroglyphic to be syllabic, and to represent a consonant with its vowel, a system which would have fallen to the ground on the very next attempt at verification. For he read two names, PTOLOMEAS and BIRENIKEN, and not, as was subsequently proved correct, PTOLMES and BRNEKS.† Dr. Young seems, therefore, entitled to little more than the praise of having practically attempted the discovery of a hieroglyphical alphabet—an attempt which, perhaps, spurred Champollion on to his more successful efforts.

* "An Account of some recent Discoveries in Hieroglyphical Literature :" *Lond.* 1823, p. 58. A writer on this subject increases the strange combination recorded in the text still farther, by asserting that both the documents were copies of a bilingual inscription in Drovetti's collection, which Dr. Young, with an illiberality most unusual in Italy, had not been allowed to copy. See the Marquis Spineto's "Lectures on the Elements of Hieroglyphics :" *Lond.* 1829, p. 68. But of this still more extraordinary coincidence not a hint is given by Dr. Young.

† "Précis du Système hiéroglyphique des anciens Egyptiens:" *Par.* 1824, p. 31.

If the merit of the very first step has been thus contested, the second has been no less an object of rival claims. This was taken as follows:—In the island of Philæ, situated high up the Nile, an obelisk was found, and thence brought to England, on which were two cartouches, or frames containing hieroglyphics, joined together. One of these presented invariably the group already explained in the Rosetta stone by the name of Ptolemy. The other evidently contained a name composed, in part, of the same letters, and followed by the sign of the feminine gender. This obelisk had been originally placed on a base bearing a Greek inscription, which contained a petition of the priests of Isis to Ptolemy and Cleopatra, and spoke of a monument to be raised to both.* There was, consequently, every reason to suppose, that the obelisk bore these two names conjointly; and observation proved that the three letters common to both, P, T, and L, were represented in the female name by the same signs as occurred for them in the king's. Thus, there could be no reasonable doubt as to this second name, which put the learned investigators in possession of the other letters which enter into its composition. All this Champollion claimed as exclusively his own.† Mr. Bankes, however, maintains that he had previously deciphered the name of Cleopatra, and endeavours to show that Champollion must have been aware of the discovery. For he says, that he had been led to the observation, that when two figures occur together on any temple, they are so repeated throughout. Now, over the portico at Diospolis Parva, is a Greek inscription to Cleopatra and Ptolemy, the only instance of the female preceding; and so, through the temple, she is always placed before the effigy of the king. Over the latter is the same hieroglyphical group as Dr. Young

---

* This inscription was illustrated by Letronne in a learned essay upon it, entitled "Eclaircissements sur une Inscription Grecque," &c. *Par.* 1822. The inscription had been copied by the diligent and accurate Cailliaud.

† "Lettre à M. Dacier:" *Par.* 1822, p. 6.

had assigned to the name from the Rosetta stone; and therefore Mr. Bankes plausibly conjectured, that the legend over the other expressed the name of the queen, Cleopatra. He then ascertained that both on the obelisk and on the temple at Philæ, which were determined, by Greek inscriptions, to be dedicated to the same two sovereigns, similar hieroglyphic groups were found. This led him to the certain conclusion, that as the one designated Ptolemy, so the other must contain the name of his consort. As these circumstances were marked by him in pencil on the very engraving of his obelisk which he presented to the Institute, as they alone could have suggested a clue to Champollion's conjectures, and as he referred to this very print, Mr. Bankes and his friends conclude, that this important step in hieroglyphic investigation should be attributed to him.*

When these first and more laborious measures had been once taken, the work was comparatively easy; and Champollion, who at first had imagined that his system could only apply to the reading of Greek or Latin names hieroglyphically expressed, soon found that the older names yielded to the key; and the successive dynasties of Pharaohs and of Persian monarchs who had ruled in Egypt, had recorded their names also, with their titles and their exploits, in the same character.† It was after his researches had reached this point, that they could be said to possess a real value for history, and aid us in unravelling the complicated difficulties of the early Egyptian annals. But, before proceeding to trace the history of their results, I must pause to explain the system which they introduced.

Many scattered passages exist in ancient writers regarding the hieroglyphical writings of the Egyptians, but there was one which seemed to treat the subject with peculiar detail. It lay treasured up in that vast repertory of philosophical learning, the Stromata of

---

* Salt, "Essay on Dr. Young's and M. Champollion's phonetic system of Hieroglyphics:" *Lond*. 1825, p. 7, note.
† "Précis du Système," &c. p. 2.

Clement of Alexandria; but so encased in impenetrable difficulties, that it may rather be said to have been explained by these modern discoveries than to have led the way towards them. It has, however, rendered them most essential service, by strongly corroborating what must be considered the essential foundation of their results, the position that alphabetical letters were used by the Egyptians. When this passage was examined, after Champollion's discovery, it was found to establish this point, which had not been suspected by older investigators, and moreover to explain the various mixture of alphabetical and symbolical writing used in Egypt, in a manner exactly corresponding to what monuments exhibit. The result of this passage as translated, and commented on by Letronne, is, that the Egyptians used three different sorts of writing: the *epistolographic*, or current hand; the *hieratic*, or the character used by the priests; and the *hieroglyphic*, or monumental character. Of the two former we have sufficient examples: the first being the *demotic* or *enchorial*, of which I have already spoken; the second a species of reduced hieroglyphical character, in which a rude outline represents the figures, and which is found on manuscripts which accompany mummies. The third, which is the most important, is composed, according to Clement, first of alphabetical words, and secondly of symbolical expressions, which again are threefold, being either representations of objects, or metaphorical ideas drawn from them, as when courage is represented by a lion, or else merely enigmatical or arbitrary signs.* Now observation has fully confirmed all these particulars; for even on the Rosetta stone it was noticed, that when some object was mentioned in the Greek, the hieroglyphics presented a picture of it, as a statue, a temple, or a man. On other occasions objects are represented by

---

* "Précis," p. 330. See also the passage in the Marquis de Fortia d'Urban's Essay, "Sur les trois Sistèmes (*sic*) d'Ecriture des Egiptieus" (*sic*): *Par.* 1833, p. 10. The passage of Clement occurs in "Stromata," lib. v. § 9, p. 245, ed. Potter.

emblems which must be considered completely arbitrary, as Osiris by a throne and eye, and a son by a bird most resembling a goose.

Suffice it to say, that new discoveries have gradually enlarged, and perhaps almost completed, the Egyptian alphabet, till we are in possession of a key to read all proper names, and even, though not with equal certainty, other hieroglyphical texts. To proper names the application is so simple, that you may be said to possess a means of verifying the system perfectly within reach. For you have only to walk to the Capitol or the Vatican with Champollion's alphabet, and try your skill upon the proper names in any of the Egyptian inscriptions.

The fate of this brilliant discovery was the same as we saw allotted to Geology and to other sciences. Scarcely was it announced to Europe than timid minds took the alarm, and reprobated it as tending to lead men to dangerous investigations. It was feared, apparently, that the early Egyptian history, thus brought to light, would be employed as that of the Chaldeans and Assyrians had been in the last century, for the purpose of impugning the Mosaic annals. Rosellini, who was the first to make the new discovery known in Italy, as he has been the means of bringing it to its perfection, justly observed, that such an outcry has been raised against every important discovery. Those who raise it, he adds, do but little justice to the truth by being so timid on its account. " This truth is founded on eternal bases, neither can the envy of man disprove it, nor can ages deface it. And if men eminent for their piety and learning, admit the new system, what has revelation to fear from it?"* In fact, the holy Pontiff who then sat in the Chair of St. Peter, expressed to Champollion his confidence, that his discovery would render essential service to religion.† In spite of this high sanction, the opposition has since

* In his Italian abridgment of "Champollion's Letters to the Duke de Blacas."
† "Bulletin Universel," 7e sect. tom. iv. p. 6: *Par.* 1825.

continued, and, I regret to say, with a degree of personal feeling, and a severe animosity, which seem hardly worthy of a just mind employed on literary pursuits.*

Perhaps the best-conducted attack on the system, because, while free from the feelings which I have just blamed, it is united to the desire of substituting something better in its place, is that lately made by the Abbé Count de Robiano, who ingeniously exposes the weak parts of the hieroglyphical system, especially through the demotic character. He institutes a very patient and successful analysis of the demotic text on the Rosetta stone, as compared with the Greek, and concludes, with great apparent reason, first, that the one is not a verbal or very close version of the other, and secondly, that nothing has been done, or well can be hoped, towards proving the identity of the Egyptian phrases thus discovered, with corresponding Coptic words.† The Abbé is himself of opinion, that the language of Egypt is of Semitic origin; and, on this hypothesis, he attempts to explain one or two inscriptions by the Hebrew language.‡ This attempt, though ingenious and learned, does not seem to me successful. However, I do not think it necessary to follow the arguments of this learned ecclesiastic; because it does not strike me that any theory which he has advanced, at all affects the only part of the system interesting to our present inquiries,—its power of deciphering proper names.

One of the first applications made by M. Champollion of his discovery, was an attempt to restore the series of

---

* I will not mention the various essays by Riccardi; but the learned Professor Lanci has been particularly zealous in his resistance. "Svanirà," he writes, "il timore che il nuovo geroglifico sistema possa mai adombrare in alcuna parte, quella storia che sola merita la universale venerazione." "Illustrazione di un Kilanoglifo," in his " Osservazioni sul Basso Rilievo Fenico-Egizio :" *Rome*, 1825, p. 47. —See Champollion's answer, in the " Memorie Romane di Antichità :" 1825, Append. p. 10.

† "Etudes sur l'Ecriture, les Hiéroglyphes, et la Langue l'Egypte :" *Paris*, 1834, 4to. with atlas of plates, pp. 16-24, &c.

‡ Page 43.

Egyptian kings. The table of Abydos* had given him a list of pronomens, and the examination of monuments exhibited the names of the kings who bore them. These corresponded pretty accurately with the eighteenth dynasty, contained in the list of kings quoted from the Egyptian priest Manetho, by Eusebius, Syncellus, and Africanus; and by combining the two documents together, he endeavoured to trace the ancient history of Egypt. As the Museum of Turin had supplied him with the greater part of his monuments, he communicated his results in letters upon that magnificent collection, addressed to his great Mecænas, the Duke of Blacas.† His relative, M. Champollion-Figeac, previously known for his learned work on the Lagides, added as an appendix to each of these letters, a chronological disquisition, having for its object to reconcile together the discrepancies in the quotations from Manetho given by ancient writers.

It was natural to expect that a comparison between the chronology thus established and that of Scripture, would soon be instituted, and in this instance the task was undertaken by the friends, not as heretofore by the enemies, of revelation. That malignant spirit, which at the last century's close had so often induced able and learned men to direct the whole force of their genius, and many years of deep research, to the overturning of sacred history, had now passed away, or at least altered its form of attack.

The first who appeared in the field was M. Charles Coquerel, a Protestant clergyman at Amsterdam, who, in a pamphlet of a few pages, in 1825, compared the two chronologies, and pointed out the advantages which one derived from the other.‡

---

* "Précis du Système," p. 241.
† "Lettres à M. le Duc de Blacas, relatives au Musée Royal Egyptien de Turin, Première Lettre:" *Paris*, 1824, 2de, 1826.
‡ "Lettre à M. Charles Coquerel sur le Système Hiéroglyphique de M. Champollion considéré dans ses rapports avec l'Ecriture Sainte." Par A. L. Coquerel. *Amst.* 1825.

I believe I had the satisfaction of being the second in the field. In making out his Egyptian chronology, Champollion-Figeac found it necessary, on one occasion, to depart from his usual guides, and adopt the term of years attributed to Horus by only one document, the Armenian translation of Eusebius's chronicle. I was fortunate enough to discover a Syriac fragment in the margin of a Vatican MS. which coincided exactly with this view, and in publishing it, I took occasion to sketch out a comparison between the sacred and the Egyptian chronologies.* I was not, however, able to see Coquerel's pamphlet till several years later.

In 1829, a learned and diligent investigation of this subject was published by M. Greppo, vicar-general of the diocese of Belley, entitled, *Essai sur le Système hiéroglyphique de M. Champollion le Jeune, et sur les avantages qu'il offre à la critique sacrée*. After a clear and popular exposition of Champollion's system, and a few remarks on some philological connections which it seems to have with early Hebrew literature, the author proceeds to a minute analysis of the biblical and Egyptian chronology, endeavouring to discover in the latter each of the Pharaohs mentioned in Scripture.

The same year, another work upon the same subject appeared in France, entitled, *Des Dynasties Egyptiennes*, by M. Bovet, formerly Archbishop of Toulouse. The parallel into which he enters of the two chronologies, is much more minute than Greppo's; but on some points, as in the attempt to find the Hyk-Shos, or shepherd kings, in the Jews, he does not seem to me so judicious. He appears to have imbibed much of the opinion introduced before the Revolution, by Boulanger and Guerin de Rocher, that a great part of all ancient annals only contains the history of the Jewish people. All these authors have undertaken the same task of demonstrating what beautiful confirmation sacred history and chronology have received from the latest discoveries in hieroglyphical and Egyptian learning.

* "Horæ Syriacæ," tom. i. *Rome*, 1828, particula iv. p. 263.

But, in the meantime, great and important advances have been made in the history of the Egyptian dynasties, by persons labouring in that country. Messrs. Burton and Wilkinson, the latter of whom only returned within a few months, remained several years in Egypt, copying, printing, and illustrating its ancient monuments. Burton's *Excerpta Hieroglyphica* was lithographed at Cairo; Wilkinson's *Materia Hieroglyphica, containing the Egyptian Pantheon, and the succession of the Pharaohs,* was published at Malta in 1828; and by reason of their appearing in such remote places, I believe both works have been comparatively little known. Burton's book is valuable for our studies merely from the accuracy of its drawings, especially of the table of Abydos. Wilkinson's contains many interesting discoveries applicable to the illustration of Scripture, and I shall refer to it more than once.

Every preceding work, however, has been eclipsed by the splendid and accurate publication now in the press at Pisa, under the direction of Professor Rosellini. He was the companion of Champollion in the literary expedition sent, at joint expense, by the French and Tuscan governments. Champollion's death threw the entire task of publication upon Rosellini, who is acquitting himself of it in a manner that leaves nothing to regret. The monuments of the kings are already published, and two volumes of text contain their illustration from historians and other monuments.

Before showing, by examples, the advantage derived by sacred chronology, and the authenticity of Holy Writ, from this modern study, I must lay before you a highly interesting document connected with our inquiry. The chronological part of the letters to the Duc de Blacas was entirely executed by Champollion-Figeac, as I before observed; but the author of the great discovery, though well known to be perfectly sound in his principles, never published anything tending to prove the conformity of his chronology with that of Scripture. But I have the pleasure of laying before you an original letter from him in my possession, wherein he not only indignantly repels the imputation that his studies tend even slightly to impugn Scripture history, but endeavours to show how exactly the two histories give and obtain mutual support. This interesting document I will read you in the original. It is dated Paris, May 23, 1827.

" J'aurai l'honneur de vous adresser sous peu de jours une brochure, contenant le résumé de mes découvertes historiques et chronologiques. C'est l'indication sommaire des dates certaines, que portent tous les monuments existants en Egypte, et sur lesquels doit désormais se fonder la véritable chronologie Egyptienne.

" MM. De San Quintino et Lanci trouveront là une réponse péremptoire à leurs calomnies, puisque j'y démontre qu'aucun monument Egyptien n'est réellement antérieur à l'an 2,200 avant notre ère. C'est certainement une très haute antiquité, mais elle n'offre rein de contraire aux traditions sacrées; et j'ose dire même qu'elle les confirme sur tous les points: c'est en effet en adoptant la chronologie et la succession des rois données par les monuments Egyptiens, que l'histoire Egyptienne concorde admirablement avec les livres saints. Ainsi par exemple; Abraham arriva en Egypte vers 1900,—c'est-à-dire, sous les *Rois Pasteurs.* Des rois de race Egyptienne n'auraient point permis à un étranger d'entrer dans leur pays,—c'est également sous un roi pasteur que Joseph est ministre en Egypte, et y établit ses frères,—ce qui n'eût pu avoir lieu sous des rois de race Egyptienne. Le chef de la dynastie des Diospolitians, dite la XVIIIe, est le *rex novus qui ignorabat Joseph* de l'Ecriture sainte, lequel étant de race Egyptienne, ne devait point connaître Joseph, ministre des rois usurpateurs; c'est celui qui réduit les Hébreux en esclavage. La captivité dura autant que la XVIIIe dynastie; et ce fut sous Ramsès V, dit Amenophis, au commencement du XVe siècle, que Moyse délivra les Hébreux. Ceci se passait dans l'adolescence de Sesostris, qui succéda immédiatement à son père, et fit ses conquêtes en Asie pendant que Moyse et Israel erraient pendant quarante ans dans le désert. *C'est pour cela que les livres saints ne doivent point parler de ce grand conquérant.* Tous les autres rois d'Egypte nommés dans la Bible, se retrouvent sur les monuments Egyptiens, dans le même ordre de succession, et aux époques précises, où les livres saints les placent. J'ajouterai même que la Bible en écrit mieux les véritables noms, que ne l'ont fait les historiens Grecs. Je serais curieux de savoir ce qu'auront à répondre ceux qui ont malicieusement avancé que les études Egyptiennes tendent à altérer la croyance dans les documents historiques fournis par les livres de Moyse. L'application de ma découverte vient, au contraire, invinciblement à leur appui.

" Je compose dans ce moment-ci le texte explicatif des *Obélisques de Rome*, que Sa Sainteté a daigné faire graver à ses frais. C'est un vrai service qu'Elle rend à la science, et je serais heureux que vous voulussiez bien mettre à ses pieds l'hommage de ma reconnaissance profonde."

But it is high time to lay before you the results of these combined labours: and always anxious to select them from the latest and best writers, I will run through the connections between sacred and Egyptian history as given in the different parts of Rosellini's work, to show you what new lights and striking confirmation the former has received from these researches, and how groundless were the alarms of their early antagonists. In the first place I must observe, that Rosellini takes the Scripture chronology as a necessary basis to all his calculations; so far that he is willing to reject every part of the early history of Egypt which cannot enter within the limits prescribed by Genesis.*

The first point in Scripture on which the labours of Rosellini throw a new light, is the origin and signification of the title of Pharaoh; though on this point he

---

* "I Monumenti dell' Egitto e della Nubia," vol. i. p. 111.

may be said to have received a hint from our learned countrymen, Wilkinson and Major Felix. By several analogies between the Hebrew and Egyptian letters, he shows the title to be identical with that of Phra, or Phre, the sun, which is prefixed to the names of the kings upon their monuments.* Coming down to a later period, we have an extraordinary coincidence between the facts related in the history of Joseph, and the state of Egypt at the period when he and his family entered it. We are told in the book of Genesis, that Joseph, upon presenting his father and brethren to Pharaoh, was careful to tell him that they were shepherds, and that their trade had been to feed cattle, and that they had brought their flocks and herds with them.† But in his instructions to them there seems to be an extraordinary contradiction:—" When Pharaoh shall call on you and say, ' What is your occupation?' ye shall say, ' Thy servants' trade hath been about cattle, from our youth even until now, both we and also our fathers;' that ye may dwell in the land of Goshen, for every shepherd is an abomination unto the Egyptians."‡ Now why make it such a point to tell Pharaoh that his family were all shepherds, because all shepherds were an abomination to the Egyptians? This contradiction is removed by the circumstance, that when Joseph was in Egypt, the greater part of its kingdom was under the dominion of the Hyk-Shos, or Shepherd Kings, a foreign race, probably of Scythian origin, who had seized upon the kingdom. Thus we have it, at once, explained how strangers, of whom the Egyptians were so jealous, should be admitted into power; how the king should be even glad of new settlers, occupying considerable tracts of his territory; and how the circumstance of their being shepherds, though odious to the conquered people, would endear them to a sovereign whose family followed the same occupation. These Hyk-Shos are supposed by Champollion to be represented by the

* Page 117. † Gen. xlvi. 33, 34; xlvii. 1.
‡ Gen. xlvi. 34, cf. xlvii. 6, 11.

figures painted on the soles of Egyptian slippers, in token of contempt.* By this state of Egypt we can also more easily explain the measures pursued by Joseph during the famine, to bring all the land and persons of the Egyptians into a feudal dependence upon their sovereign.† And before leaving this period, I may observe, that the name given to Joseph of "Saviour of the world," has been well explained by Rosellini from the Egyptian language.

After the death of Joseph, the Scripture tells us that a king arose who knew not Joseph. This strong expression could hardly be applied to any lineal successor of a monarch who had received such signal benefits from him. It would lead us rather to suppose that a new dynasty, hostile to the preceding, had obtained possession of the throne. "The Scripture," says James of Edessa, "does not mean one particular Pharaoh, when it says a new king, but all the dynasty of that generation."‡

Now, this is exactly the case. For, a few years later, the Hyk-Shos, or Shepherd Kings, who correspond to the 17th Egyptian dynasty, were expelled from Egypt by Amosis, called on monuments Amenophtiph, the founder of the 18th or Diospolitan dynasty. He would naturally refuse to recognize the services of Joseph, and would consider all his family as necessarily his enemies; and thus, too, we understand his fears lest they should join the enemies of Egypt, if any war fell out with them.§ For the Hyk-Shos, after their expulsion, continued long to harass the Egyptians, by attempts to recover their lost dominion.‖ Oppression was, of course, the means employed to weaken first, and then extinguish, the Hebrew population. The children of Israel were employed in building up the

---

* Champollion, Lettre i. pp. 57, 58.
† Rosellini, *ib.* p. 180.
‡ Cod. Vat. Syr. 104, fol. 44.
§ Exod. i. 10. Also Maretho, ap. "Joseph. cont. Appion." lib. i.
‖ Rosell. p. 291.

cities of Egypt. It has been observed by Champollion, that many of the edifices erected by the 18th dynasty are upon the ruins of older buildings, which had been manifestly destroyed.* This circumstance, with the absence of older monuments in the parts of Egypt occupied by the Hyk-Shos, confirms the testimony of historians, that these usurpers destroyed the monuments of native princes; and thus was an opportunity given to the restorers of a native sovereignty, to employ those whom they considered their enemies' allies, in repairing their injuries. To this period belong the magnificent edifices of Karnak, Luxor, and Medinet-Abu. At the same time, we have the express testimony of Diodorus Siculus, that it was the boast of the Egyptian kings, that no Egyptian had put his hand to the work, but that foreigners had been compelled to do it.†

It was under a king of this dynasty—according to Rosellini, of Ramses—that the children of Israel went out from Egypt.‡ The Scripture narrative describes this event as connected with the destruction of a Pharaoh, and so the chronological calculation adopted by Rosellini, would make it coincide with the last year of that monarch's reign.§

* Champollion, 2de Lett. pp. 7, 10, 17.
† 14 tom. ii. p. 445, ed. Havercamp.
‡ Lib. i. p. 66, ed. Wesseling. I omit noticing the opinion, formerly held by Josephus, and others (*ubi sup.*), repeated by many modern writers, as Marsham (*Canon Ægypt. Lips.* 1676, pp. 90, 106) and Rosenmüller (Scholia in Vet. Test. Pa. i. vol. ii. § 8, ed. tert.), and upheld even since the discovery of the hieroglyphical alphabet by a few, as Bovet and Wilkinson (*Materia Hieroglyphica, Malta*, 1828, part ii. p. 80), that the shepherd kings were no other than the children of Israel. This opinion appears now quite untenable, and not likely to find many supporters. The Hyk-Shos, as represented on monuments, have the features, colour, and other distinctives of the Scythian tribes.

§ As the Scripture speaks, with the exception of one poetical passage, of the destruction of Pharaoh's host, rather than of the monarch's, some writers, as Wilkinson (p. 4, Remarks, at the end of *Materia Hieroglyph.*) and Greppo, to whom I cannot now refer, maintain, that we need not necessarily suppose the death of a king to coincide with the exit from Egypt. In Rosellini's scheme this departure from the received interpretation is not wanted.

T

At this point we are met with a serious difficulty. Ancient historians speak of Sesostris as of a mighty conqueror, who, issuing from Egypt, and passing along the coast of Palestine, subjected innumerable nations to his sceptre. The Scripture never once alludes to this great invasion, which must have passed over the country inhabited by the Israelites. And this silence has been charged against sacred history as involving a serious omission, ruinous to its authenticity. For a long time it was supposed that the Sethos Ægyptus of Manetho was identical with the Sesostris of Herodotus. Even Champollion, from a want of sufficient monuments, had fallen into an error on this point, and subsequently changed his opinion. Rosellini has taken great pains to prove that the two were distinct, and by this discovery entirely removes all difficulty. For he shows that the great conqueror, Ramses Sethos Ægyptus, a totally different person from Ramses Sesostris, or the Sesostris of Herodotus and Diodorus, was the sovereign who conducted that mighty expedition, and founded the nineteenth Egyptian dynasty. As the Israelites had left Egypt shortly before the conclusion of the eighteenth, it follows that the exploits of this conqueror, and his passage through Palestine, happened exactly during their forty years' wandering through the wilderness, and could have no influence on the state of that people, and consequently needed not to be recorded in their national annals.*

Connected with this application is a curious and interesting monument, which has for some time formed the topic of discussion among our Roman antiquaries, and deserves a passing notice. Herodotus mentions that the great conqueror Sesostris marked the route which he took by a series of monuments, some of which he himself saw in Palestine, while others existed in Ionia.† Maundrell was the first to notice "some strange figures of men, carved in the natural rock, in

---

* Rosell. p. 305.   † Lib. ii. c. 105.

mezzo rilievo, and in bigness equal to life," on the mountain which overhangs the ford across the river Lycus, or the Nahr-el-Kelb, not far from Beirut.

Champollion, in his *Précis*, noticed this monument as Egyptian, and as appertaining to Ramses or Sesostris. It appears that his information came from a sketch made of it by Mr. Bankes; but an earlier one, by Mr. Wyse, had led Sir W. Gell to the same discovery of the hero whom it represents. Mr. Levinge, at Sir William's request, examined the monument, and pronounced that the hieroglyphical legend was quite defaced.* Mr. Lajard published a farther notice, from a sketch by MM. Guys, but turned his attention chiefly to the Persian monuments which are on the same rock. Later he collected all the information he could from M. Callier, who had not, however, any drawings to illustrate his description.† Mr. Bonomi at length fully investigated this interesting matter, and his observations, with the drawings that accompany them, both published by Mr. Landseer, leave little more to be desired.

It appears, then, that on the side of the road, which passes along the side of a mountain skirted by the Lycus, are ten ancient monuments. Two of these are comparatively of small interest, being a Latin and Arabic inscription regarding some repairs done to the road. Of the others, Mr. Bonomi speaks as follows: "The most ancient, but unfortunately the most corroded of the antiquities, are three Egyptian tablets. On these may be traced, in more places than one, the name, expressed in hieroglyphics, of *Ramses the Second;* to the period of whose reign any connoisseur in Egyptian art would have attributed them, even if the evidence of the name had been wanting, from the beautiful proportions of the tablets, and their curvetto mouldings."‡ I will content myself

---

* "Bulletino dell' Instituto di Corrispondenza Archeologica:" Gennaro, 1834, No. I. *b*, p. 30; No. VI. Luglio, p. 155.
† *Ibid.* and "Bulletino," No. III. *a*, Marzo, 1825, p. 23.
‡ "Landseer's Sabean Researches continued:" *Lond.* 1835, p. 5. See the drawing prefixed to his essay.

with mentioning, that beside this is a Persian *rilievo*, representing a king, with astronomical emblems, and covered with an arrow-headed inscription. Of this precious monument a cast was made with great difficulty, by Mr. Bonomi.* Mr. Landseer supposes it to represent Salmanasor, or some other early Assyrian invader.† The Chevalier Bunsen, without having inspected the cast or drawing, conjectures, with great appearance of reason, that its hero is Cambyses.‡

But to return to our Egyptians:—Champollion, and after him Wilkinson, considered the Sesostris of history to be identical with Ramses II., to whom Bonomi attributes the hieroglyphical legend on the Syriac monument;§ but, probably, he added the number to his name only on account of that received idea. Champollion changed his opinion, I believe, before his death, and was followed, as you have seen, by Rosellini. But M. Bunsen, who has long been occupying himself with an attempt to unravel the complications of Egyptian chronology, has observed that Ramses III. is undoubtedly the Sesostris of the Greeks; and that there is a mistake of three or four centuries in the date assigned by Champollion to the commencement of his reign.‖

Proceeding downwards in order of time, Rosellini, with all other chronologists, places the fifth year of Rehoboam, when Shishak overran the kingdom of Judah, and conquered Jerusalem, in the year 971 B.C.¶ Now, in Egyptian monuments, we find that Sheshonk began his reign with the twenty-first dynasty precisely at the same period.**

* The original cast is at present in the possession of my friend W. Scoles, Esq. † *Ib.* p. 14.
‡ "Bulletino," No. III. *a*, 1835, p. 21.
§ "Lettres écrites d'Egypte et de Nubie en 1828 et 1829:" *Par.* 1833, pp. 362, 438. Wilkinson's "Topography of Thebes:" *Lond.* 1835, p. 51 ; also "Materia Hieroglyph."
‖ "Bulletino," *ib.* p. 23. ¶ 3 or 1 Kings xiv. 25.
** Rosell. p. 83. See also Champollion, 2de Lett. pp. 120, 164. Also his Letter to Mr. G. A. Brown, in "Les Principaux Monumens Egyptiens du Musée Britannique, par le T. H. Charles York, et M. le Col. M. Leake:" *Lond.* 1827, p. 23.

Rosellini has published many monuments of Shishak, one of which particularly affords the strongest confirmation of sacred by profane history hitherto anywhere discovered. But this morning I am treating only of pure chronology, and must, therefore, reserve this interesting monument for our next meeting, when we shall discuss archæology.

The Zarach of the second book of Chronicles (xiv. 9-15), has been supposed by Greppo and others to be the Osorchon of monuments. Rosellini, however, rejects this opinion, though, I confess, I do not think his reasons very satisfactory: they consist in the slight difference of the name and in his being called an Ethiopian, a circumstance which rather confirms the coincidence, for the dynasty to which he belonged was the Bubastian, considered by Champollion Ethiopian.*

Rosellini, however, has added new monuments to those already furnished by Champollion, as commemorating two other kings mentioned later in sacred history: Sua, the Sevechus of the Greeks, and the Shabak of monuments, commemorated in the palaces of Luxor and Karnak, and by a statue in the Villa Albani; and Teraha, commemorated at Medinet-Abu, under the name Tahrak.†

To conclude these chronological details, one of the most striking confirmations of Scriptural accuracy yet remains. In Ezechiel, xxix. 30-32, and Jerem. xliv. 30, we have a donation made by God of Pharaoh and his land to Nabuchodonosor; and " there shall be no more a prince of the land of Egypt." Yet we find mention made of Amasis by Herodotus and Diodorus as king of Egypt after that period.

How are these two facts to be reconciled? By his monuments, first published by Mr. Wilkinson. Upon them Amasis never receives the Egyptian titles of royalty, but, instead of a pronomen, has the Semitic

---

* *Ubi sup.* p. 122.
† Pages 107, 109. Wilkinson, pp. 98, 99.

title of *Melek*, showing that he reigned on behalf of a foreign lord.* Two circumstances put this, I may say, beyond a doubt. First: Diodorus tells us that Amasis was of low birth; consequently he did not *inherit* the kingdom. Secondly: a son of Amasis seems to have governed Egypt under Darius, for he bears the same title. Now, certainly under the Persian conquest, there was no native king, for monuments bear the names of the Persian monarchs. The title Melek will thus be proved to denote viceregal authority; which again is still farther confirmed by a monument published by Rosellini, who does not seem to have observed Wilkinson's remark. This is an inscription at Kosseir, belonging to the times of the Persian domination, recording "the Melek of Upper and Lower Egypt."† Thus is a serious difficulty removed; Amasis was not a king, but only a viceroy.

But it is time to turn to another application of Egyptian researches,—to the illustration of its astronomical representations. The attention to Egyptian monuments and literature in modern times, has been, indeed, fertile in objections to sacred history, which, like every other study, it has overthrown in its advance. The controversy upon the zodiacs of Dendera, the ancient Tentyris, and Esneh, or Latopolis, is a remarkable proof of this assertion.

The expedition into Egypt under Napoleon, which shed as much lustre on the literary ardour of France as it cast shadow upon her martial prowess, first made us acquainted with these curious monuments. At Dendera were found two; one was an oblong painting, formed by two parallel but separated bands, enclosed within two monstrous female figures. Upon these bands, in an inner subdivision, were disposed the zodiacal signs, with numerous mythological representations; on the outside were a series of boats, representing the decans

---

* "Materia Hierogl." pp. 100, 101.
† Page 243.

of each sign. This zodiac was painted in the portico of a temple, where, like all the others, it occupied the ceiling. The second zodiac, or rather planisphere, is circular, and has been transported to France from an upper chamber of the same temple by MM. Saulnier and Lelorrain. Esneh contributed also two zodiacs, one from the greater, the second from the smaller of its temples. These two, with the rectangular zodiac of Dendera, can alone claim particular attention; the circular planisphere must follow the fate of the zodiac painted in the same temple.

No sooner were representations of these monuments published, than Europe, and particularly France, teemed with memoirs and dissertations discussing their antiquity. It was in general taken for granted that they represented the state of the heavens at the period when they were projected, and when the edifices which they adorned were erected. Some discovered in them the point in which the solstitial colures cut the ecliptic at that time, and, with Burckhardt, attributed to the great zodiac of Esneh the frightful antiquity of 7,000, to that of Dendera of 4,000 years; while Dupuis, upon the same premises, stinted the latter to 3,562.[*] Others assumed that they represented the state of the heavens at the commencement of a Sothic period; and, like Sir W. Drummond, assigned to that of Dendera 1,322,[†] to that of the great temple of Esneh 2,800 years before our era.[‡] A third class, in fine, saw in them the heliacal rising of Sirius at some given period, and concluded, with Fourier, that the zodiacs of Esneh were constructed 2,500, that of Dendera 2,000 years before Christ,[§] or with Nouet, that the latter was traced 2,500, the greater of the former 4,600 years anterior to that era.[||] I need not weary you farther by enumerating

---

[*] See Cuvier, *ubi sup.* p. 251.
[†] "Memoir on the Antiquity of the Zodiacs of Esneh and Dendera:" *Lond.* 1821, p. 141; vid. p. 7.
[‡] *Ib.* p. 59.
[§] See Guigniaut, p. 919.
[||] Volney's "Recherches nouvelles," 3e partie : *Par.* 1814, p. 336.

such systems as these. The same basis led different speculators to opposite conclusions; and error thus betrayed itself by the characteristic variety of its hues.

Early in the contest there was a class of investigators who ventured to suggest, that the alarming antiquity thus conceded to these curious monuments, should be examined, not upon astronomical, but upon archæological principles. The venerable and learned Monsignor Testa, and the celebrated antiquary Visconti, were among the number.* The latter remarked, in particular, that the temple of Dendera, though of Egyptian architecture, bore characteristic marks which could not be more ancient than the Ptolemies, and that Greek inscriptions upon it referred to a Cæsar, who, he thought, must be Augustus or Tiberius. This reasoning, however, was overlooked for twenty years, and astronomical illustrations were alone admitted. Mr. Bankes, during his visit to Egypt, paid considerable attention to this interesting investigation; and, in a letter to Mr. David Baillie, communicated his grounds for believing these temples to be of no greater antiquity than the reigns of Adrian and Antoninus Pius.† He remarked, that while the capitals of the most ancient columns of Thebes are a simple bell, and placed on polygonal or fluted shafts, those of Esneh and Dendera are laboriously rich with foliage and fruit. More than this, the hieroglyphics upon the columns are not certainly Egyptian, for Mr. Bankes found an inscription, stating that they were traced in the reign of Antoninus.‡

The archæological arguments, however, for the modern construction of these monuments, received their full development from the hand of M. Letronne. This learned scholar collected all necessary information

---

* "Testa sopra due Zodiaci novellamente scorperti nell' Egitto:" *Rome*, 1802. Visconti, in Larcher's Herodotus, vol. ii. p. 567, *seqq*.
† Sir W. Drummond's Memoir, p. 56.
‡ *Ib*. p. 57. This, I suppose, is meant of the temple at the north of Esneh, known by the name of the small temple.

from the publications and reports of travellers regarding their architecture, and illustrated the inscriptions still existing upon them. MM. Huyott and Gau furnished him with interesting particulars on the former subject. Among other facts, they proved from its style, and from the colours employed, that the pronaon of the small temple of Esneh, in which the zodiac is painted, is of the same date with the temple itself. Now an inscription, probably the same alluded to by Mr. Bankes, was copied by these artists from a column of the latter, in which it is stated that two Egyptians caused the *paintings* to be executed in the tenth year of Antoninus—the 147th after Christ.* Such, then, is the date of the small zodiac of Esneh, to which an age had been assigned of from two to three thousand years anterior to Christ. The temple of Dendera has shared the same fate. A Greek inscription on its portico, which had been overlooked, declares it to be dedicated to the safety of Tiberius.†

While Letronne was thus occupied in examining the Greek inscriptions on these supposed vestiges of hoary antiquity, M. Champollion was maturing his alphabet of hieroglyphics, and soon confirmed, by his researches, the conclusion of his friend. On the pronaon of the temple of Dendera he also read the hieroglyphical legend of Tiberius.‡ On the circular planisphere of the same temple, he deciphered the letters AOTKRTR; or, supplying the vowels, ΑΥΤΟΚΡΑΤΩΡ, the title which Nero takes upon his Egyptian medals.§ Only the zodiac of the great temple of Esneh remains, and M. Champollion has disposed of its antiquity, together with the temple on which it is painted, in an equally unceremonious manner. When at Naples, in August, 1826, Sir William Gell communicated to him accurate draw-

* "Recherches pour servir à l'Histoire de l'Egypte pendant la domination des Grecs et des Romains:" *Paris*, 1823, p. 456.
† *Ib.* p. 180.
‡ Lettre à M. Letronne, at the end of "Observations," &c., as below, p. 111.
§ Lettre à M. Dacier, p. 25, Letronne, p. xxxviii.

ings of the Esneh zodiac, taken by Messrs. Wilkinson and Cooper; and he discovered that this monument was dedicated, not as the astronomers would have conjectured, under the reign of some rough-named Egyptian Pharaoh, but under the Roman emperor Commodus.* The sculptures of this temple he had before demonstrated to have been executed in the reign of Claudius.†

It was with justice, then, that the Minister of the Interior, the Viscount de la Rochefaucauld, in a letter addressed to the King of France, dated May 15th, 1826, attributed to M. Champollion the merit of having decided the controversy in the opinion of every unprejudiced person.

"The public suffrage," says he, "of the most distinguished learned men in Europe, has consecrated results, the application of which has already been very useful to the truth of history, and the assurance of sound literary doctrines. For your Majesty has not forgot that the discoveries of M. Champollion have demonstrated, without opposition, that the zodiac of Dendera, which appeared to alarm public belief, is only a work of the Roman epoch in Egypt."

It was not, however, to be expected that the resistance of adversaries would be fully overcome by these vigorous attacks. Too much learning had been expended in the support of elaborate theories, too much confidence had been exhibited in asserting favourite systems, for their authors to yield them up without a pang, and, in some instances, without a struggle.

"Difficile est longum subitò deponere amorem:"‡

The temples, it might be granted, were indeed proved to be modern, and consequently the zodiacs which they bear; but the latter must have been copied from others of an ancient date. "Thus, the original scheme of the round zodiac of Dendera must have been formed at

---

* "Bulletin Universel," *ut sup.* tom. vi. † Letronne.
‡ Catul. Car. lxxvi. 13.

least seven centuries before our era." Such was the defence raised by the late Sir William Drummond in his last work;* and when he penned it, he cannot have been acquainted with the learned dissertation published a few months before, in which Letronne gave the finishing stroke to this and every other defence of the absurd antiquity of the zodiacs.†

The enterprising traveller, Cailliaud, on his return from Egypt, brought, among other rarities, a mummy discovered at Thebes, and distinguished by several peculiarities. The two most important were, a Greek legend much defaced, and a zodiac, very exactly resembling that of Dendera.‡ In the dissertation to which I have alluded, M. Letronne undertakes the illustration of these two points, and their application to the zodiacal representations in the Egyptian temples. The inscription he restores with a felicity that must satisfy the most supercilious critic, and discovers the mummy to be that of Petemenon, son of Soter and Cleopatra, who died at the age of twenty-one years, four months, and twenty-two days, in the nineteenth year of Trajan, the 8th Payni, or June 2, A.D. 116.§

The zodiac on the interior of the case, I have already said, resembles that of Dendera. Like it, protected by a disproportioned female figure, whose arms are extended, it exhibits the zodiacal signs in two parallel bands, ascending and descending precisely in the same order, and in a similar style of design. Even the cow reposing in a boat, and emblematic of Isis or of Sirius, is not wanting. The identity, therefore, of the two representations, may be said to be fully established. But there is one peculiarity in the miniature representation. The sign of Capricorn is withdrawn from the

* "Origines; or, Remarks on the Origin of several Empires," vol. ii. p. 227 : *Lond.* 1825.
† "Observations critiques et archéologiques sur l'objet des Représentations Zodiacales :" *Paris,* Mars, 1824. Sir W. Drummond's dedication is dated Sept. 17, 1824.
‡ "Voyage à Méroé, au Fleuve Blanc," &c. : *Par.* 1823, fol. vol. ii. pl. lxxi. § Page 30.

series, and placed over the head of the figure, in an isolated situation, where it appears to dominate.*

The very existence of a zodiac upon the case of a mummy, must suggest the idea that it has a reference to the embalmed; in other words, that it is *astrological*, and not astronomical. In this case, the detached sign may be supposed to represent that under which the individual was born, and which consequently was to rule his fate through life. This hypothesis is easily verified. We have the exact age of Petemenon, with the date of his death. Calculating from these, we find that he was born on January 12, A.D. 95. On that day the sun is situated at nearly two-thirds of Capricorn. If instead of the sign we prefer the constellation, the conclusion will be the same; for, calculating from Delambre's table, according to the annual precession, we find that at the period in question the whole constellation was comprised in the sign, and that on the 12th of January the sun was about the 16th degree of the former.†

We can therefore entertain no doubt that the zodiac expresses a natal theme; and analogy would lead us to the same conclusion regarding that of Dendera, even if the appearance of the decans, recognized by Visconti, and demonstrated by Champollion, who has read beside them the names given them in Julius Firmicus, did not already authorize us to consider it astrological.

M. Letronne, however, does not content himself with this general conclusion, but enters into an elaborate examination of the astrology of the ancients. This, originally the offspring of Egypt, passed into Greece and Rome, and returned to its mother country, ennobled and consecrated, by the patronage of the Cæsars.‡ Precisely at the moment when the celebrated zodiacs were sketched, this science, if it may bear that name, had attained its zenith, and culminated over its native soil. Manilius, in the reign of Augustus, Vettius Valens in that of M. Aurelius, wrote their treatises concerning it; but the

* Page 49.   † Pp. 53, 54.   ‡ Pp. 58–86.

numerous astrological medals of Egypt, under Trajan, Adrian, and Antoninus, demonstrate its prevalence in that country.* This was likewise the age of astrological sects, of Gnostics, Ophites, and Basilidians, whose Abraxes, exhibiting various astrological combinations, had been gravely taken by some of the illustrators of the zodiacs, for monuments of 3,863 years before the Christian era.† This concentration of evidence, the modern and nearly contemporary dates of *all* the zodiacs, the decided astrological character of one, the decans upon another, and above all, the prevalence of astrological ideas at the *only* time when any zodiac existing in Egypt was made, leaves no room to doubt that *all* such representations are purely remnants of the occult science, and only exhibit genethliacal themes.‡

What a waste of talents, of time, and of learning, has not truth to deplore, in retracing the history of this memorable controversy! Over what a glittering heap of ruined systems has not error to mourn—systems where all was brilliant, all was imposing, all was confident, but where all was, at the same time, hollow and brittle, and unsound. We have, indeed, many cases, where a sportive or malicious fraud has deluded the ingenuity and study of an antiquary, and made him pay, like Scriblerus, to modern rust, the veneration and homage reserved to that of antiquity.§ But never before did the world see an instance where " a spirit of giddiness " had so completely invaded such a large portion of learned and able men, as that they should ascribe countless ages to monuments comparatively modern, undeterred by the fall of system after system:

"And still engage
Within the same arena where they see
Their fellows fall before, like leaves of the same tree."
CHILDE HAROLD, *Canto* iv. 94.

---

* Pp. 86-92. † Page 70. ‡ Pp. 105-108.
§ See D'Israeli's "Curiosities of Literature," 2nd series, 2nd edit.: Lond. 1824, vol. iii. pp. 49, *seqq*. But many other curious examples might be added to those cited by D'Israeli.

U

Never, in fact, did error bear more completely its hydra form. Each head was cut off the moment it appeared, but a new one rose instantly at its side, equally bold, and equally "speaking great things." For more than twenty years, this galling warfare continued; but, as prejudice was gradually exhausted, and true science gained strength, the vital powers of the monster became less vigorous, and the wounds which it received more fatal. Its last gasp has long since died away; the last flap of its mortal struggles has ceased; and only existing among the records of history, it can now present no more terrors to the most simple and timid, than the " gaunt anatomy," or well-preserved coils of some desert monster, in the cabinet of the curious.

Still, it is a pleasure to see the catalogue of great names who did not bend their knee to this favourite idol, and it is only justice to record them. A writer in an English journal, long after the last researches which I have detailed, had the boldness to assert, that " on the Continent,"—and he is speaking of France in particular —" the antiquity of the zodiacs of Dendera has been considered as quite sufficiently established, to prove that the Egyptians were a learned and scientific people long before the date which our belief affixes to the creation of man;" while in England, not only was this denied, but the contrary demonstrated, *for the first time*, by Mr. Bentley!* By a logical process, unfortunately too common in the pages of that journal, the writer finds the cause of this phenomenon in the religions of the countries. " The baneful influence of Popery," he says, induces the philosophical inquirer " to reject all revelation as no better than priestcraft;" while, " in our own free country, the encouragement given to a full and free examination of the evidence of Christianity, has taught acute reasoners to know its strength."† All this was written *two years* after the last work of Letronne

---

* "British Critic," April, 1826, p. 137, cf. 149.
† Pages 136, *seq.*

had closed the lists in France on the subject of the zodiacs. But if the critic had been less borne away by the desire of tilting against Catholicity, even where his challenge was with infidelity—the common adversary— he surely would have recollected the names, not only of Letronne and Champollion, but of Lalande, Visconti, Paravey, Delambre, Testa, Biot, Saint-Martin, Halma, and Cuvier, every one of whom had assigned a modern epoch to these monuments. And where not numbers, but astronomical science is required, such names as those of Lalande, Delambre, and Biot, may surely weigh in the balance against many others, and redeem the French *savans* from the sweeping imputation so injuriously cast upon them.

LECTURE THE NINTH;

ON

ARCHÆOLOGY.

INTRODUCTORY remarks.—MEDALS: Reconciliation of an apparent contradiction between Genesis and the Acts.—Fröhlich's application of Medals to the defence of the chronology of the Maccabees.—Alexander called the first king among the Greeks: Death of Antiochus Evergetes.—Acknowledgments of his opponents; accordance of Eckhel.—M. Tochon d'Annecy's objections.—Apamean Medals: History of them; comparison with other monuments.—INSCRIPTIONS: Verbal illustrations of Scripture from them.—Gibbon and Dodswell's assertions regarding the small number of Christian martyrs, and Burnet's objections, answered by Visconti, from inscriptions.—MONUMENTS: Use of Wine in Egypt denied, and the Scripture consequently assailed.—Confutation of this cavil from Egyptian monuments.—Costaz, Jomard, Champollion, and Rosellini.—Curious vase found in the Roman Campagna, referable to the Deluge.—Conquest of Juda by Shishak, represented at Karnak.—Concluding remarks.

OUR last inquiries have gradually led us amongst the monuments of antiquity: and, from the examination of such great chronological points as touched on the authenticity of sacred history, we found ourselves almost imperceptibly brought to the discussion of individual monuments of kings, and of their people. It might, therefore, be said, that the study on which we have now to enter has been already introduced; or, at least, that the connection between what has been said and what will follow, is so close and natural, as hardly to warrant a separation into two distinct pursuits. But, in all the histories hitherto examined, we have had one specific object in view, the reconciliation of their early monuments with sacred chronology, and the process we have pursued has been consequently uniform and simple. We have followed the actual progress of science, and, comparing its results with our sacred records, have invariably discovered that it removed all difficulties, and gave us a variety of new and interesting chronological coincidences.

There are, however, a multitude of monuments bearing upon the Christian evidences which could not enter into this class, and which, if introduced under the same science, would have disturbed our process, and broken the unity of our design. These, therefore, I will throw together into a distinct class, under the name of archæology. Obviously, its character will hardly allow us to pursue so uniform and progressive a method as in our last researches; for, like the objects which it discusses, it is necessarily of a fragmentary nature. It owns not the unities of time, place, or action; it professes to deal with the remains of every age, and of every country, composed of every sort of materials, and shaped in every possible form. Thus, as it turns its attention from Greece to Italy, from Sicily to Egypt, as it deciphers an inscription, discusses a medal, fixes the locality of an edifice, or judges of its age, it must vary its rules, its methods, and its direction. Hence, as a science, it cannot be said to have one definite onward movement, tending to the development of any general conclusion. Our course must be of a similar nature; we will here pick up a medal; there will pore over an inscription; we will content ourselves with such monuments as chance shall throw in our way, and carefully store up in our cabinet such illustrations or confirmations, however slight, as they may seem to afford to our sacred convictions.

To these remarks I must further add, that here I can only pretend to glean what others have left behind. Of the species of confirmatory evidences which these lectures pursue, none has been oftener or more fully handled than the illustrations from such antiquarian remains. Every elementary introduction to Scripture dedicates a chapter to this subject; though, in some instances, as in the monument of the Assyrian captivity, given by Horne from Kerr Porter, the examples are far from certain; in others, as in the Apamean medal, by no means accurate. Now, I have pledged myself to bring forward no examples already given in works upon the evidences, and therefore I must be content with such as the industry of others may have overlooked.

I cannot avoid mentioning, in this place, a work which has taken one class of monuments out of our hands—those that relate to the history of Christianity. I mean Walsh's *Essay on ancient coins, medals, and gems, as illustrating the progress of Christianity in the early ages.*[*] It is a work, however, which must disappoint expectation. Most of its materials are but of a secondary interest; a great portion of the volume is taken up with an account of the Gnostics, and their doctrines, and makes but a sorry figure beside the profound researches of such continental writers as Neander and Hahn. The second part of the work gives a series of medals, illustrative of the imperial history from Diocletian to John Zemiscus, in 969, and so far is interesting; but it contains many inaccuracies, and gives the author opportunities of displaying an ill-timed illiberality.

With these disadvantages, we will enter upon our researches among the medals, inscriptions, and monuments of antiquity.

I. There is an apparent contradiction between the narratives in Gen. xxxiii. 19, and in Acts, vii. 16, relating to the purchase of a field by Jacob from the Hemorites. For St. Stephen, in the latter passage, tells us that the price was paid in a sum of money, τιμῆς ἀργυρίου, whereas the original text of Genesis says that it was paid by a *hundred lambs* or sheep. At least, the Hebrew word there used, קשיטה (*Kesita*), is so rendered by every ancient version. Hence, the English version, which renders it by *pieces of money*, has added in the margin, as

---

[*] *London*, 1828.

nearer the original, the other interpretation. Supposing this rendering of the ancient versions to be correct, and there must have been some reason for their all giving that meaning to the word, there was a very simple method of reconciling the two passages, by considering the same term to have expressed both objects; in other words, by conjecturing that the ancient Phenician coin bore upon it the figure of a lamb, for which it was an equivalent, and that from this emblem is also derived its name. For nothing is more common than such a substitution. Among our ancestors, the *angel* and *cross*, so often alluded to in Shakspeare, received their names from the representation they bore; and among the Romans, the very name of money, *pecunia*, is allowed to be derived from the exactly similar case of a sheep being stamped upon it. Any apparent difficulty would thus be satisfactorily removed, by a highly probable conjecture. But the publication of a medal, found by Dr. Clarke near Citium in Cyprus, has given us all the evidence we might desire. The late learned Dr. Munter presented a dissertation on this subject to the Royal Danish Academy, inserted in their Acts for 1822.* In it he observes that the coin, which is of silver, is undoubtedly Phenician, as it bears upon the reverse a legend in Phenician characters. On the obverse is the figure of a sheep; and no doubt can be entertained of its extreme antiquity. Here, then, he concludes, it is extremely probable, that we have the very coin alluded to in Scripture; at least, we now know for certain that the Phenicians had a coin with a symbol corresponding to the meaning of the word Kesita; and the element alone wanting to make the conjectural reconciliation morally certain now exists.†

---

* Philosophical and Historical Class.
† On the reverse, with the legend, is a crown of *pearls*. One would be tempted to suspect, that such a circumstance may account for the strange translation of the two Targums of Onkelos and Jerusalem, which both render מאה קשיטה a hundred Kesites, by מאה מרגליין a hundred *pearls*.

A most complete and valuable application of numismatics, to the vindication of sacred chronology, has been made in reference to the latest historical works of the Jews, the two books of Maccabees. No books of Scripture had been subjected to a stricter examination than these, because they entered among the topics of religious dispute, after the Reformation. The Catholic, who believes them to form part of the canonical Scriptures, feels necessarily a livelier interest concerning them; but to all Christians they must appear of immense value, from forming the last and only historical link in the connection between the old and new dispensations, and the only record of the fulfilment of those promises, which foretold the restoration and continuation of the Jewish sceptre till the Messiah should come. Great difficulties, however, existed regarding the dates assigned by them to events related no less in classical history, and the manner in which they recounted them. By some strange inconsistency, it has almost always happened, that when the evidence of any sacred book is compared with that of a profane author, it is taken for granted that the former must be in error, if both do not agree. This we have seen to be the case in treating of Indian and Egyptian antiquities. Where they did not harmonize with Scripture chronology, this was pronounced in fault; though, critically speaking, it must be allowed at least an equal weight with them. Now, precisely the same course was pursued here. Discrepancies were undoubtedly found to exist between the dates assigned to events in these and in other authors later in time, and more distant in country from the scene of those actions; and, of course, the sacred book was condemned as inaccurate. Erasmus Fröhlich, in the preface to his *Annals of the Kings and Events of Syria*, a numismatic work of great authority and research, has undertaken the task of comparing the chronology of these books, not with the vague testimony of other historians, often differing among themselves, but with the contemporary and incontestable evidence of medals. And the result has been a table confirming, in every respect, the order and epochs of events recorded in the inspired history.*

You will easily suppose, that the objections were not given up without a struggle. The first edition of Fröhlich's work appeared in 1744, and two years later, Ernest Fred. Wernsdorff appeared in the field against him.† His efforts were not considered satisfactory by his party, and his brother, Gottlieb, came to his assistance in the following year.‡ Both were fully answered by an anonymous work in 1749;§ and, in spite of the virulence exhibited by the two brothers, I think, whoever reads the controversy, will be satisfied that the victory was not with them. However, in giving two or three examples of Fröhlich's illustrations, I will select such as the Wernsdorffs themselves acknowledge to be satisfactory.

In the first book of Maccabees, vi. 2, Alexander the Great is introduced with this description,—ὃς ἐβασίλευσε πρῶτος ἐν τοῖς Ἕλλησι—*who first was king among the Greeks.* This, it has been alleged, is false; inasmuch as Alexander had several predecessors in Macedon, who certainly were kings, and reigned among the Greeks. It may be answered, indeed, that he was the first among them who founded an empire bearing their name; but the solution given by Fröhlich is far more satisfactory. For it is extraordinary, that whatever may have been the power of other monarchs before him, not one ever took the title of Βασιλεύς, or king, upon his coin, before him. "Certainly," says Fröhlich, "it is not without

---

* "Annales compendiarii Regum et Rerum Syriæ." Ed sec. *Vien.* 1754. The second part of his Prolegomena is entirely taken up with the vindication of these books.

† "De fontibus Historiæ Syriæ in Libris Maccabæorum prolusio." *Lips.* 1746.

‡ "Gottlieb Wernsdorffii Commentatio historico-critica de fide historica librorum Maccabaicorum." *Wratislau,* 1747.

§ "Auctoritas utriusque libri Maccab. canonico-historica adserta. .... a quodam Soc. Jesu sacerdote, Curante Casparo Schmidt bibliopego." *Vien.* 1749.

importance, that no medal of undoubted genuineness of sovereigns in Macedon, anterior to Alexander, should bear the title of *king*. They have barely the names of the monarchs, as Amyntas, Archelaus, Perdiccas, Philip; and some coins have simply Alexander, but many more King Alexander."* Gottlieb Wernsdorff acknowledges that this solution is correct. "This," he says, "is right; I could hardly suppose that any doubt could exist on this point. For Jewish historians, under the name of Greeks (τῶν Ἑλληνῶν), always understand the Macedonians, and by *kingdom*, the Macedonian empire, or more peculiarly that of the Seleucidæ." He, however, charges Fröhlich with a double fraud; first, in attributing to Philip Aridæus a medal of Philip Amyntor, given by Spanheim, on which the title of king occurs; secondly, in overlooking a medal of Argæus.—" Dicitur quoque extare numus Argæi, regis antiquissimi cum epigraphe Αργειου Βασιλεως."† To these objections the anonymous defender of Fröhlich replies, that the supposed Amyntor of Spanheim is manifestly, from the style of art, a coin of a Gallo-Grecian king; and that the Argæus of Tollius, no one had ever seen, or could pretend to trace. He assures us also, that he and Fröhlich had carefully examined every medal in the imperial and other cabinets, and had never found the title upon any prior to Alexander.‡

Again, the second book gives us, in the first chapter, a letter from the Jews of Palestine to their brethren in Egypt, dated in the year of the Seleucidæ 188, and containing a detailed narrative of the death of King Antiochus in Persia. What Antiochus, it has been asked, could this be? Independently of chronological objections, it could not certainly be Antiochus Soter,

---

* "Sane non de nihilo est, veterum qui ante Alexandrum fuissent Macedoniæ regum certa numismata Βασιλεως titulum non præ se ferre: sola comparent regum nomine: Αμυντα vel Αμυντου, Αρχελαου, Περδικκου, Φιλιππου, et quædam numismata Αλεξανδρου legimus, alia plura Βασιλεως Αλεξανδρου."—FRÖHLICH, p. 31.
† "Commentatio," § xxii. p. 39.
‡ Oper. cit. p. 170.

who died at Antioch; not his successor, Antiochus Theus, who was poisoned by Laodice; nor Antiochus Magnus, who was friendly to the Jews. Of Antiochus Epiphanes' end we have quite a different account in the very same book (ix. 5). Antiochus Eupator, his successor, after a reign of two years, was killed by Demetrius, and the infant of the same royal name, who was proclaimed king by Tryphon, was soon poisoned by him as well. No other sovereign of this name remains, but Antiochus Sidetes, called also Evergetes, whose reign alone coincides with the time of the letter. But a difficulty, apparently as serious as any of the preceding, seemed to exclude him; for this monarch commenced his reign in 174, and Porphyrius and Eusebius agree in assigning less than nine years as the term of its duration. He must, therefore, have died in war, according to them, about the year 182. How, then, could the Jews, in 188, give an account of his death as of a recent event? Could we imagine, for instance, the members of any religious community nowadays writing a common letter to their brethren in a very near country, to convey the intelligence that the sovereign who oppressed them was dead, full six years after that event? This concurring testimony of two historians was considered decisive against the Jewish historian, and Prideaux unhesitatingly adopted it as correct.* Now Fröhlich has proved, beyond a doubt, that *they* must be wrong. First, he produced two medals bearing the name of Antiochus, with dates, one of 183, the other 184; consequently later by two years than the time which those historians assign to his death. One is as follows:

ΒΑΙCΛΕΩC. ΑΝΤιοχου ΤΥΡ: ΙΕΡ: ΑCΥ. ΔΠΡ.

Of King Antiochus; of Tyre, the sacred Asylum, 184.†
The controversy upon these medals has been carried

---

* "Old and New Testaments connected." Chronolog. Table at the end of vol. iv. ed. 1749.
† Page 24. See the medals in his plate xi. Nos. 27, 29.

down into our own times. Ernest Wernsdorff acknowledges the genuineness of the medal, and allows that it satisfactorily proves Antiochus Sidetes to have lived beyond the period assigned to him by profane history; and even seems to add his own testimony to that of Fröhlich. For he thus expresses himself: "Quamquam igitur quod ad numismata et annos iisdem inscriptos attinet facile assentior; eidem cum ipsi mihi, beneficio consultissimi viri complures ab Antiocho procusos numos oculis usurpare manibusque tractare contigerit."* His auxiliary, however, was more unyielding, for he suggests that the legend has been misread, and that, probably, a slight alteration in a letter has changed the number 181 into 184.† But if even we allow all that has been written against these two medals to be valid, there are others, produced subsequently to the animadversions of the two brothers, which seem to place the matter out of doubt. For Fröhlich afterwards published a medal of the same king with the date of 185;‡ and Eckhel added a fourth, struck in 186.§

This point of sacred chronology was re-examined a few years ago by M. Tochon d'Annecy,|| who was manifestly guided by no desire to weaken the authority of the books of Maccabees. He proves what every one will allow, that serious difficulties surround every hypothesis, and that the concurrent testimony of historians should not be lightly rejected. Apparent contradictions, indeed, must meet us in every part of history; the difficulty is where to lay the blame. The medals struck for the coronation of Louis XIV. give a different day from

---

* "De fontibus historiæ Syriæ," p. xiii.
† "Commode legi possct ΑΠΡ 181, cum elementum A et Δ adeo similibus lineis exaretur, ac numus ipse mutilus sit, ut ne nomen quidem Antiochi distincte exhibeat."—*Ubi sup.* sec. xlii. p. 79; cf. the reply, p. 288.
‡ "Ad numismata regum veterum anecdota et rariora accessio nova," p. 69.
§ "Sylloge Numorum veterum," p. 8. "Doctrina Numorum veterum," tom. iii. p. 236.
|| "Dissertation sur l'Epoque de la Mort d'Antiochus VII. Evergetès Sidétès:" *Paris*, 1815.

that which all contemporary historians accord in fixing for the date of that event. Of them all, only one, D. Ruinart, has noticed a circumstance which reconciles this discrepancy. For he alone has recorded, that the coronation had been appointed to take place on a certain day, the one given by the medals, which were accordingly prepared, but circumstances caused a delay till the one which historians assign. Nothing can be more simple than all this; yet, in a thousand years had no such explanation been given, antiquaries might have been sadly perplexed to find a reconciliation. In that case, then, the medals were wrong, and the historians right; in ours we are equally driven to condemn one class of authorities, and I think the critic will hardly hesitate which to prefer. For, in the example given, the medals are inaccurate, from the date once placed on them not having been changed, when the event which they commemorated was deferred; but here we must suppose the incredible error of successive false dates, in consequence of new medals being struck to a monarch who was long before dead.

M. Tochon rejects the two earlier medals, chiefly that of 184, on grounds different from Wernsdorff's, but admitted by Eckhel, that the supposed Δ, or 4, which is somewhat indistinct, appears to be a B, or 2, of peculiar shape.* But against the two later medals he urges nothing but plausibilities; the difficulties which we incur by considering them genuine, to the disparagement of so many historical authorities.† In some respects he is hardly just to Fröhlich; for he assumes throughout that the learned Jesuit places the death of the king in 188.‡ and consequently asks how it happens, that we have medals of his successor, Antiochus Grypus, with the date of 187.§ Now Fröhlich places the death

---

* "Dissertation," p. 22.   † Page 64.
‡ Pages 24, 29, &c.
§ "Comment alors supposer, que la mort d'Antiochus Evergetès puisse être arrivée l'an 188? Elle serait postérieur au ègne de son fils" (p. 61).

of Antiochus Evergetes in 186.* In this manner the circumstance of no medal of Antiochus Grypus bearing an older date, forms a negative confirmation of his opinion. Thus far, therefore, it should seem, that the application of medals has served to defend the chronology of these sacred records.

I will now call your attention to a class of medals long the subject of serious disputes and endless conjectures, and allusive to that great revolution which has already several times occupied our notice. After the proofs we have seen of the Deluge in the traditions of every country, "from China to Peru;" after the visible evidences of its action, which we have discovered piled up on the mountains, and scooped out in the valleys of our globe, it will perhaps appear mere trifling to occupy ourselves about the petty monuments on which any particular nation, much more any city, may have thought proper to inscribe its traditions concerning it. Still must we not neglect small things on account of greater; but make all contribute, where they can, to the noble and glorious cause of religion. It is evident that the ancients had two very different legends of the Deluge, one a popular fable adapted to their national mythology, another far more philosophical, derived from the traditions of the East, and consequently much more in accordance with the scriptural narration. The former is the deluge of the poets, such as Ovid has described it; and Millin has observed, that no monument exists whereon it is represented.† The other account of this event is preserved in the writings of Lucian and Plutarch. According to this tradition, Deucalion is represented as making an ark or chest (λάρνακα), into which he retired, taking with him a couple of every species of animals as well as his wife and children. In this ark they sailed so long as the inundation lasted, and "this," says Lucian, at the end of his narrative,

---

* "Anno CLXXXVI. Circa hoc tempus contigisse existimo cædem Antiochi VII. Evergetis" (p. 88).
† "Galerie Mythologique:" *Par.* 1811, tom. ii. p. 136.

PLATE 3. _Page 339._

APAMEAN MEDAL

Fig. 1.

Fig. 2.

"is the *historical* account given by the Greeks, concerning Deucalion."* Plutarch adds, that the return of a dove first gave notice to Deucalion of the waters being dried up.† Now the medals, of which I am going to treat, with another monument, which I shall by-and-by describe, contain the representation of this traditional history.

These imperial bronze medals of the city of Apamea, in Phrygia, bear on one side the head of different emperors, of Severus, Macrinus, and Philip the elder. The reverse is uniform, having the representation drawn on the lithograph placed in your hands (pl. 3, fig. 1). It is thus described by Eckhel:—" A chest swimming upon the waters, in which a man and woman appear from the breast upwards. Without it, advance with their faces turned from it, a woman robed, and a man in a short garment, holding up their right hands. On the lid of the chest stands a bird, and another, balanced in air, holds in its claws an olive branch."‡ The small compass of a medal could hardly give a more expressive representation of this great event. We have two different scenes, but manifestly the same actors. For the costume and heads of the persons standing outside, do not allow us to consider them others than the figures in the ark. We have these individuals first floating over the waters in an ark, then standing on dry land in an attitude of admiration,§ with the dove bearing the symbol of peace above them.

But the most interesting circumstance yet remains. On the front panel of this ark are some letters, and the discussion of their import has been the subject of many learned dissertations. The first who published these medals was Octavius Falconieri, in Rome, in 1667.

---

* "De Dea Syra," vol. ii. p. 661, ed. Beued. *Amst.* 1687.
† "Utrum animalia terrestria aut aquatica magis sint solertia." Oper. *Par.* 1572, tom. iii. p. 1783.
‡ "Doctrina Numorum veterum:" *Vienna*, 1793, part 1. vol. iii. p. 130.
§ Eckhel, *ibid.* p. 136.

The engravings which he gives of the Paris Severus, has the letters NHTΩN; which he reads in continuation of ΜΑΓ *μαγνητων*.* Vaillant pretended to read on it, and on the Chigi medal of Philip, NEΩK, for *νεωκορων*. The Rev. Mr. Mills gave an essay on this subject, inserted in the fourth volume of the *Archæologia*, by the Royal Antiquarian Society, in which he maintains all to be spurious which read not thus. Bianchini published two copies of this medal, on one of which he reads NΩE, and on the other NEΩ,† the former of which readings Falconieri also gives upon another medal. Thus we had four versions of this legend, and every new inquiry seemed still more to involve the controversy. The reading NΩE appeared too favourable to the object proposed in the first publication of these medals, not to be held in suspicion; and such was the dread of admitting anything so good to be true, that Mr. Barrington, allowing this to be the correct legend, would not believe it to have any allusion to the scriptural name, but rather supposed it to stand for NΩI, *we*, dual of εγω, and be a compendious representation of Ovid's words: "Nos duo turba sumus!"‡ The fact is, that of all these readings not one is correct; for Eckhel has proved that the medals only bear two letters, NΩ. This he has proved from his own and Fröhlich's observation of the Vienna and Florence medals, from Venuti's of that in the Albani cabinet, and Barthelemy's, of the Paris Severus. Indeed, in some only the N is visible, but at the same time, in most, trace of a third letter is discernible, which has not been purposely erased, but worn out from being the most prominent point in the relief. Eckhel, after examining the different explanations given by others to this legend, rejects them, and concludes, that, as the entire scene, represented on the medal, bears manifest

---

* "De nummo Apamensi Deucalionei diluvii typum exhibente Dissertatio, ad P. Seguinum:" *Rome*, 1667.

† "La Storia universale provata con monumenti:" *Rome*, 1697, pp. 186, 191.

‡ "Archæologia," vol. iv. p. 315.

reference to the Noachian Deluge, so must the inscription on the ark; and that, consequently, it is the name of that patriarch. This he illustrates from the coins of Magnesia in Ionia, on which is the figure of a ship, bearing the inscription ΑΡΓΩ: no doubt for the purpose of clearly specifying the mythological event to which it refers, the expedition of the Argonauts.*

But here an obvious difficulty occurs: what could have induced the Apameans to choose such an event for their symbol on their coins? This difficulty, too, is satisfactorily removed. It was customary for cities to take, as their emblems, any remarkable event which was fabled to have happened there. Thus the city of Thermæ, in Sicily, has Hercules upon its coins, because he is supposed in mythology to have there reposed. Now, this is precisely the case with Apamea; or, as it anciently was called, Celæne. For the Sibylline books, which, however spurious, are sufficient testimony of the existence of a popular tradition, expressly tell us, that in the neighbourhood of Celæne stands the mountain Ararat, upon which the ark reposed. This tradition, evidently having no reference to Deucalion's deluge, the seat of which was Greece, is sufficient to account for the adoption of such a representation upon the Apamean coins. Hence, too, probably arose another ancient name of this city, Κιθωτος, the *Ark*, as Winkelmann has shown; and this name is the very word used by the Septuagint and Josephus in describing Noah's ark.†

Here, then, we have an instance of a monument illustrative of Scripture, which owes its certainty and authority to the progress of the very science which first presented it. For we have seen the learned medalist, who may be said to have first reduced the study of coins into a systematic order, and incorporated the whole science into one plan, was also the first to

---
* Page 132.
† See Winkelmann's "Monumenti antichi inediti:" *Rome*, 1767, tom. ii. p. 258. Eckhel, *ib.* pp. 132, 139.

clear away all uncertainty from these interesting documents, and place their meaning above all doubt.

But it might be objected that such a representation of the ark can hardly be considered in accordance with either the sacred or the profane description of the Deluge before rehearsed; inasmuch as these suppose not merely Noah and his wife, but all his family, and many animals, to have been shut up in the ark. Such circumstances can hardly be expressed by the representation of a small chest, containing two individuals. To remove this difficulty, I would propose a comparison between the early Christian monuments and the representations on the medals, for in the former, no one can doubt that the Scripture narrative was kept in view. In them the ark is always represented as a square chest, floating upon a stream of water. In it is seen only the figure of the patriarch from the waist upwards; and above, the dove bearing the olive branch towards him. Such is the representation on four marble sarcophagi given by Aringhi,* and in the painting of the second chamber in the cemetery of Callistus.† An exactly similar representation is given from a metal lamina by the senator Buonarotti,‡ and illustrated by Ciampini.§ Some of these paintings seem to show the cover of the chest raised open above the head of the patriarch, as in the Apamean medals.‖ Again, as in these, the figure of Noah is sometimes seen out of the ark, standing on dry land, with the symbolic dove to specify who he is. For so Boldetti enumerates, among the common Christian

---

* "Roma subterranea:" *Rome*, 1651, tom. i. pp. 325, 331, 333; tom. ii. p. 143.

† *Ib.* p. 539. See also pp. 551, 556.

‡ "Osservazioni sopra alcuni frammenti di vasi antichi di vetro," tom. i. fig. 1.

§ "Dissertatio de duobus emblematibus Musæi Card. Carpinei:" *Rome*, 1748, p. 18. Bianchini has also published, from an ancient glass, a miniature representation of the same scene. (Demonstratio historiæ ecclesiasticæ quadripartitæ comprobatæ monumentis: *Rome*, 1753, p. 585.) It is marked No. 159, in the last sheet of the second plate, illustrative of the second century.

‖ See examples in Aringhi, tom. ii. pp. 67, 105, 187, 315.

symbols: "Noè dentro e talvolta fuori dell' arca, colla colomba."* In fine, the dove is sometimes seen perched upon the ark, as on the medal; but then the figure of the patriarch is wanting. Thus it is on the Fogginian gem, described by Mamachi.† To enable you better to make the comparison between the sacred and profane representations, I have had a painting from the cemetery of Callistus drawn beside the Apamean medal (Fig. 2). And I think, after seeing the two together, you will conclude, not only that thereby is removed every difficulty as to whether such an ark as Noah's could ever have been represented as we see it on the medals, but that the resemblance between the two classes of monuments is such as to warrant our considering their subjects identical. Add to this, that the difference of age between the two cannot be very great; and that it is evident the Christians, in these paintings, which are so uniform in different monuments, had a common type, quite distinct from the sacred narrative, for their designs, and that this type was probably borrowed from other traditions.

II. From medals let us turn to inscriptions, a higher order of monuments, inasmuch as they are generally more detailed in the information they convey. The greatest advantage which has been derived from this class of ancient remains, consists in verbal illustrations of obscure passages in Scripture, which they have often afforded; but were I to enlarge upon this species of philological confirmation or explanation, which the sacred text has received from them, it is plain that I should lead you into minute detail and learned disquisition, hardly suitable to the purport of these lectures. Yet, whatever throws new light upon any passage of Scripture, and whatever vindicates its phraseology from any charge of inconsistency or barbarism, tends likewise to increase our clear apprehension of it, and gives

---

* "Osservazioni sopra i Cimiterii, &c. *Rome*, 1720, lib. i. p. 22.
† "Originum et antiquitatum Christianar." lib. xx. tom. iii. *Rome*, 1731, p. 22, tab. ii. fig. 6.

us additional evidence of its authenticity. I will, therefore, content myself with one example, taken from a learned dissertation by Dr. Fred. Münter, entitled, *Specimens of Sacred Observations from Greek Marbles;* inserted a few years ago in the Copenhagen Miscellany.* In John, iv. 46, mention is made of a τις βασιλικος, a *certain nobleman*, or *ruler*, or *courtier*, for in all these ways it is rendered. The English version has the first, with the other two in the margin; and of this interpretation a modern commentator observes, that it "conveys the notion of hereditary rank, and certain dignities, to which there was nothing in Palestine, or even in Syria, that corresponded."† Some have thought it meant one of the royal blood, another a royal soldier; others have considered it a proper name. The most probable explanation of the word seemed that of Krebs, that it signified a minister or servant of the kings.‡ The examples he brought from authors did not satisfy many commenta-

---

* "Symbolæ ad interpretationem N. T. ex marmoribus, numis, lapidibusque cælatis, maxime Græcia." In the "Miscellanea Hafnensia theologici et philologici argumenti," tom. i. fascic. i. *Copenhag.* 1816.

† Campbell, *in loc.*

‡ "Observationes Flavianæ," p. 144. Six of Griesbach's codices read βασιλίσκος, and it is evident that the translator of the Vulgate read it so; for that version has "quidam *regulus*," or as we have rendered it, "a certain ruler." Schleusner supposes this reading to have arisen from the Vulgate, but the contrary is much more probable. It may not be out of place to remark in this note, that although the Vulgate has rendered the word by a diminutive, in Hellenistic Greek it has by no means that signification. This appears from an inscription of Silco, King of Nubia, first published from a less perfect copy of M. Gau, by Niebuhr, in his "Inscriptiones Nubienses," *Rome*, 1820; and again, from one of M. Caillaud, by Letronne, in the "Journal des Savans," Feb. 1825, pp. 98, 99. This king begins the magnificent recital of his victories by Εγω Σιλκω βασιλισκος των Νουβαδων και ὁλων των Αιθιοπων. Even if the judicious axiom of M. Salverte, in his "Essai sur les Noms propres," "Jamais peuple ne s'est donné à lui-même un nom peu honorable," did not apply to monarchs, in the proclamation of their titles, the words in the tenth and eleventh lines would leave no doubt of the true meaning. For he there says: ὁτε εγεγονε μην βασιλισκος, "I was not behind other princes, but I have been superior to them." M. Letronne illustrates many phrases of this inscription from the Greek of the Septuagint and New Testament.

tors. A new one produced by Münter, from an inscription on Memnon's statue, written in the same Greek dialect, the Hellenistic, as the New Testament, puts this translation on a more secure footing. For in it mention is made of Αρτεμιδωρος Πτολεμαιου βασιλικος, Artemidorus, the *courtier*, or servant of Ptolemy. For the addition of the king's name will admit of no other translation.*

To come now to instances of more general importance and interest, and from words to things, I will give you an example of the services which inscriptions may render to the great evidences of Christianity. Whoever has but superficially studied these, is aware of the importance of the argument drawn from the alacrity with which the early Christians encountered death in defence of their religion. From the visions of the Revelations to the great ecclesiastical history of Eusebius, the Church annals present us a cloud of witnesses, a host of martyrs, who returned love for love, and life for life, sealing their confession with their blood, and setting at nought the malice and cruelty of relentless persecutors. And in this firmness of conviction, this steadfastness of faith, this boldness of profession, and this enthusiasm of love, we have surely proof of the powerful might with which a thousand evidences, now read, but then seen and felt, laid hold of their minds; and in the strength which supported them through every cruel trial, we have a demonstration of a strong inward principle counteracting in them the feebleness of our nature; and in the nothingness of every effort to overcome them or utterly destroy them, we have evidence of a protecting arm, of the secure promise of One who could bring to nought every weapon forged against his work. Who, then, can be surprised at the ingenuity with which every discredit has been thrown upon that interesting fact of ecclesiastical history, and that Gibbon should have employed all the meretricious brilliancy of

* "Miscellanea," p. 18.

his own style, and borrowed all the learning of his predecessors, to prove that Christianity had but few martyrs, and that these suffered death rather from their own imprudence than from any malice or hatred to Christianity in their enemies; that they were driven to the scaffold by an ambitious or restless spirit, rather than by any hallowing and inspired motive—" Their persons," he concludes, "were esteemed holy, their decisions were admitted with deference, and they too often abused, by their spiritual pride and licentious manners, the predominance which their zeal and intrepidity had acquired. Distinctions like these, whilst they display their exalted merit, betray the inconsiderable number of those who suffered, and of those who died for the profession of Christianity."* The learned Dodwell, in his dissertations on St. Cyprian, had prepared the way for this attack upon the historical evidences of Christianity, by maintaining that the number of martyrs was but inconsiderable, and that, after the reign of Domitian, the Church enjoyed perfect tranquillity.† Doubtless Ansaldi and others have well performed the task of confuting these assertions upon historical grounds; but monumental inscriptions afford the most direct and satisfactory means of overthrowing them. Visconti has taken the pains to collect, from the voluminous works on Christian antiquity, such inscriptions as show the number of those who shed their blood for Christ.‡

The cruelty of the heathen persecutions, even under emperors of mild principles and gentle rule, is sufficiently attested by a pathetic inscription given by Aringhi from the cemetery of Callistus. " Alexander is not dead but liveth above the stars, and his body rests in his tomb. He finished his life under the Emperor Antoninus, who, when he saw that much favour was due, instead of kindness returned him hatred. For, when

---

* " Decline and Fall," ch. xvi.
† " Dissertationes Cyprianicæ." Dissert. xi. p. 57, ed. calc. Cypr. Opp. *Oxon.* 1682.
‡ In the " Memorie Romane di Antichità," tom. i. *Rome*, 1825.

bending his knee about to sacrifice to the true God, he was dragged off to punishment. Oh unhappy times! wherein amidst our sacred rites and prayers we cannot be safe even in caverns. What is more miserable than life? But, on the other hand, what more miserable than death? for we cannot be even buried by our friends and families."* This pathetic lamentation will explain the difficulties which the Christians must have experienced in recording the names of their martyrs, and why they were so often obliged to content themselves with giving their numbers. Thus we have the following inscriptions in the catacombs:†

> MARCELLA ET CHRISTI MARTYRES CCCCCL.
> (Marcella and 550 martyrs of Christ.)
>
> HIC REQUIESCIT MEDICUS CUM PLURIBUS.
> (Here rests Medicus with Many.)
>
> CL MARTYRES CHRISTI.
> (150 Martyrs of Christ.)

These inscriptions clearly prove the cruelty of the persecutions, and the great number of the martyrs.

Having thus seen the custom of commemorating in one short inscription so many sufferers for the faith of Christ, we are led to the natural conclusion, that when a simple number is found inscribed upon a stone, it may refer to the same circumstance. This, the antiquarian to whom I have referred, seems satisfactorily to have proved; for it had often been supposed that such numerals referred to some series in which the inscriptions

---

* "Alexander mortuus non est, sed vivit super astra, et corpus in hoc tumulo quiescit. Vitam explevit cum Antonio Imp. qui ubi multum benefitii antevenire previderet pro gratia odium reddit: genua enim flectens, vero Deo sacrificaturus, ad supplicia ducitur. O tempora infausta! quibus inter sacra et vota ne in cavernis quidem salvari possimus! Quid miserius vita? sed quid miserius in morte, cum ab amicis et parentibus sepeliri nequeant?"—Aringhi, "Roma Subterranea," tom. ii. p. 685.

† Visconti, pp. 112, 113.

had been **arranged**. But not to say that any such series, or any approximation to it, cannot be discovered, these ciphers are sometimes inscribed in a manner which could hardly have been adopted were they simple progressive numbers. For instance, they are sometimes surrounded by a wreath supported by doves; in one place the word TRIGINTA, *thirty*, is written at full, with the monogram of Christ's name before and after, which excludes all idea of its being merely a reference to a progressive series: in another the number xv is followed by IN *pace, in peace*. The conjecture that such simple inscriptions record the death of as many martyrs as the numbers signify, passes into absolute certainty when confirmed by a passage in Prudentius, writing on the catacombs while the traditions regarding them were yet fresh:—"There are many marbles," he tells us, "closing tombs, which only indicate a number; you thus know how many bodies lie piled together; but you read not their names. I remember I learnt there that the remains of sixty bodies were buried under one heap."

"Sunt et multa tamen tacitas claudentia tumbas
Marmora quæ solum significant numerum.
Quanta virum jaceant congestis corpora acervis
Scire licet, quorum nomina nulla legas.
Sexaginta illic defossa mole sub una
Reliquias memini me didicisse hominum."*

These verses leave us nothing to desire; they put us in possession of a great many inscriptions, which, while they only record numbers, prove most sufficiently that they were truly many, who, in those first ages, bore testimony to the Lord Jesus.

But a new antiquarian difficulty here meets us. For Burnet has asserted, that no monument has been found whereby it can be proved that the Christians possessed the catacombs before the fourth century.† General

* "Carmina:" *Rome*, 1788, tom. ii. p. 1164, Carm xi.
† "Some Letters from Italy:" *Lond.* 1724, p. 224.

negative assertions are always easy to make, and doubtless hard to prove; but, on the other hand, they are the easiest to confute, for one instance to the contrary will suffice. So it is here. One only of the numeral inscriptions already explained will demonstrate all that we want. It runs thus:—

N. XXX· SURRA· ET SENEC· COSS·
(30. In the consulate of Surra and Senecio.)

Now Surra and Senecio were consuls in the year of Christ 107, the very era of Trajan's persecution. But there is another most valuable inscription given by Marangoni, which places this question out of doubt. It is that of Gaudentius, an architect, whom this learned antiquarian believes to have been the director in building the Colosseum. The inscription in the Catacombs tells us that he suffered death under Vespasian. Nor can it be supposed that it was erected later to his honour. For it is distinguished by a particular sort of accents, or apices, over some syllables, which the learned Marini has shown to have been in use only from Augustus to Trajan.* Consequently the inscription must have been engraved before this emperor's reign.

These inscriptions are a strong additional evidence what numbers must have laid down their lives for the faith, and have thus conduced towards confuting a powerful objection against one of the most interesting and beautiful confirmations of Christianity.

III. Although medals and inscriptions may justly be considered monuments, yet I have reserved this term rather for the class of more completely commemorative symbols, which, by representations speaking to the eye, preserve the remembrance of great events, or of the practices and customs of ancient times. The value of such monuments must be very great; for they are the deliberate committal of the fame of generations to those

---

* "Atti dei Fratelli Arvali," p. 760.

that follow them; the representatives and substitutes of nations, who, knowing themselves to be perishable and mortal, have erected them, fashioning them as best they could to their own image and likeness, have clothed them with that grandeur and splendour which might best symbolize their own estate, have written on them all the thoughts of pride which influenced their own hearts, have embodied in them all the vastness of their ambition, and the immeasurableness of their wishes, and have breathed into them a soul of silent recollections, an appealing power, which fastens on the sympathies, and speaks to the heart of living generations as though they communed with the concentrated energy of the whole extinguished race. And, alas! too well have they made them in general typical of themselves: epigraphs, like their history, an enigma for the scholar to pore over; ground-plans, like their constitutions, a ruinous labyrinth for the antiquarian to restore; sculptured images, like their national character, time-worn and featureless, for the poet to muse on; mighty fabrics, like the mighty men who raised them, disjointed, mouldered, scattered into dust, whereon the philosopher may meditate, and whereby human pride may be humbled. But a far sweeter lesson will they speak to us if man's design, or Providence's guidance, shall have somewhere caused them to bear any slight uneffaced memorial of things sacred to us, though worthless to those who noted them, if, as among the sculptured images on Titus's triumphal arch, the emperors who erected them, and who ride thereon in triumph, shall have been mutilated, disfigured, and almost blotted from the very record of their greatness; but the golden candlestick of the temple, the lamp of holy evidence, shall remain upon them, a trophy then of war, now of prophecy, a token to them of victory, and to us of unconquerable strength.

In the last century, the books of Moses were often attacked on account of grapes and vineyards being mentioned in them,* and perhaps wine,† as used in

---

* Gen. xl. 9; xliii. 13. † Num. xx. 5.

Egypt.* For Herodotus expressly tells us, that in Egypt there were no vineyards,† and Plutarch assures us, that the natives of that country abhorred wine, as being the blood of those who had rebelled against the gods.‡ So conclusive did these authorities appear, that the contrary statements of Diodorus, Strabo, Pliny, and Athenæus, were considered by the learned authors of the *Commentaries on the Laws of Moses*, as quite overbalanced by the testimony of Herodotus alone.§ Hence, he concluded, that wine was ordered in the Jewish sacrifices, expressly to break through any Egyptian prejudice regarding it, and detach the chosen people still more from their overweening affection for that country and its institutions. In this opinion he has been followed by many able men. Dr. Prichard mentions oblations of wine among those rites, which stand either "in near relation or contradiction to the laws of Egypt;"‖ and as it cannot certainly enter into the first of these classes, I presume we must consider him of the same opinion as Michaelis. So long as the authority of Herodotus was thus held superior to the concurrent testimonies of other writers, the reply to the objection was necessary feeble. Accordingly, we find the authors who undertook this reply, either having recourse to conjecture, from the improbability of such a statement, or else supposing a chronological difference of circumstances, and a change of custom between the ages of Moses and Herodotus.

But Egyptian monuments have brought the question to issue, and have, of course, decided in favour of the Jewish legislator. In the great description of Egypt, published by the French government, after the expedition into that country, M. Costaz describes the minute representation of the vintage in all its parts, as painted

---

* See Bullet, "Réponses critiques," *Besançon*, 1819, tom. iii. p. 142; Duclot's "Bible vengée," *Brescia*, 1821, tom. ii. p. 244.
† Lib. ii. cap. lxxvii.   ‡ "De Iside et Osiride," § 6.
§ Vol. iii. pp. 121, *seqq.* English trans.
‖ "Analysis of Egyptian Mythology," p. 422. Guénée, "Lettres de quelques Juifs :" *Par.* 1821, tom. i. p. 192.

in the hypogeæ, or subterraneans of Eilithyia, from the dressing of the vine to the drawing-off of its wine; and he takes Herodotus severely to task for his denial of the existence of vineyards in Egypt.*

In 1825, this question was mooted once more in the *Journal des Débats*, where a critic, reviewing a new edition of Horace, took occasion to observe, that the *vinum mareoticum*, mentioned in the 37th Ode of the first book, could not be an Egyptian wine, but the production of a district in Epirus called Mareotis. This was in the paper of June 26; and on the 2nd and 6th of the following month, Malte-Brun examined the question in the same paper, chiefly in reference to the authority of Herodotus; but his proofs went no farther back than the times of Roman and Grecian dominion. M. Jomard, however, took occasion to discuss the point more fully; and in a literary periodical, better suited than a daily paper to such discussions, pushed his inquiries into the times of the Pharaohs. In addition to the painted representations already quoted by Costaz, he appeals to the remains of amphoræ, or wine-vessels, found in the ruins of old Egyptian cities, and as yet encrusted with the tartar deposited by wine.† But since Champollion's discovery of the hieroglyphic alphabet, the question may be considered as quite decided; as it now appears certain, not only that wine was known in Egypt, but that it was used in sacrifices. For, in the paintings of offerings, we have, among other gifts, flasks coloured red up to the neck, which remains white as if transparent; and beside them is read in hieroglyphics the word EPΠ, which, in Coptic, signifies wine.‡

Rosellini has given, in the plates of his splendid work, representations of every department of a vintage and wine manufactory. But before this, he had published at Florence an Egyptian basso-rilievo, from the Grand-

---

* "Description de l'Egypte, Antiquités Mem." tom. i. *Par.* 180 p. 62.
† "Bulletin Universel," 7e section, tom. iv. p. 78.
‡ "Lettres à M. le Duc de Blacas," 1st Lett. p. 37.

Ducal gallery, containing a prayer in hieroglyphics, as he supposes, to the goddess Athyr. She is requested to bestow upon the deceased, wine, milk, and other good things. These objects are symbolized by vessels supposed to contain them, with their names written in hieroglyphics around them. Round the first are the feather, mouth, and square, the phonetic characters of the letters EPΠ.* And here I will observe, that the learned Schweighäuser, in his observations on Athenæus, appears to doubt the correctness of Casaubon's assertions, that ἔρπις was the Egyptian for wine,† though proved clearly from Eustathius and Lycophron. Had he written after this discovery of the word in hieroglyphics, he would doubtless have altered his opinion. And, on the other hand, I doubt not but Champollion and Rosellini would have confirmed their interpretation from those ancient writers, had they been aware of their testimony.

Allow me now to claim your attention to an extremely curious monument, which seems to bear no other explanation but such as we saw given to the Apamean medals; the considering it as commemorative of the deluge. In the year 1696, in excavating a monument in the neighbourhood of Rome, a workman found an earthen vase, covered with a tile. In removing this, the cover fell and broke. The workman then drew out a number of seals and amulets, consisting of closed hands, oxen's heads, and olive-berries, all rudely worked in stone. Below these he felt something hard and even;

---

* "Di un basso-rilievo Egiziano della I. e. R. Galleria di Firenze." —*Ib.* 1826, p. 40. Wilkinson has also read the same word, "Materia hieroglyphica," p. 16, note 5.

† Athenæus, "Deipnosoph. Epit." lib. ii. tom. i. p. 148, ed. Schweighäuser, has the word ἔρπις in a quotation from Sappho, though, in another passage (lib. x. tom. iv. p. 55), he reads ὄλπιν. The learned critic seems to have proved, that the latter is the correct reading. (Animadv. in Athen. Argentor. 1804, tom. v. p. 375.) This discovery, however, of the Egyptian name given to wine by ancient writers, in hieroglyphic characters, under the circumstances noticed in the text, must be considered a strong corroboration of the correctness of the phonetic system.

x 2

and in his impatience to discover it, broke the vase in two, and not so satisfied, broke it open below; upon which there dropped out a bronze circle, which had fitted exactly into the lower portion of the vase, and a thin plate which evidently had covered it. It had no bottom; but, from the fibres of wood which were found mixed with the earth, it was conjectured that this was originally formed of that material. At the same time, there fell out a number of figures which I will presently describe. This curious monument came into the possession of the antiquarian Ficoroni, and a minute account of it was published by Bianchini in the following year.* An engraving accompanies it, very rudely executed; but a later edition of this exists, without date, but stating below that the objects were in the house of the Ab. Giovanni Domenico Pennacchi. From this I have had a copy made, without attending to the imperfect drawing exhibited in both the engravings, which are sufficiently different from each other to show that perfect accuracy of design was not an object in either. You have it before you,† and I proceed to explain it.

The figure is divided into three compartments. The first, on the left hand, represents the vase A, made of earthenware, of a different quality from ordinary *terracottas*, inasmuch as it was mixed up with shining metallic fragments, and bits of marble. In shape it somewhat resembles a small barrel, or the vase represented on the Isiac pomp in the Palazzo Mattei. The figure represents it as it was broken, and shows the distribution of the trinkets within at C. Beside it, B is the cover which is found upon it. Passing to the second compartment, you have the shape and proportion of the lower part of the vase, two-thirds the size of the reality. In the same proportion nearly are the figures distributed in this and the third compartment. D represents the metal circle which lined the lower portion of the vessel,

---

* "La Storia Universale provata coi Monumenti," pp. 178, *seqq.*
† See Pl. IV.

LUGE

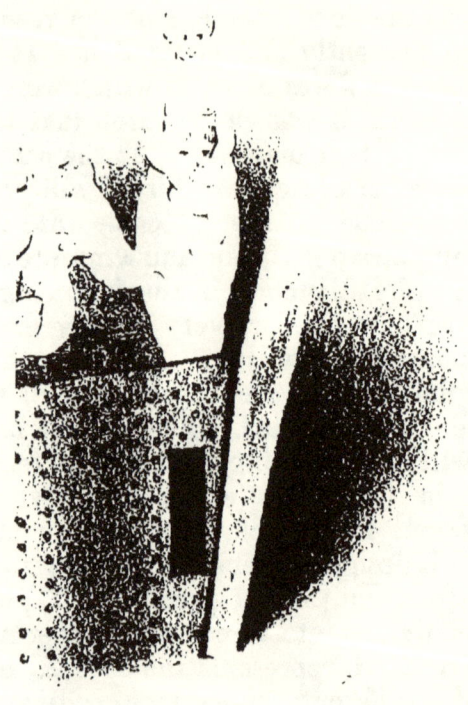

PLATE 4. *Page 354*

composed of small plates nailed together, as if in imitation of a wooden framework. At intervals are windows or open spaces, with shutters over them. There is no door, but, to supply this deficiency, there is a bronze ladder of five steps, as if intended to give entrance above. The structure of this metal box seems thus evidently to indicate a desire of representing a building or edifice, probably of wood, not to be entered from the ground. At certain distances, the side is raised higher than the rim of this little chest, like the breastworks of a battlement; two of these elevations appear in the design, these seemed to hold on the cover, which was fastened to them by certain metal pins, one of which, fastened in the cover, is seen at E, in the left division

The figures consisted of twenty couple of animals,[*] twelve of quadrupeds, six of birds, one of serpents, and one of insects. There were two other unpaired insects, the fellows of which were probably lost in the excavation. The animals were a lion and lioness, a couple of tigers, horses, asses, deer, oxen, wolves, foxes, sheep, hares, and two others not specified. There were, besides, thirty-five human figures, some single, some grouped; but all, with two or three exceptions, showing signs of trying to escape from drowning. The hair of the females is all dishevelled, and they are borne away on the shoulders and backs of the men. In this case they perform the task of closing the mouth and nostrils of their protectors. Single figures do the same for themselves. All are represented as raised to their utmost pitch of stature, and on the right you have a group of three figures standing upon a corpse apparently drowned, as if to add somewhat to their height. The figures were all of exquisite workmanship, indicating a very perfect state of art, with the exception of four, which seem to have been supplied by a much ruder hand. The same may be said of the animals, in

---

[*] Bianchini, in his description, says there were nineteen couple: but this does not accord with his enumeration of them in detail.

which pieces broken or lost seemed to have been supplied in later times. In the description we are nowhere told of what materials the figures were composed. If of bronze, we might compare them to the number of little images of animals, always in pairs, found in Pompeii, of which many may be seen in the museum of Naples. Neither am I aware what has since become of this curious relic.

I will not follow the learned illustrator of this monument into the variety of arguments which he brings to prove that this was a vase used in the festival of the *hydrophoria,* or commemoration of the deluge. The different amulets are certainly very like what Clement Alexandrinus, Arnobius, and others have described as placed by the heathens in their mystic baskets; but if the one given in the acts of the Academy of Cortona be correct,* as it seems most probable, this vessel could hardly be considered as belonging to that class of monuments. I must observe that a chain and lock were found close to our vase, as if belonging some way to it.

But be this as it may, it is difficult to give any other explanation of this singular little monument, than what must obviously strike at once, that it alludes to the destruction of the human race, with the exception of a few, who, with pairs of animals, were saved in some species of ark or chest.

In my last lecture, treating of the chronology of Egypt, as now established by monuments, I mentioned one remarkable synchronism of Shishak and Rehoboam, as given by Rosellini. This king of Egypt is totally omitted by Herodotus and Diodorus, though Manetho mentions him under the name of Sesonchis, as founder of the 22nd dynasty. I mentioned the discovery of several monuments bearing the name of this king as Shishonk. This agreement between the two annals in so definite a

---

* "Atti dell' Academia di Cortona :" *Rome,* 1742, tom. i. p. 65 ; cf. also, the dissertation of Prof. Wunder, "De discrimine verborum *cistæ* et *titellæ,*" in his "Variæ Lectiones librorum aliquot M. T. Ciceronis ex cod. Erfurt :" *Lips.* 1827, pp. clviii. *seqq.*

manner, makes this point the proper basis of any system of Egyptian chronology, and as such Rosellini takes it. But I reserved for this meeting, one monument completely establishing this harmony, and affording, at the same time, one of the most striking confirmations yet discovered of sacred history. This I proceed to lay before you.

The first book of Kings (xiv. 24) and the second of Chronicles (xii. 2) inform us, that Shishak, king of Egypt, came against Juda, in the fifth year of Rehoboam, with 1,200 chariots and 60,000 horsemen, and a countless host; that, after taking the fortified places of the country, he approached to besiege Jerusalem; that the king and people humbled themselves before God, and that he, taking pity on them, promised them, that he would not destroy them, but still should give them into the invader's hand to be his slaves; " nevertheless they shall be his servants, that they may know my service, and that of the kingdoms of the nations." Shishak therefore came and took the spoil of the temple, and among it the golden shields which Solomon had made.* In the great court of Karnak, the exploits of this mighty conqueror, and restorer of the Egyptian power, are represented at full. We might naturally expect this conquest of Juda to be included among them, the more so as that kingdom might be considered at its zenith, just after Solomon had overawed all neighbouring nations by his splendid magnificence. Let us see if this is so. In the representations at Karnak, Shishak is exhibited, according to an image familiar in Egyptian monuments, as holding by the hair a crowd of kneeling figures heaped together, and with his right hand raised up, ready with one blow of his battle-axe to destroy them all. Besides these, the god Ammon-Ra drives forwards towards him a crowd of captives, with their hands tied behind them. If the first group represent those whom he destroyed, the second

---

* 2 Chron. xii. 8.

may well be supposed to contain those whom he only made his servants, or simply overcame, and subjected to tribute. According to the promise made him, the king of Juda was to be in this class, and in it we must look for him. Among the figures of captive kings we accordingly find one, with a physiognomy perfectly Jewish, as Rosellini observes. He has not as yet given the copy of this monument, though he has the legend;* but that you may convince yourselves how truly *un-egyptian*, and how completely Hebrew the countenance of this personage is, I have had it exactly copied for you, from the engraving published of it at Paris, by Champollion.† (Pl. V.) The profile, with its beard, is every way Jewish; and to make this more apparent, I have placed beside it an Egyptian head, quite characteristic of the natural type. Each of these captive monarchs bears a shield, indented as if to represent the fortifications of a city; and on this is written a hieroglyphic legend, which we may suppose to designate who he is. Most, if not all the shields are so far defaced, as to be no longer legible, except that borne by our Jewish figure, which remains, as you see it in the drawing. The two feathers are the letters J. E.; the bird, OU.; the open hand, D. or T.; thus we have *Jeoud*, the Hebrew for Juda. The next five characters represent the letters, H. A. M. L. K., and, supplying the vowels, usually omitted in hieroglyphics, we have the Hebrew word with its article, Hamelek, the king. The last character always stands for the word *Kah*, a country. Thus we have a clear demonstration that this was the king of Juda, treated just as the Scriptures tell us he was, reduced to servitude by Shishak, or Shishonk, king of Egypt. Well may we say, that no monument ever yet discovered gives such new confirmatory evidence to the authenticity of Scripture history. I will close my observations, by remarking, that

---

* "I monumenti dell' Egitto," Parte i. Monum. stor. tom. ii. p. 79.
† In his "Lettres écrites d'Egypte."

PLATE 5. Page 358.

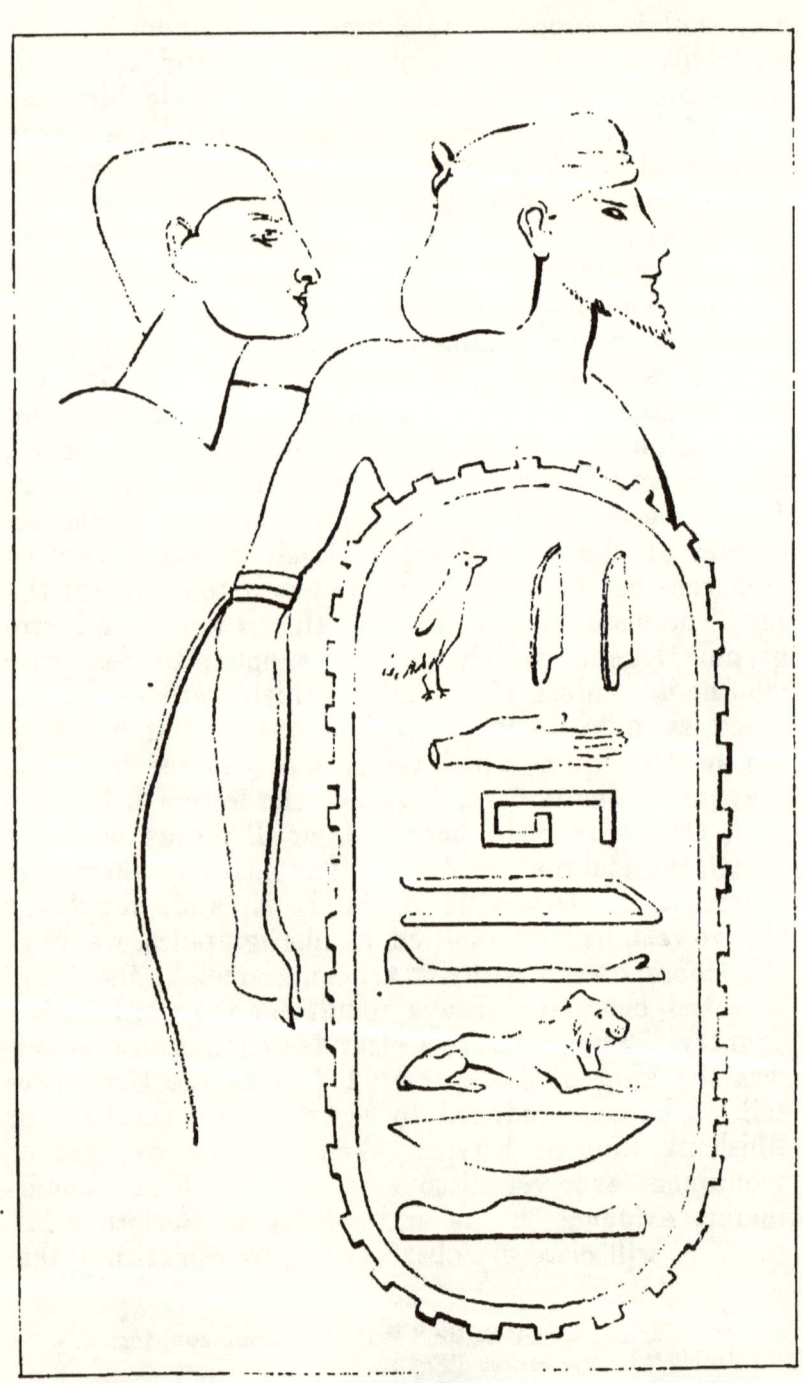

J. Lewis Lith. Dublin.

Paravey thinks a resemblance clearly discernible between the face of the king of Juda and the received type of our Saviour's countenance, particularly in the lower part; and thus a family likeness would exist between the ancestor and descendant.

Let these examples suffice; for when I remember where we are, in the very heart and citadel of this science, where its great influences are drunk in by every sense, and we ourselves become as it were identified with the recollections of its sacred monuments, I feel as if the detailing of a few insignificant instances of its power to aid our faith, must appear almost a needless importunity. There has been one who sat upon the ruins of this city, and was led, by the train of reflections they suggested, to plan that work upon its later history to which I have to-day referred,

"Sapping a solemn creed with solemn sneer."

But surely a believing mind must rise from such a meditation with very different feelings, oppressed, indeed, with the whole weight of his natural feebleness, humbled in spirit before the colossal wrecks of matchless grandeur, more than ever sunk into littleness before the memorials of almost superhuman power; but at the same time cheered by other and more consoling thoughts. For even those heathen monuments have many holy recollections; of the three triumphal arches, one records the fulfilment of a great prophecy, the other the triumph of Christianity over heathenism: and the Flavian amphitheatre was once the scene of the martyrs' witnessing. And surely, whatever creed any may profess, he cannot visit, but with soothed and solemn feeling, those many old and venerable churches which stand alone amidst the ruins of ancient buildings, not because they were erected in solitude, but because, like the insulated cones that rise on the flanks of mountains, the inundations of many ages have washed down around them the less durable masses that enclosed and

connected them together. And if he enter some of
these, and see them yet retaining all their parts and
decorations, even as they were in early times, so unmoved, so unchanged, as if the very atmosphere
breathed in them by the ancient Christians had not
been disturbed; methinks it were not difficult for you
to feel, for some short space, as they did, to wish that
all else had suffered as small mutation, and long that
religion could once more strike its roots as deeply into
our hearts as it did into theirs, and if it produce no
more the martyr's palm, put forth at least the olive
branch of peace. And wherever we move among the
remains of the ancient city, whether in search of amusement or instruction, there is caught a tone of mind
which the most thoughtless cannot escape, essentially
subduing of all selfish and particular feelings, an approximation to a religious frame of soul, which shows
how necessarily the destruction of all mere earthly
power was a preliminary step to the introduction of a
more spiritual influence, even as the contemplation of
that destruction opens the way to that influence's personal action. And thus may we say, that archæology,
the study of ruins and of monuments, while it enlightens
and delights us, may well form the basis of the strongest religious impressions and individual evidences.

LECTURE THE TENTH;
ORIENTAL STUDIES.

PART I.
SACRED LITERATURE.

INTRODUCTORY remarks on the connection of these studies with Religion. CRITICAL SCIENCE: Its objects and principles. *Old Testament.*—Houbigant, Michaelis, Kennicott, De Rossi.—Encouragement given by Rome to these studies. *New Testament.*—Anticipations of Freethinkers.—Wetstein, Griesbach. Results: 1. Proof obtained of the purity of the text in general; 2. Authentication of particular passages; 3. Security against future discoveries.—Confutation of an anecdote related by Michaelis and Dr. Marsh. SACRED PHILOLOGY.—*Hebrew Grammar.*—Its origin among Christians.—Reuchlin and Pellicanus, &c. Application of cognate Dialects, De Dieu, Schultens: Dutch School of Sacred Literature. German School; Michaelis, Storr, Gensenius.—His application of it to invalidate the prophecy of Is. lii. liii.—Confutation of his rule by later Grammarians; Ewald. *Hermeneutical Studies.*—1. Use made of this science to attack the character of the Fathers.—Vindication of them, drawn from the very progress of the study. Winer, Clausen, Rosenmüller.—2. Vindication of old Catholic Commentators by the same advance.—3. Attacks upon Scripture, principally the Prophecies, drawn from the imperfect state of Biblical hermeneutics; the Rationalist School.—Return to sound principles.—Hengstenberg.—4. Practical application of Philology to the refutation of objections made to the genuineness of Matt. i. ii. from expressions therein used.

THE East has already more than once engaged our attention; and assuredly it would be vain to look for collateral evidences of Christianity, or documents confirmatory of its sacred writings, with greater chance of success in any other country than in that which gave it birth. The East bears a character in regard to us and the entire human race, which no relative situation can ever alter; to the scholar and philosopher it opens a mine of reflections, sacred and historical, which yields, every time it is farther explored, new and exhaustless treasures. It is the womb of nations, not only where the species originally came into being, and was renewed after the deluge, but whence, by a power given to no other portion of the globe, successive races of men have come forth, pushing forward each other as waves to the shore, from the unmoved calm of the ocean. Apparently without the power of giving the last development of intellectual energy to its own inhabitants, it hath so fitted and prepared them, that, under proper influences, they have advanced to every possible degree of civilization, of culture, and of power.

For so long as they remain in their native birthplace, as though it were but a nursery wherein their growth is stunted, the nations of Asia appear incapable of rising above a certain degree of moral pre-eminence. While physical life seems brought to the highest possible perfection; while every luxury which nature has bestowed upon the world is there a gift rather than a production; while the outward vesture of man, his corporal endowments of beauty, agility, strength, and temperate endurance, is dressed out in surpassing excellence; while every institution, of government, of morality, of society, and religion, bears the impress of a sensuous happiness, carried to its highest stretch of gratifying power; there is a boundary set upon all these qualities, a separation impassable between them and a nobler order of excellence; the civilization there can never give full growth to the spirit's wings, to raise it into the higher regions of pure intellectual enjoyment; the inventive powers are for ever supplied by mere contriving skill; the steadiness of rule is replaced by boisterous and transitory conquest, or by stagnant despotism; and civilization stands, age after age, at a dull, unvarying level, seldom sinking below, and never rising above an appointed mark.

But this strange contrast between the inhabitants of Asia and those races which, when once issued from it, have shown such marvellous powers of thought and design, is withal a source of great and interesting advantages. For it gives to the former a fixed and unaltering character, which enables the latter to trace back their history and institutions into the remotest ages, and gives connections between the present and the past, which must otherwise have been effaced, and which afford us now many rich and valuable illustrations of our most sacred monuments. Vain would be the attempt to discover the state of any country in Europe, of Germany for instance, of Britain or of France, two thousand years ago, from such institutions, habits, or appearances as yet remain. Except the great unchangeable features of nature, mountains, seas, and rivers, nothing is there which has not been altered and modified; languages, government, arts, and cultivation, the face of the field, and the countenance of man, all is different, and gives tokens of complicated change. But if we travel to the East it is far otherwise. We find the Chinese just as his oldest literature describes him; we have the wandering Monguls and Turcomans, with their waggon-houses and herds, leading the Scythian's life; we see the Brahman performing the same ablution in the sacred river, going through the same works of painful ceremony, as did the ancient gymnosophists, or rather as is prescribed in his sacred books of earlier date; and still more we discover the Arab drinking at the same wells, traversing the same paths, as did the Jew of old, on his pilgrim journeys; tilling the earth with the same implements and at the same seasons; building his house on the same model, and speaking almost the same language as the ancient possessors of the promised land.

Hence, it follows, that innumerable illustrations of holy writ may be found, at every step, through that blessed country. But, independently of this, there is comprised in that unchanging uniformity of more eastern nations, a tenacious grasp of all great traditions, an earnestness in the preservation of all that records the primeval history of man; and thus is given us, in the present, a test which cannot deceive us, when used to assay what is delivered of the past; a means of connecting links, otherwise irretrievably dispersed, of that chain which continues the history of man's mind, from the first-taught lessons of his childhood, to the bolder thoughts of his manlier years.

Having now entered upon that department which more strictly forms my own particular pursuit, and feeling the materials whereof it is composed more immediately under my hand, my principal difficulty to-day, and in my next lecture, will consist in selecting out of innumerable examples, a few of more general interest, and in confining myself to such simple outlines of things capable of much higher finish, as may be easily retained. And I will divide my subject into two portions, treating to-day of sacred, and at our next meeting of profane, Oriental literature.

The portion of my task which I have allotted to this day, I shall divide under the two heads of critical and philological pursuits. For, to preserve some measure of proportion between this and our next entertainment, I must place under the head of profane studies, such antiquarian illustrations as are drawn from uninspired sources. The subject of this day's lecture will wholly consist of such studies as have the Scriptural texts alone in view.

Of all these pursuits, critical science may be justly considered the very foundation. For, if the understanding the words of Scripture aright, necessarily form the groundwork of all true interpretation, the reading of them correctly must be a preliminary step to that accurate understanding. Now, the science of sacred criticism undertakes this office. First, it investigates what are the true words of any single text, it examines all the varieties which may exist therein; and, weighing the arguments in favour of each, decides which reading the commentator or translator should prefer. But then it goes farther, and generalizes its results, by inquiring into the correctness of the entire sacred volume, after the revolutions of so many ages.

The influence of this study upon the Christian evidences is manifestly very great. For, as to its particular application, very much may be gained or lost, by a word or a syllable. The application to Christ of the beautiful prophecy, Ps. xxii. 16, "They pierced my hands and feet," is disputed by the Jews, and by all theologians of the rationalist school; and the dispute turns entirely upon the reading of the words. For, the present reading of the Hebrew text gives a totally different meaning to the passage, that is, "as a lion are my hands and feet;" and innumerable are the disquisitions published upon the true reading of the text. In the New Testament, it is singular that the most important passages affecting the Socinian controversy should be in the same condition, and form the subject of the most complicated critical investigations. I hardly need mention the endless dispute, whether the celebrated verse of the Three Witnesses, 1 John, v. 7, be a part of the original text, or a later interpolation. But besides this, another most important passage, bearing upon the same dogma, is in a still more curious position. This is 1 Tim. iii. 16, where a serious dispute exists, whether we should read, "God appeared in the flesh," or "*who* appeared in the flesh;" and this dispute has been not only contested with the pen, but has literally been made the object of microscopic investigation. For it turns upon this; whether the word in the most celebrated manuscripts be OC, *who*, or ΘC., the abbreviation for Θεος, God. Now, the pronoun and the abbreviation are the same, excepting in the transverse stroke which passes through the Θ, distinguishes it from the O, and in the line drawn over it, as a sign of abbreviation. Some, for instance, assert, that in the celebrated Alexandrian manuscript in the British Museum, these lines are added by a later hand; all agree that they have been most imprudently retouched. Others have maintained, that some remnants of the original stroke might be seen in a strong light, with the aid of a good lens; and their opponents again rejoin, that it was only the transverse stroke of a letter on the other side of the page, which appeared through the vellum, when raised to the sun.* In fine, this dispute has been continued, and the passage positively handled, till strokes and letters, retouchings and originals, have been equally cancelled, and the decision for posterity must rest on what judgment it can form from so many conflicting testimonies. A similar variety of opinion exists regarding the passage in another most celebrated Paris manuscript, called the "Codex Ephrem;" Woide, Griesbach, and Less examined it, yet could not ascertain which is its true reading.

But the great and most important office of this study, particularly in connection with the object of these lectures, consists in giving us the means of deciding how far the text of Scripture, as we now possess it, is free from essential alterations, and corruptions; and consequently, in removing all our anxiety and uneasiness regarding its interpretation. And to show how far it has been successful in its researches, I will briefly sketch out the history of the science as exercised upon the texts of both Old and New Testaments.

I need not say, that, from the earliest ages of the Church, the necessity of having correct texts, and the duty of taking pains to procure them, were fully admitted;† with this difference, that, as the language of the Old Testament was little known to Christians, their labours were chiefly directed to the perfecting of their versions. Origen, Eusebius, Lucian, and other learned Greeks, dedicated their talents to this object, purged the Septuagint version of the errors which had gradually crept into it, and produced different texts, yet discernible

---

* See Woide, "Notitia Cod. Alexandrini." *Lips.* 1788, p. 172, § lxxxvii.

† "Codicibus emendandis primitus debet invigilare solertia eorum qui Scripturas nosse desiderant." St. Aug. "De Doctrina Christiana," lib. ii. cap. 14, tom. iii. pa. i. p. 27, ed. Maur.

in the different manuscripts of that translation. In the West, St. Jerome, Cassiodorus, and Alcuin, took no less pains with the Latin version. But all the ecclesiastical writers who, besides those already enumerated, occupied themselves with critical subjects, particularly St. Augustine and Ven. Bede, repeatedly acknowledged the necessity of having recourse to the originals, and endeavouring, as far as possible, to procure a correct text.*

When the study of Hebrew began to be more cultivated among Christians, and the invention of printing made its text accessible to all, there sprang up an important controversy upon its accuracy. In many most important passages, as the one I have cited from Ps. xxii., it was found to differ from the versions then in use; and suspicions were raised against the Jews, who had so long monopolised it, as though they had taken advantage of that circumstance, to alter and strangely corrupt the original text, in divers places. Hence, many assumed that the versions were to be preferred to the original;—others of more moderate principles, that this was at least to be corrected by them. But, even before critical studies had received their full development, or been reduced to principles, which in every science must follow, not precede observation, the accurate examination of almost every passage quoted in support of these opinions, was found to lead to their confutation; and the Jews were proved, upon incontestable evidence, to have preserved the sacred volume free from all intentional alteration. Such is the judgment which all now agree in pronouncing on the animated folio controversies between Cappellus and the Buxtorfs.

Still there were many who were not convinced; and their obstinacy led to the most important step in this branch of sacred literature, to laying the foundation of

* "Ubi cum ex adverso audieris proba, non confugias ad exempla veriora, vel plurium codicum, vel antiquorum, vel linguæ præcedentis, unde hoc in aliam linguam interpretatum est." Adv. Faust. lib. x. cap. 2, tom. viii. p. 219.

all satisfactory critical investigation, by the collection of various readings from the examination of MSS., versions, and ancient quotations. Such at least was the motive which excited the industry of F. Houbigant. He fancied that the Hebrew text was essentially corrupt; and therefore attempted, in 1753, to publish it in four splendid folios, purged of its errors, and restored to its original purity, by the examination of several manuscripts in the libraries of Paris, and by the comparison of the oldest versions. Rash as were at once his theories and their application, no alarm was felt by the friends of religion, lest they might lead to any serious consequences,—no obstacles were thrown in his way by his ecclesiastical superiors, and the Pope sent him a splendid gold medal, as a testimony of approbation for his industry and zeal.*

This same path was, however, pursued upon higher and better motives by other learned men. John Henry Michaelis, whose reputation has been unjustly much eclipsed by that of his nephew, published in 1720, after thirty years' incessant labour, an edition of the Bible, with notes, in which, among other valuable matter, are given the varieties discoverable in three manuscripts preserved at Erfurt. Our own country, however, has the merit of producing the greatest and most valuable work on this important science, the one to which all later researches must necessarily be attached as supplements and appendixes. The learned Benjamin Kennicott occupied more than ten years in preparing the materials for his great critical Bible, which issued from the Clarendon Press in 1776 and 1780. For this purpose, he did not content himself with collating all the manuscripts in England, but extended his researches over all the Continent, and everywhere received the most liberal encouragement. The results of his labours, and every interesting discovery which they made, he communicated to the public every year in an annual

* See Orme's "Bibliotheca Biblica:" Art. Houbigant.

report, which kept alive the interest of the learned, from the first announcement, to the completion of his herculean work.

Nothing has been more common than to charge us who dwell in Rome, and particularly those who have authority here, with discouraging all critical research, especially in sacred literature, and with throwing every obstacle in the way of those who cultivate it. I shall have to advert, a little later, to a specific charge of this nature; but the conduct and feeling manifested in Rome towards Kennicott and his undertaking, affords sufficient proof of how groundless are such accusations. He himself tells us, that the first place which gave him encouragement, and offered him assistance, was Rome; and he gave us the following letter, written to him by Cardinal Passionei, librarian to the Vatican, dated May 16, 1761, and entitled by him, "The Roman Testimonial."

"The undertaking of a new edition of the Bible to be made at Oxford upon all the Hebrew MSS. existing in the most celebrated libraries, has here met as many approvers as persons who have heard it mentioned. And to favour the author of so important a work, I have permitted, with pleasure, the collation of the ancient Hebrew MSS. existing in the Vatican Library, and I have granted it officially as Librarian of the Holy Roman Church."*

In 1772, F. Fabricy, a Dominican, published in Rome two very large volumes, directed almost entirely to prove the great benefit which religion must receive from a free and complete examination of the critical state of our present Hebrew text, such as was promised by Kennicott. "What must chiefly interest us," he says, "is, that it will infallibly give religion powerful arms to confound a fundamental error of the impious and the libertine, on the actual state of our Hebrew text. From the inspection of Hebrew MSS. compared with our common text, and with the most ancient

---

* Kennic. Vet. Test. Pref. p. viii.

versions, an interesting fact must result, the assurance of our divine Scripture being essentially incorrupt. We cannot give a better confutation of their hypothesis, who call themselves philosophers in our days, and who refuse credit to the sacred books, on the pretence that the originals of Scripture are essentially corrupt, and are now in extreme confusion and disorder."*

It was only, indeed, by the existence of such kind encouragement, that the next and last labourer in this field could have accomplished his extraordinary undertaking. This was John Bernard de Rossi, a poor and modest professor of Parma. In an interesting account of his labours, which he published shortly before his death, he considers himself only a humble instrument in the hands of Providence, for the work which occupied his life, the collection of manuscripts and rare editions of the Hebrew text. Without fortune, influence, or connections, he dedicated himself to this task; he devoted to it all his little means; he employed every art to overcome the repugnance which the Jews had to part with their written records; and by his steady, undeviating attention to one great and religious object, succeeded in his design beyond his most sanguine expectation. Kennicott, through the whole of Europe, had only been able to collate 581 Hebrew manuscripts; nor does any public library in England, or on the Continent, possess more than fifty such documents. In 1784, De Rossi published the first volume of his various readings, as supplementary to Kennicott's collection, and in it he gives the catalogue of 479 manuscripts in his own possession. Before the completion of the fourth volume in 1788, his collection had increased to 612; and in 1808 he published a supplementary volume, in which 68 new manuscripts are described, making in all 680 Hebrew manuscripts. As he went on amassing till his death, a few years ago, this invaluable collection is now

---

* "Des Titres primitifs de la Révélation," tom. prem. p. 3. See tom. ii. pp. 332, 373, 521, &c.

much greater. Every temptation was held out to this worthy ecclesiastic to part with his literary treasure. The Emperor of Russia offered him an enormous price; but he replied that it should never go out of Italy. Pius VI. had before proposed to purchase it, and the thought of having his library united to that of the Vatican, perhaps tried him more keenly than gold; but he preferred accepting a trifling compensation for himself and his niece from his own sovereign, and bequeathed it to the library of his native city. With the valuable labours of this humble, but enterprising individual, the history of this department of sacred criticism may be said to close; its results we shall see united to those of the other more interesting branch, the critical examination of the New Testament.

Very early after the first publication of this sacred collection, it became the custom to examine the manuscripts of it, which abounded in every library, though with no great accuracy, and on no uniform plan. It was not till the great edition of Mill, in 1707, which condensed all the labours of his predecessors, corrected their errors, and greatly increased their stores, that sacred criticism could be said to have assumed a systematic form. After him the task of collecting rapidly advanced, and successive critical editions occupied the attention of the learned, through the whole of the eighteenth century. That of Wetstein, in 1751 and 1752, far eclipsed all that had gone before; but he, as well as they, has yielded the pre-eminence which he long enjoyed to the great reformer of the science, John James Griesbach. To him we owe the leading principles which have swayed it ever since, almost with an iron rule.

It was chiefly with reference to this branch of critical science, that the interest of the learned, and of theologians in particular, was much excited. For it was chiefly here that the opposers of religion, or of its most essential dogmas, had hoped for something useful to their cause. It had been anticipated, indeed, that some various readings would probably be discovered more favourable to Socinian opinions; and, at any rate, many believed that such an uncertainty would arise concerning the entire text, such difficulty of choice between conflicting readings, as would unsettle all belief, and utterly destroy the authority of Scripture as a guide to truth. Such was the view taken of the critical labours of Mill and others, by the celebrated Anthony Collins, in his " Discourse on Freethinking." He took advantage of the differences between Mill and Whitby, about some passages, and about the value of various readings in general, to conclude that the entire New Testament was thereby rendered doubtful. He was soon, however, chastised by the heavy lash of Bentley, who, in his disguise of Phileleutherus Lipsiensis, thoroughly exposed the folly of Collins's assertions, and vindicated the condition of the inspired text.

And, in fact, we may well inquire, what has been the result of this laborious and acute research,—of this toilsome collation of manuscripts of every age, of the many theories for classifying critical documents; in fine, of all the years which able and learned men have dedicated to the zealous task of amending and perfecting the sacred book? Why truly, if we exclude the great and important conclusions which we have at present in view, the result is so trifling, that we should say, there had been much unthrifty squandering of time and talents thereupon. Not indeed that there has been lack of abundant differences of readings; on the contrary, the number is overpowering. Mill's first effort produced 30,000, and the number may be said daily to increase. But in all this mass, although every attainable source has been exhausted; although the fathers of every age have been gleaned for their readings; although the versions of every nation, Arabic, Syriac, Coptic, Armenian, and Ethiopian, have been ransacked for their renderings; although manuscripts of every age, from the sixteenth upwards to the third, and of every country, have been again and again visited by industrious swarms to rifle them of their treasures; although having exhausted the stores of the West, critics have travelled like naturalists into distant lands to discover new specimens,—have visited, like Scholz, or Sebastiani, the recesses of Mount Athos, or the unexplored libraries of the Egyptian and Syrian deserts—yet has nothing been discovered, no, not one single various reading, which can throw doubt upon any passage before considered certain or decisive in favour of any important doctrine. For in the instances which I before quoted, as 1 Tim. iii. 16, the doubt existed already from the variety found in the ancient versions. These various readings, almost without an exception, leave untouched the essential parts of any sentence, and only interfere with points of secondary importance, the insertion or omission of an article or conjunction, the more accurate grammatical construction, or the forms rather than the substance of words. For instance, the first verse of St. John's Gospel had been the subject of various critical conjectures, with a view of destroying its force in proving the divinity of Christ. One author had maintained that the reading should be in the genitive, "and the Word was of God;" another, that the sentence should be differently pointed, and that we should read, "and God was," leaving "the Word" to be joined to the next period. Now, after examining all the evidence within the reach of unexampled industry, exercised by men noways unfavourable to the cause supported by those conjectures, what discoveries have been made in this passage? Several various readings, to be sure; such as Clement of Alexandria's having once "the Word was *in* God," instead of *with* God; one manuscript, and St. Gregory of Nyssa, reading the word *God* with an article, "was *the* God." These are the only variations found in the text, while the great doctrine which it contains, remains perfectly untouched, and the presumptuous conjectures of Photinus, Crellius, and Bardht, are proved to be frivolous and ungrounded.

In fact, if we look through the new text published by

Griesbach, the first critic who ventured to insert a new reading into the received text, and see, as we may in a moment, from the difference of type, how few are the instances where the great quantity of documents which he consulted suggested to him any improvement, we cannot but be surprised at the accuracy of our ordinary text, formed as it was, without selection, from the first manuscripts that came to hand after the invention of printing; or rather we must feel great satisfaction at the small difference between the best and the most inferior manuscripts, and consequently at the consoling manner in which the integrity of the inspired records has been preserved.

So completely did this result disappoint the expectations of those who opposed religion, that we are told by a celebrated scholar of the last century, that they began to think less favourably of that species of criticism which they at first so highly recommended, in the hope of its leading to discoveries more suitable to their maxims than the ancient system.*

This result is precisely the same as has been obtained from the critical study of the Old Testament. It has been acknowledged by the learned Eichhorn, that Kennicott's various readings hardly present any of consequence, or sufficiently interesting to repay the labour bestowed on their collection.† Even within these few years we have had a new and striking confirmation of this result. Dr. Buchanan, in 1806, procured and brought to Europe a Hebrew manuscript used by the black Jews, settled from time immemorial in India, where they had for ages been cut off from all communication with their brethren in other parts of the world. It is a fragment of an immense roll, which, when complete, must have been about ninety feet long. Even as it now is, it is made up of pieces written by different persons, at different epochs, and contains a considerable portion of the Pentateuch. It is written on skins dyed

---

* Michaelis, tom. ii. p. 266.
† "Einleitung," ii. Th. S. 700, ed. *Leipzig*, 1824.

red. An interesting collation of this MS. has been made and published by Mr. Yeates; and the result is, that, comparing it with the edition of Van der Hooght, considered always as the standard edition in such collations, it presents not more than *forty* various readings, not one of which is in the least important, for the most part affecting letters, such as *jod* or *vau*, which may be inserted or omitted with perfect indifference. Indeed, comparing it with other printed, and very correct editions, this number is considerably reduced. The collator well observes, that here we have "specimens of at least three ancient copies of the Pentateuch, whose testimony is found to unite in the integrity and pure conservation of the sacred text, acknowledged by Christians and Jews in these parts of the world."*

But, once more returning to the New Testament, and the critical attention paid to its text, the advantages which this has procured us, are far from stopping at the assurance, that nothing has been yet discovered which could shake our belief in the purity of our sacred books. This advantage was but the first step gained by it in the earliest labours of Mill and Wetstein. The critic, with whose name I closed my list, went much farther; he gave us, in addition, a security for the future. His great theory of the classification of manuscripts, was, however, first suggested by an amiable and profound scholar, John Albert Bengel. This learned man is a noble model of the principles in action which I have been striving to inculcate through this course of lectures. He was perplexed by the quantity of various readings discovered in the New Testament, and feared that, by them, all security in its correctness was essentially destroyed. He had no one to consult; he feared to open the state of his mind: and with an uprightness and courage which do him honour, he resolved to face every difficulty, to dedicate himself to critical inquiries, and to find, in the science itself that suggested them,

---

* "Collation of an Indian Copy of the Pentateuch," p. 8.

the solution of his scruples. The result was what might have been anticipated—his own individual conviction of the purity of the text, and the simplification of the inquiry to all who might find themselves in a similar position. He soon observed that it was lost labour to count manuscripts upon any passage; for a great number of them always herded together, so that when you knew how one read, you might consider it a type or representative of many more, which belonged, as it were, to the same family. Thus he suggested, that if you found upon any text one celebrated old manuscript, agreeing with any very ancient version, you might safely consider their joint reading as certain.

This, however, was but a rude germ of the system discovered and introduced by Griesbach. He found, by a long and diligent research, that all known manuscripts are divided into three classes, to which he has given the name *Recensions*, because he supposes them to have been produced by corrected editions of the text in different countries; and he, consequently, gives them the titles of the Alexandrian, the Western, and the Byzantine Recensions. Every known manuscript belongs to one of these classes; and though it may occasionally depart from its type, it accords with it on the whole. The consequence of this arrangement is obvious. We no longer speak of twenty manuscripts being in favour of one reading, and as many on the other side, nor think of examining their individual value; nor have we to weigh numbers against intrinsic worth, and decide between them. Individual manuscripts have now no value; but we only decide between families. If two families agree, their joint reading is probably correct; if they are so blended together, that manuscripts of all families are confusedly mixed on both sides, the question cannot be decided. But here we have a security against the discovery of any future documents. For, if any manuscript, however venerable and precious, were to be discovered, it must enter into the ranks, and submit to be classified with one of the families, whose weight it might increase, while it lost all individual authority; and thus it could noways disturb our security. And if it presented such anomalies as would exclude it from them all, and prevent its classification, it must be considered a vagrant and outlaw, and could no more derange the system than a comet cutting through the orbits of the planets could be said to disturb their order, by refusing to come into their arrangement.

This great and important step in the critical study of the New Testament, has received important modifications, all tending to simplify it farther. Nolan, Hug, Scholz, and many others, have proposed various arrangements, and distributions of manuscripts; but they have gone little farther than varying the names and numbers of the classes; the principles they have preserved entire. Scholz, indeed, may be said to have proposed the most important change. After travelling all over Europe, and a great part of the East, to collate manuscripts, he published in 1830 the first volume of a new critical edition; in the preface to which he reduces the families to two, thus rendering the application of Griesbach's principle still more attainable. By a letter which I lately received from him, I learn that the second volume is now in the press.

Thus, may we say, that critical science has not only overthrown every objection drawn from documents already in our possession, but has given us full security against any that may be yet discovered; and has, at the same time, placed in our hands simple and easy canons, or rules for deciding complicated points of difference. And these results will be still more within our reach, when a new edition, now preparing, shall have appeared, in which only select readings, examined with great care, and given with great accuracy, shall have been completed.

Besides these general advantages, we may moreover say, that many particular passages, over which a cloud of doubt before hung, have been cleared of their difficulty, and fully secured. For instance, the eleven last verses of

St. Mark, containing very important and interesting matter, had been doubted of by many critics; and the same may be said of Luke, xxii. 43-45, wherein the account is given of our Saviour's bloody sweat in the garden. Now, the progress of critical research has so completely placed these two passages on a level with every other part of the New Testament, that it is quite impossible they can ever again be called in question.

There is an anecdote connected with this science, to which I before alluded, and which it would be unjust not to inquire into before concluding it. The Vatican library possesses, as all of you must be aware, the most valuable manuscript of the Septuagint version, and the New Testament, now in existence. It is known by the name of the Codex Vaticanus, and was published in 1587, by order of Pope Sixtus V. Michaelis, and his annotator, Dr. Marsh, have informed us, upon the authority of Adler, that, in 1783, the Abbate Spaletti, or, as they call him, Spoletti, applied to Pope Pius VI. for permission to publish a fac-simile of the entire manuscript upon the same plan as the Anacreon which he had printed: that the Pope was favourable to the scheme, but "referred the matter, according to the usual routine, to the Inquisition, with the order that F. Mamachi, the *magister sacri palatii*, should be consulted in particular; whose ignorance, and its usual attendant, a spirit of intolerance, induced him to persuade the Pope to prevent the execution of the plan, under the pretence that the Codex Vaticanus differed from the Vulgate, and might, therefore, if made known to the public, be prejudicial to the interests of the Christian religion." A second memorial was presented to the Pope, "but the powers of the Inquisition prevailed against arguments, which had no other support than sound reason." De Rossi, in a letter to Michaelis, answered this accusation against the character of his patron, the Pope; but Dr. Marsh replies, "that this at least is certain, that no public permission was ever given to Spoletti, though he repeatedly asked it; he was therefore obliged to abandon the design, since the private indulgence of the Pope would have been no security against the vengeance of the Inquisition."* It is really a pity to see such a tissue of misrepresentations as are here strung together, repeated by writers of authority, from whom they are, of course, copied into popular works, and become universally current. Mr. Horne, naturally, has not overlooked it.†

When I first read this story, some years ago, I lost no time in examining its accuracy. The leading fact is indeed true, that the Abbate Spaletti applied for permission to publish a fac-simile of that immense manuscript; and, doubtless, had he applied for permission only, it would have been soon obtained. But, unluckily, his demand was, that he should publish it at the expense of the government; and this was the sole ground of refusal. This I was told by one who had known Spaletti intimately, and was acquainted with the whole transaction, and had no idea that any different account, or, indeed, any account of it at all, had been ever published.‡ It would have been a pity, he added, if Spaletti had been allowed; for he was but a superficial scholar, and merely desired to undertake this immense task, as a good speculation. When we consider that it required the interference of Parliament, and its engagement to pay all expenses, before Mr. Baber's fac-simile of the Alexandrian manuscript of the *Old* Testament alone could be undertaken; and that, even then, on account of the enormous expense, only 250 copies have been printed, we surely have reason enough for the government here declining the extravagant outlay necessary for carrying Spaletti's projects into execution. Besides this leading incorrectness, there are others of minor importance in the anecdote. The Inquisition could not have been ever referred to, according to the "ordinary routine," as Dr. Marsh expresses it; for, to

---

* Michaelis, vol. ii. part i. p. 181; part ii. p. 644.
† Vol. ii. p. 125.
‡ The late Canonico Baldi, sotto-custode of the Vatican library.

any one acquainted with the course of business here, such an assertion sounds as probable as if some foreigner were to state, that Mr. Baber's proposal to publish the Alexandrian manuscript was referred, according to the " usual routine," to the Horse-Guards, or the Board of Control. Nor, in fact, was it ever referred to the Inquisition at all. So far from any misunderstanding having ever existed between Spaletti and the members of that office, he continued to the end of his life to spend all his Sunday mornings in their society, within the walls of that dreadful tribunal. Nor can I pass over the learned Bishop of Peterborough, speaking of the *ignorant* Mamachi; a man who holds a place among the illustrators of ecclesiastical antiquity second to none, and whose works will fortunately last as long, at least, as this aspersion on his memory. However, Dr. Marsh himself affords the best confutation of the motive attributed to this *ignorant* clergyman, who surely knew that the Vatican manuscript had been published nearly two centuries before, when he tells us that Dr. Holmes found no obstacles in the way of collating the manuscripts of the Vatican for his edition of the Septuagint.* And in fact, Spaletti was employed among others in making it, and the very manuscript in question was one of those examined.

When Monsignor Mai, lately librarian of the Vatican, suggested to Leo XII. the propriety of publishing the New Testament of the Codex Vaticanus, his Holiness replied, that he would wish the whole, including the Old, to be accurately printed. Upon this, the learned prelate undertook the task, and advanced as far as St. Mark's gospel. Not satisfied with the execution of the work, he has since recommenced it on a different plan. The New Testament is finished, and the Old

---

* The collation of this manuscript was interrupted by the French revolution. Why it was not resumed after the restoration of the Codex, the officers of the library were at a loss to discover. Surely a critical edition of the Septuagint, in which a collation of the best and oldest manuscript is wanting, labours under an essential defect.

considerably advanced. This publication will be the most satisfactory proof how little apprehension is felt in Rome of any "injury to the Christian religion" from the critical study of the Holy Scriptures.

But, to conclude this last portion of my task, we have thus seen this science run precisely the same course as so many others; afford, in its imperfect state, some ground of objection to freethinkers against the basis of Christian revelation, and then, by pursuing its own natural direction without fear, not only overthrow all the difficulties which it had first raised, but replace them by such new and satisfactory assurances, as no farther inquiry can possibly weaken or destroy.

After the text has been settled by critical research, the next task is to interpret. This is primarily the province of philology, which examines the signification of the words, whether singly, or combined in phrases, and, by deciding on their value, arrives at the sense of entire sentences and paragraphs. Now, the different parts of this study, strange as it may seem, have been progressive, and their progress has uniformly tended to the vindication of Scripture, and the confirmation of the evidences. Grammar is necessarily the basis of all study which has words for its object: and I commence with it.

You will, perhaps, be inclined to smile, when I speak of the grammar of a language dead two thousand years, as in a state of progress and improvement. You will, doubtless, be no less tempted to incredulity, when I assert that its progress has even slightly added to our security in essential doctrines. And yet both assertions are really true. For the sake of such as may feel an interest in such researches, I will sketch you an outline of its history, and then exemplify the useful and important applications to which it may be directed.

The grammar of the Hebrew language naturally originated with the Jews; nor did any Christian, in modern times, commence its study, until it had received from them all that perfection which their defective methods could bestow on it. Still the study amongst us may be said to have been conducted upon independent grounds. Elias Levita was employed, in giving to the grammatical researches of the Kimchis, all the improvements which they were ever to receive from writers of his nation, when Conrad Pellicanus, in 1503, and Reuchlin, three years later, published the first rudiments of Hebrew intended for Christian education. The former a monk at Tübingen, had made himself acquainted with the language at the age of twenty-two, with no other help than a Latin Bible; and embodied, consequently, in his grammar, only such imperfect elements as he had thus gleaned. Reuchlin took lessons at Rome, from a Jew, at the extravagant price of a golden crown an hour: and to him we are indebted for most of the grammatical terms now used in the study of the sacred language. Sebastian Münster, a scholar of Elias, soon eclipsed his predecessors; and his labours, which were copied almost entirely from the Rabbins, yielded, in their turn, to the more comprehensive and more lucid method of the elder Buxtorf. Nor were grammatical researches wanting in other parts of Europe besides Germany. Santes Pagnini in Italy, and Chevalier in France, published introductions to the study of the sacred language. This may be styled the first period of Hebrew grammar among Christians, a period ending with the middle of the seventeenth century.[*] Its characteristics are those of the Jewish school, from which it sprang—a minute attention to the complicated changes of letters and vowel-points, and to the derivation and formation of nouns; while the general structure of the language is, in a great measure, overlooked. Besides Buxtorf, one other honourable exception must, however, be made. Solomon Glass, whose *Philologia Sacra*, especially in the improved edition of Dathe, should never be absent from the table of the biblical student, collected a treasure of syntactical

---

[*] Gensenius, "Geschichte der hebräischen Sprache und Schrift:" *Leipzig*, 1825, pp. 101, 107.

remarks, which, besides their utility for Hebrew grammar, had the merit of first bringing the language of the New Testament into relation with the Old.

While the study of Hebrew grammar was thus slowly advancing, the cognate Semitic dialects, then known by the general name of the Oriental languages, were cultivated with considerable attention. At the period which, after Gensenius, I have assigned to the termination of the first Christian school, the study of them began to exercise an influence on Hebrew grammar, and thus marked the commencement of a second epoch. Louis De Dieu, in 1628, first published a comparative grammar of Hebrew, Chaldaic, and Syriac. He was followed by Hottinger (1649), and Sennert (1653), who added the Arabic to the languages previously compared. The celebrated polyglot lexicon of Castell, in its prolegomena, further contributed the Ethiopic or Abyssinian.

This was a new and important instrument for the study of Hebrew grammar; but the syntax of these kindred languages was itself imperfectly developed, and the application of them was therefore principally confined to the declensions and conjugations. At the beginning of the last century, a more extensive application of one branch at least of this comparative philology, was introduced by the learned and sagacious Albert Schultens. Deeply versed in Arabic literature, and having at command a treasure of Oriental manuscripts in the Leyden library, he devoted most of his life to the illustration of Hebrew philology from these new sources. Great as his merits are, his devotion to the system which he was the first to introduce, necessarily led him too far. He sacrificed the advantages, which a comparison with all the kindred dialects affords, to his predilection for one. He went farther still; for he often neglects the peculiar structure and idiomatic uses of the Hebrew language for a parallelism, however faint, with Arabic.*

* *Ibid.* page 128.

He was the founder of what is called the Dutch school in Hebrew philology. As might be expected, many of his scholars copied the faults of their master, though a few, more judicious, were careful to avoid them. While rash Arabisms, as they were called, and forced etymologies, disfigure the works of Venema, Lette, and Scheid, others, like Schröder, have brought a more chastened judgment to the study of grammar. The *Institutiones* of this judicious author,* was for many years the standard work in Germany, and is, I believe, as yet considerably used, and deservedly esteemed in England. His syntax is copious and accurate, and may be reckoned the best substitute by those who have not access to the larger German works of Gensenius and Ewald.

While the Dutch school was in its perfection, the Germans were laying the foundation of that system, which, though not matured so early, was the only true and solid method of proceeding. This consisted in not attempting to reach at once a full and comprehensive system of grammar, but in illustrating particular points, either from the cognate dialects, or by a collation of numerous passages in the Bible itself. Christian Benedict Michaelis laudably attended to both methods; Simonis, Storr, and numerous others, contributed valuable observations towards methodizing the Hebrew syntax, and its analogies. Materials were thus accumulated at the commencement of this century, which only required a learned, judicious, and patient investigator, to arrange, discuss, and complete them.

From the first school, the modern one differs, much in the same manner as the tactics of the present day do from those of ancient times. As these trained the phalanx, or legion, through a maze of manœuvres which depended chiefly upon the exact movements and positions of individuals, so the whole system of ancient grammar depended upon the minute changes which occurred in every single word, upon the complicated evolutions of

---

* "Institutiones ad Fundamenta Linguæ Hebraicæ." The last German ed. *Ulm*, 1792. It was reprinted at Glasgow in 1824.

each point, its advance, its retreat, or its charge. The modern grammarian, on the other hand, neglects not, indeed, these minor movements, but bestows his greatest attention on the co-ordination of the parts of speech, on the force of the particles in every varied circumstance, on the different powers of peculiar forms of words, and on the mutual dependence of the lesser and greater members of the sentence: he looks mainly to more extensive combinations, and more important effects.

The first school, however, used one advantage, which its successor neglected or despised, the Rabbinical grammarians. All, indeed, at the beginning, was Jewish, whether in grammar or in lexicography; while, during the following period, the Rabbins were discarded in both. Forster (1557) published his lexicon, " non ex Rabbinorum commentis nec nostratum Doctorum stulta imitatione;" and Masclef determined to purge Hebrew grammar of the points, " aliisque inventis Masorethicis." I know not whether his followers consider the existence of syntax and construction in Hebrew as a Rabbinical invention; but those grammars which treat of the language without points, generally unshackle it no less of grammatical ties, and thus represent the language of inspiration as a speech, wherein almost every word is vague and indeterminate, and every sentence devoid of rule and fixed construction.

But be this as it may, the moderns make it a point to neglect no source of information; and much that is valuable in the grammar and lexicography of the present day, must be attributed to a proper attention to Jewish sources. The grammar also of the cognate dialects has improved in like manner. The Baron de Sacy has totally changed the face of Arabic grammar. Hoffman has left little hope to those who cultivate the field of Syriac philology.*

* Hoffman's work, however, must be considered rather a consequence of the latest advances in Hebrew and Arabic grammar, than as a co-ordinate improvement.—"Grammaticæ Syriacæ, Libri tres," *Halæ*, 1827, p. viii.

With these principles and these advantages, it was that Gensenius undertook the task of publishing a complete Hebrew grammar, which appeared in 1817.* This work, with his lexicon, forms an era in biblical literature: though many severe strictures were at first passed, it gained very general and merited approbation; and many writers hesitate not to consider its author as almost monopolizing the Hebrew learning of the day.

I have detained you too long with the history of so barren a district of science as Hebrew grammar; it is time that I should apply it to the object of these lectures.

The influence of grammar upon the interpretation of any passage, is too obvious to require explanation. No modern commentator would advance an illustration of a text, without showing that the meaning of each word, and its connection with the passage, warrant the sense which he has selected. To demonstrate, on the other hand, that his opinion involves the text in a conflict with the established rules of grammar, would be its most unanswerable refutation. But hence, you must instantly see the importance of having the standard rules, to which every one appeals, certain and satisfactory; and how easily a general grammatical canon may be laid down, upon the authority of a few instances, which will fatally deprive us of an important dogmatical proof, or give a totally new meaning to passages hitherto deemed clear. In such a case, it becomes our duty to examine the universality of the rule; we may have to enter into the *minutiæ* of philological discussion; and in vain shall we aspire to be commentators without being grammarians. The progress of study may, therefore, refute these difficulties, and regain the ground which such partial researches appear to have conquered.

All this has, in fact, happened. When I inform you, that the most magnificent and most circumstantial

---

* "Ausführliches grammatisch-kritisches Lehrgebäude der hebräischen Sprache, mit Vergleichung der verwandten Dialekte:" *Leipzig*, 1817, 8vo. pp. 908.

prophecy in the Old Testament had been denied; that the dispute concerning it had been mainly reduced to a grammatical discussion of the force of one little word, supposed to be the key to the entire passage; that a rule had been framed by the standard grammarian whom I have just eulogized, depriving this word of the only signification compatible with a prophetic interpretation; that, in fine, the researches of later grammarians have overthrown this rule; you will allow that important results may be gained by the progress of this study, for the vindication of prophecy, and consequently, for confirming the truth of Christianity. For there could hardly be pointed out a passage in the Old Testament from which this class of evidence can be established so satisfactorily, as from the fifty-second and fifty-third chapters of Isaiah. Nothing, therefore, remains for my proof, but briefly to sketch out the history of this controversy, making it as intelligible as possible to those who are unacquinted with the Hebrew language.

In the three last verses of the fifty-second, and through the whole of the following chapter, are represented the character and fate of the *Servant of God*. Perhaps no portion of the same extent in the Old Testament is so honoured by quotations and references in the New; it is the passage which divine Providence used as an instrument to convert the eunuch of the Queen of Ethiopia.* As early as the age of Origen, the Jews had taken care to elude the force of a prophecy which described the *Servant of God* as afflicted, wounded, and bruised, and as laying down his life for his people, and even for the salvation of all mankind.† Though the Targum, or Chaldee paraphrase of Jonathan, understood it of the Messiah, the later Jews have explained it either of some celebrated prophet, or of some collective body. The modern adversaries of prophecy have generally adopted

---

* Acts, viii. 32, 33.
† Chap. liii. 12. Compare Mat. xxvi. 28; Rom. v. 19; Is. lii. 15: on which see Jahn, "Appendix Hermeneuticæ," fasc. ii. *Vien.* 1815, p. 5.

the latter interpretation, though with considerable diversity as to the particular application. The favourite theory seems, that it represents, under the figure of the Servant of God, the whole Jewish people, often designated under that title in Scripture, and that it is descriptive of the sufferings, captivity, and restoration of the whole race.* Others, however, prefer a more restricted sense, and apply the whole passage to the prophetic body. This explanation has met with an ingenious and learned patron in Gensenius.†

It is true, that this servant of God is represented as one individual, but the advocates of the *collective* application appeal to one text as containing a decisive argument in their favour. This is the eighth verse of the fifty-third chapter, "for the sin of my people a stroke (was inflicted 'upon *him* ')." The pronoun used here is one of rare occurrence, found chiefly in the poets (לָמוֹ *lamo*). This, it is asserted, is only plural, and the text should therefore be rendered, "a stroke is inflicted on *them*." Now this meaning would be absolutely incompatible with a prophecy regarding a single individual, and is therefore assumed as giving the key to the entire passage, and proving that a collective body alone can be signified under the figure of God's servant. The prophecy therefore would be totally lost; instead of a clear prediction of the mission and redemption of the Messiah, we should only have a prophetic elegy over the sufferings of the prophets, or of the people! To this word the learned Rosenmüller appeals in his prolegomena to the chapter for a decisive termination of the contest, and supposes the prophet to have used this pronoun for the express purpose of clearing up any difficulty regarding his meaning.‡ To it Gensenius in

---

* Eckermann, " Theologische Beyträge," Erst. St. p. 191. Rosenmüller, "Jesajæ Vaticinia:" *Lips.* 1820, vol. iii. p. 326.
† " Philologisch-kritischer und historischer Commentar über den Jesaia," Zweiter Th. *Leips.* 1821, p. 168.
‡ Omnino autem quo minus de singula quadam persona vatem loqui existimemus, illud vetat, quod versu 8, exeunte, de illa, qui loquentes

like manner refers for the same purpose;* and he considers it a mere prejudice to render the passage in the singular, as has been done by the Syriac version and by St. Jerome.† But Gensenius, as I have before hinted, had already prepared the way for his commentary, and prevented the necessity of any discussion in it, by framing a rule in his grammar, evidently intended for this passage.

There he has laid down that the poetical pronoun לָמוֹ is only plural; and that though sometimes referred to singular nouns, it is only when they are collectives. After noticing a certain number of examples, he adds the text under consideration. "In this passage," he remarks, "the grammatical discussion has acquired a dogmatical interest. The subject of this chapter is always mentioned in the singular, except in this text, but it is perfectly intelligible how it should be changed in verse 8 for a plural, since, as appears to me certain, that *servant of God* is the representative of the prophetic body."‡ You see, therefore, how important a discussion, in itself of small consequence, may become; how the inquiry, whether an insignificant pronoun is only plural or may be singular, has become the hinge on which a question of real interest to the evidence of Christianity has been made to turn.§

The grammatical labours of Gensenius were not so

inducuntur, dicunt. . . . לָמוֹ enim *collective* duntaxat pro לָהֶם usurpari videbimus ad eum locum, voluitque vates illa voce usus ipse significare, ministrum illum divinum, de quo loquitur, esse certam quandam plurium hominum ejusdem conditionis collationem unius personæ imagine repræsentatam. Quum igitur omnis interpretatio, quæ singulari alicui personæ hanc pericopam accommodare student, plane sit seponenda," &c. *ubi sup.* 330, cf. p. 359.

* *Ubi sup.* pp. 163, 183.
† Erst. Th. erste Abth. pp. 86, 88. The Targum, Symmachus and Theodotion, who are not Christian interpreters, render the word in the same manner.
‡ Lehrgebäude, p. 221.
§ It must be remembered that the discussion of this particular prophecy is closely connected with the principle whether prophecy exists at all in the Old Testament. It is by such special explanations that

perfect as to deter others from cultivating the same field. In 1827, a very full critical grammar was published by Ewald, who necessarily discussed the grammatical rule laid down by Gensenius on the subject of this pronoun. He brings together more examples, and by an examination of their context or parallel passages, determines satisfactorily, that this unusual form may well bear a singular signification.* The difficulty against the prophetic interpretation is thus removed by one of the most modern grammarians, and all those internal arguments in its favour are restored to their native force, by perseverance in the very study which had been brought to confute them.

Hermeneutics, or the principles of biblical interpretation, will scarcely appear to you a science more capable of improvement than Hebrew grammar. Did not the early writers of the Church understand the sacred volume, and must they not have been, therefore, guided

---

rationalists get rid of the whole system of prophecy, whereby the truth of Christianity is so much confirmed. This passage, moreover, is of peculiar importance in proving the mission of Christ, and his identity with the promised king of the Jews. I must also observe, that besides the solutions in the text, others have been given which secure the prophecy, and yet leave the pronoun in the plural. One is in Jahn, *ubi sup.* p. 24; another, I think more conformable to Hebrew usage, in Hengstenberg's "Christologie des alten Testaments:" *Berlin*, 1829. Erst. Th. zweit. Abth. p 339.

* Kritische Grammatik der Hebräischen Sprache ausführlich bearbeitet von D. Georg. H. A. Ewald:" *Leipzig*, 1827, p. 365. It would be out of place, in a popular lecture, to enter into the minute confirmations of a grammatical rule. I will therefore observe in this note, that, besides the examples given by Ewald from Job, xxvii. 23, but especially Is. xliv. 15, 17, which is quite satisfactory, other considerations confirm the singular rendering of לָמוֹ 1. The suffix מוֹ attached to nouns is certainly singular in Ps. xi. 7.—פָּנֵימוֹ "*his* face," speaking of God. A plural suffix is never referred to the name יְהוָה as a *plurale majestatis* (Ewald, *ib.*), and hence Gensenius supposes the use of the suffix to have been a mistake of the author's (*ubi sup.* p. 216). 2. In Ethiopic the suffix יֹמֵי is certainly singular. Lud. De Deu. *Crit. Sacra.* p. 226. *Animad.* in V. T. p. 547. This pronoun seems to be common not only to both numbers, but also to both genders, as it seems to be feminine in Job, xxxix. 7.

by fixed and correct rules in its interpretation? I well understand the force of this question, which will receive, perhaps, a sufficient answer in what I shall presently say. But when I speak of hermeneutics as a science, I mean that regular digest of principles and rules which qualifies the student to study, with comparative facility, God's holy word; and just as we have certainly better grammars of the Greek and Latin languages than those who spoke them, without our therefore claiming to know or understand them better than they, so has modern diligence collected and arranged with care those principles of sacred hermeneutics, founded on reason and logic, which are to be found scattered in the writings of the ancients, and were applied by them when interpreting literally, without referring to them as rules.

I am not afraid of this last assertion being disputed. It is true that the Fathers often run into allegories and mysteries which the taste of the age required, and which conduced to the moral instruction of their readers or hearers. It is true, that when commenting even literally, they do not always follow those theoretical maxims which they have themselves clearly laid down, but prefer appropriate theological discussions, to the less engaging occupation of the scholiast. But, notwithstanding this, I do not hesitate to affirm, that the best principles of biblical interpretation are to be found in their treatises, and the most judicious and acute application of them in their commentaries.

The Fathers knew very well the difference between literal and allegorical interpretation. St. Ephrem, for instance, is careful to warn his readers when he is going to neglect the literal for the mystical sense.* Indeed, Junilius has assured us, that a course, introductory to Scripture, was delivered in the Syriac school of Nisibis, in which St. Ephrem lived; and has given a compendium of the principles there taught. These he collected from

* See "Horæ Syriacæ," p. 54; and Gaab's Essay on the method of commenting followed by St. Ephrem in the "Memorabilien" of Paulus. No. i. pp. 65, *seqq.*

the mouth of a Persian scholar, and they certainly compress in a few words the chief substance of modern hermeneutics.* The merit of St. Chrysostom as a literal commentator, who knows how to use all the pretended improvements of modern biblists, is acknowledged by Winer, a critic of the severest school.† Nor does he deny unequivocal praise to his disciple Theodoret.‡ But as I am upon the subject, you will, I trust, indulge me a few moments while I trace an important revolution in the opinions of the moderns, and show how the increasing attention to this branch of theology, has served to vindicate the early writers of Christianity. A few years ago it was the fashion to consider the Fathers of the Church as devoid of fixed or solid principles of interpretation, and their commentaries as a tissue of blunders or mistakes. The progress of hermeneutics has produced this fruit, among others, that this prejudice has worn away, and those learned and pious men have regained, in modern works, that respect and deference which had been so inconsistently refused them. Two examples of this change of sentiment will fully justify my assertion.

Of St. Augustine, the candid Ernesti has written, that "had he been acquainted with Hebrew and Greek, the greatness and subtlety of his genius would have raised him to a pre-eminence above all ancient commentators."§ Guarded as this praise may be, it is the language of panegyric when compared with the unmeasured censure and scurrilous language of the elder

---

* "De Partibus Divinæ Legis," in "Biblioth. magna Pat. Col." tom. vi. p. ii.
† "In iis enim, quas ad singulos SS. libros confecit homilias, nihil antiquius habet, nisi sensuum et singulorum verborum et integrorum commatum e loquendi usu, ex historiis, e scriptorum denique sacrorum consiliis explicare, eaque in re idoneam probavit solertiam, ita ut si qua parum recte nihil tamen temere dictum reperiatur."—"Pauli ad Galatas Epistola Græce, perpetua annotatione illustravit Dr. G. Ben. Winer;" Lips. 1828, p. 15. Of what modern commentator can as much be said?
‡ Ib. p. 16.
§ "Instit. Interp. N. T." Lips. 1809, p. 342.

Rosenmüller. In his *History of the Interpretation of Scripture in the Christian Church,** which had been for some years a book of reference in Germany, he undertakes to discuss the character and merits of that holy bishop. He details the wanderings of his youth, in order to conclude that he rather "obscured than illustrated the sacred writings;" and that, as " he preferred the authority of his master, St. Ambrose, to all the principles of sound reason, it is no wonder that the disciple was no wiser than his master."† That St. Augustine was not unacquainted with the principles of interpretation, Rosenmüller is not bold enough to deny; but his conclusion is, " Augustinum nomine interpretis vix esse dignum;" nor does he even allow him that acuteness and talent which Ernesti so unrestrictedly concedes.‡ Such a character of the learned and pious Bishop of Hippo, is, however, worthy of a history which gives the first rank, among Christian commentators, to the heretics Pelagius and Julian !§

But a vindicator has not been wanting; and the merits of this great Father have been diligently canvassed, and solidly demonstrated, within these few years, by Dr. Henry Clausen. His interesting little volume, published at Copenhagen, has placed the merits of St. Augustine, as a biblical scholar, in a new and honourable light.‖ It is there proved, that he was sufficiently acquainted with Greek to make a useful application of it in his commentaries;¶ that he has laid down clearly all those principles " which are the stamina and first elements of chaste and sound criticism;"** that

---

* " D. Jo. Georg. Rosenmülleri Historia Interpretationis Librorum SS. in Ecclesia Christiana," 5 parts: *Hildburg* and *Leips.* 1798, 1814.
† Pars iii. *Lips.* 1807, pp. 404, 406.
‡ " Augustine is not worthy of the name of an interpreter."—Pages 500, *seqq.*
§ Pages 505, 537.
‖ " Aurelius Augustinus Hipponensis Sacræ Scripturæ Interpres ;" *Haunæi,* 1827, 8vo. 271 pp. The author is a Protestant.
¶ Pages 33, 39 ; cf. Rosenmüll. l. c. p. 404.
** Page 135.

he has both diffusely given, and condensed all the best maxims of hermeneutics;* that by the good use of these, joined to his natural sagacity, he has been frequently most happy in elucidating the obscurities of Scripture;† in confuting, by accurate research, the erroneous interpretations of others;‡ and that he has frequently removed difficulties by acutely penetrating the views of the inspired writers, and adducing parallel texts.

St. Jerome, the illustrious contemporary and friend of St. Augustine, has been the object of still falser obloquy, conveyed in even coarser terms. Of him Luther had said, that, instead of reckoning him a Doctor of the Church, he considered him a heretic, though he believed him to have been saved through his faith in Christ. He adds, " I know none among the Doctors to whom I am more an enemy than Jerome, because he writes only of fasting, meats, and virginity."§ But the elder Rosenmüller is more definite, and more violent in his charges against him as a biblical expositor. He scarcely allows him a single good quality. According to him, his knowledge of the languages, and of Palestine, is fully counterbalanced by his groundless etymologies, his rabbinical subtleties,

---

* Pages 137, *seqq.* St. Augustine names three qualities, with which any one attempting the illustration of Scripture should be furnished : 1. A knowledge of the Hebrew and Greek languages (*scientia linguarum*, or, as he elsewhere explains himself, *linguæ Hebræ et Græcæ cognitio*). 2. A knowledge of biblical archæology (*cognitione rerum quarundam necessarium*), elsewhere detailed as a knowledge of the philosophy, history, physics, and literature of the Bible. 3. An acquaintance with the critical rules for discussing the proper reading of the text (*adjuvante codicum veritate quam solers emendationis diligentia procuravit*).—De Doct. Christ. l. i. c. i. *Clausen*, p. 140.
† Pages 181, *seqq.*
‡ Pages 207, *seqq.*
§ "Hieronymus soll nicht unter die Lehrer der Kirche mitgerechnet noch gezählet werden; denn er ist ein Ketzer gewesen; doch glaube ich, dass er selig sey durch den Glauben an Christum. Ich weiss keinen unter den Lehrern dem ich so feind bin, als Hieronymus; denn er schreibt nur von Fasten, Speisen, und Jungfrauschaft."— "Luther's sämmlichte Schriften :", Th. xxii. p. 2070, ed. Walch.

and his total inability to seize the views of his author!* Nay, these are the lightest of his failings; what erudition he did possess, he only employed to pervert the doctrines of Christianity, nor can he be considered as possessing the slightest pretensions to theological knowledge!†

For a change of opinion among modern scholars, upon the merits of this Father, we need not step beyond the family of his accuser. The younger Rosenmüller, by his eulogiums and practical approbation, has compensated for the scurrilous and indecent censures of his father. He has observed, that the commentaries of this learned doctor must be held in the greatest estimation, on account of the learning with which he always supports whatever interpretations he embraces.‡ He is not content with verbal praise, for the constant use made in his commentaries, of the exegetical labours of our Father, amply shows the sincere estimation in which he holds them. Through his *Scholia* on the minor prophets, he seldom has occasion to depart from the sentiments of his illustrious guide.

I have detained you long on an early period of biblical literature, because it proves, that even the *history* of hermeneutics is an advancing science; and

---

* Rosenmüller, *ubi sup.* p. 346.
† I trust it will be with deserving indignation, that the following bitter passages are read, by all who value the venerable ornaments of early Christianity:—" Maxime autem dolendum, est, hunc tantum virum eruditione sua tam turpiter abusum esse, ad pervertendam doctrinam Christianam, in sacris literis traditam, atque ad omnis generis superstitiones defendendas et propagandas." He then proceeds to attribute to him, " immodicum studium suas absurdissimas opiniones tuendi, incredibilis animi impotentia et superstitio, furor quo abreptus," &c., p. 369.—" Ex hactenus dictis satis, ut opinor, apparet, Sanctum (si Diis placet) Hieronymum cum omni sua eruditione hebraica, græca, latina, geographica, &c. fuisse Monachorum superstitiosissimum, omnis veræ eruditionis theologicæ expertem. Ut paucis dicamus, religioni plus nocuit quam profuit."—Page 393.
‡ " Ezechielis Vaticinia:" *Lips.* 1826, vol. i. p. 26. We may forgive filial affection, when he refers us to the work of his father for the character of St. Jerome, whom he himself portrays so differently.— Page 25.

that its advance has served to remove prejudices against the early writers of Christianity, and to vindicate their character from the rash and unwarranted aggressions of the liberal school.

Having thus shown that, however modern this science may be in its code, it is as ancient as Christianity in its principles, we must pass over the lapse of a thousand years of its history, and approach nearer our own times. Upon the revival of letters, numerous commentators arose among our divines, whose works have shared the obloquy heaped upon those of the fifth century. It has been esteemed a duty to decry the voluminous productions of these diligent, and often sagacious, expositors, as a mere mass of literary rubbish, fit, perhaps, to fill the shelves of a library, but not to encumber the table of the student.

But though they are often too prolix, and tend too much to allegorical interpretation, it would be injustice to deny, that in the diligent collection and discussion of others' opinions, in a sagacious examination of the context and bearing of a passage, and in the happy removal of serious difficulties, they have cleared the way for their successors, and effected much more than these are always careful to acknowledge. The commentary, for instance, of Pradus and Villalpandus, on Ezechiel, which was published at Rome, from 1596 to 1604, is still the great repertory to which every modern scholiast must recur, in explaining the difficulties of that book, and is acknowledged, by the most learned of them, to be "a work replete with varied erudition, and most useful to the study of antiquity."[*] The annotations of Agelli upon the Psalms, published also at Rome in 1606, have been pronounced by the same writer, after Ernesti, the work of a "most learned and most sagacious author, who is peculiarly happy in explaining the relations of the Alexandrian and Vulgate versions."[†] Even

---

[*] Rosenmüller, "Ezechielis Vaticinia," vol. i. *Lips.* 1826, p. 32.
[†] "Psalmi," vol. i. *Lips.* 1821, Præf. (p. 5).

greater commendations are lavished by the learned and ingenious Schultens, upon the Spanish Jesuit Pineda, whose notes upon Job (*Madrid*, 1597) he acknowledges to " have eased him of no small part of his labours." He styles their author, " Theologus et Literator eximius, magnus apud suos, apud nos quoque."* Maldonatus on the Gospels has been praised and recommended by Ernesti, though, as might be expected, the recommendation is recalled in harsh terms, by his annotator Ammon.† When, some years ago, it was proposed in Germany to republish Calmet's commentaries, the very mention of such a scheme excited the ridicule of the liberal school;‡ yet I have been assured by a very sound scholar, that he had compared his notes on Isaiah with Lowth's, and had generally found the most beautiful illustrations of the English bishop anticipated by the learned Benedictine. Another learned friend has pointed out to me considerable transcriptions from him, in modern annotators, without the slightest acknowledgment.§ But no one has put the truth of these observations in a stronger light than my late amiable and excellent friend, Professor Ackermann, in his commentary on the Minor Prophets ‖ Through the whole of this work, the opinions of the old Catholic divines have been collected and honourably mentioned. It is pleasing to see these writers, whose names it has become so unfashionable to quote, once more treated with respect; and there is something almost amusing in the frequent juxtaposition of Rosenmüller and Cornelius a Lapide, Oedmann and Figueiro, Hort and De Castro.

---

* " Liber Jobi cum nova versione et commentario perpetuo :" *Lug. Bat.* 1737, tom. i. Præf. (p. 11).

† " Inst. Jut." p. 353.

‡ If I remember right, there is a paper on this subject, somewhere in " Eichhorn's Allgemeine Bibliothek."

§ For instance, Rosenmüller's " Prophetæ Minores," vol. ii. *Lips.* 1813, pp. 337, *seqq.* is taken almost verbatim from Calmet's preface on Jonas, " Commentaire litéral," vol. vi. p. 893, fol. *Par.* 1726.

‖ " Prophetæ Minores perpetua annotatione illustrati a Dre. P. F. Ackermann :" *Vienna*, 1830.

If I have wandered into such long digressions upon the older commentators, you will allow that the results obtained bear strongly upon my subject, and unite their conclusions with the general issue of these discourses. For it will, I trust, have appeared, that the study and application of hermeneutics, though not digested into a system, have always been followed in the Church, and that the progress of the science has removed old prejudices, and vindicated the memory of men entitled to the respect and gratitude of every Christian.

From them I must turn to a very different class. After the middle of the last century, Semler gave the first impulse to what he denominated the liberal interpretation of the Scriptures. A denial of inspiration, the resolution of every miracle into an allegory, or a vision, or a delusion, or a natural event clothed in oriental exaggeration, and a total denial of prophecy, are the characteristics of his school. That belief in inspiration cannot be required from any Protestant divine, Semler argues from the acknowledged principles of all the Reformed Churches.* For this impious explanation of miracles, actual rules have been laid down by Ammon;† and practical applications of them abound in the works of Eichhorn, Paulus, Gabler, Schuster, Rettig, and many others. But it is chiefly on the progress of hermeneutics in the interpretation of prophecy, that I wish to detain you a few moments; because, by it the Old Testament principally is connected with the evidences of Christianity.

Any one accustomed, as you have been, to hear the prophecies of the Old Testament treated, not merely with respect, but with veneration, must be shocked to see with what open liberty they are handled by authors of this school. De Wette, for instance, never thinks,

* In his preface to "Vogel's Compendium of Schultens on the Proverbs:" *Halle*, 1769, p. 5.
† "De interpretatione narrationum mirabilium N. T." prefixed to his Ernesti, ed. *sup. cit.* He seems, however, to allow some miracles, p. xiv.

in his Introductory Manual, of even noticing the belief that there is such a thing as real prediction, in the writings of Isaiah, or of his fellow prophets. The only difference between them and the seers of pagan nations is, that " these wanted the true and moral spirit of monotheism, by which the Hebrew prophecy was purified and consecrated."* I will not farther shock you by following the history of this wretched school, the impieties of which have unfortunately so widely prevailed on the Continent, as to be openly taught by persons holding theological chairs in Protestant universities, and published by men who call themselves, on their title-page, pastors of Protestant congregations. It will be sufficient to state, that the late Professor Eichhorn reduced to system the rationalist theory of prophecy, and pretended to establish a complete parallelism between the messengers of the true God and the soothsayers of heathenism.†

With such principles as these, we must expect to find the interpretation of prophecies dreadfully perverted. Hence, in many modern commentaries, the predictions relating to the Messiah are either totally overlooked, or systematically attacked. Jahn, though a rash unsound writer, did something towards vindicating and illustrating many of them;‡ and the prophecies in the Psalms are much indebted to Michaelis for an able defence.§ In Rosenmüller there is much inequality; on some occasions, he takes the side of our adversaries, as on the 53rd chapter of Isaiah, and in impugning the genuineness of the latter portion of that book. On other occasions, he stands forth as a learned and able advocate for the prophetic sense; and I need only instance his annotations

---

* "Lehrbuch der historisch-kritischen Einleitung. Zweyte verbesserte Auflage :" *Berlin*, 1822, p 279.
† "Einleitung in das Alte Testament," 4th ed. *Götting.* 1824, vol. iv. p. xlv.
‡ "Appendix Hermeneut." *Vienna*, 1813, 1815.
§ "Critisches Collegium über die drey wichtigsten Psalmen von Christo :" *Frankf. & Götting.* 1759.

on the 45th Psalm, and his dissertation on the celebrated prediction in Isaiah vii.*

The depraved state into which hermeneutical science had thus sunk, was sure to produce a reaction, and, through it, a return to better principles. This has already in a great measure been the case, and works have appeared, which, having profited by the great erudition brought into play on the other side, have drawn some good out of the mass of evil accumulated on this study. For they have fully shown that the learning and ingenuity displayed in attacking divine prophecy, may be well enlisted in the better cause, and retain all their brilliant, though they lose their dazzling power. I will only notice the work of Hengstenberg upon the prophecies regarding Christ, in which the series of prophetic announcement is analysed and vindicated with great sagacity, and solid learning. The doctrines of a suffering Messiah, and of Christ's divinity, as foretold in the Old Testament, are admirably exposed; all that Rabbins and Fathers, oriental and classical writers, can contribute, is lucidly and effectively brought together; the objections of adversaries are skilfully solved or removed, and a great felicity and tact is exhibited in unravelling the sense of obscure phraseology.† We may, indeed, say, that in his hands the very science, which till lately appeared ruinous to the cause of inspired truth, becomes a most efficient instrument for its vindication.

Allow me now to give you what I consider an example of a higher order of application; and, pardon me if, for a few moments, I depart from the popular form which I have endeavoured to preserve throughout these Lectures; for the subject may well seem to merit, and certainly requires, more learned disquisition. Among some arguments urged by Michaelis for rejecting the two first chapters of St. Matthew's gospel, is one founded on

---

* "Jesajæ Vaticin." tom. i. p. 292.
† "Christologie des alten Testaments, und Commentar über die messianischen Weissagungen der Propheten:" *Berlin*, 1829, vol. i. parts i. ii. Other parts have since been published.

the following circumstance. They contain several references to the Old Testament, introduced by the formulas, "all this was done, *that it might be fulfilled* which the Lord spoke by the prophets;"[*] "*for so it is* written by the prophet;"[†] "*that it might be fulfilled* which the Lord spoke by the prophet;"[‡] "*then was fulfilled* that which was spoken.[§] According to him, the texts thus quoted do not appear literally to correspond to the events to which they are applied; and he refuses to consider them as mere quotations, or adaptations, on account of the strong forms of introduction. No examples, he observes, can be brought, of any phrase, so strong as the ones which I have quoted, being used to introduce a mere accommodation of a text. He must, therefore, consider the writer's meaning to be, that the circumstances which he describes, truly formed the fulfilment of those ancient prophecies. Now, proceeding on the principle of private interpretation, he thinks they cannot be so taken; and, as an inspired writer could not have committed an error, he will rather attribute those chapters to some other, and that an uninspired author, than bend these phrases to signify simply an adaptation of Scripture texts.[‖]

It is this objection which I wish to meet. I am not going to examine the texts singly, and prove that they may well be considered applicable to the events of our Saviour's life; I wish to meet the broad question, and show how the progress of oriental research cuts away the ground from under the rationalist's feet, and totally overthrows the chief argument on which the rejection of those two important chapters has been based.

Most commentators, Catholic and Protestant, will be found to agree, that some texts, even when thus introduced, may be mere allegations, without its being intended to declare that the literal fulfilment took place on the occasion described. Many writers have taken

---

[*] Matt. i. 22.   [†] Matt. ii. 5.   [‡] Matt. ii. 15.   [§] Matt. ii. 17.
[‖] Michaelis's "Introduction to the New Testament," vol. i. pp. 206, 214, Marsh's translation.

great pains to prove, that even the forms of expression which I have cited, are not incompatible with this idea; and for this purpose, they have chiefly used the writings of the Rabbins, and of classical authors. Thus, Surenhusius produced a large volume upon the forms of quotation used by the Rabbins; but did not adduce a single passage where the word *fulfilled* occurs.* Dr. Sykes asserts, that such expressions are to be found in every page of Jewish writers; but does not quote one single example.† Knapp repeats the same assertion, saying "that the Hebrew and Chaldaic verb, מלא, and the Chaldaic and Rabbinical words, אשלים, תקן, and גמר, signify to *consummate*, or *confirm* a thing."‡ He then gives an example of the first word, from 1 Kings, i. 14, where the meaning is only, " I will *complete* your words." Prof. Tholuck has, indeed, brought several examples from the Rabbins to establish this meaning. The two strongest are these:—" He who eats and drinks, and afterwards prays, *of him it is written,* ' Thou hast cast me behind thy back.' "—" Since the שמיר (*Shamir*, a fabulous animal) has destroyed the temple, the current of divine grace, and pious men, has ceased, *as it is written,* Psal. xii. 2." To these he has added a passage from the chronicle of Barhebræus, a Syriac writer of a much later age. It simply says—"They saw the anger *whereof the prophet says,* I will bear the anger of the Lord, because I have sinned."§ The force of which

* Βιβλος καταλλαγης. *Amsterd.* 1713.
† "Truth of the Christian Religion:" *Lond.* 1725, pp. 203, 296.
‡ Georgii, Christ. Knapp. "Scripta varii argumenti maximam partem exagetici et historici argumenti," ed. 2, *Halle,* 1823, tom. ii. p. 523.
§ "Commentar zu dem Evangelio Johannis:" *Hamb.* 1827, p. 68. Some years ago this learned professor asked me whether, in the course of reading, I had met with passages, in Syriac writers, calculated to remove these difficulties, and to illustrate the phrases in question. I pointed out the examples given in the text; and, at his request, furnished him with a copy, and gave him full permission to use them. It is possible, therefore, that they may have appeared in some German work which I have not seen; and I consequently feel it right to mention the circumstance, lest I should be suspected of taking to myself credit for any other person's industry.

words extends no farther than this—"they saw the anger of the Lord." Mr. Sharpe, and others, have quoted a few passages from Greek classics; but they are far from coming up to the determinate and strong form of the phrases in the New Testament.* For, after all, Michaelis's observation stands good, that none of them equal in force the words, "Then was fulfilled that which was spoken by the prophet;" and his annotator's question remains unanswered, " was this expression used in this sense by the Rabbins?"†

One example, however, may seem to escape this censure. It is a passage quoted by Wetstein from the compendium of St. Ephrem's life given in Assemani's *Bibliotheca Orientalis;* where an angel thus addresses the saint:— ܐܙܕܗܪ ܕܠܡܐ ܢܬܡܠܐ ܒܟ ܗܘ ܕܟܬܝܒ "Take care lest that *be fulfilled in thee which is written,* 'Ephraim is a heifer,'" &c.‡ This instance, however, did not appear to Michaelis satisfactory, because, I suppose, it was unsupported by others, and on account of its admonitory form.§

The field, therefore, may be considered open, and worthy to occupy the attention of scholars. Now, though it may appear presumptuous, I think I have it in my power to solve the difficulty, simply by the course which I have been endeavouring to suggest through these Lectures, by the prosecution, however feebly, of the very study to which it belongs. In endeavouring to meet it, I need not premise that I, by no means, allow any validity to Michaelis's arguments, or mean to admit that the quotations in St. Matthew's first chapters may not be proved accurately applicable to the events there described. On these points there is very much to be said; but I wish to waive the long

---

* Ap. Horne, "Introduction," vol. ii. p. 444, note.
† "Notes on Michaelis," vol. i. p. 487.
‡ "Assem. B. O." tom. i. p. 35. "Acta S. Ephr. Oper." tom. iii. p. 36. Wetstein in Mat. i. 22.
§ Vol. i. p. 214.

investigation into which they would lead us, and simply take up the question upon the objector's own grounds, and prove that, even granting all that he assumes, he has no reason for rejecting that portion of Scripture, or impugning the inspiration of its writer. In other words, I wish to show, that, even if those texts could not be applied to certain events, otherwise than by accommodation, the phrases which introduce them will easily bend to that explanation, and so destroy the argument drawn from their force. For I will show you, by examples from the earliest Syriac writers, that in the East similar expressions were used for accommodating Scriptural phrases to individuals, to whom the writers could not possibly have believed them primarily or originally to refer.

1. The phrase "to be fulfilled" is so used, and that in a declaratory form, and not merely as in the instance given by Wetstein. In a fuller life of St. Ephrem than the one which he quotes, we have this remarkable passage:—ܠܚܢܢܝܐ. ܕܡܐܢܐ ܗܘ ܠܝ ܘܫܠܡܬ ܠܟܠܗܘܢ ܓܒܝܐ. ܕܐܬܐܡܪܬ ܡܠܬܐ ܡܛܠ ܦܘܠܘܣ—"And *in him was fulfilled* the word which was spoken concerning Paul to Ananias: he is a vessel of election to me."* The author is here speaking of St. Ephrem, and clearly expresses himself, that the words which he applies to him were really spoken of another. But the saint himself, the oldest writer extant in that language, uses this phrase in a more remarkable manner. For thus he speaks of Aristotle:—ܕܩܕܡܝܐ ܘܐܚܪܝܐ ܠܐ ܗܘܐ ܕܢܣܝܒܘܬܐ ܐܫܬܠܡܬ ܐܚܘܬܗ ܡܛܠ ܫܠܝܡܘܢ ܚܟܝܡܐ ܗܘ ܕܟܬܝܒܐ ܒܟܠܗܘܢ "*In him was fulfilled* that which was written concerning Solomon the Wise; 'that of those who were before or after, there has not been one equal to him in wisdom.'"†

* "St. Ephrem Oper." tom. iii. p. xxiv.
† Serm. i. tom. ii. p. 317.

2. The expression, *as it is written*, or *as the prophet says*,* is used precisely in the same manner. St. Ephrem uses it manifestly to introduce a mere adaptation of a scriptural text.—ܕܟܠܝܗܘܢ ܐܠܝܢ ܕܒܛܥܝܘ ܐܣܪ ܕܟܕ ܘܩܡ ܣܢܘ ܠܥܘܕܪܢܐ ܕܟܬܝܒ ܕܐܝܟ ܕܕܡܟ "Those who are in error have hated the source of assistance: *as it is written*, 'The Lord awoke like one who slept.'"† To see the force of this application, the entire passage must be read. I pass over some less decided examples,‡ and hasten on.

3. Even the strongest of all such expressions, "this is he of whom it is written," is used with the same freedom by these early oriental writers. In the Acts of St. Ephrem, which I have more than once quoted, it is so applied. For example, speaking of the Saint—ܕܐܡܪ ܥܠܘܗܝ ܕܐܚܘܕ ܗܘ ܕܐܡܪ ܦܪܘܩܢ ܕܐܬܝܬ—"This *is he of whom our Saviour said*, 'I came to cast fire upon the earth.'"§ In another place the same text is applied to him by St. Basil, in still more definite terms.‖

Still further to confirm these illustrations, I will observe that the Arabs, in quoting their sacred book, the Koran, apply it in this manner to passing events. I will give you one or two instances out of many which I have noticed. In a letter from Amelic Alaschraf Barsebai to Mirza Schahrockh, son of Timur, published

* Matt. ii. 6.
† Serm. xxxiii. Adv. Hæres. tom. ii. p. 513. To such as are conversant with the Syriac language, I would observe, that the Latin version translates the word ܛܥܝܐ by *amentes*, whereas throughout all these sermons it means *wanderers*, or heretics. Cf. pp. 526, 527, 559, &c. By it St. Ephrem seems to mean the Manicheans.
‡ For instance, in the Acts of St. Ephrem, p. xxv. where, however, only a moral precept is cited, which in fact does not occur in the Bible. Again, tom. ii. p. 487, where "as it is written" introduces a quotation.
§ Page xxxviii.
‖ Page xlviii. He expressly says, "This is he *of whom* our Saviour said," &c., whereas in the other text the words in italics are understood. Assemani, the translator of this life, renders the phrase by "propterea ipsi *accommodatum iri* illa Domini verba," &c.

by De Sacy, we have these words:—" We, indeed, if the Most High had wished it, could not prevail over you; but *he has promised us victory* in the venerable book of God, saying, ' Then we gave you the advantage over them.' "* Which words were clearly spoken of a quite different person. The following example approaches more to the phrases in question:—ما أوديت

"فلنا اسوة برسول الله في قوله ماأردي نبي—" We resemble the Prophet, *when he says*, ' Never did prophet suffer what I suffer.' "†

I fear lest this disquisition may have proved tedious to many; if so, I will only request them to consider how important its object may well appear. For it is directed to wrench out of the hands of rash scholars, a pretended argument for rejecting two of the most important and beautiful chapters of gospel history. It serves, too, as another illustration, of how continued application to any pursuit, is sure to obtain possession of a sufficient clue to unravel the difficulties drawn from its lower stages.

Desultory as the subjects of which I have treated may appear, they have, I trust, presented a variety of points illustrative of the object pursued in these Lectures. In every one of the members which compose the direct study of the Bible, we have seen a natural onward progress; and in every instance the spontaneous consequence of that progress has been the removal of prejudice, the confutation of objections, and the confirmation of the truth. I will only add, that the personal and practical application of the various pursuits which have been grouped together in this Lecture, will satisfy any one, that even in that confined form they have the same power of development, and the same saving virtue. Experience has long since satisfied me, that

---

* De Sacy, "Chrestomathie Arabe," 1st ed. Arab. text, p. 256, vers. tom. ii. p. 325.
† Humbert, "Anthologie Arabe:" *Paris*, 1819, p. 112.

every text, which Catholics advance in favour of their doctrines controverted by Protestants, will stand those rigid tests to which modern science insists upon submitting every passage under discussion. This, however, is the province of dogmatic or polemic theology, and therefore must not be intruded upon here.

The study of God's word, and the meditation upon its truths, surely forms our noblest occupation. But when that study is conducted upon severe principles, and with the aid of deep research, it will be found to combine the intellectual enjoyment of the mathematician, with the rapture of the poet, and ever to open new sources of edification and delight, to some of which I hope to open you a way in my next discourse.

LECTURE THE ELEVENTH;

ORIENTAL LITERATURE.

PART II.

PROFANE STUDIES.

INTRODUCTORY Remarks. *Illustrations* of particular passages —Collections of Oriental customs and ideas from travellers.—The growing nature of such illustrations exemplified in Gen. xliv. 5, 15.—Difficulties raised by earlier writers; illustrations furnished by later authors.—Luke, ii. 4, supposed to be not comformable to any known law among the ancients; difficulties removed by a passage of an Oriental author.—Geographical elucidations lately made by Messrs. Burton and Wilkinson.—*Philosophy of Asia*. General remarks on the confirmation it gives of the fundamental principles of Christian faith, by the unity of its conclusions in different countries.—On the Oriental philosophy.—Its influence on the Jewish doctrines; Scriptural phrases illustrated by Bendsten.—Sabian doctrines; their use in explaining some parts of the New Testament.—Opinions of the Samaritans, lately ascertained, remove a difficulty in John, iv.—Chinese school of Lao-tseu; its doctrine of the Trinity shown to be probably derived from the Jews.—Indian philosophy; excessive antiquity attributed to it; opinions of the moderns; Colebrooke, the Windischmanns, Ritter. Supposed antiquity of the Ezour Vedam; the work discovered to be modern.—*Historical researches.* Serious historical difficulty in Is. xxxix. removed by a newly-discovered fragment of Berosus.—Attack on the origin of Christian rites, from their resemblance to the Lamaic worship. Discovery, from Oriental works, of the modern origin of that system.

IN my last Lecture, I treated of those illustrations of the sacred text which had its own substance for their object, whether in the letter or in its signification. There are obviously many of another class, which oriental studies must afford, similar to those which we have seen furnished by other sciences. In fact, there is no branch of literature so rich in biblical vindications and illustrations, as those studies which I have characterized as " Profane Oriental Literature." The epithet here given is unfortunately equivocal, and I wish we had some other to substitute in its place. The term "profane," when applied to studies not essentially connected with sacred subjects, seems almost to cast a reproach upon them. Being often used to express not merely the absence of a peculiarly sacred character, but the addition of positive unholiness, and applied to express the guilt of acts otherwise indifferent, it has unfortunately the same force in the minds of some, when applied to literary pursuits. Among the errors of thought which the use of equivocal words has introduced, there are few more hurtful, and yet few more common, than this. In my concluding Lecture I may have occasion to notice the opposition made at all times by many to human learning; for the present I will only observe, that they are the epithets by which it has been distinguished from more sacred studies, which have chiefly led weak minds to their rash decision. The names of *secular*, or *human*, or still more *profane* learning, have in reality suggested or encouraged the abhorrence which such men have felt and expressed for all but theological pursuits.

These terms, however, are all relative, and only framed thus strongly to exalt the other, which necessarily excels them, as all things directed to the spirit and its profit, must surpass whatever is but the offspring of earth. But wisdom and knowledge, wherever found, are gifts of God, and the fruits of the right use of faculties by him given; and as we find that the Christians of former ages scrupled not to represent on their most sacred monuments the effigies of men whose science or graceful literature had adorned the world even in ages of paganism, so may we consider the learning of such men well worthy of a place among the illustrations and ornaments of the holy religion to which those buildings were devoted.

At the same time, therefore, that I esteem such pursuits most worthy of our attention, the consideration of what I have remarked leaves me no scruple in placing among profane literature, such illustrations of Holy Writ, as may be found in oriental writers of the most venerable character, and of the most holy minds. For I use the term in no other sense than as a conventional distinctive of a class of learning most useful and most commendable.

I shall divide the subject of this morning's entertainment into three parts: first, I will treat of such particular illustrations as eastern archæology may glean in the East; secondly, I will give a few instances of the influence which our growing acquaintance with the philosophy of Asia has had upon the vindication of religion; and thirdly, I will try to select one or two examples of the use to be made of oriental historical records.

The first of these classes has been long justly popular in this country. No other nation has sent so many enterprising travellers to explore the East; and it was natural to expect that it would take the lead in applying the results of their observations, which became a part of its literature, to the illustration of Scripture. Accordingly, we have been almost overrun with collections from travellers, of manners, customs, and opinions existing in Asia, and tending to throw some light upon the biblical narrative. Often the examples which follow the order of the books and chapters of Scripture, are quite unnecessary, sometimes they are insufficient; on all occasions they do not possess the value of systematic treatises on Scriptural antiquities, in which the results are digested, and compared with all the passages on which they seem to bear. It is hardly necessary to remark, that whatever advantage such compilations may present to religion and its sacred volume, is necessarily of a growing character. The mine is inexhaustible; every traveller succeeds in discovering some new coincidence between the ancient and modern occupants of Asia, and at every new edition, the works to which I have alluded swell in bulk, and increase the number of their volumes. Burder's "Oriental Customs and Literature," when translated by Rosenmüller into German, received great and valuable accessions, which have, in their turn, been translated, and added to the original work. I believe I should have to add to the number of my Lectures, were I to offer you the gleanings which I have made in this branch of literature, after the plentiful harvest of my predecessors. Well might the Oriental Translation Committee pronounce, not only that "the sacred Scriptures abound in modes of expression, and allusions to customs, in many cases imperfectly understood in Europe, but still prevailing in the East," but also, that many additional illustrations might be expected from the publication of more oriental authors.*

I will select one instance, almost at random, which seems to exemplify the increasing nature of such researches.

In Gen. xliv. 5, 15, mention is made of a cup in which Joseph divined; of course, keeping up the disguise which he had thought it necessary to assume. "The cup which you have stolen is that in which my lord drinketh, and *in which he is wont to divine* . . . . . . And he said to them, Why would you do so? know ye not that there is no one like me in the science of divining?" Now, formerly this gave rise to such a serious objection, that very able critics proposed an alteration in the reading or translation of the word; for it was supposed to allude to a custom completely without any parallel in ancient authors. "Who," exclaims Houbigant, "ever heard of auguries taken by the agency of a cup?"† Aurivillius goes still further: "I acknowledge," says he, "that such an interpretation

---

* "Report," *Lond.* 1829, p. 7.   † Note *in loc.*

might be probable, if it could be proved by the testimony of any creditable historian, that, either then or at any later period, the Egyptians used this method of divination."* Burder, in the first edition of his *Oriental Customs*, produced two methods of divining with cups, given by Saurin from Julius Serenus and Cornelius Agrippa, neither of them very applicable to this case.† The Baron Silvestre de Sacy was the first to show the existence of this very practice in Egypt in modern times, from an incident recounted in Norden's travels. By a singular coincidence, Baram Cashef tells the travellers that he had consulted his cup, and discovered that they were spies, who had come to discover how the land might best be invaded and subdued.‡ Thus we see the condition complied with on which alone Aurivillius, half a century ago, agreed to be satisfied with the sense at present given by the text. In the *Revue des Deux Mondes*, for August, 1833, a very curious and well-attested instance was given of the use of the divining-cup, as witnessed by the reporters in Egypt, in company with several English travellers, which bears a character highly marvellous and mysterious.

But so far from its being any longer difficult to find a single instance of this practice in Egypt, we may say, that no species of divining can be proved more common throughout the East. For instance, in a Chinese work, written in 1792, which contains a description of the kingdom of Thibet, among the methods of divining in use there, this is given: "Sometimes they look into a jar of water, and see what is to happen."§ The Persians, too, seem to have considered the cup as the principal instrument of augury; for their poets constantly allude to the fable of a celebrated

---

* "Dissertationes ad Sacras Literas et Philologiam Orientalem pertinentes," *Götting.* and *Lips.* 1790, p. 273.
† "Oriental Customs:" *Lond.* 1807, vol. i. p. 25.
‡ "Chrestomathie Arabe:" *Paris*, 1806, vol. ii. p. 513.
§ "Quelquefois ils regardent dans une jatte d'eau, et voient ce que doit arriver."—" Nouveau Journal Asiatique," *Oct.* 1829, p. 261.

divining-cup, originally the property of the demigod Dshemshid, who discoved it in the foundations of Estakhar, and from whom it descended to Solomon and Alexander, and formed the cause of all their success and glory. Guigniaut adds Joseph to the list of its possessors; but I know not on what authority.* All these examples suppose the augury to be taken by inspection. I will add another example of a different manner. This, the authority of the oldest Syriac Father, St. Ephrem, who tells us, that oracles were received from cups, by striking them, and noticing the sound which they emitted.† Thus, then, we see a growing series of illustrations of a passage not many years ago considered untenable, from its being unsupported by any.

And having produced this last example from a class of oriental literature too much neglected at present, I cannot refrain from giving one more illustration from it, of a difficulty which I believe has not as yet been removed. It is stated in Luke, ii. 4, that Joseph was obliged to go to Bethlehem, the city of David, there to be enrolled and taxed with his virgin spouse, on occasion of a general census. This was evidently an obligation; and yet there appears no other example of such a practice. Lardner proposes this difficulty, and suggests a solution from Ulpian, who tells us that all should be enrolled where their estate lies. " Though Joseph," says he, " was not rich, yet he might have some small inheritance at or near Bethlehem."‡ He was not, however, himself satisfied with this answer; because, as he observes, had Joseph possessed any land there (*ager* is the word used by Ulpian), some house would probably have been attached to it, or at least his tenant would have received him under his roof. And, moreover, the reason given is, " *because* he was of the house and family of David." Lardner, therefore,

---

* " On Creuzer," tom. i. part i. p. 312.
† " Opera omnia," tom. i. Syr. et Lat. *Rome*, 1737, p. 100.
‡ " Lardner's Works:" *Lond.* 1827, vol. i. p. 281.

further suggests, that it was some custom of the Jews, to be enrolled in tribes and families: but there could be no necessity for this troublesome method of observing it, nor has it been shown that such a custom ever existed. But the fact is, we have an example of this very practice in the same country in later times. Dionysius, in his chronicle, tells us, that " Abdalmelic made a census of the Syrians in 1692, and published a positive decree, that every individual should go to his country, his city, and his father's house, and be enrolled, giving in his name, and whose son he was; with an account of his vineyards, his oliveyards, his flocks, his children, and all his possessions." This, he adds, was the first census made by the Arabs in Syria.* This one instance is sufficient to take away all strange appearance from the circumstance as recorded in the Gospel, and makes it unnecessary to assign a reason for it.

I can hardly give any motive for allowing these instances a preference over many others, which would have equally shown how this branch of oriental pursuits, the inquiry into the habits and state, physical and moral, of the East, goes on, so long as it is pursued, removing all difficulties, and shedding new light upon Scriptural narratives.

To conclude this branch of my subject, I will notice the information lately gained upon Scripture geography by the discoveries in Egyptian literature. For instance, Mr. Burton has made us acquainted with the Zoan of Numbers (xiii. 22), and Ezechiel (xxx. 14), the hieroglyphic name for which he has discovered and published.†
In like manner, Mr. Wilkinson has cleared up the controversy respecting the No-Ammon, or No of Nahum (iii. 8), Jeremiah (xlvi. 25), and Ezechiel (*ib*.); for he has proved it to be the Egyptian name for the Thebais.‡
The Septuagint has indeed translated it by Diospolis,

---

* Assemani, " Biblioth. Orientalis," vol. ii. p. 104.
† " Excerpta Hieroglyph." No. iv.
‡ Communicated by Sir W. Gell, in the " Bulletino dell' Instituto di Corrispondenza Archeologica :" *Rome*, 1829, No. ix. pp. 104–106.

the ancient name of Thebes' among the Greeks. In fact, the name Thebes, or Thebæ, is supposed by Champollion to be the Egyptian word *Tapè*, the *head* or *capital*, in the Theban dialect. The Hebrew name, No-Ammon, is purely Egyptian, and signifies the *possession* or *portion* of the God *Amun*, by which the same version once renders it μερις Ἀμμων (Nahum, iii. 8).*

It must not be thought that the department of biblical illustration on which I have so long dwelt, has been entirely in the hands of such popular writers as I have before alluded to. On the contrary, the natural history of the East has been profoundly studied, since the time of Bochart and Celsius, by Oedmann and Forskäl, with wonderful success; the manners and costumes of the Jews have received invaluable light from Braun and Schröder; nay, we have a volume by Bynæus, replete with much curious erudition, *de calceis Hebræorum*,—on the shoes of the Hebrews. But let us pass forward to more important subjects.

The philosophy of the East may be viewed in many lights, and in each reflects differently upon sacred truths. We may simply consider the philosophy of different nations as the characterizing indication of their mind, as that distinctive which, in reference to the operations of their understandings, takes the place held by the outward features in regard to their characteristic passions. Every national philosophy must necessarily bear the impress of that peculiar system of thought which nature or social institutions, or some other modifying cause, has stamped upon the mind; it will be mystical, or merely logical, profound or popular, abstract or practical, according to the character of thought prevalent in the people. The experimental philosophy, which we owe to Bacon, is the exact type of the habit of thought pervading the English character, from the highest meditations of our sages, to the

---

* "Handbuch der biblischen Alterthumskunde," or "Biblische Geographie, von E. F. K. Rosenmüller," *Leipz.* 1828, dritter Band, p. 299.

practical reasoning of the peasant. The abstracting and contemplative, half-dreaming mysticism of the Hindoo, is no less the natural expression of his habitual calm and listlessness, the flow of bright deep thought, which must be produced in one who sits musing on the banks of his majestic streams. Where there are many sects, we may rely upon most of them professing foreign, and often uncongenial, doctrines. Hence arise those almost contradictory appearances in some parts of the best Greek philosophies, that admission of great truths, and yet the weakness of proofs, which we meet in their sublimest writer.

But hence it follows, that when we see all the philosophical systems of nations quite distinct in character, perfectly unlike each other in their logical processes, arriving at the same consequences, on all great points of moral interest to man, we are led to a choice of one of two conclusions; either that a primeval tradition, a doctrine common to the human species, and consequently given from the beginning, has flowed down to us through so many channels; or else, that these doctrines are so essentially, so naturally true, that the human mind, under every possible form, discovers and embraces them. Ancient philosophers concluded, from the consent of mankind in some common belief, that it must be correct; and thus did prove many precious and important doctrines. By the deeper study of the philosophy of many nations, we have advanced the force of this reasoning an immense step; for we now can tell the grounds on which they received them. Had we met one system in which the future and perpetual existence of man's soul was denied, and the denial supported by processes of reasoning, conducted on principles perfectly independent of foreign teaching, we certainly should have felt before us a difficulty, of some weight to overcome. But when we find the mysticism of the Indian arriving at the same conclusion as the synthetic reasoning of the Greek, we must be satisfied that the conclusion is correct. In the portions of the *Akhlak e Naseri*, a Persian work upon the soul, which Colonel Wilks has translated, all the questions relating to that portion of man are discussed with marvellous acuteness; and though, from some resemblance to the Greek philosophers, the translator thinks the reasoning is borrowed from them,* it seems to me that the turn of thought, and form of argumentation, display a decidedly original character.

Thus have we gained an additional force for our convictions upon points of belief essentially necessary, as the groundwork of Christianity, and still further developed by its teaching. But there are several systems of Asiatic philosophy, which come into close contact with the Scriptures, from their being alluded to in it, or perhaps attacked; and which being known, may throw considerable light upon particular passages.

The principal of these is what is commonly known under the name of the *Oriental philosophy*. This consists of that peculiarly mysterious system which formed the basis of the old Persian religion, and from which the earliest sects of Christianity sprung up; the belief in the conflict between opposite powers of good and evil, and in the existence of emanated influences, intermediate between the divine and earthly natures; and the consequent adoption of mystical and secret terms, expressive of the hidden relations between these different orders of created and uncreated beings. This philosophy pervaded all the East: there can be no doubt but that its influence was felt among the Jews at the time of our Saviour's coming, and that in particular the sect of Pharisees held much of its mysterious doctrines. It penetrated into Greece, affected greatly the Pythagorean and Platonic philosophies, and acted on the people through the secret religious mysteries. In many of its doctrines it approached so near to the truth, that the inspired writers were led to adopt some of its terms to expound their

---

* "Transactions of the Royal Asiatic Society of Great Britain and Ireland," vol. i. pp. 514, *seqq.* Lond. 1827.

doctrines. Hence it is, that our great acquaintance with its system of philosophy, from the greater attention paid to it, has tended to confirm and illustrate many phrases and passages formerly obscure. For instance, when Nicodemus either understood not, or affected not to understand, our Lord's expression that he must be "born again," we should be rather inclined to think such an expression by no means easy, and to consider the censure as severe: "Art thou a master in Israel, and understandest not these things?"* But when we discover that this was the ordinary figure by which the Pharisees themselves expressed, in their mystic language, the act of becoming a proselyte, and that the phrase belongs to that philosopy, and is used by the Brahmans of such as join their religion;† we at once perceive how such an obscure phrase should have been well understood by the person to whom it was addressed. Bendsten has carefully collected such ancient inscriptions as contain mystical allusions drawn from this hidden philosophy, and has produced several illustrations of phrases in the New Testament.‡ It may suffice to say, that such expressions as *light* and *darkness*, the *flesh* and the *spirit*, the representation of the body as a *vessel* or *tabernacle* of the soul, images so beautifully adapted for expressing the purest doctrines of Christianity, as none other at that time could be, all have been found to belong to this philosophy, and have thus lost the obscurity wherewith they used to be reproached.

But to come to one particular sect or modification of this system; a curious elucidation has been obtained of a difficult portion of the New Testament, by our acquaintance with a sect of Gnostics yet existing, but of whom little or nothing was known till the end of the last century. From a small treatise, of no great celebrity, published above a hundred years ago by F. Ignatius à Jesu, a

---

* John, iii. 3.
† See the author's "Lectures on the Real Presence:" *Lond.* 1836, p. 95. See Windischmann's "Philosophie," &c. p. 558.
‡ In the "Miscellanea Hafnensia," tom. i. *Copenhag.* 1816, p. 20.

missionary in Asia, Europe first became acquainted with a semi-Christian sect, settled chiefly in the neighbourhood of Bassora, evidently descended from the ancient Gnostics, but having a peculiar veneration for St. John the Baptist.* They are called Nasareans, Sabians, Mendeans, or disciples of John. The last is the name they give themselves. Evidence is not wanting to prove that they have existed from the earliest ages; and the whole of their belief is grounded upon the oriental philosophy, the system of emanations from the Deity. Prof. Norberg was the first who made this strange religion better known, by publishing, not many years ago, their sacred book, the Codex Adam, or Codex Nasaræus.† It is written in a peculiar character and dialect of very corrupt Syriac, and is extremely difficult to be understood. Their principal work, which Norberg so much desired to see published, is yet inedited. It is an immense roll covered with curious figures, and is called their Divan. The original copy is in the Museum of the Propaganda; from this I have had two fac-similes made, whereof one is in my possession, and I have brought it for your inspection; the other I have deposited in the Library of the Royal Asiatic Society in London.

It had been well known that St. John, in his writings, entirely attacked Gnostic sects, principally those known by the name of Ebionites, and Cerinthians. This circumstance explained many expressions otherwise obscure, and led us to understand why he so constantly insisted upon the reality of Christ's being in the flesh. It was evident that the first chapter of his gospel contained a series of aphorisms directly opposed to their tenets. For instance, as these Gnostics maintained the existence of many Æons, or emanated beings inferior to God, one of which they called "the Word," and another

* Ignatius à Jesu, "Narratio originis et errorum Christianorum S. Johannis."
† "Codex Nasaræus liber Adami appellatus," tom. i. *Hafniæ.* No date.

" the only begotten," another " the light," &c.; and
asserted the world to have been created by a malignant
spirit; St. John overthrows all these opinions, by showing that only *One* was born from the Father, who was
at once light, the word, and the only begotten, and by
whom all things were made.*

But there were other things in this sublime prologue,
not so easily explained. Why is the inferiority of the
Baptist so much insisted upon? why are we told that
he was not the light, but only a witness to the light;
and why is this twice repeated? Why are we told that
he was a mere man. These reiterated assertions must
have been directed against some existing opinions, which
required confutation as much as the others: yet we
knew of no sect that could appear to have suggested
them. The publication of the Sabian books has, to all
appearance, solved the difficulty.

When the Codex Nasaræus was first published, several
learned men applied its expressions to the illustration of
St. John's gospel. The evidence for this application was
at first considered strong,† but was afterwards, particularly, if I remember right, by Hug, rejected as of small
weight. Still, on looking over the book, I think we cannot
fail to be struck with opinions, manifestly ancient, which
seem exactly kept in view by the apostle, in the introduction to his gospel. First, the marked distinction
between light and life; secondly, the superiority of
John the Baptist to Christ; thirdly, the identification of
John with "the light."

The first of these errors was common, perhaps, to
other Gnostic sects; but, in the Codex Nasaræus, we
have the two especially distinguished as different beings.
In it the first emanation from God, is the king of light;
the second, fire; the third, water; and the fourth, life.‡
Now, this error St. John rejects in the fourth verse,
where he says, "and the light was life." The second

---

* St. Irenæus, " Adv. Hæres." lib. i. c. i. § 20.
† Michaelis, "Introduction," vol. iii. pp. 285, *seqq.*
‡ Norberg, p. viii.

error, that John was superior to Christ, forms the fundamental principle of this sect. Its members are called *Mende Jahia*, disciples of John, from this very circumstance. And an Arabic letter, from the Maronite Patriarch in Syria, published by Norberg, tells us that they worship John before Christ,* whom they carefully distinguish from " the life." In the third place, they identify John with " the light." These two last errors will be at once brought home to them by one passage, which I take without selection, upon opening the book. " Going forward, and coming to the prison of Jesus, the Messiah, I asked, ' Whose place of confinement is this?' I was answered, ' It overshadows those who have denied the life, and followed the Messiah.' "† The Messiah is then supposed to address the narrator in these words: " Tell us thy name, and show us thy mark, which thou receivedst from the water, the treasure of splendour, and the great baptism of the *Light*." And on seeing the mark, the Messiah adores him four times.‡ After this, the souls that are with him ask permission to return into the body, for three days, that they may be baptized in the Jordan, " in the name of this man who has passed above him."§ Here, then, we have John and his baptism superior to Christ; the Messiah distinguished from " the light," and the baptism of John called " the baptism of the Light." Now, we can hardly fail to observe, how pointedly the evangelist contradicts every one of these blasphemous opinions, when he tells us, that in Christ " was life;" that John " was not the light, but only a witness to it " (vv. 7, 8); and that John was inferior to Christ, according to his own testimony. And on this point, the very words of the gospel seem selected to meet the error. " John beareth witness, and crieth out, saying: ' This was he of whom I spake, *He that shall come after me shall be preferred before me*, because he was before me.' " (v. 15.)

---

* Notes to the Preface. † Tom. ii. p. 9.
‡ *Ib*. p. 11.
§ *Ib*. p. 13. " In nomine hujus viri qui te præteriit."

That the opinions of this strange sect have been much changed in the lapse of ages, we have every reason to suppose; but their conformity to the Gnostic system, and some historical evidence, prove that the religion is not modern; indeed, it seems to have sprung from those who only received the baptism of John. At any rate, the publication of these documents, and our better acquaintance with this sect, have shown opinions to have existed among the Gnostics, exactly corresponding to the errors condemned by St. John. Expressions, which before were unintelligible, have thus become clear; and the series of apparently unconnected propositions, or axioms, which compose his proem, and which seemed unnecessarily to insist upon points to us of little interest, have been shown to point at blasphemous doctrines confuted in the gospel.

Another example of a difficulty being cleared away, by our becoming acquainted, in modern times, with the opinions of an oriental sect, may be drawn from the Samaritan literature. This sect sprung from the Jews, in part, at least, at an early period of their history; and acknowledged, as is well known, no sacred books but those of Moses. Their religious hatred to the Jews was violent; and as they never could be united together in friendship, so does it appear improbable that one sect would have ever borrowed opinions from the other. In the fourth chapter of St. John, a Samaritan woman professes her belief that a Messiah would speedily come (v. 25); and afterwards the inhabitants of the city publicly avow the same expectation (vv. 39, 42). Does not this seem highly improbable? For, surely, the Pentateuch alone could hardly have furnished grounds for so rooted and general a belief. This difficulty increases when we reflect, that the only passage in those books, which could appear to suggest the doctrine with sufficient clearness, is not interpreted by them of the Messiah. I allude to Deut. xviii. 15: "The Lord thy God shall raise up unto thee a prophet," &c., which Gensenius, in his essay on the theology of the

Samaritans, has shown they do not apply at all to his coming.* And yet we have now every evidence that we can desire upon this point. For, the Samaritans, who are reduced to about thirty houses in Naplous, yet profess to expect such a Messiah under the name of Hathab. In the last century, a correspondence was entered into with them, for the purpose of clearing up this question; it was published by Schnurrer,† and the result is precisely such as we could desire, to confirm the gospel narrative. This conclusion has been still farther illustrated by the Samaritan poems in the Bodleian library, which Gensenius has published. For in them the expectation of a Messiah seems clearly expressed.‡ Thus, then, is an important illustration obtained by our modern acquaintance with the doctrines of this remnant of the Samaritans, for a passage otherwise presenting some difficulty.

Having seen the influence exercised by foreign philosophy upon the expressions, and consequently upon the explanation, of Scripture, let us turn the tables, and see if from this we can throw any light upon the philosophy of other oriental nations, and thereby remove objections made against our religion; and by this course we shall return to the Oriental philosophy, from which we have somewhat wandered.

An extraordinary resemblance had been discovered between some of the most mysterious dogmas of Christianity, and expressions found in this philosophy. Some

* "De Samaritanorum Theologia:" *Halæ*, 1822, p. 45.
† "Eichhorns Biblisches Repertorium," ix. Th. S. 27. There had been other similar correspondences between the few remaining Samaritans, and Scaliger, Ludolf, and the University of Oxford. See De Sacy, "Mémoire sur l'état actuel des Samaritains," p. 47.
‡ "Carmina Samaritana e codicibus Londinensibus et Gothanis:" *Lips.* 1824, p. 75. On the objections made by several reviewers, Gensenius is not disposed to enforce the allusion to the Messiah in this verse, and allows that it may be differently interpreted. But, knowing that the word there used, *Hathab*, "the converter," is the Samaritan name for the Messiah, there seems no reason to depart from his original interpretation. At any rate, his commentary places our proofs of the expectations of a Redeemer among the Samaritans upon a more secure footing than it had before.

traces of a belief in a Trinity, you are probably aware, may be found in Plato's celebrated epistle to Dionysius of Syracuse. Philo, Proclus, Sallustius the philosopher, and other Platonists, contain still clearer indications of such a belief. It was agreed that it could only be derived from the Oriental philosophy, in which every other dogma of Platonism is to be discovered.

The progress of Asiatic research placed this supposition beyond controversy. The *Oupnekhat*, a Persian compilation of the Vedas, translated and published by Anquetil Duperron, contains many passages in still clearer unison with Christian doctrines than the hints of the Greek philosophers. I will only quote two from the digest of this work, made by Count Lanjuinais:— " The *word* of the Creator is itself the Creator, and the great *Son* of the Creator."—" *Sat* " (that is, truth) " is the name of God, and God is *trabrat*, that is, three making only one."*

From all these coincidences, nothing more ought to be deduced, than that primeval traditions on religious doctrines had been preserved among different nations But instead of this conclusion being drawn, they were eagerly seized by the adversaries of Christianity, and used as hostile weapons against its divine origin. Dupuis collected every passage which could make the resemblance more marked, not even neglecting the suspicious works of Hermes Trismegistus, and concluded that Christianity was only an emanation of the Philosophical school which had flourished in the East, long before its divine Founder appeared.†

But if one did borrow this doctrine from another, it must now be acknowledged that the very research, which extended still farther this connection between the different philosophic schools of the East and West, has discovered the stock from which they all originally descended. China, too, is now proved to have possessed

---

* "Journal Asiatique:" *Par.* 1823, tom. iii. pp. 15, 83. The name Oupnekhat is a corruption of the Indian Upanishad.
† " Origine de tous les Cultes :" *Paris*, l'an III. vol. v. pp. 283, *seqq.*

its Platonic school; and the doctrines of its founder, Lao-tseu, bear too marked a resemblance to the opinions of the Academy, not to be considered an offspring of the same parent. The early missionaries had presented the public with some extracts from his writings, and some account of his life. The former, however, were incomplete, the latter was mixed with fable. To Abel-Rémusat we are indebted for a satisfactory and highly interesting memoir upon both.* Not only are the leading principles of Platonism expressed in his works, but verbal coincidences have been traced in them by this learned orientalist, which cannot be explained without admitting some connecting link between the Athenian and Chinese sages.† The doctrine of a Trinity is too clearly expounded in his writings to be misunderstood; but in one passage it is expressed in terms of a most interesting character.

" That for which you look, and which you see not, is called *I*: that towards which you listen, yet hear not, is called Hi (the letter H): what your hand seeks, and yet feels not, is called Wei (the letter V). These three are inscrutable, and being united, form only one. Of them the superior is not more bright, nor the inferior more obscure...... This is what is called form without form, image without image, an indefinable Being! Precede it, and ye find not its beginning; follow it, and ye discover not its end."‡

It is not necessary to comment at any length upon this extraordinary passage, which obviously contains the same doctrine which I have quoted from other works. I need only remark, with Abel-Rémusat, that the extraordinary name given to this Triune essence, is composed of the three letters, I H V; for the syllables expressed in the Chinese have no meaning in that language, and

---

* "Mémoire sur la Vie et les Opinions de Lao-tseu, philosophe Chinois du VI. siècle avant notre ère, qui a professé les opinions communément attribuées à Pythagore, à Platon, et à leurs disciples :" *Paris*, 1823.
† See pp. 24, 27.   ‡ Page 40.

are, consequently, representative of the mere letters. It is, therefore, a foreign name, and we shall seek for it in vain anywhere except among the Jews. Their ineffable name, as it was called, which we pronounce Jehovah, is to be met, variously distorted, in the mysteries of many heathen nations; but in none less disfigured than in this passage of a Chinese philosopher. Indeed, it could not have been possibly expressed in his language in any manner more closely approaching to the original.*

The learned French orientalist is far from seeing any improbability in this etymology; on the contrary, he endeavours to support it by historical arguments. He examines the traditions, often disguised under fables, which yet exist among the followers of Lao-tseu; and concludes, that the long journey which he made into the West, can only have taken place before the publication of his doctrines. He does not hesitate to suppose that his philosophical journey may have extended as far as Palestine; but though he should have wandered no farther than Persia, the captivity of the Jews, which had just taken place, would have given him opportunities of communing with them.† Another singular coincidence of his history is, that he was nearly contemporary with Pythagoras, who travelled into the East to learn the same doctrine; and perhaps brought to his own country the same mysteries.

With these conclusions of Abel-Rémusat, authors agree, of no mean name, whether we consider this a question of philosophy or philology. Windischmann,

---

† Iaω is probably the Greek form approaching nearest to the true pronunciation of the Hebrew name. Even pronouncing the Chinese word according to its syllables, I-hi-wei, we have a nearer approach to the Hebrew, Ie-ho-wa, as the oriental Jews rightly pronounce it, than in the Chinese word Chi li-su-tu-su to its original *Christus*.

* "Effectivement, si l'on veut examiner les choses sans préjugé, il n'y a pas d'invraisemblance à supposer, qu'un philosophe Chinois ait voyagé dès le VIe siècle avant notre ère, dans la Perse ou dans la Syrie" (p. 13). One tradition among his followers is, that, before his birth, his soul had wandered into the kingdoms west of Persia.

whom I have before quoted, and of whom I shall have occasion again to speak, seems to consider the grounds given by Abel-Rémusat for his opinion, as worthy of great consideration.* Klaproth, in like manner, defends his interpretation against Pauthier's strictures; observing that, though he does not think it probable that the name Jehovah is to be found in Chinese, he sees no impossibility in the idea, and maintains that his learned friend's interpretation has not been solidly answered.†

This instance renders it sufficiently probable, that, if any connection be admitted between the doctrines delivered to the Jews, and those which resemble them in other ancient nations, these derived them from the depositories of revealed truths. It satisfies us, that in other instances similar communications may have taken place; and there is an end to the scoffing objections of such writers as I before quoted, that Christian dogmas were drawn from heathen philosophy.

Let us now, after these partial applications, look at the general progress made by one branch of research in Oriental philosophy, which long used to be employed as a formidable weapon against Scripture. You will remember how the Hindoo astronomy and chronology, exaggerated to an excessive degree, were found to have come down wonderfully in their pretensions, and that I reserved for this place, the examination into the age of philosophical literature in India. I need not say, that the unbelievers of the last century did not confer a more reasonable antiquity on those sacred books of the Indians, wherein are contained their philosophical and religious systems, and which are well known by the name of the Vedas: in fact, so extravagant an antiquity was attributed to them, that the writings of Moses were represented as modern works in comparison with them. It must, therefore, be a matter of some interest to

---

* "Die Philosophie im Fortgang der Weltgeschichte," Erst. Th. *Bonn*, 1827, p. 404.
† "Mémoire sur l'Origine et la Propagation de la Doctrine du Tao," p. 29.

ascertain how far this opinion has been confirmed or confuted by the great progress made in our acquaintance with Sanskrit literature.

The first consideration which must strike us is, that works of this character are the most easy to invest with appearances of age; since a certain simplicity of manner, and mysticism of thought, will lead the mind to attribute to them an antiquity which cannot be tested, as in the other branches of literature or science, by dates or scientific observations. But, at the same time, we may further remark, that when other portions of a nation's literature have been proved, in spite of high pretensions, to be comparatively modern, any other class which shared their unmerited honours, may also, with great show of justice, be made partaker of their degradation, and condemned to aspire no higher than its associates. Thus, therefore, the moral philosophy of the Hindoos, having been considered a part of the very ancient literature of India, may well, in part at least, yield to those investigations which have deprived the rest of its fancied antiquity.

But specific researches have not been wanting; and they present much more detailed and striking results. And first, let us take the extreme most favourable to our opponents. The authority of Colebrooke will be considered perfectly competent to decide questions connected with Sanskrit literature; and he certainly has never shown a disposition to underrate its importance and value. Now, he takes as the basis of his calculations, the astronomical knowledge displayed in the Vedas: and concludes from such data as it presents, that they were not composed earlier than fourteen hundred years before Christ.* This, you will say, is a great antiquity; but, after all, it does not go back, by nearly two hundred years, to the age of Moses, and the time when the arts had reached their maturity in Egypt.

* "Asiatic Researches," vol. vii. p. 284.

There is a more recent investigation into this question, which seems to me still more remarkable for its results, no less than interesting from the character of its author. This is Dr. Frederick Windischmann, whom I have a real delight in calling my friend, not merely on account of his brilliant talents, and his profound acquaintance with Sanskrit literature and philology, but far more on account of qualities of a higher order, and of a more endearing character, and for virtues which will be one day an ornament to the ecclesiastical state to which he has devoted his future life. Free from the remotest idea of either exaggerating or diminishing the antiquity of these books, which he has minutely studied, he has ingeniously collected all the data which they afford for deciding their true age. Now, what strikes us particularly in his investigation is, how manifestly the struggle of Sanskrit philologers now is to prevent their favourite literature being depressed too low, and how, instead of claiming, on its behalf, in the spirit of older writers, an unnatural term of ages, they contend, with eagerness, to have it raised to a reasonable period before the Christian era. The course of argument followed by my amiable young friend, is simply this. The Institutes of Menu appear, from internal evidence, to have been drawn up before the custom of self-immolation was prevalent, at least completely, throughout the peninsula of the Ganges. As we learn from Grecian writers of the time of Alexander, that this rite was then practised, this work must have been composed anterior to that age. Now the Institutes suppose the existence of the Vedas, which are therein quoted, and said to have been composed by Brahmah.* The argument, as thus stated, does injustice to the great acquaintance manifested by the young author with the minutiæ of the language and the contents of these sacred volumes. Every position is supported by a profusion of erudition, which few can fully

---

* "Frederici Henr. Hug. Windischmanni Sancara, sive de Theologumenis Vedanticorum:" *Bonnæ*, 1833, p. 52.

appreciate. The same must be said of the remainder of his arguments, which principally consist in proving, by philological disquisitions, interesting only to the initiated, that the style of the Vedas is much more ancient than that of any other work in the language.* Still the conclusions to which he comes are noways definite; they allot a high antiquity to the Vedas, but not such as can startle the most apprehensive mind.

After doing so little justice to this learned author, I fear it is less in my power to render a proper tribute to the labours of his father, whose reputation in Europe, as a philosopher, must raise him above the necessity of any preliminary remarks from me; especially as, in making them, I should certainly appear to be carried away by my feelings towards him, as an admiring and revering friend. The work of this extensive and profound scholar, which I have already quoted to-day, has arranged, in the most scientific and complete manner, all that we know of Indian philosophy. He does not so much consider it chronologically, as inquire into its internal and natural development, and endeavour to trace, through every part of the systems which compose it, the principles which animated it, and pervaded all its elements. Now, in this form of investigation, which requires at once a vast accumulation of facts, and an intellectual energy, that can plunge into their chaos, and separate the light from the darkness, Windischmann has been, beyond all other writers, successful. The epochs of the Brahmanic system, he examines by the doctrines and principles which they contain; and his results are such as, while they attribute great antiquity to the Indian books, bring them forward as confirmatory evidence of what is described in the inspired records. For the earliest epoch or period of Brahmanic philosophy exhibits, according to him, the exact counterpart of the patriarchal times as described in the Pentateuch.†

---

* Pages 58, *seqq.*
† "Die Philosophie im Fortgang der Weltgeschicte," Zweites Buch, pp. 690, *seqq.*

But there is another author of deserved reputation among the historians of philosophy, who is far from being disposed to admit the claims or the arguments advanced by Oriéntalists in favour of this high antiquity. Ritter, professor in the University of Berlin, has sifted, with great acuteness, all that has been advanced on its behalf. The astronomical reasonings, or rather conjectures, of Colebrooke, he rejects, as not amounting to any positive or calculable data;* and he is inclined to concede very little more force to the arguments drawn from the apparent antiquity of Indian monuments, or the perfection of the Sanskrit language. For, he observes, the taste for colossal monuments is not necessarily so ancient, seeing that some have been erected in comparatively modern days: and language receives its characteristic perfection often at one moment, and cannot form a sure criterion of antiquity, unless relatively considered by epochs discoverable within itself.† The entire reasoning pursued by Ritter, tends more to throw down the supposed antiquity of Indian philosophy, than to build up any new theory. However, his conclusion is, that the commencement of true systematic philosophy must not be dated further back than the reign of Vikramaditja, about a century before the Christian era.‡

Before quitting the subject of Indian philosophical works, I will give you an example of the facility with which men, who took pride in being called unbelievers, swallowed any assertion which seemed hostile to Christianity. In the last century, an Indian work, extremely Christian in its doctrines, was published by Ste. Croix, under the title of the *Ezour Vedam*.§ Voltaire pounced upon it, as a proof that the doctrines of Christianity were borrowed from the heathens, and pronounced it a

---
* "Geschichte der Philosophie," 1 Th. *Hamburg*, 1829, p. 60.
† Page 62.
‡ Pages 120, 124.
§ "Ezour Vedam, ou ancien Commentaire du Vedam:" *Yverdun*, 1728.

work of immense antiquity, composed by a Brahman of Seringham.* Now, hear the history of this marvellous work.

When Sir Alex. Johnston was Chief Justice in Ceylon, and received a commission to draw up a code of laws for the natives, he was anxious to consult the best Indian works, and, among the rest, to ascertain the genuineness of the Ezour Vedam. He therefore made diligent search in the southern provinces, and inquired at the most celebrated pagodas, particularly that of Seringham; but all in vain. He could learn no tidings of the Brahman, nor of the work which he was said to have composed. Upon his arrival at Pondicherry, he obtained permission from the governor, Count Dupuis, to examine the manuscripts in the Jesuits' library, which had not been disturbed since they left India. Among them he discovered the Ezour Vedam, in Sanskrit and French. It was diligently examined by Mr. Ellis, principal of the College at Madras; and his inquiry led to the satisfactory discovery, that the original Sanskrit was composed in 1621, entirely for the purpose of promoting Christianity, by the learned and pious missionary, Robert de Nobilibus, nephew of Card. Bellarmin, and near relative to Pope Marcellus II.†

From philosophy, we may now proceed to examine what has been done for religion by the progress of Oriental history; and I shall content myself with one or two examples.

The thirty-ninth chapter of Isaiah informs us, that Merodach-Baladan, king of Babylon, sent an embassy to Ezekiah, king of Judah. This king of Babylon makes no other appearance in sacred history; and even this one is attended with no inconsiderable difficulty. For, the kingdom of the Assyrians was yet flourishing, and Babylon was only one of its dependencies. Only nine

---

* "Siècle de Louis XV."
† "Asiatic Researches," vol. xiv. "British Catholic Colonial Intelligencer," No. ii. *Lond.* 1834, p. 163.

years before, Salmanassar, the *Assyrian* monarch, is said to have transported the inhabitants of *Babylon* to other parts;* and Manasses, not many years after, was carried captive to *Babylon* by the king of *Assyria.*† Again, the prophet Micheas, about this very period, speaks of the Jews being carried away to Babylon, while the Assyrians are mentioned as the enemies whom they have principally to fear.‡

All these instances incontestably prove, that at the time of Ezekiah, Babylon was dependent on the Assyrian kings. Who, then, was this Merodach-Baladan, king of Babylon? If he was only governor of that city, how could he send an embassy of congratulation to the Jewish sovereign, then at war with his liege lord? The canon of Ptolemy gives us no king of this name, nor does his chronology appear reconcilable with sacred history.

In this darkness and doubt we must have continued, and the apparent contradiction of this text to other passages would have remained inexplicable, had not the progress of modern oriental study brought to light a document of the most venerable antiquity. This is nothing less than a fragment of Berosus, preserved in the Chronicle of Eusebius. The publication of this work, in a perfect state, from its Armenian version, first made us acquainted with it;§ and Gensenius, whom I have so often quoted as opposed to us in opinion, I have now the pleasure of citing, as the author to whose ingenuity we owe its application.‖

This interesting fragment informs us, that after Sennacherib's brother had governed Babylon, as Assyrian viceroy, Acises unjustly possessed himself of the supreme command. After thirty days he was murdered by Merodach-Baladan, who usurped the sovereignty for six months, when he in his turn was killed, and

---

* 2 (4) Reg. vii. 24.   † 2 Chron. xxxiii. 11.
‡ Mic. iv. 10; cf. v. 5, 6.
§ "Eusebii Chronicon₄:" *Venet.* 1818, tom. i. p. 42.
‖ Commentar über den Jesaia," Erst. Th. 2 Abth. pp. 999, *seqq.*

2 c

succeeded by Elibus. But after three years, Sennacherib collected an army, gave the usurper battle, conquered and took him prisoner. Having once more reduced Babylon to his obedience, he left his son Assordan, the Essarhaddon of Scripture, as governor of that city.

There is only one apparent discrepancy between this historical fragment and the Scripture narrative; for the latter relates the murder of Sennacherib, and the succession of Essarhaddon before Merodach-Baladan's embassy to Jerusalem.* But to this Gensenius has well replied, that this arrangement is followed by the prophet, in order to conclude the history of the Assyrian monarch, which has no further connection with his subject, so as not to return to it again.

By this order also, the prophecy of his murder is more closely connected with the history of its fulfilment.† But this solution, which supposes some interval to have elapsed between Sennacherib's return to Niniveh and his death, is rendered probable by the words of the text itself—"He went and returned, *and abode in Niniveh;* and it came to pass," &c.; and moreover becomes certain from chronological arguments. For it is certain, that Sennacherib's expedition into Egypt must have been made in his first or second year (714 B.C.); since the twentieth chapter of Isaiah mentions Sargon as reigning just before that event (716). Now, according to Berosus, at the conclusion of the above-quoted fragment, Sennacherib reigned eighteen years before he was murdered by his sons. He must, therefore, have survived, by many years, his return to Niniveh.‡ The account of Berosus, that the Babylonian revolt happened in the reign of Sennacherib, is thus nowise at variance with the sacred text; and this only difficulty being once removed, the fragment clears up every possible objection to its accuracy.

For we have it perfectly explained, how there was a

---

* Isaiah, xxxvii. 38.
† Isaiah, xxxvii. 7.
‡ "Gensenius," p. 1002; cf. the Table, 2 Th. p. 560.

king, or rather a usurper, in Babylon, at a time when it was in reality a provincial city of the Assyrian Empire. Nothing was more probable than that Merodach-Baladan, having seized the throne, should endeavour to unite himself in league and amity with the enemies of his master, against whom he had revolted. Ezekiah, who, no less than himself, had thrown off the Assyrian yoke,* and was in powerful alliance with the king of Egypt, would be his first resource. No embassy, on the other hand, could be more welcome to the Jewish monarch, who had the common enemy in his neighbourhood, and would be glad to see a diversion made in his favour, by a rebellion in the very heart of that enemy's kingdom.† Hence arose that excessive attention which he paid to the envoys of the usurper, and which so offended the prophet Isaiah, or rather God, who through him foretold, in consequence, the Babylonian captivity.‡

Another instance of the advantage which the progress of oriental historical research may bring to matters of religious interest, is afforded us by the light lately thrown upon the religious worship of Thibet. When Europe first became acquainted with this worship, it was impossible not to be struck with the analogies it presented to the religious rites of Christians. The hierarchy of the Lamas, their monastic institutes, their churches, and ceremonies, resembled ours with such minuteness, that some connection between the two seemed necessarily to have existed. "The early missionaries were satisfied with considering Lamaism as a sort of degenerate Christianity, and as a remnant of those Syrian sects which once had penetrated into those remote parts of Asia."§

---

* 2 (4) Reg. xviii. 7.
† From what has been said in the text, it appears probable that the revolt in Babylon took place during Sennacherib's expedition against Judea and Egypt.
‡ Isaiah, xxxix. 2, 5.
§ Abel-Rémusat, "Aperçu d'un Mémoire intitulé Recherches chronologiques sur l'Origine de la Hiérarchie Lamaique," reprinted in the "Mélanges Asiatiques:" *Paris*, 1825, vol. i. p. 129.

LECTURE THE ELEVENTH.

But there have been others who have turned this resemblance to very different purposes. "Frequent mysterious assertions and subdued hints, in the works of learned men," says a lamented orientalist, to whose memoir on this subject I shall have to refer just now, "led many to doubt whether the Lamaic theocracy was a remnant of Christian sects, or, on the contrary, the ancient and primitive model, on which were traced similar establishments in other parts of the world. Such were the views taken in the notes to Father D'Andrada's Journey, to the French translations of Thunberg and of the *Asiatic Researches*, and in many other modern works where irreligion has sought to conceal itself under a superficial and lying erudition."*
"These resemblances," says Malte-Brun, "were turned into arguments against the divine origin of Christianity."† In fact, we find these analogies affording matter for peculiar merriment to Volney.‡

At first these objections were only met by negative answers. It was well argued by Fischer, that no writer anterior to the thirteenth century, gives a hint of the existence of this system, nor could any proof be brought of its antiquity. But it had been the fashion to attribute an extravagant date to all the institutions of Central Asia, upon the strength of plausible conjecture. The venerable age given to this religious establishment, was in perfect accordance with Bailly's scientific hypotheses regarding the same country, and formed a natural counterpart to the romantic system which made the mountains of Siberia, or the steppes of Tartary, the cradle of philosophy. Since that period the languages and literature of Asia have made a wide step; and the consequence has been, the thorough confutation of these extravagant hypotheses from the works of native writers.

---

* *Ib.* note 2. "Mélanges," p. 132.
† "Précis de la Géographie universelle :" *Paris*, 1812, vol. iii. p. 581.
‡ "Ruines ;" *Paris*, 1820, p. 428.

Abel-Rémusat is once more the author to whom we are indebted for this valuable exposition. In an interesting memoir, he has made us acquainted with a valuable fragment preserved in the *Japanese Encyclopædia*, and containing the true history of the Lamaic hierarchy. Without this, we should, perhaps, have been for ever left to vague conjectures; with its assistance we are able to confute the unfounded, though specious, dreams of our assailants. The god Buddha was originally supposed to be perpetuated upon earth in the person of his Indian patriarchs. His soul was transfused in succession, into a new representative chosen from any caste; and so confident was the trustee of his divinity, that he possessed an amulet against destruction, that he usually evaded the sufferings of age, by ascending a funeral pile, whence, like the phœnix, he hoped to rise into a new life. In this state the god remained till the fifth century of our era, when he judged it prudent to emigrate from Southern India, and fix his residence in China. His representative received the title of *preceptor of the kingdom;* but only added, like the later khalifs at Bagdad, a religious splendour to the court of the Celestial Empire.

In this precarious condition, the succession of sacred chiefs was continued for eight more centuries, till, in the thirteenth, the house of Tchingkis-khan delivered them from their dependence, and invested them with dominion. Voltaire has said, that Tchingkis-khan was too good a politician to disturb the spiritual kingdom of the Grand Lama in Thibet;* and yet, neither did a kingdom then exist in Thibet, nor did the high priest of Shamanism yet reside there, nor was the name of Lama yet an appellation. For, it was the grandson of the conqueror, thirty-three years after him, who first bestowed sovereignty on the head of his religion; and, as the living Buddha happened to be a native of Thibet,

---

* "Philosophie de l'Histoire ; Essai sur les Mœurs." Abel-Rémusat, p. 137.

that country was given him for his government. Thus was the mountain of Pootala, or Botala,* made the capital of this religious kingdom, and the term *Lama*, which signifies a priest, first applied as distinctive title to its ruler.

This account of the origin of the Lamaic dynasty accords perfectly with another interesting document lately brought before the public. This is a description of Thibet, translated from the Chinese into Russian, by the Archimandrite, F. Hyacinth Pitchourinsky;† and from the Russian into French, with corrections upon the original, by Julius Klaproth.‡ From this document we learn that Tchingkis-khan overran that country, and established a government which comprised Thibet and its dependencies. The emperor Khoubilai, seeing the difficulty of governing this distant country, devised a method for rendering it submissive, which was conformable to the usages of the people. "He divided the country of the *Thou-pho* into provinces and districts; appointed officers of different degrees, and subjected them to the authority of the *Ti-szu* (preceptor of the emperor). At that time, *Bhâchbah*, or *Pagba*, a native of Sarghia, in Thibet, held this office. At the age of seven years he had read all the sacred books, and comprehended their most sublime ideas, for which reason he was called the *spiritual child*. In 1260 he received the title of *king of the great and precious law*, and a seal of oriental jasper. Besides these, he was invested with the dignity of *chief of the yellow religion*. His brothers, his children, and descendants, have enjoyed eminent posts at court, and have received seals of gold and oriental jasper. The court received Bhâchbah with distinction, entertained towards him a superstitious faith, and neglected nothing which could contribute to make him respected."§

---

* See the "Nouveau Journal Asiatique," *Oct.* 1829, p. 273, note 1.
† St. Petersburg, 1828.
‡ In the "Nouveau Journal Asiatique," *Aug.* and *Oct.* 1829.
§ "Nouveau Journal Asiatique," *August*, 1829, p. 119.

At the time when the Buddhist patriarchs first established themselves in Thibet, that country was in immediate contact with Christianity. Not only had the Nestorians ecclesiastical settlements in Tartary, but Italian and French religious men visited the court of the Khans, charged with important missions from the Pope and St. Lewis of France. They carried with them church ornaments and altars, to make, if possible, a favourable impression on the minds of the natives. For this end, they celebrated their worship in presence of the Tartar princes, by whom they were permitted to erect chapels within the precincts of the royal palaces. An Italian archbishop, sent by Clement V., established his see in the capital, and erected a church, to which the faithful were summoned by the sound of three bells, and where they beheld many sacred pictures painted on the walls.*

Nothing was easier than to induce many of the various sects which crowded the Mongul court, to admire and adopt the rites of this religion. Some members of the imperial house secretly embraced Christianity, many mingled its practices with the profession of their own creeds; and Europe was alternately delighted and disappointed by reports of imperial conversions, and by discoveries of their falsehood.† It was such a rumour as this, in reference to Manghu, that caused the missions of Rubriquis and Ascellino. Surrounded by the celebration of such ceremonies, hearing from the ambassadors and missionaries of the West accounts of the worship and hierarchy of their countries, it is no wonder that the religion of the Lamas, just beginning to assume splendour and pomp, should have adopted institutions and practices already familiar to them, and already admired by those whom they wished to gain. The

---

* Abel-Rémusat, p. 138. Compare Assemani, *inf. cit.*
† "Assemani Biblioth. Orient." tom. iii. part ii. pp. ccclxxx. *seqq.* "Di Marco Polo e degli altri viaggiatori Veneziani più illustri Dissertazione del P. Ab. (afterwards Cardinal) Zurla:" *Ven.* 1818, vol. i. p. 287.

coincidence of time and place, the previous non-existence of that sacred monarchy, amply demonstrate that the religion of Thibet is but an attempted imitation of ours.

It is not my province to follow the learned academician in the later history of this religious dynasty. It has continued in dependence on the Chinese sovereigns till our days, at one and the same time revered and persecuted, adored and oppressed. But its claims to antiquity are forfeited for ever, and its pretensions as a rival, still more as the parent of Christianity, have been fully examined and rejected.

I have prolonged my disquisition so far, that I must forego the many reflections which its subject might well suggest. But it would be unjust to take leave of it without alluding to the proud pre-eminence which our country is taking in the prosecution of these studies; and if our education have not qualified us, like our continental neighbours, for such deep research into the abstruser parts of Asiatic literature, we are at least learning to contribute those vast means which Providence has placed at our disposal, towards bringing to light much which otherwise would have remained concealed. It would, indeed, be disgraceful to us, if, in after-ages, the history of all our colonies should present to the inquiring philosopher, only pages ruled into balances of imports and exports, and statements of annual returns to our national coffers; or, if the annals of our mighty empire in India should present nothing better than a compound establishment of commercial and military agents, passing through varied scenes of mercantile warfares and kingly speculations. It is, indeed, an honour to our national character, and the greatest proof of its moral energies, that so much has been done by those whose professions seemed necessarily at variance with literary and scientific pursuits; and I know not whether the public discredit will not be hidden by the honour reflected from the personal merit of so many illustrious individuals. For posterity will not fail to observe, that while the French, in their Egyptian expedition, sent scientific and literary men, to accompany their army, and bring home the monuments of that country, England has needed not to make such a distinction; but found among those who fought her battles, and directed her military operations, men who could lay down the sword to take up the pen, and record for us every interesting monument, with as much sagacity and learning, as though letters had been their sole occupation.* But still there is a hope of a higher national feeling; and the foundation, under royal patronage, of the Commitee for the translation of oriental works, has already greatly increased our stock of oriental lore. It has interested in these pursuits, those who otherwise could hardly have been led to patronize them; it has cheered many a scholar who otherwise would have drooped in silent obscurity: and it has encouraged many, who otherwise would not have felt the necessary strength,—

"Eoam tentare fidem, populosque bibentes
Euphratem—
Medorum penetrare domos, Scythiosque recessus
Arva super Cyri Chaldæique ultima regni,
Qua rapidus Ganges, et qua Nyssæus Hydaspes
Accedunt pelago." (*Lucan.* viii. 213.)

---

* The author's lamented friend, Colonel Tod, was among the number.

LECTURE THE TWELFTH;

CONCLUSION.

OBJECT of this Lecture.—Character of the confirmatory Evidence obtained through the entire course, arising from the variety of tests to which the truth of religion has been submitted. Confirmed from the nature of the facts examined, and of the authorities employed. Auguries thence resulting for the future.—Religion deeply interested in the progress of every science.—Opponents of this opinion. First, timid Christians; confutation of them by the ancient Fathers of the Church. Second, the enemies of religion, in former and in later times.—Duty of ecclesiastics to apply to study, with a view of meeting all objections: and of all Christians, in proportion to their ability.—Advantages, pleasure, and method of such pursuits.

I HAVE now accomplished the task on which I entered, encouraged by your kindness. I promised to pass through the history of several sciences, and to prove, by that simple process, how their progress has ever been accompanied by the accession of new light and splendour to the evidences of Christianity. I promised to treat my subject in the most unostentatious manner, to avoid such exemplifications as had already found their way into elementary books upon the subject, and to draw my materials, as much as possible, from works which were not directed to a defence of Christianity.

And now having, to the best of my small ability, discharged my duty towards you, it may be given us to rest a little, and look back upon the course we have followed; or, like those who have journeyed together awhile, sit down at the end of our travel, and make a common reckoning of what we have therein gained. Our road may have seemed in part to lie over barren and uninteresting districts; I have led you through strait and toilsome ways, and perhaps sometimes have bewildered and perplexed you; but if, while we have kept company, you have to complain of having found but an unskilful guide, he in his turn may perchance rejoin, that he has found but too much. encouragement to prolong his wanderings, and too much indulgence to have easily discovered his going astray. But there has been sufficient variety, at least in the objects which have passed under our observation, to make compensation for the labours of our journey; and we have throughout it kept one great point in view, which sooner or later could always bring us back to our right track, and give a unity of character, and uniformity of method, to our most devious wanderings. And by looking for one moment upon this again, we shall be able, in a few moments, to run over the road through which our course hath led us.

And first, I may naturally be asked, what addition I consider myself to have made to the evidences of Christianity. Now, to this question I should reply with most measured reserve. I hold those evidences to be something too inwardly and deeply seated in the heart, to have their sum increased or diminished easily by the power of outward considerations. However we may require and use such proofs of its truths, as learned men have ably collected, when reasoning with the opponents of Christianity, I believe no one is conscious of clinging to its sublime doctrines, and its consoling promises, on the ground of such logical demonstration; even as an able theorist shall show you many cogent reasons, founded on the social and natural laws, why ye should love your parents, and yet both he and you know that not for those reasons have you loved them, but from a far holier and more inward impulse. And so, when we once have embraced true religion, its motives, or evidences, need not longer be sought in the reasonings of books; they become incorporated with our holiest affections; they result from our finding the necessity, for our happiness, of the truths they uphold; in our there discovering the key to the secrets of our nature, the solution of all mental problems, the reconciliation of all contradictions in our anomalous condition, the answer to all the solemn questions of our restless consciousness.

Thus is religion like a plant, which drives its roots into the centre of the soul; having in them fine and subtile fibres, that pierce and penetrate into the solidest framework of a well-built mind, and strong knotty arms, that entangle themselves among the softest and purest of our feelings. And if without it also put forth shoots and tendrils innumerable, wherewith, as with hands, it apprehends and keeps hold of mundane and visible objects, it is rather for their benefit and ornament than from any want of such support; nor does it from them derive its natural and necessary vitality. Now, it is with this outward and luxurious growth, that our husbanding hath been chiefly engaged, rather than with its hidden foundations and roots; we have, perhaps, somewhat extended its beneficial connections; we have sometimes wound it round some decayed and neglected remnant of ancient grandeur; we have stretched it as a garland to some vigorous and youthful plant, and mingled the fruits of its holiness with less wholesome bearing; and we have seen how there is a comeliness and grace given to both, by the contact; how it may cast an interest and an honour and a beauty over what else were useless and profane. And we may also, by this partial tilling, have given to the plant itself some additional energy and power to strengthen.

In other words, these Lectures have been mainly directed to watch the relation between the evidences of Christianity and other pursuits; to trace the influence which the necessary progress of these must have upon the illustration of the former. With the true internal proofs of the Christian religion, we have not dealt: but, by removing objections against the external form of manifestation in which this religion appears, and against the documents in which its proofs and doctrines are recorded, and against many of the specific events therein registered, we may in some measure hope, that the native force of those grounds of evidence will be something increased and fitted for receiving a more powerful development in our minds. This consideration admits of many different views, and leads the way to many even more important conclusions, which will form the subject of this my last address. And first, I will say a few words upon the direct application of what has been hitherto treated, to the general evidences of Christianity, and to the vindication of those sacred documents whereby the principal evidences are authentically enforced.

The great difference between specious error, and a system of truth, is, that the one may present certain aspects, under which, if viewed, it gives no appearance of fault; it is like a precious stone that has a flaw, but which may be so submitted to the eye, that the play of light, aided by an artful setting, may conceal it; but which, when only slightly turned, and viewed under another angle, discovers its defect. But truth is a gem which need not be enchased, which, faultless and cloudless, may be held up to the pure bright light, on any side, in any direction, and will everywhere display the same purity, and soundness, and beauty. The one is an impure ore, that may resist the action of several reagents brought to act upon it, but in the end yields before one of them: the other is as annealed gold, which defies the power of every successive test. Hence, the more numerous the points of contact which any system presents to other orders of intellectual or scientific research, the more opportunities it gives of assaying its worth; and assuredly, if it noways suffer by their continued progress towards perfection on different sides, we must conclude, that it hath so deep a root in the eternal truth, as that nought created can affect its certainty. Nothing has been oftener attempted than the forgery of literary productions, but nothing has been more unfortunate. Where the author, like, perhaps,

Synesius, has confined himself to philosophical speculation, which may have been the same in any age, it may be more difficult to decide on the imposture. But where history, jurisprudence, manners, or other outward circumstances, enter into the plan of the work, it is almost impossible for it to succeed in long defeating the ingenuity of the learned. The most celebrated literary frauds of modern times, the history of Formosa, or, still more, the Sicilian code of Vella, for a time perplexed the world, but were in the end discovered.

Now, such has been the object and tendency of our investigation, to examine the different phases which revealed religion presents, from the reflected light of so many various pursuits; to see what are its aspects under the influence of such diversified powers, and thus ascertain how far it is capable of resisting the most complicated assay, and defying the most obstinate and most unfriendly examination. And surely we may say, that no system has ever laid itself open more completely to detection, if it contained any error, than this of Christianity; no book ever gave so many clues to discovery, if it tell one untruth, than its sacred volume. In it we have recorded the earliest and the latest physical revolutions of our globe; the dispersion of the human race; the succession of monarchs in all surrounding countries, from the time of Sesostris to the Syrian kings; the habits and manners, and language of various nations; the great religious traditions of the human race; and the recital of many marvellous and miraculous events, not to be found in the annals of any other people. Had the tests whereby all these different ingredients were to be one day tried, existed when they were thus compounded together, some pains might have been taken to secure them against their action. But against the future, no skill, no ingenuity, could afford protection. Had the name of a single Egyptian Pharaoh been invented to suit convenience, as we see done by other oriental historians, the discovery of the hieroglyphic alphabet, after 3,000 years, would not have been one of the chances of detection against which the historian would have guarded. Had the history of the creation, or of the deluge, been a fabulous or poetical fiction, the toilsome journeys of the geologist among Alpine valleys, or the discovery of hyænas' caves in an unknown island, would not be the confirmations of his theory, on which its inventor would have ever reckoned. A fragment of Berosus comes to light, and it proves what seemed before incredible, to be perfectly true. A medal is found, and it completes the reconciliation of apparent contradictions. Every science, every pursuit, as it makes a step, in its own natural onward progress, increases the mass of our confirmatory evidence.

Such, then, is the first important result which we have gained; the acquisition of that powerful proof which a system receives from multiplied verifications. This proof will be greatly enhanced in value by a few obvious considerations. And first I would remark, that the sacred volume is not the work of one man, nor of one age, but is a compilation rather of the writings of many. Now, if one very skilful writer had attempted the task of forging the annals of a people, or of writing the fictitious biography of some distinguished person, or of drawing up imaginary systems of nature, or of describing from fancy the great events of her history, he might, by possibility, have guarded himself on every side against detection, and measured every phrase, so as to suit the specific purpose which he held in view. But to imagine, that during the 1600 years from Moses to St. John, such a system could have been carried on, by a series of writers having no connection, of the most unequal abilities, writing—if we, for one moment, admit the impious hypothesis—under the most diverse influences, necessarily viewing the past and the future under different aspects, is to imagine a stranger combination of moral agents for an evil work than the world ever beheld. But this is not our present consideration. It is evident that the power could not have seconded the will to deceive, supposing this to have existed; the points of contact with other facts would have been too infinitely multiplied to fit exactly in every case: if we supposed Moses to have been accurately acquainted with the Egypt of his time, it would be improbable that every succeeding annalist should have possessed a similar acquaintance; if the opinions of his time, concerning the physical constitution of the world, were so accurate as to give no chance of their being falsified by modern discoveries, this would not have secured to Isaiah accuracy in recounting the affairs of Babylon. In fine, the greater the extent of time and territory, events and usages, embraced by the sacred Book, the greater the dangers of discovery, had it contained aught untrue or incorrect.

Secondly, we may remark, that the points which our researches have verified, have seldom been leading events, or the direct subject of which the inspired authors treated; but generally incidental, and almost parenthetic observations, or narratives, on which they could hardly have expected much research to be made. The common origin of all mankind, or the miraculous dispersion of our race, are not matters paraded at length; but the former is left almost to inference, and the latter is recorded in the simplest manner. Yet we have seen what a long process of study has been required to bring out the proofs of these events, against the strong prepossessions of first appearances, and the boasted conclusions of ill-studied science. The various historical incidents, on which light has been shed by our modern application, are mostly episodes to the general narrative of Jewish domestic history; all are such passages as would have been penned with a less guarded hand, and with the smallest suspicion that they would be used for assaying the work. Yet even such passages as these have been searchingly assailed without any unfavourable result.

Thirdly, we might have been somewhat jealous of the experiment, had it been conducted exclusively by friends. But though these have laboured much in the work of verification and illustration, the greater part has been done by two other classes of men, equally above suspicion. The first consists of those who have quietly conducted their studies, without intending at all to apply them to sacred purposes, or even suspecting that they would be so applied. The antiquarian, when he garners up, and then deciphers, a new coin, knows not, till the process is complete, what tidings from the olden world it will bear him. The orientalist pores over his defaced parchments, unable to conjecture what information it will give him of distant usages, till he has overcome its difficulties. Neither the one nor the other pursues his studies from a surmise that what he shall discover will prove of use to the theologian; no possible anticipation of mind could have led the learned Aucher to hope, that a fragment of Berosus would be found in the Armenian version of Eusebius, which had been lost in the original; still less that such a fragment, if discovered, would disperse a difficulty which clouded an important narrative. Now, this has been essentially a portion, or rather a condition, of my plan, to have recourse chiefly to authors that have conducted their researches, without attention to any advantages thence accruing to Christian evidences.

But the second class of writers, to whom we are indebted for a large portion of our materials in this investigation, are removed a step farther from all suspicion of partiality to our cause. You will naturally understand me to signify such as are decidedly hostile to our opinions. These, again, may be subdivided into two classes. The first may contain such writers as do not admit the conclusions which we draw from our premises, though they assist us in establishing them; or who do not impugn, though they admit not our belief. Thus, you have seen Klaproth deny the dispersion, and Virey the unity of the human race, yet both accumulating evidence of importance towards establishing these two points. Others have been pressed into our service much more unwillingly; for their ingenuity and talents have been exercised to combat the very propositions which I have endeavoured to establish. Nay, the genius of Buffon seems to have been quickened by the idea that he was taking a bolder flight than men are wont to attempt, and striving to pass the limits of universal conviction. The miserable fragments then possessed of Hindoo astronomy, never would have occupied the genius of the unfortunate Bailly, had not his eagerness been sharpened by the vain hope of thereby constructing a chronological scheme, more in accordance with the irreligious opinions of his party, than with the venerable belief of former ages. And yet the imagination of the former first devised the theory of a gradual cooling of the earth's mass, which now is considered by so many as a sufficient solution of the difficulties regarding the Deluge; and the latter may be said, by trying to reduce that astronomy to a scientific expression, to have laid the train for its total exposure.

These considerations must add greatly to the power of the argument proposed in these Lectures. For they must remove every suspicion that the authorities on which it is based have been carefully prepared by a friendly hand.

The first result of this reasoning is obvious; that every security which an endless variety of tests, applied to a system without injuring it, can give us of its truth, the Christian religion, and its evidences, may justly boast. But this consequence has also an important prospective force, for it presents a ground of confidence for the future, such as no other form of argument could present. For, if all that has yet been done has tended to confirm our proofs, we surely have nothing to fear from what yet remains concealed. Had the first stages of every science been the most favourable to our cause, and had its further improvement diminished what we had gained, we might indeed be alarmed about any ulterior prosecution of learning. But seeing that the order of things is precisely the reverse, that the beginnings of sciences are least propitious to our desires, and their progress most satisfactory, we cannot but be convinced that future discoveries, far from weakening, must necessarily strengthen the evidences we possess.

And thus we come to form a noble and sublime idea of religion, to consider it as the great fixed point round which the moral world revolves, while itself remains unchanged; or rather as the emblem of Him who gave it, the all-embracing medium in which every other thing moves, increases, and lessens, is born and destroyed, without communicating to it essential mutation, but, at most, transiently altering its outward manifestation. We come to consider it as the last refuge of thought, the binding link between the visible and invisible, the revealed and the discoverable, the resolution of all anomalies, the determination of all problems in outward nature and in the inward soul; the fixing and steadying element of every science, the blank and object of every meditation. It appears to us even as the olive, the emblem of peace, as described by Sophocles—a plant not set by human hands, but of spontaneous and necessary growth in the great order of creative wisdom, fearful to its enemies, and so firmly grounded, as that none, in ancient or later times, hath been able to uproot it.

> Φύτευμ' ἀχείρωτον, αὐτόποιον
> ἐγχέων φόβημα δαΐων·
> τὸ μέν τις οὔτε νέος οὔτε γήρᾳ
> σημαίνων ἁλιώσει χερὶ πέρσας.*

After what I have said, it may appear superfluous to conclude that the Christian religion can have no interest in repressing the cultivation of science and literature, nor any reason to dread their general diffusion, so long as this is accompanied by due attention to sound moral principles and correctness of faith. For if the experience of the past has given us a security that the progress of science uniformly tends to increase the sum of our proofs, and to give fresh lustre to such as we already possess, in favour of Christianity, it surely becomes her interest and her duty to encourage that constant and salutary advance. Yet, from the beginning of the

* Œdip. Col. 694.

Church, there have been found men, who professed a contrary opinion, and they may be divided into two classes, according to the motives which have instigated their opposition to human learning.

The first consists of those well-meaning Christians, who, in all ages, have fancied that science and literature are incompatible with application to more sacred duties, or that they draw the mind from the contemplation of heavenly things, and are an alloy to that constant holiness of thought, which a Christian should ever strive to possess; or else that such pursuits are clearly condemned in Scripture, wherever the wisdom of this world is reproved. This class of timid Christians first directed their opposition to that philosophy which so many Fathers, especially of the Alexandrian school, endeavoured to join and reconcile with Christian theology. They were, however, strenuously attacked and confuted by Clement of Alexandria, who devoted several chapters of his learned *Stromata* to the vindication of his favourite studies. He observes very justly, that "varied and abundant learning recommends him who proposes the great dogmas of faith, to the credit of his hearers, inspiring his disciples with admiration, and drawing them towards the truth;"* which is in like manner the opinion of Cicero, when he says, "magna est enim vis ad persuadendum scientiæ."† Clement then illustrates his arguments by many quotations from the Holy Scriptures, and from profane authors. I will read you one remarkable passage.

"Some persons having a high opinion of their good dispositions, will not apply to philosophy or dialectics, nor even to natural philosophy, but wish to possess faith alone and unadorned: as reasonably as though they expected to gather grapes from a vine which they have left uncultivated. Our Lord is called, allegorically, a vine, from which we gather fruit, by a careful cultivation, according to the eternal Word. We must prune,

---

* "Stromata," lib. i. cap. 2, tom. i. p. 327, ed. Potter.
† "Topica," Oper. tom. i. p. 173, ed. *Lond.* 1681.

and dig, and bind, and perform all other necessary labour. And, as in agriculture and in medicine, he is considered the best educated who has applied to the greatest variety of sciences, useful for tilling or for curing, so must we consider him most properly educated who makes all things bear upon the truth; who from geometry, and music, and grammar, and philosophy itself, gathers whatever is useful for the defence of the faith. But the champion who has not trained himself well, will surely be despised."*

These words, I must own, afford me no small encouragement. For if, instead of geometry and music, we say geology, and ethnography, and history, we may consider ourselves as having, in this passage, a formal confirmation of the views which we have taken in these Lectures, and an approbation of the principles on which they have been conducted.

As this opposition continued in the Church, so was it met by zealous and eloquent pastors, as most prejudicial to the cause of truth. St. Basil the Great seems particularly to have been thought a most strenuous defender of profane learning, in his age. He himself earnestly recommends the study of elegant literature, at that age when, according to him, the mind is too weak to bear the more solid food of God's inspired Word. He expressly says, that by the perusal of such writers as Homer, the youthful mind is trained to virtuous feelings; at the same time, however, that care must be taken to withhold all that can corrupt the innocence of the heart.†

St. Gregory of Nyssa speaks of him with great praise, because he practically brought these principles to bear upon religion, and illustrated them by his great learning. "Many," he writes, "present profane learning as a gift to the Church; among whom was the great Basil, who, having, in his youth, seized on the spoil of Egypt, and consecrated it to God, adorned with its wealth the tabernacle of the Church."‡

* *Ibid.* c. ix. p. 342.   † "Basilii Opera," tom. i. hom. 24.
‡ "De Vita Mosis." "S. Gregorii Nysseni Opera:" *Paris*, 1638, tom. i. p. 209.

But the illustrious friend of St. Basil has entered more at length into the merits of this question. St. Gregory Nazianzen had been his schoolfellow at Athens; where both, animated by the same religious spirit, had devoted themselves with signal success to the prosecution of study, considering truth, according to the expression of St. Augustine, "wherever found, to be the property of Christ's Church." Indeed, so well did their schoolmate, Julian, understand the value which they and other holy men of their time, attached to human learning, and the powerful use which they made of it to overthrow idolatry and error, that, upon his apostacy, he issued a decree, whereby Christians were debarred from attending public schools, and acquiring science.* And this was considered by them a grievous persecution. One passage from St. Gregory's funeral oration over his friend, will be sufficient to satisfy you concerning his opinion.

"I think that all men of sound mind must agree, that learning is to be reckoned the highest of earthly goods. I speak not merely of that noble learning which is ours, and which, despising all outward grace, applies exclusively to the work of salvation, and the beauty of intellectual ideas, but also of that learning which is from without, which some ill-judging Christians reject as wily and dangerous, and as turning the mind from God." After observing, that the abuse of such learning by the heathens is no reason for its rejection, any more than their blasphemous substitution of the material elements for God, can debar us from their legitimate use, he thus proceeds:—" Therefore must not erudition be reproved, because some men choose to think so; on the contrary, they are to be considered foolish and ignorant who so reason, who would wish all men to be like themselves, that they may be concealed in the crowd, and no one be able to detect their want of education."†

---
* "Socrates Hist. Ecclea." lib. i. cap. 12.
† S. Gregor. Nazianzeni, "Funebris oratio in laudem Basilii Magni," Oper. *Par.* 1609, tom. i. p. 323.

The terms here used are indeed severe; but they serve to show, in the strongest manner, the sentiments of this holy and learned man, on the utility of human science and literature. Turning to the great lights of the Western Church, we find no less severity of reproof used in dealing with those that oppose profane learning. St. Jerome, for instance, speaks even harshly of those who, as he says, "mistake ignorance for sanctity, and boast that they are the disciples of poor fishermen."* On another occasion, he illustrates the Scripture from many topics of heathen philosophy, and then concludes in these words:—" Hæc autem de Scriptura pauca posuimus, ut congruere nostra cum philosophis doceremus."—" We have alleged these few things from Scripture, so to show that our doctrines agree with those of the philosophers."† Which words clearly intimate, that he considered it an interesting study, and not unworthy of a good Christian, to trace the connections between revealed truths and human learning, and to see if the two could be brought into harmony together.

His learned friend, St. Augustine, was clearly of the same mind. For, speaking of the qualities requisite for a well-furnished theologian, he enumerates mundane learning among them, as of great importance. Thus he writes:—" If they who are called philosophers have said any true things, which are conformable to our faith, so far from dreading them, we must take them for our use, as a possession which they unjustly hold." He then observes, that those truths, which lie scattered in their writings, are as pure metal amidst the ore of a vein, " which the Christian should take from them, for the rightful purpose of preaching the Gospel."‡ " Have so many of the best faithful among us," he continues,

---

* " Responsum habeant non adeo me hebetis fuisse cordis, et tam crassæ rusticitatis, quam illi solam pro sanctitate habent, piscatorum se discipulos asserentes, quasi idcirco sancti sint, si nihil scirent."— Ep. xv. ad Marcellum, Oper. tom. ii. part ii. p. 62, ed. Martianay.

† " Ad Jovinianum," lib. ii. *ib.* p. 200.

‡ " Debet ab eis auferre Christianus, ad usum justum prædicandi evangelium."

"acted otherwise? With what a weight of gold and silver and precious garments, have we not beheld Cyprian, that sweetest doctor and most blessed martyr, laden as he went forth from Egypt? How much did Lactantius, Victorinus, Optatus, Hilary, bear away? How much innumerable Greeks?"*

It is not difficult to reconcile with such passages as these, those many places where the Fathers seem to reprobate human learning; as where St. Augustine himself, in one of his letters, speaking of the education he was giving to Possidius, says, that the studies usually called liberal deserve not that name, at that time honourable, which properly belongs to pursuits grounded on the true liberty which Christ purchased for us; or where St. Ambrose, to quote one passage out of many, tells Demetrius, that "they who know by what labour they were saved, and at what cost redeemed, wish not to be of the wise in this world."† For it is plain that they speak, on those occasions, of the foolish, vain, and self-sufficient learning of arrogant sophists and wily rhetoricians, and of that science, which, void of the salt of grace, and of a religious spirit, is insipid, vapid, and nothing worth. And how can we, for a moment, think otherwise, when we peruse their glorious works, and contemplate the treasure of ancient learning therein hoarded, and trace in every paragraph their deep acquaintance with heathen philosophy, and in every sentence their familiarity with the purest models of style? Who can doubt, or who will dare to regret, that Tertullian and Justin, Arnobius and Origen, were furnished with all the weapons which pagan learning could supply, towards combating on behalf of truth? Who can wish that St. Basil and St. Jerome, St. Gregory and St. Augustine, had been less versed than they were, in all the elegant literature of the ancients? Nay, even in the very letter to which I have alluded, St. Augustine,

---

* "De Doctrina Christiana," lib. ii cap. 40, Opera, tom. iii. part i. p. 42, ed. Maur.
† "Epistolar." lib. iv. Epist. xxxiii. Oper. tom. v. p. 264, ed. *Par.* 1632.

if I remember right, speaks without regret, and even with satisfaction, of the books on music which his friend had expressed a wish to possess.

The sentiments of the early Church have undergone no change from time, on this, any more than on other points. Mabillon has proved, beyond dispute, that even among men of monastic life, learning was encouraged and promoted from the beginning.* Bacon writes with great commendation of the zeal for learning which has been always shown in the Catholic Church. God, he writes, "sent out his divine truth into the world, accompanied with other parts of learning, as her attendants and handmaids. We find that many of the ancient bishops and fathers of the Church were well versed in the learning of the heathens, insomuch that the edict of the Emperor Julian, forbidding the Christians the schools and exercises, was accounted a more pernicious engine against the faith, than the sanguinary persecutions of his predecessors. It was the Christian Church, which among the inundations of the Scythians from the north-west, and the Saracens from the east, preserved in her bosom the relics of even profane learning, which had otherwise been utterly extinguished. And of late years the Jesuits have greatly enlivened and strengthened the state of learning, and contributed to establish the Roman see."

"There are, therefore," he concludes, "two principal services, besides ornament and illustration, which philosophy and human learning perform to religion; the one consists in effectually exciting to the exaltation of God's glory, the other affording a singular preservation against unbelief and error."†

Between the two extremes which Bacon has named, the ancient Fathers and the Society of Jesus, there is a long interval, during which, in spite of ordinary prejudice, we must not allow ourselves to imagine that the

* "Traité des Etudes monastiques," pt. i. cap. xv. p. 112: *Par.* 1691.
† "De augmentis Scientiarum."—Bacon's Works, *Lond.* 1818, vol. vi. p. lxiii.

fostering spirit of the Church was not exerted in favour of profane learning. "I would observe," writes a learned and amiable author, "that to a Catholic, not only the philosophical, but also the literary history of the world, is prodigiously enlarged; objects change their relative position, and many are brought into resplendent light, which before were consigned to obscurity. While the moderns continue, age after age, to hear only of the Cæsars and the philosophers, and to exercise their ingenuity in tracing parallel characters among their contemporaries, the Catholic discovers that there lies, between the heathen civilization and the present, an entire world, illustrious with every kind of intellectual and moral greatness; the names which are on his tongue are no longer Cicero and Horace, but St. Augustine, St. Bernard, Alcuin, St. Thomas, St. Anselm; the places associated in his mind with the peace and dignity of learning, are no longer the Lycæum or the Academy, but Citeaux, Cluny, Crowland, or the Oxford of the middle ages."*

I will only refer you to his rich and glowing page for sufficient proof that classical and philosophical pursuits were zealously and ably followed in the solitude of the cloister, by—

> "The thoughtful monks, intent their God to please,
> For Christ's dear sake, by human sympathies
> Pour'd from the bosom of the Church."†

But I cannot withhold from you the opinion of one who was a bright ornament of those calumniated ages. Among the exquisite sermons of St. Bernard on the Canticles, is one on this very theme; "that the knowledge of human learning is good;" in which the eloquent Father thus expresses himself:—" I may, perhaps, appear to depreciate learning too much, and almost to reprove the learned, and forbid the study of letters. God forbid! I am not ignorant how much learned men have

---

* "Mores Catholici, or Ages of Faith," book iii. *Lond.* 1833, p. 277.   † "Yarrow revisited," 2nd ed. p. 254.

benefited, and now benefit the Church, whether by confuting those who are opposed to her, or by instructing the ignorant. And I have read, 'because thou hast rejected knowledge, I will reject thee; that thou shalt not do the office of the priesthood to me.'"*

Such, then, have been the feeling and conduct of the Catholic Church regarding the application of profane learning to the defence and illustration of truth: and perhaps the best answer which can be given to such inconsiderate Christians as say that religion needs not such foreign and meretricious aids, is that of Dr. South: "If God hath no need of our learning, he can have still less of your ignorance."

The second class of writers who assert that religion is not interested in the progress of learning, is actuated by very different motives. For it comprises those enemies of revelation, against whom these Lectures have been principally directed, and who pretend that the onward course of science tends to overthrow, or weaken, the evidences of revealed religion. I have had so many opportunities of practically confuting these men, that I shall not stay to expose any farther the folly of their assertions. I will only observe, that this ungrounded reproach was not made for the first time, by the modern adversaries of Christianity, but is in fact the oldest charge brought against it. For Celsus, one of the most ancient impugners of its truth, whose objections are on record, especially taunted us with this hostility to science, from a fear of its weakening our cause. But he met with an able and victorious opponent in the learned Origen, who triumphantly rebuts the calumny, and draws from it a conclusion which I cannot refrain from quoting:—" If the Christian religion shall be found to invite and encourage men to learning, then must they deserve severe reprehension who seek to excuse their own ignorance, by so speaking as to draw others away from application."† This remark, while it shows the

---

* "Serm. xxxvi. super Cantica," Opera, p. 608 : *Basil,* 1566.
† "Contra Celsum," lib. iii. Opera, tom. i. p. 476, ed. De la Rue.

security felt by Origen, that Christianity could not suffer by the encouragement of learning, is also a just rebuke to that timid class of friends who are alarmed at its progress.

More than once I have had opportunities of vindicating Italy, and Rome especially, from silly calumnies in this regard. I have proved that this city has been the foremost in encouraging and aiding science and literature, the tendency of which was to probe the foundations of religion to their very centre, without jealousy and without alarm. There is no country, perhaps, where the higher departments of education are so unreservedly thrown open to every rank, where the physical sciences are more freely pursued, and where oriental and critical literature have been more fostered than here. This city possesses three establishments in the form of a University, in which all the branches of literature and science are simultaneously cultivated under able professors; and there is a chair in the great University of a character perfectly unique, wherein the discoveries of modern physics are applied to the vindication of Scripture.* In my own case, I should be unjust to overlook this opportunity of saying, that on every occasion, but principally in reference to the subject of these Lectures, I have received the most condescending encouragement from those whose approbation every Catholic will consider his best reward on earth.†

---

* The chair of "Fisica sagra."

† I feel a pleasure in relating the following anecdote:—A few years ago, I prefixed to a thesis held by a member of my establishment, a Latin dissertation of ten or twelve pages, upon the necessity of uniting general and scientific knowledge to theological pursuits. I took a rapid view of the different branches of learning discussed in these Lectures. The essay was soon translated into Italian, and printed in a Sicilian journal; and I believe appeared also at Milan. What was most gratifying, however, to my own feelings, and may serve as a confirmation of the assertions in the text, is, that when two days after I waited upon the late Pope, Pius VIII., a man truly well versed in sacred and profane literature, to present him, according to form, with a copy of the thesis prepared for him, I found him with it on his table; and in the kindest terms, he informed me, that having

But from all that I have hitherto said, and I hope proved, we may surely draw some practical conclusions. And first I beg to turn myself, with all becoming deference, to those who share the duties and the dangers of my own calling; and without presuming so far as to instruct or even to advise them, as a friend and brother, entreat them to lose no opportunity of giving the lie, by their deeds, to the persevering reproach of religious enemies. It is not by abstract reasoning that we shall convince mankind of our not dreading the progress of learning; it is by meeting it fairly, or rather accompanying it in its onward march, treating it ever as an ally and a friend, and exhibiting it as enlisted on our side, that we can reasonably hope to satisfy them that truth is God's alone, and that his servants and their cause may fear it not. The reason why infidelity proved so mischievous in France, during the last century, was, that its emissaries presented it to the acceptance of the people, tricked out with all the tinsel ornaments of a mock science; because they dealt in illustration and in specious proofs drawn from every branch of literature; because they sweetened the edge of the poisoned cup with all the charms of an elegant style and lively composition; while unfortunately they who undertook to confute them, with the exception of Guenée, and perhaps a few others, dealt in abstract reasoning, and mere didactic demonstration.* And is it too much to demand that equal pains be taken by us to deck out religion with those charms that are her own

heard of my little essay, he had instantly sent for it; and added, in terms allusive to the figure quoted above from the ancient Fathers, "You have robbed Egypt of its spoil, and shown that it belongs to the people of God."

* As an instance of this defect, in one who has taken a higher ground than I have thought necessary, and tried to carry the war into the enemy's country, I might mention a work, published at Naples towards the end of the last century, "L'irreligiosa libertà di pensare nemica del progresso delle scienze." It is a large quarto, but from the first page to the last, does not contain a single illustrative fact, to prove that infidelity has been hostile to the progress of science. It is a work of dry reasoning with a good deal of declamation.

vesture, given unto her by God, which her enemy has impiously usurped?

The shifting forms which infidelity takes, the Proteus-like facility with which its shape and motions vary, should keep us in a state of unwearied activity, to face it in all its changes, with a suitable resistance, and so be able to quell it in all its fantastic apparitions. " The versatility of error," says an eloquent writer of our times, " demands a correspondent variety in the means of defending truth: and from whom have the public more right to expect its defence, in opposition to the encroachments of error and infidelity, than from those who profess to devote their studies and their lives to the advancement of virtue and religion?... As the Christian ministry is established for the instruction of men, throughout every age, in truth and holiness, it must adapt itself to the ever-shifting scenes of the moral world, and stand ready to repel the attacks of impiety and error, under whatever form they may appear."*

But these sentiments, spoken of the instructors of any religion, have been uttered more than a thousand years ago, concerning our ministry, by the glorious Chrysostom, in the golden book which he wrote for those of our profession. For thus he speaks upon this very point:—" Wherefore we must take all pains that the doctrine of Christ dwell abundantly within us. For the preparations of the enemy's battle are not of one form; for the war is in itself various, and waged by divers foes. All use not the same arms, nor conduct their assault on the same plan. He, therefore, who undertakes to fight them all, must understand the arts of each. He must be at once an archer and a slinger, subaltern and commander, soldier on horseback or on foot, equally able to fight in the ship and on the bulwark. For in ordinary warfare, each one opposes his adversary after that manner whereunto he hath been trained; but in this conflict

* " Modern Infidelity considered with respect to its Influence on Society," in a sermon by R. Hall, M.A. *Lond.* 1822, pp. iv. & 11.

it is far otherwise; since, should he who must gain the victory be not intimately acquainted with every separate art, the devil well knows how to take advantage of some unguarded point, and introduce his despoilers to seize and tear the flock. This is not the case where he knows the shepherd to be provided with every acquirement, and aware of his deceits. It behoveth us, therefore, to be prepared on every side."*

To this encouraging testimony of the correctness of the views which I have taken, I can add that of an illustrious Father of the Latin Church. For St. Jerome, commenting on Eccles. ii. 8, "I heaped together for myself silver and gold, and the wealth of kings," thus expresses himself:—" By the wealth of kings we may understand the doctrines of the philosophers and profane sciences, which the ecclesiastic understanding, by his diligence, he is able to catch the wise in their own toils."†

It is, you will say, a toilsome task to acquire the necessary preparation for this varied warfare; but such, no less, is the qualification for every other noble office of society—

———"Pater ipse colendi
Haud facilem esse viam voluit."‡

Shall the Roman orator declare that no one need hope to attain the perfection of his profession, " unless he shall have acquired the knowledge of all the sciences;"§ and this to cajole a multitude, and, perhaps, even to turn the course of justice:|| and shall we be deterred from a similar application, sweet in itself and full of

---

* "De Sacerdote," lib. iv. § iv. p. 177 : *Cantab.* 1710.
† "Possunt regum substantiæ et philosophorum dici dogmata et scientiæ sæculares, quas ecclesiasticus vir diligenter intelligens, apprehendit sapientes in astutia eorum."—Comment. in Eccles. tom. ii. p. 726.   ‡ Virgil. Georg. i. 121.
§ "Ac mea quidem sententia, nemo poterit esse omni laude cumulatus orator, nisi erit omnium rerum magnarum atque artium scientiam consequutus."—De Orat. lib. i. p. 89, ed. cit.
|| "Discitur innocuas ut agat facundia causas ;
  Protegit hæc sontes, inmeritosque premit."
  Trist. ii. 273.

fruit, by an idea of labour and of difficulty; when our object is the noblest and the holiest which earth can propose; when the sciences themselves, daughters as they are of the uncreated wisdom, will receive consecration, and be made the priestesses of the Most High, by the very errand whereon we lead them? That time will be consumed in the preparation necessary for this method of meeting error and illustrating truth, cannot be denied: but how, I may confidently ask, could time be better spent? Surely not on the flitting topics which occupy for a day the public mind; not on the flimsy literature which issues in an unfailing stream from our national press; not upon the insipid gratifications which general society can offer. "Break," I would say with the poet, "through the trammels of such chilling cares, and follow the guidance of heavenly wisdom, that we may be an honour to our country, and possess a fund of happiness within ourselves."

―――――― "Quod si
Frigida curarum fomenta relinquere posses,
Quò te cœlestis sapientia duceret, ires.
Hoc opus, hoc studium parvi properemus et ampli,
Si patriæ volumus, si nobis vivere cari."*

Yes; *parvi properemus et ampli;* let all, great and little, forward this noble work. It is in every one's power so to order his literary occupation, as to render it subservient to his religious improvement, to the strengthening of his own solemn convictions; even though he be not blessed with talents sufficient to add unto the sum of general evidence, for the public benefit. For if few are destined by Divine Providence, to be as burning lights in his Church, not to be hidden under the bushel, yet hath each one a virginal lamp to trim, a small but precious light to keep burning within his soul, by feeding it ever with fresh oil, that it may guide him through his rugged path, and be not found dim and clogged when the bridegroom shall come.

And yet I know not why any one who possesses but

* Horace, "Epist." l. i. ep. iii. 25.

ordinary abilities, may not hope, by persevering diligence, somewhat to enlarge the evidences of truth. There are humble departments in this as in every other art; there are calm, retired walks, which lead not beyond the precincts of domestic privacy, over which the timid may wander, and, without exposure to the public gaze, gather sweet and lowly herbs, that shall be as fragrant on the altar of God as the costly perfume which Bezaleel and Oholiab compounded with so much art.* The painted shell which the child picks up on the hill-side, may well be sometimes as good evidence of a great catastrophe, as the huge bones of sea-monsters, which the naturalist digs out of the limestone rock; a little medal may attest the destruction of an empire, as certainly as the obelisk or triumphal arch. " While others," says St. Jerome, " contribute their gold and their silver to the service of the tabernacle, why should not I contribute my humble offerings, at least, of hair and skins?"† To this beautiful figure, which each one may utter in his own name, I will only add, that while the gold and silver are for the ornament of God's house, those humbler gifts—the skins and haircloth—are for its shelter and protection.

You all, I doubt not, have often admired those exquisite paintings on the ceilings of the Borgia apartments in the Vatican, wherein the sciences are represented as holding their separate courts; each enthroned upon a stately chair, with features and mien of the most noble and dignified beauty, surrounded by the emblems and most distinguished representatives of its power on earth, and seeming to claim homage from all that gaze upon it. And judge what would have been the painter's conception, and to what a sublimity of expression he would have risen, had it been his task to represent that noblest of all sciences, our divine religion, enthroned as ever becomes her, to receive the fealty and worship of those her handmaids. For if, as hath been

---

* Exod. xxx. 35; xxxi. 11.
† " Prologus Galeatus," prefixed to the Vulgate.

proved, they are but ministers unto her superior rule, and are intended to furnish the evidences of her authority, how much above theirs must be the comeliness and grace, and majesty and holiness, with which she must be arrayed! And what honour and dignity must be conferred on him who feels himself deputed to bear the tribute of any of these fair vassals; and how must his admiration of their queen be enhanced, by finding himself thus brought so near unto her presence!

But whosoever shall try to cultivate a wider field, and follow, from day to day, as humbly we have striven here to do, the constant progress of every science, careful ever to note the influence which it exercises on his more sacred knowledge, shall have therein such pure joy, and such growing comfort, as the disappointing eagerness of mere human learning may not supply. Such a one I know not unto whom to liken, save to one who unites an enthusiastic love of nature's charms, to a sufficient acquaintance with her laws, and spends his days in a garden of the choicest bloom. And here he seeth one gorgeous flower, that has unclasped all its beauty to the glorious sun; and there another is just about to disclose its modester blossom, not yet fully unfolded; and beside them, there is one only in the hand-stem, giving but slender promise of much display; and yet he waiteth patiently, well knowing that the law is fixed whereby it too shall pay, in due season, its tribute to the light and heat that feed it. Even so, the other doth likewise behold one science after the other, when its appointed hour is come, and its ripening influences have prevailed, unclose some form which shall add to the varied harmony of universal truth, which shall recompense, to the full, the genial power that hath given it life, and, however barren it may have seemed at first, produce something that may adorn the temple and altar of God's worship.

And if he carefully register his own convictions, and add them to the collections already formed, of various converging proofs, he assuredly will have accomplished the noblest end for which man may live and acquire learning,—his own improvement, and the benefit of his kind. For, as an old and wise poet has written, after a-wiser saint:—

> "The chief use then in man of that he knowes,
> In his paines-taking for the good of all,
> Not fleshly weeping for our own made woes,
> Not laughing from a melancholy gall,
> Not hating from a soul that overflowes
> With bitterness breathed out from inward thrall;
> But sweetly rather to ease, loose, or binde,
> As need requires, this fraile fallen human kinde.
>
> "Yet some seeke knowledge, meerely to be knowne,
> And idle curiosity that is;
> Some but to sell, not freely to bestow,
> These gaine and spend both time and wealth amisse,
> Embasing arts, by basely deeming so;
> Some to build others, which is charitie;
> But these to build themselves who wise men be."*

When learning shall once have been consecrated by such high motives, it will soon be hallowed by purer feelings, and assume a calmer and more virtuous character than human knowledge can ever possess. An enthusiastic love of truth will be engendered in the soul, which will extinguish every meaner and more earthly feeling in its pursuit. We shall never look with a partisan's eye upon the cause, nor estimate it by personal motives, but, following the advice of the excellent Schlegel, we shall "eschew all sorts of useless contention, and uncharitable hate, and strive to keep alive a spirit of love and unity."† We shall consider the cause as too sacred to be conducted under the influence, or with the aid, of human passions. In the words of the poet, it

---

* Lord Brooke: "Treatise on Humane Learning." These lines are but a paraphrase of the following beautiful passage of St. Bernard: "Sunt namque qui scire volunt eo tantum fine ut sciant, et turpis curiositas est. Et sunt qui scire volunt, ut sciantur ipsi, et turpis vanitas est. Et sunt item qui scire volunt, ut scientiam suam vendant, verbi causa pro pecunia, pro honoribus, et turpis quæstus est. Sed sunt quoque qui scire volunt ut ædificent, et charitas est. Et item qui scire volunt ut ædificentur, et prudentia est."—Sermo xxxvi. super Cant. p. 608.

† "Philosophische Vorlesungen," p. 265.

will seem to address us; inciting us indeed to seek victory, but only in the power of God:

Βούλου κρατεῖν μὲν, ξὺν Θεῷ δ' ἀεὶ κρατεῖν.

But these motives will have a still stronger power; they will insure us success. For if once a pure love and unmixed admiration of religion animate our efforts, we shall find ourselves inflamed with a chivalrous devotion to her service, which will make us indefatigable and unconquerable, when armed in her defence. Our quest may be long and perilous, there may come in our way enchantments and sorceries, giants and monsters, allurements and resistance; but onward we shall advance, in the confidence of our cause's strength; we shall dispel every phantasm, and fairly meet every substantial foe, and the crown will infallibly be ours. In other words, we shall submit with patience to all the irksomeness which such detailed examination may cause: when any objection is brought, instead of contenting ourselves with vague replies, we shall at once examine the very department of learning, sacred or profane, whence it hath been drawn; we shall sit down calmly, and address ourselves meekly to the toilsome work; we shall endeavour to unravel all its intricacies, and diligently to untie every knot; and I promise you, that however hopeless your task may have appeared at first, the result of your exertions will be surely recorded in the short expressive legend, preserved on an ancient gem, which I trust I may consider as the summary and epilogue of these my Lectures:

"RELIGIO, VICISTI."

RELIGION, THOU HAST CONQUERED.

THE END.

www.ingramcontent.com/pod-product-compliance
Lightning Source LLC
Chambersburg PA
CBHW020834020526
44114CB00040B/777